EDUCATION AND THE SCOTTISH PEOPLE

EDUCATION AND THE SCOTTISH PEOPLE 1750–1918

R. D. Anderson

CLARENDON PRESS · OXFORD

1995

Oxford University Press, Walton Street, Oxford OX2 6DP

Oxford New York
Athens Auckland Bangkok Bombay
Calcutta Cape Town Dar es Salaam Delhi
Florence Hong Kong Istanbul Karachi
Kuala Lumpur Madras Madrid Melbourne
Mexico City Nairobi Paris Singapore
Taipei Tokyo Toronto
and associated companies in
Berlin Ibadan

Oxford is a trade mark of Oxford University Press

Published in the United States
by Oxford University Press Inc., New York

First Published 1995

British Library Cataloguing in Publication Data
Data available

Library of Congress Cataloging in Publication Data
Anderson, R. D. (Robert David)
Education and the Scottish people, 1750–1918 / R. D. Anderson.
p. cm.
Includes bibliographical references and index.
1. Education—Scotland—History—18th century. 2. Education—
Scotland—History—19th century. 3. Education—Scotland—
History—20th century. I. Title.
LA651.A53 1995
370'.9411'0903—dc20 94–49084
ISBN 0–19–820515–5

1 3 5 7 9 10 8 6 4 2

Typeset by Graphicraft Typesetters Ltd., Hong Kong
Printed in Great Britain
on acid-free paper by
Bookcraft Ltd., Midsomer Norton, Bath

Preface

No apology seems needed for presenting this study of Scottish popular education, since the last general accounts of the subject, by H. M. Knox and James Scotland, appeared in 1953 and 1969 respectively. My original intention was to write a short textbook synthesizing recent research, but I soon realized that the gaps in scholarly coverage were so great that a more extensive treatment based on original sources was needed. For a book covering more than 150 years, the use of these sources is necessarily selective, and I have tried to incorporate the findings of other scholars with the results of my own research.

In 1983 I published *Education and Opportunity in Victorian Scotland*, which was devoted to secondary and university education. This book is complementary to it, and there is some common ground, since in Scotland the histories of 'popular' and 'élite' education were less distinct than in many countries. The core of the present book is the development of the national educational system. It expands in one direction into an account of educational politics, debates, and ideas. In another, it seeks to study how the system worked in practice, which involves looking at the relationship of education and social class, at the wide regional and local variations within Scotland, and at those outcomes of education which can be measured statistically. The book also seeks to relate Scotland to some of the general ideas about educational development put forward by recent historians. By comparison with some recent work on English education, the approach is a traditional one, in focusing on institutions and the decision-making élite, rather than on how education was seen and used by those at the receiving end. It also does no more than touch on the wider relationship of education to Scottish culture, literature, and daily life. Nevertheless, there is a lot in this book which is new, and it should act both as a foundation for the further research which is very much needed, and to make the history of Scottish education more accessible to comparative historians, and indeed to British social historians, who seem inclined to steer clear of the subject as a specialist preserve. The actual relationship of English and Scottish education was very close; yet their history has usually been written as if they were on different planets.

This book could hardly have been written without the resources of

Edinburgh University Library and the National Library of Scotland. I owe a special debt to Tony Morris at Oxford University Press for his patience and encouragement, and to Donald Withrington, whose profound knowledge and generosity in sharing it are known to all working in this field. Other colleagues or friends who have helped with information, advice, or inspiration include Paul Addison, Andrew Bain, John Brown, Peter Burnhill, Jennifer Carter, Terry Cole, Ian Donnachie, Owen Dudley Edwards, Rab Houston, the late Jack Howells, Ian MacDougall, Richard Mackenney, Andrew McPherson, Lindsay Paterson, Nicholas Phillipson, Thomas Velek, Ian Wood, and John Young. Any errors of fact and interpretation are my own responsibility.

Contents

List of Tables, Figures, and Maps

Figures

Maps

List of Abbreviations

BJES	*British Journal of Educational Studies*
CCE	Committee of Council on Education
CCES	Committee of Council on Education in Scotland
CCs & CIs	Continuation Classes and Central Institutions
DSA	Department of Science and Art
EIS	Educational Institute of Scotland
EN	*Educational News*
JEAH	*Journal of Educational Administration and History*
NEA	National Education Association
NSA	*The New Statistical Account of Scotland* (Edinburgh, 1845)
OSA	*The Statistical Account of Scotland, 1791–1799* (reprinted, Wakefield, 1975–83), the Old Statistical Account
PP	Parliamentary Papers
SAPTSE	Scottish Association for the Promotion of Technical and Secondary Education
SCHSR	*Scottish Church History Society Records*
SEA	Scottish Educational Association
SED	Scotch (later Scottish) Education Department
SER	*Scottish Educational Review*
SES	*Scottish Educational Studies*
SESH	*Scottish Economic and Social History*
SHR	*Scottish Historical Review*
SRO	Scottish Record Office
SSBA	Scottish School Boards Association
SSPCK	Society in Scotland for Propagating Christian Knowledge
TGSI	*Transactions of the Gaelic Society of Inverness*
UP	United Presbyterian

1

Scottish Education before 1800

THE historian Lawrence Stone has claimed that 'for a brief period in
the late eighteenth century Scotland enjoyed the largest elementary
educational system, one of the best classical secondary systems, and the
best university system in Europe, all catering for an unusually wide
range of social classes. At every level Scotland in the middle and late
eighteenth century—the Scotland of Adam Smith and David Hume—
was one of the best educated countries in Europe.'[1] This favourable
picture, which dates back to the eighteenth century itself, has generally
been endorsed by modern specialists in Scottish history, like Donald
Withrington and Christopher Smout. In recent years, however, historians have been working to establish a comparative context for schooling
and literacy in Europe, and this work makes Scotland look rather less
exceptional. R. A. Houston, in particular, has questioned the traditional
assumptions of Scottish superiority.

It is important to note that literacy and schooling were distinct phe-
nomena; the school was only one of the ways in which literacy was
acquired, and literacy could be widespread long before the establishment of public systems of education and compulsory school attendance.
François Furet and Jacques Ozouf, in an influential study of literacy
in France, stress that it was a social phenomenon which developed
independently of political events, and that compulsory education, not
imposed until 1882, was the 'institutional expression of the consequences of literacy, not its cause'.[2] The development of a school system
by the élites of church and state interacted with a cultural revolution
from below. Mary Jo Maynes, in a pioneering attempt to treat European
popular education as a whole, sees a formal 'schooling movement',
leading in the long run to the disappearance of the distinction between
literacy and schooling, beginning around 1760.[3] It was taken up by

[1] L. Stone, 'Literacy and Education in England, 1640–1900', *Past and Present*, 42
(1969), 135.
[2] F. Furet and J. Ozouf, *Reading and Writing: Literacy in France from Calvin to Jules
Ferry* (Cambridge, 1982), 45.
[3] M. J. Maynes, *Schooling in Western Europe: A Social History* (Albany, NY, 1985),
34–5.

governments and by the educated classes, and in many countries was part of a reform programme inspired by Enlightenment ideas. But it usually had conservative aims, and the first rulers to attempt to impose universal education were the absolutist monarchs of central Europe. There were edicts setting up local schools and making attendance compulsory in Prussia in 1763, in Austria and Bohemia in 1774, although it was many years before these became effective. The motives were various: economic development and the need for a disciplined industrial workforce, the desire to make religious piety and political loyalty depend on positive indoctrination rather than outward conformity, the need for the state to establish more direct contact with its citizens as serfdom became obsolete, the first stirrings of a sense of national community, the reinforcement of social barriers by underlining the distinction between élite and popular education. But most historians would agree that, contrary to what is taken for granted in the twentieth century, education was not seen primarily as a form of individual emancipation or an instrument of personal social mobility. So too Harvey Graff has warned against any simple equation of literacy and 'modernization', preferring to interpret it as a means of enforcing social and cultural hegemonies.[4] In the 1790s, more radical conceptions of education were spread by the French Revolution, which saw universal education as a way of forming democratic citizens and creating loyalty to the sovereign nation-state, but the revolutionaries were not in power long enough to carry out their plans.

The question why some countries developed national systems of education earlier than others, and in particular why England was slow to do so, has been discussed by Andy Green.[5] He argues that the decisive factor was 'state formation', and that the historical development of power and class relations in England left it with a decentralized state which had no need to make education an instrument of policy. Since Scotland was part of the same state as England, this theory does not explain why Scottish and English educational development differed. But an explanation might be found in the notion that the political union of 1707 was a bargain in which the Scottish élite retained control of 'civil society'—of those areas of social and cultural life on which their

---

[4] H. J. Graff, *The Legacies of Literacy: Continuities and Contradictions in Western Culture and Society* (Bloomington, Ind., 1987).

[5] A. Green, *Education and State Formation: The Rise of Education Systems in England, France and the USA* (London, 1990).

influence depended.[6] These included the universities and the schools as well as the Presbyterian Church. Although Britain had no bureaucratic state to take the initiative in promoting school reform, in Scotland the church took its place, and was able both to formulate a national programme of cultural and religious uniformity and to enforce it through its parochial organization. In fact the development of educational institutions by the church, to be taken over at a later stage by the state, is a common European pattern.

1. THE PARISH SCHOOL AND THE RURAL LOWLANDS

The popular view that the Scottish educational tradition can be traced back to John Knox and the reformers is not incorrect. The *First Book of Discipline* of 1560 envisaged a national system in which schools at all levels were linked with each other and with the universities, and the need for all Christians to be instructed in the elements of their faith and to be able to read the Bible was a fundamental tenet of Calvinism. But it took many years to apply this ideal in practice. The first aim was to ensure that each parish had a school, and this was pursued in the course of the seventeenth century by a series of enactments of the Scottish Parliament. Statutes of 1616, 1633, and 1646 culminated in the act of 1696 which remained the legal foundation of the parish schools down to 1872, with no further legislation until 1803. The 1696 Act was itself part of the religious and political settlement following the 1688 revolution, which sought to entrench the victory of Presbyterianism, and education was seen thereafter as an instrument of religious authority as much as an independent cultural force, reflecting the church's determination to impose conformity and root out dissent.

The central feature of the school legislation was that the landowners of each parish—the 'heritors'—had to appoint a schoolmaster, who then had life tenure, and to provide him with a schoolhouse and a small fixed salary, paid for by a rate levied on landed property. For parents, education was neither compulsory nor free, for the schoolmaster depended on fees to bring his income up to a reasonable level. Poor children had their fees paid by the kirk session, which was responsible for poor relief. In areas where the system was well established, pressure from

---

[6] C. Harvie, *Scotland and Nationalism: Scottish Society and Politics, 1707–1977* (London, 1977), 61; D. McCrone, *Understanding Scotland: The Sociology of a Stateless Nation* (London, 1992), 3.

the landowner, the minister, or community opinion ensured that most children did attend school and learnt at least to read. The ministers were especially important, because part of their duties was to visit families in their homes, 'catechize' the children, and ensure that the disciplines of the church were enforced. The aim was to promote an active piety based on family devotion. At one time, the lives of all parishioners—especially in matters of sexual morality—came under the scrutiny of minister and kirk session. But in the eighteenth century changing manners and the rise of religious dissent meant that for adults these disciplines were relaxed, and the Presbyterian vision of a godly village community grouped around parish church and school began to crumble. But perhaps this made the church all the more anxious to hold on to its influence over children, which few were yet prepared to challenge.

The heritors were laymen, and the daily supervision of the school fell to the minister and session; the presbytery, the ecclesiastical authority at the level above parishes, was responsible for inspecting schools and testing the qualifications and orthodoxy of teachers, and the General Assembly of the church, meeting annually in Edinburgh, exercised a general role of supervision and encouragement. The system thus rested on a partnership between state and church. Its basis was statutory, but its regular working depended on local initiative and the zeal of landowners and ministers rather than on government intervention, and no funds were provided from central sources. Local energy was greater at some times than others, but historians generally agree that the church pursued a consistent 'literacy campaign' over two centuries, that much had already been achieved by the beginning of the eighteenth century, and that by its end the network of schools in the lowlands—the highlands were a different matter—was more or less complete and working as the law intended.[7] Evidence about parish schools is especially abundant for the 1790s, when it was collected and published in the 'Statistical Account' compiled by Sir John Sinclair, which contained few statistics in the modern sense, but included a description of each parish and its resources, usually written by the minister.

Every parish schoolmaster had to subscribe to the Westminster Confession of 1643, the church's test of orthodoxy, and in many respects he acted as the minister's assistant, performing subordinate tasks which

[7] R. A. Houston, *Literacy in Early Modern Europe: Culture and Education, 1500–1800* (London, 1988), 42–3; D. J. Withrington, 'Schooling, Literacy and Society', in T. M. Devine and R. Mitchison (eds.), *People and Society in Scotland, I: 1760–1830* (Edinburgh, 1988), 163–87.

also made useful additions to his income: he was usually the clerk to the kirk session, the precentor who led the singing at services, and the person who proclaimed banns and kept the register of marriages and baptisms. It followed that religious instruction was the first function of the school. Children were expected to learn the church's Shorter Catechism by heart, as well as to master the reading of the Bible. Of the skills which the Victorians were to call the three Rs, reading was the most fundamental, and it was taught separately from writing. This was reflected in the pattern of fees, which were charged by the quarter, and invariably had different rates for simple reading (usually called 'English' at the time) and for reading with writing and arithmetic. Most but not all children moved on from one stage to another, and it was common for girls to learn sewing rather than writing. If children stayed on at school, they might learn other subjects like grammar or geography, and parish schoolmasters were also expected to offer more advanced subjects (for higher fees) where a demand existed. The most popular were practical and commercial applications of arithmetic, such as bookkeeping, land measurement, or navigation. In large parishes with an active economic life, schoolmasters could make a good living by teaching such subjects.

In an ideal parish, like one in Kirkcudbrightshire described in the Statistical Account, the schoolmaster was 'able to teach Latin and Greek, with accompts and some practical parts of the mathematics; in short, every thing necessary to prepare the young student for the university, as well as to qualify the man of business for acting his part well in any ordinary occupation'.[8] This university connection was a distinctive feature of the Scottish system, around which much sentiment accumulated. It was possible because university education itself started at a low level, requiring little more than a rudimentary knowledge of Latin, and because boys could go there at fourteen or even younger. This custom suited the church because it created a pool of recruits for the clergy, with the aid of bursaries which paid part of the cost of a university education. Thus the system came to be seen as one by which 'lads of parts' from remote villages, or from humble social origins, used education to climb the social ladder. In reality, this function of the parish school was more limited than the democratic myth suggests, and the presence of Latin might not mean much: on the one hand, its traditional

---

[8] *The Statistical Account of Scotland, 1791–1799* (20 vols., Wakefield, 1975–83), v. 129 (Dalry). This is usually known as the 'Old Statistical Account', and is referred to hereafter as *OSA*; in this modern reprint, the volumes are arranged by county.

prestige meant that it was taken for a year or two by children who had no intention of going further; on the other, it was often the local middle classes, even sometimes the landowners, who benefited from the convenience and cheapness of the parish school before sending their sons off to complete their education in a town, or direct to a university.

The link between schools and universities worked in both directions, and lads of parts often returned to the schoolhouse once qualified. Since schoolmasters were expected to teach Latin, presbyteries usually required some university attendance, if only for one or two sessions. Parish teachers thus shared the cultural world of ministers, though not their social status and salary; some had already qualified in divinity but failed to find a parish, while others saw teaching as a temporary phase while they continued to study for the ministry. In a society where professional and business openings were limited, the schools could attract men over-qualified for the modest duties demanded. But the professional status of the schoolmaster and his recognized position in the community did distinguish Scotland from England, and most other countries at this time, where elementary teaching was seen as a last resort for men who could find no other profession, a sideline to manual work or shopkeeping, or something to which anyone literate could turn their hand. The education decrees in Prussia and Austria were accompanied by the foundation of training schools for teachers, but in Scotland the supply of qualified men was such that these were not thought necessary until the 1830s.

The remarks on education in the Statistical Account were naturally conditioned by the clergy's religious perspectives, and they were perhaps inclined to conceal deficiencies which reflected on their own pastoral zeal. But they generally presented the parish schools as a success story and a source of national pride. They had less to say about other sorts of school, for by this time the parish schools were only part of a wider network of schools provided by various voluntary, private, or charitable efforts. These unofficial schools left few traces in the historical record, but they were becoming an essential supplement to the statutory system. For the law only obliged the heritors to provide one school and pay one salary, and this was often inadequate. It was notoriously so in the highlands, but even in the lowlands Scottish parishes could be very large, and the concentration of population in a single centre was uncommon. More often there were hamlets or scattered settlements outside walking distance from the school. In the 1790s there were still many small parishes where a single school sufficed, but in others the growth of urbanized villages, or the appearance of mines and factories, created a demand quite beyond the capacity of a single schoolmaster. He therefore acquired various rivals or auxiliaries.

In the eighteenth century, unlike the nineteenth, the church faced little competition from other religious denominations. Roman Catholics were still subject to penal legislation, and the church could use its powers to license schoolmasters against both Episcopalians and the Presbyterian dissenters produced by the various 'secessions' from the Church of Scotland. In the second half of the century these powers were falling into disuse, but there was no serious challenge to the church's educational role, and no denomination tried to set up a rival network. At most, there was local competition from individuals, as at Newburgh in Fife, where the parish school had sixty scholars (thirty learning 'English', i.e. reading, twenty-two writing and arithmetic, and eight Latin), while a private teacher who was a Seceder had fifty-five scholars—thirty-one learning reading, twenty-one writing and arithmetic, and three Latin; in the winter, both had evening classes for 'grown up persons'.[9] This was typical of populous parishes, where the market could support more than one well-qualified teacher, teaching the same kind of commercially useful subjects; in this context, the parish teacher himself could be seen as one entrepreneur among many, with the advantage of the house and salary to support his activities. Teachers who could establish a reputation for classical teaching could exploit another possibility: to take a large house and attract boarders from other parts of Scotland, or from families living abroad. This could be quite lucrative. At Dalmeny in West Lothian, for example, there were thirty to forty children from the parish in the school, but also twenty to thirty boarders who paid twenty guineas a year.[10] Schools of this kind were to be found all over the lowlands, and commentators who have celebrated the streams of distinguished men coming from village schools have not always appreciated that these might not be local boys.

The parish school was supplemented, rather than threatened, by the many small schools which tried to serve the outlying parts of parishes, with varying degrees of affluence and permanence.[11] The parish of Dirleton in East Lothian, for example, contained 'several small villages, where old and infirm people keep schools for young children'.[12]

---

[9] *OSA* x. 681.   [10] *OSA* ii. 730.
[11] Cf. R. T. D. Glaister, 'Rural Private Teachers in 18th-Century Scotland', *JEAH* 23/2 (1991), 49–61.
[12] *OSA* ii. 463 (Dirleton).

Sometimes a charitable endowment or a benevolent landowner stepped in to pay a small salary or provide a schoolhouse, but more often parents were left to their own devices. It was common to club together to hire a teacher for part of the year; these improvised schools usually operated only in the winter, and were especially common in the upland areas of the southern lowlands, serving isolated communities of small farmers and shepherds, and taught by an ever-changing succession of young men, who lodged in rotation with the families they served. At New Galloway (Kirkcudbrightshire), 'such as are further distant, hire young lads into their families, that have been bred at the public school, to teach their children English, and the first principles of writing and arithmetic. . . . by this means all the children in the parish are taught to read and write.' At Kirkpatrick Irongray in the same county, the parish teacher himself taught for alternating two-year periods in one house near the church and another '3 miles up the parish', while the more distant parents 'hire a lad for themselves, who goes from one family to another, along with his scholars, by turns'. At Dunoon (Argyll), 'the winter schools are taught by children from 12 to 15 years of age, who go from house to house, for about 20*s*. and their maintainance [*sic*], to teach younger children than themselves.'[13] For ambitious lads, this could be the first rung on the ladder to the university or to a permanent post.

A very common type of unofficial school was for girls and younger children. All parish schools were open to girls as well as boys, and there was nothing to prevent them studying any subject. But parents were often content that they should learn to read and not to write, and girls were also expected to learn sewing and knitting, a custom encouraged by the authorities in order to promote industrial employment. Thus many smaller schools appeared, taught by women, and concentrating on sewing and reading; usually there were young boys as well, learning their first letters before passing on to the large school. Many of the teachers in these 'dame schools' seem to have been widows or other elderly women. They relieved some of the pressure on the parish school, which in large parishes took on the role of a school for more advanced subjects into which other schools could feed. The parish schools had no monopoly, but their presence encouraged the habit of education and served as a model for others; as one minister put it, the parish school 'keeps alive a sense of education in the country, and

---

[13] *OSA* v. 153 (Kells); 255; viii. 92. Twenty shillings (*s.*) made one pound, twelve pence (*d.*) one shilling.

induces those who stand in need, to provide schoolmasters for the instruction of their own families and friends'.[14]

2. THE HIGHLANDS AND THE TOWNS

In the lowlands, the inadequacies of the parish schools were supplemented by private effort. In the highlands, poverty made this more difficult. The highland region as a whole still held a fifth of the Scottish population in 1801, though it was in the Western Isles and the adjoining mainland areas that conditions were most difficult. Most parishes did have the school required by law, but it was difficult for the statutory system to work properly. Poor communications and harsh weather often made travel to distant schools impossible. Highland parishes could be of enormous size, making a single school quite inadequate, and some included separate islands without schools of their own. Landownership was on a large scale (the 'heritors' could be a single person, as happened in the lowlands too), and landlords were often absentees. The 'clearances' of the population from their traditional settlements were only just beginning in the eighteenth century, but the region was already undergoing a demographic crisis, with the population outrunning the scanty resources of agriculture and resorting to large-scale migration, both temporary and permanent. The parish school worked on the assumption that most parents would pay fees, with the community supporting poorer children. But when the whole community was poor, there were no resources to support the school. Salaries were low, and it was difficult for teachers to collect enough fees to make a living. Able men were thus not attracted to teach in the highlands, and there were few pickings for private teachers. Sometimes the parish salary was divided in an attempt to overcome the problems of distance, and as in the lowlands parents could club together to make their own rudimentary provision; but the whole web of schools was much thinner and more precarious than in more prosperous areas.

Some of the gaps were filled by the Society in Scotland for Propagating Christian Knowledge, founded in 1709. This was really an arm of the Church of Scotland, and was supported by the government; it long remained the only official attempt to supplement the parish schools. The SSPCK raised funds in the lowlands, and used them to support

---

[14] *OSA* ii. 94 (Midcalder).

teachers in the outlying parts of highland parishes; they were not meant to compete with parish schools. The Society appointed and paid the teachers, but the heritors were expected to provide a schoolhouse and a garden or croft; the parents seldom paid fees. Few SSPCK schools went beyond reading, writing, and arithmetic, and the teaching of Latin was not allowed. Under its 'second patent' of 1738 the SSPCK also introduced practical training for agriculture and industry, and after the 1745 Jacobite rising government agencies like the Board of Manufactures and the Forfeited Estates Commissioners sought to use education to promote the linen industry. These efforts had little success, the only legacy being a number of 'spinning schools', which were transferred to the SSPCK in the 1780s, and came to resemble ordinary girls' schools teaching reading and sewing.[15]

The work of the SSPCK was part of a general national strategy of integrating the highlands into a united Scotland and bringing them the benefits of lowland, English-speaking culture. This seemed especially urgent after 1745, when the secular authorities sought to combine the restoration of political order with economic development; but from the start the church had been concerned to consolidate a parochial system which had not yet taken deep roots, and to eliminate the remains of Episcopalian and Roman Catholic loyalties. State and church agreed that the 'extirpation' of the Gaelic language was central to these aims. At first the SSPCK schools taught entirely in English. From the 1760s the preliminary teaching of Gaelic reading was allowed, but only as an aid to learning English, which remained the medium of teaching and the language enforced for conversation in school. Parish schools had the same policy. This war on Gaelic has generally been condemned from the perspective of later ages as the deliberate destruction of an ancient culture. But contemporaries saw little alternative to teaching in English if literacy was to be used, as in the lowlands, to promote religion, morality, and civilization. Much of Gaelic culture was in any case transmitted orally, and Gaelic reading matter was very limited: the New Testament in Scottish Gaelic appeared only in 1767, and the complete Bible in 1801. The result was that, while Gaelic remained the language of the home and of religious worship, it failed to make

---

[15] M. G. Jones, *The Charity School Movement: A Study of Eighteenth Century Puritanism in Action* (Cambridge, 1938), 165–214; J. Mason, *A History of Scottish Experiments in Rural Education from the Eighteenth Century to the Present Day* (London, 1935); D. J. Withrington, 'The S.P.C.K. and Highland Schools in Mid-Eighteenth Century', *SHR* 41 (1962), 89–99.

the transition to the new world of written culture, and when literacy in Gaelic was acquired it was a 'restricted literacy' used for reading religious books, while English was used for access to modern, secular ideas. This 'alienation of language from literacy'[16] not only had grave implications for the future of the language, but added one more barrier to the effectiveness of highland schooling, as children struggled with an alien tongue.

In the late eighteenth century the Gaelic-speaking area, though smaller than the geographical highland region, still extended far to the east and south. It included Arran and Bute, the whole of Argyll, northern Perthshire, the whole of Inverness-shire, and all the mainland north-wards except for Caithness.[17] But within this area, educational stand-ards varied. The SSPCK tackled the fringe areas first, and its schools—about 150 in 1800—were thickest in the south and east.[18] One authority has concluded that in the highland counties generally school attendance was 'nowhere very impressive',[19] but in areas like southern Argyll, northern Perthshire, or Easter Ross (and in English-speaking Orkney and Caithness, though in Shetland provision was poorer) the Statistical Account suggests that conditions could approach those in the lowlands. Parish and SSPCK schools, with local schools maintained by parents, were adequate to basic needs, though there was a wider gulf in the highlands between the literacy of men and women, more pressure on children to leave school to start work, and widespread desertion of the schools in summer, sometimes made worse by the migration of children to temporary jobs elsewhere. Since there were few towns in the highlands, apart from Inverness, and since well-qualified schoolmasters able to teach Latin or mathematics were thin on the ground, highland children also had very limited chances, until basic schooling was better developed, of using education to climb the social ladder.

It is significant that the SSPCK usually confined its work to the highlands, while in England the corresponding 'charity school' movement was especially active in towns. In Scottish royal burghs, the parish school legislation did not apply, but there seems to have been no perceived

---

[16] V. E. Durkacz, *The Decline of the Celtic Languages: A Study of Linguistic and Cultural Conflict in Scotland, Wales and Ireland from the Reformation to the Twentieth Century* (Edinburgh, 1983), 25.

[17] C. W. J. Withers, *Gaelic in Scotland, 1698–1981: The Geographical History of a Language* (Edinburgh, 1984), 81.

[18] Ibid. 120 ff.   [19] *OSA* xvii. 1 (introduction by M. Gray).

shortage of schools. It was normal, though not legally compulsory, for town councils (at this time self-perpetuating oligarchies rather than elected bodies) to support a burgh school with a salaried schoolmaster, although they did not have the power to levy a school rate. In small towns the burgh school was much like a parish school, but in larger ones it was traditionally a 'grammar' school specializing in the classics. In the course of the seventeenth and eighteenth centuries burgh councils began to appoint extra schoolmasters to teach mathematics and other commercial or modern subjects, and by 1800 they were beginning to consolidate these separate schools into rebuilt 'academies' which distanced themselves from elementary instruction. All these schools charged relatively high fees, and became chiefly middle-class preserves. Town councils had no statutory obligation to meet the needs of the poor. Sometimes they maintained separate 'English' schools for this purpose, but more often this task was left to charitable effort, or to the enterprise of private teachers. Private education met much of the middle-class demand, especially for girls' education, but for the lower social strata too it was probably small private schools, charging modest fees without any public subsidy, and giving a correspondingly modest education, which were the commonest resource.

The Statistical Account is generally uninformative about urban conditions. Fortunately we have a detailed study of Edinburgh by Alexander Law, which illustrates the variety of choice available in a large city. Here an active part was played both by the town council, which set up its own English schools in 1759, and by the SSPCK—this was untypical, but Edinburgh was the society's headquarters. The city had some notable endowed charities, including George Heriot's Hospital which dated from the seventeenth century, and there was a good deal of charitable effort directed at orphans and the poor. Law identifies a large expansion of schools after 1760, but the evidence available does not allow him to say how many children actually attended school, or whether provision was keeping up with the rapid population increase of this period.[20] In most towns, developments were on more modest lines than in Edinburgh, but showed the same mixture of public, private, and charitable effort. When ministers commented on urban education in the Statistical Account, they did not usually express any sense of backwardness or crisis. The only real exception was Greenock, the main landing-point for highland immigrants, where it was said that out of

[20] A. Law, *Education in Edinburgh in the Eighteenth Century* (London, 1965).

4,772 children under 12, there were 1,185 'whose parents are unable to defray the expence [*sic*] of their education'; 883 of them were from highland families. In neighbouring Renfrew and Paisley, however, education was thought to be well provided for.[21] In Glasgow, the situation was more mixed—there were many schools, including free charity schools, but the results were mediocre: a survey by the presbytery had 'found in this city above 60 schools, in which the masters were entirely supported by school wages [fees], from 5*s*. to 1*s*. 6*d*. the quarter. In the greater part of these, nothing was taught but reading English, the Catechism, and perhaps a little writing.' Parents were urged to send their children to school young, as manufactures attracted them away from the ages of 7 or 8; Sunday schools could also be valuable in preventing 'such education as they have got being lost'.[22]

Sunday schools were an innovation of the 1780s directed at young children who started full-time work, especially in the new factories. But this problem was still very limited. Scotland had long-established textile industries, notably linen, but they were mostly organized on the domestic system with families working in their own homes. Spinning and weaving were found in towns and villages of all sizes, and were sometimes a part-time rural occupation rather than a specialized activity. Children were expected to play their part, but it was possible to fit education into their pattern of work, in much the same way as in farming families. Factories, with their demand for full-time labour outside the home, were a different matter. Cotton-spinning mills, the first manifestation of mechanized industry, began to spread from the 1780s onwards, and they created a special demand for the labour of young children. In the early years, when water rather than steam power was used, mills were set up in remote locations far from the parish school. Many mill-owners saw it as their responsibility to provide a school, and in company towns like Catrine in Ayrshire or New Lanark, both founded by David Dale, it was provided, like housing and churches, as part of the new community which clustered around the mill.[23] Colliery owners, also responsible for the creation of new and raw communities, often did the same. But such philanthropy was less likely when the factory system spread to large towns like Glasgow, and the rapid expansion of industry in the early nineteenth century was to expose the weaknesses of a school system based on the parish structure of a stable, agrarian

---

[21] *OSA* vii. 705–6; cf. 834 (Paisley), 864 (Renfrew).
[22] *OSA* vii. 324; cf. 351–2 (Barony Parish).   [23] *OSA* vi. 567–8 (Sorn).

society. Neither in the towns, nor in the newly urbanized parishes in which so much of the new industry appeared, was there any public authority responsible for keeping up with new needs, or possessing the resources to do so. This was, in T. C. Smout's view, 'the Achilles heel of the national system of education'.[24]

None the less, both Smout and Withrington stress the wide provision of schools in the lowlands by the eighteenth century. Even before the 1696 Act, qualified schoolmasters able to teach the classics were to be found in quite small parishes, and in later years the presbyteries filled most of the gaps. Even where formal provision was scanty, Withrington has argued, small private schools and various forms of informal learning, too easily overlooked by historians, reflected a persistent demand for education. Families and local communities exploited scanty human and financial resources with ingenuity. The quality varied, and the opportunities open to individuals depended on the prosperity of the parish and the location of the family home, but by the 1790s the basic network was complete, and one can speak of a genuinely national system with an accepted pattern of standards and institutions.[25] But did widespread schooling necessarily support universal literacy? This is the question which Houston has reopened.

3. LITERACY

Literacy as a social phenomenon has become the focus of much historical attention. In Europe before the nineteenth century, the ability to read and write varied greatly between and within countries, but there are some quantitative measures which allow the levels of achievement to be measured and compared. The main one is the ability of men and women to sign documents rather than making a mark, and in many countries marriage registers provide a standard source for studying literacy trends. In Scotland, unfortunately, married couples and witnesses did not have to sign their names until the introduction of state registration of marriages in 1855. Houston's achievement is to have found alternative evidence of this kind, mainly court depositions, and he uses it to challenge the 'myth' of Scottish superiority.

[24] T. C. Smout, *A History of the Scottish People, 1560–1830*, paperback edn. (n.p., 1972), 443.

[25] D. J. Withrington, 'Lists of Schoolmasters Teaching Latin, 1690', *Miscellany of the Scottish History Society*, x (Edinburgh, 1965), and 'Schooling, Literacy and Society'.

Lawrence Stone's view is that while England may have been ahead of Scotland in the seventeenth century, Scotland then pulled ahead while England stagnated. He estimates that adult male literacy in Scotland was 33 per cent in 1675, 75 per cent in 1750, 88 per cent in 1800, compared with 45, 53, and 65 per cent in England at the same dates.[26] Houston, however, estimates that by 1750 literacy in the lowlands stood at no more than 65 per cent for men; for women, it was 15 per cent by one of his calculations, 30 per cent by another. In the highlands, the figures would be lower—40 to 45 per cent for men is his estimate.[27] Houston's main source of evidence ends in the 1750s, and there is then a large gap until the first official statistics in 1855, when 89 per cent of Scottish bridegrooms and 77 per cent of brides could sign their names.[28] On Stone's estimate there was little progress in male literacy over a hundred years, on Houston's a great deal; the latter seems more plausible, and we shall return to this question in Chapter 5.

The interpretation of literacy evidence demands some caution. In the first place, the link between schooling and literacy is not a direct one in the age before compulsory education. Literacy could be acquired, and maintained or improved in later life, in a variety of informal ways, and it was possible (the case of Sweden being the most commonly cited) to combine high literacy, taught through the agency of churches and families, with the absence of a developed school system. Informal modes of acquiring literacy persisted well into the nineteenth century. However, in Scotland the literacy campaign seems to have emphasized schooling from the first, and there is no evidence of high literacy preceding the development of parish schools. Schools of some kind were within reach of most families; but we cannot infer from their presence that attendance was universal, or that those who used them automatically acquired full literacy. For a second problem lies in the definition of literacy itself. It is quite clear from the Scottish evidence that reading and writing were taught as separate skills, and that children might not learn to write if they left school early, or if it seemed a skill without any functional value. Evidence about signatures is not direct evidence

[26] Stone, 'Literacy and Education', 120. Cf. Graff, *Legacies of Literacy*, 161.

[27] R. A. Houston, 'The Literacy Myth?: Illiteracy in Scotland, 1630–1760', *Past and Present*, 96 (1982), 98–9; *Scottish Literacy and the Scottish Identity: Illiteracy and Society in Scotland and Northern England, 1600–1800* (Cambridge, 1985), 56, 70 ff.; and 'Scottish Education and Literacy, 1600–1800: An International Perspective', in T. M. Devine (ed.), *Improvement and Enlightenment* (Edinburgh, 1989), 52–3.

[28] C. M. Cipolla, *Literacy and Development in the West* (Harmondsworth, 1969), 122–3.

about the ability to read, nor does it necessarily mean that the signer had a real command of writing skills. Historians have argued among themselves about the real significance of signature evidence, but the soundest conclusion is that it is an 'intermediate' measure: anyone who could sign could almost certainly read, but signatures by themselves underestimate the existence of reading literacy. The degree of this underestimate was not constant, but depended on educational practices, and on where a society stood in the long transition from partial to total literacy.

These points need to be borne in mind when interpreting contemporary sources such as the Statistical Account. The ministers did not report systematically on literacy, but when they did it was generally with a note of satisfaction. As Withrington put it, 'readers of the *Account* must be struck by the matter-of-fact way in which high levels of literacy are reported—with no obvious indication of special pride in their achievement, more as a normal expectation which had been quietly fulfilled.'[29] This is true, yet individual comments suggest that the ministers' expectations were confined to the basic ability to read. 'I know nobody in the parish, above 8 or 10 years of age, who cannot read, and not a few can write and do a little in accounts' was a typical comment from Midlothian; at Cleish (Kinross) there was scarcely a child of 8 or 9 'that cannot read pretty distinctly'; at Speymouth (Moray), 'even the poorest of the people take care to have all their children taught to read, and most of the boys learn a little writing and arithmetick.'[30] But not, one may infer, the girls. The distinction between reading and writing is underlined by Smout in a study of the men and women involved in the religious revival at Cambuslang, near Glasgow, in 1746. It was reported that all of these without exception had learnt to read. But the proportion who could also write was as low as in Houston's sample: between 60 and 72 per cent for men, 11 per cent for women.[31] This seems to confirm that low signature literacy, the main basis for Houston's critique of the Scottish myth, was quite compatible with widespread reading literacy, although the Cambuslang sample of religious zealots may well have been untypical of the countryside as a whole. At any rate, Houston himself is prepared to grant that by 1800 Scotland may have had 'nearly complete reading ability',[32] and one may fairly conclude that a minimal

[29] Withrington, 'Schooling, Literacy and Society', 173.

[30] *OSA* ii. 94 (Midcalder); xi. 641; xvi. 663.

[31] T. C. Smout, 'Born Again at Cambuslang: New Evidence on Popular Religion and Literacy in Eighteenth-Century Scotland', *Past and Present*, 97 (1982), 122.

[32] Houston, *Literacy in Early Modern Europe*, 132.

ability to read had become a normal part of the cultural expectations and everyday experience of the lowland population.

Houston's work is especially valuable because he seeks to put the Scottish experience in a European context, challenging the customary association of educational superiority with Calvinism and with the supposedly unique features of Scottish society. On the one hand, Scotland contained in the highlands one of the least literate areas in Europe; on the other, literacy rates in the lowlands resembled those in adjoining parts of northern England: thus a regional rather than a national framework of explanation might be in order. In the European context, Scotland belonged to a high-literacy group which included Catholic areas like north-eastern France as well as Protestant countries like Holland, Prussia, and Scandinavia. A male signature literacy rate of 65 per cent was high for the eighteenth century, but not unique. Moreover, most characteristics of Scottish literacy fitted into a pattern familiar elsewhere. Three features in particular may be commented on: literacy was lower among women than men, it had a close relationship with the social hierarchy of occupations, and it was higher in towns than in the countryside.

The large gender gap in literacy is hardly surprising, given the role of men in family contacts with the outside world. Even from the religious point of view, it was not necessary for every member of a family to be literate, provided that its male head, like the father in Burns's 'Cottar's Saturday Night', could read the Bible and conduct family prayers. The differential between reading and writing was especially wide for women; the closing of this gap was to be a major part of the educational progress of the nineteenth century, and reflected a still poorly documented change of mentality. It is also unsurprising that literacy spread from the top of society, and first became indispensable among those who needed it for public transactions or for business. In the seventeenth century, it was still possible for town councillors or heritors to be unable to sign their names.[33] By the mid-eighteenth, Houston's evidence shows, nearly all landlords and professional men (though not their wives and daughters) were literate. In the period 1700–60, the masculine rate was 87 per cent among merchants and craftsmen, the group where literacy had probably been growing most quickly, but at the bottom of the social scale, for labourers and servants, the rate was only 51 per cent for men and 13 per cent for women.[34] Finally, since the groups for whom literacy

[33] J. M. Beale, *A History of the Burgh and Parochial Schools of Fife* (n.p., 1983), 40.
[34] Houston, 'The Literacy Myth?', 94.

was most valuable were concentrated in towns, literacy was consistently higher there than in the countryside, and highest of all in the large cities of Edinburgh and Glasgow.[35] This is perhaps unexpected in view of the traditional Scottish emphasis on the parish schools, but is in line with other countries in the pre-industrial age. Urban life provided intellectual stimulus, integration into a market economy, and opportunities for individual mobility, all of which favoured the acquisition of literacy. But when industrialization began to overwhelm the towns, this was to change.

4. SCHOOL ATTENDANCE AND SOCIAL MOBILITY

Literacy is one way of measuring the output of education. Another is school attendance, and in the nineteenth century it becomes possible to count children at school, and estimate what proportion of them attended and for how long. For earlier years, no general statistics of this kind are available. In some individual parishes, the Statistical Account allows the numbers at school to be related to the total population, but the ratios revealed by this exercise vary so much that it is difficult to attach much meaning to them.[36] For before the era of legal compulsion families and individuals used schools in ways which suited their own priorities, not necessarily coinciding with the ideas of the social authorities. When there was no defined minimum period and no official 'leaving age', the patterns of attendance could vary widely. In a rural society, with its seasonal rhythms and its fluctuating demands for child labour, there was no clear division between work and school, and whatever amount of literacy was thought desirable could be achieved by a mixture of full-time schooling, irregular attendance in slack periods, and informal or private study, often continuing well into adolescence or even adult life. Children were expected to contribute to the family economy as soon as they were old enough, beginning by herding and watching animals, but the demand for labour was highest in the summer, and in Scotland, as in other countries, school attendance fell off sharply after the spring. In the winter 'quarter', on the other hand, adolescents could return to brush up or extend their basic knowledge. The wide dispersion of parish and private schoolmasters in the countryside made it relatively

---

[35] Houston, 'The Literacy Myth?', 95–8. Cf. R. A. Houston, 'Literacy, Education and the Culture of Print in Enlightenment Edinburgh', *History*, 78 (1993), 373–92.

[36] Withrington, 'Schooling, Literacy and Society', 172.

easy to return to education as funds allowed, or as the desire for instruction of some specific kind arose, and many teachers gave evening as well as day classes. But accounts which concentrate on the supply of teachers and schools underestimate both the complexities of educational demand, and the degree to which it was a force independent of provision from above.

The irregular and intermittent nature of school attendance can be illustrated by some individual biographies, which are also relevant to the question of how far the parish school helped 'lads of parts'. One well-known case is Robert Burns, born in Ayrshire in 1759. His father was a not very successful small farmer, and Burns's services on the farm were needed at an early age. He was sent at the age of 6 to a small local school, then for a few years his father clubbed together with four neighbours to engage a schoolmaster. He later attended the parish school to improve his writing, and went briefly to the 'English' school at Ayr, where his former teacher was now the master. Later again he studied surveying with another local teacher. He thus assembled enough education to arouse his interest in literature, though not at first to emancipate him from farming. Burns's education, though fragmentary, gave him a better start than his successor as a peasant poet, James Hogg, born in 1770 in the Borders. Hogg had very little formal schooling, began herding sheep at 7, and worked as a shepherd. It was only at the age of 26 that he 'began with great difficulty to write his verses, his school training having merely introduced him to large text'.[37] Like many poor children Hogg had presumably learnt to read but not to write; yet independently of the written word, both he and Burns had access to a rich oral tradition of songs and ballads.

Self-education after minimal school attendance was also the experience of the great engineer Thomas Telford, born in Dumfriesshire in 1757, who began life as a stonemason (and who also made his first bid for fame with poetry). It figures too in the biographies of several country lads who went on to eminence in church or university, such as Alexander Murray, a Galloway shepherd-boy who became professor of oriental languages at Edinburgh.[38] Watching sheep was a lonely and boring occupation, and for those who knew how, reading was a natural way of passing the time. A similar case was that of Alexander Christison, born in 1753 at Longformacus in Berwickshire. He stayed long enough

---

[37] *Dictionary of National Biography.*
[38] R. D. Anderson, *Education and Opportunity in Victorian Scotland: Schools and Universities* (Oxford, 1983), 6–7.

at the parish school to encounter Latin, which first stimulated his ambition, but was soon taken away to herd sheep, and studied entirely by himself before qualifying for a schoolmaster's post; he was to become rector of Edinburgh High School, and professor of Latin at the university.[39] More use was made of schools by John Cruickshank, born in 1787, the son of a small farmer and handloom weaver in Banffshire. His full-time attendance was short, but an uncle 'appears to have allowed him once or twice the customary winter-quarter, or "raith," as it was called, at the parish school of Rothiemay'; collective family support of this kind for a promising boy was common. Cruickshank carried on intermittent attendance at parish schools until he was 18, when he managed to get a bursary to Marischal College in Aberdeen, where he was eventually to become professor of mathematics. As a student, he came back to the parish school in the summer to improve his knowledge, then accepted a post as a schoolmaster, teaching in the summer and paying a substitute during the university term—a common practice.[40] In cases like these, local schools played an important role as a stimulus to initial intellectual interest, as an accessible source of part-time education, and as a means of support during the years of study.

Another pattern of social mobility through education was for able boys to be spotted in their local schools by ministers or benevolent landowners, and sent to the nearest burgh school, as happened to James Mill, the son of a rural shoemaker, born in 1773, and sent to Montrose Academy.[41] It was the burgh school too, in this case at Annan, which was the road to the university for Thomas Carlyle, born in 1795. Mill and Carlyle were the classic cases used by Élie Halévy to illustrate 'the life of every poor Scotsman who desired to win through to success'.[42] In fact examples of 'lads of parts' following the supposedly standard route direct from parish school to university prove surprisingly elusive. Those who did this were more likely to be the sons of the minister or of a well-off farmer, using the parish school because of its local convenience; Nicholas Hans's study of élite careers in the eighteenth century showed that of 130 prominent Scots who were educated at parish schools, 37 were the sons of professional men, 9 of merchants and

[39] R. D. Anderson, 'Scottish University Professors, 1800–1939: Profile of an Elite', *SESH* 7 (1987), 30–1.

[40] J. Ogilvie, *John Cruickshank, Professor in the Marischal College and University of Aberdeen* (Aberdeen, 1896), 7.

[41] A. Bain, *James Mill, a Biography* (London, 1882), 6–7.

[42] É. Halévy, *A History of the English People in 1815, iii: Religion and Culture*, Pelican edn. (Harmondsworth, 1938), 90.

traders, 47 of farmers, 15 of craftsmen and retailers, and (with 20 unknown) only 2 identifiably the sons of workers.[43] When men from poor backgrounds reached the university, it was usually in their twenties after a period of struggle combining work and self-education, and might owe as much to enlightened patronage as to democratic striving. Even then, the careers open to them were relatively modest and ill-paid ones in the church or teaching. The real breadth of opportunity in Scottish society lay as much in the excellent and reasonably priced education available to the urban middle classes as in the narrow and haphazard path of social mobility which education offered to the poor.[44]

Discussion of the relationship between education and democracy in Scotland owes much to two influential books. In his *Scottish Democracy 1815–1840* (1950) Laurance Saunders painted an attractive picture of pre-industrial Scotland as an 'egalitarian and progressive society'. The 'parochial tradition', with its link between parish schools and universities, made the school both an 'equalising agency' which initiated all classes into a common national tradition, and a 'selective agency' which prepared an élite for the universities and the professions, but with 'a premium on general intellectual and moral training rather than on specialised instruction'.[45] This last point became the theme of George Davie's *The Democratic Intellect* (1961). This phrase has become celebrated, and is used to refer to such 'democratic' features as mass literacy and the 'lad of parts' phenomenon, but Davie's book concentrated on the university curriculum, arguing that it embodied a traditional 'social ethics' which linked the country's intellectual leadership with the common people.[46] Both authors see these traditions coming under attack in the nineteenth century, in Davie's case through 'anglicization' of the universities, in Saunders's by the threat which industrialization posed to the radical artisans and literate peasants who were at the heart of popular culture. Both too would see the roots of the tradition in a blend of reformed religion and secular enlightenment. The role of the church in the development of Scottish education is incontrovertible, and Lawrence Stone argued that the advanced state of education in Scotland arose from its peculiar political history, which saw the

[43] N. Hans, *New Trends in Education in the Eighteenth Century* (London, 1951), 26–7.

[44] Smout, *History of the Scottish People*, 449–50, 471–2.

[45] L. J. Saunders, *Scottish Democracy, 1815–1840: The Social and Intellectual Background* (Edinburgh, 1950), 241–3, 261.

[46] G. E. Davie, *The Democratic Intellect: Scotland and her Universities in the Nineteenth Century* (2nd edn., Edinburgh, 1964), pp. xi–xii.

Presbyterian clergy becoming 'the nationalist leaders of the people' against the upper classes, creating 'a society which politically and socially was very democratic, but spiritually was very authoritarian'.[47]

It is to views of this kind that Houston has applied his scepticism, and if he is right about levels of literacy then much of Saunders's picture becomes unconvincing; nor was it ever true that all classes passed through the parish schools. More fundamentally, one can question whether eighteenth-century Scotland was more 'democratic' in any real sense than other societies of the time. It was an agrarian society dominated by its landowners, whether the social structure was one of small tenants or (as in most of the lowlands) of capitalist tenant-farmers and labourers. There were some aristocratic absentees, but most of the lairds were very much on the spot, and whatever may have been the case earlier on, they had now made their peace with the church. They appointed the ministers and the schoolmasters, and if the kirk sessions which superintended the daily affairs of the school can be seen as representatives of a 'village community', it was a body dominated by the larger farmers and other local notables. Thus the undoubtedly 'democratic' features of rural education—widespread provision of schools, and universal literacy as a social norm—did not spring from the soil of a peasant democracy, but owed most to encouragement by the social authorities. In this process the church was predominant, and was guided chiefly by religious aims, including the enforcement of orthodoxy, and by practical considerations like the need to recruit young men to the ministry. When social mobility took place, it was within a framework of patronage and sponsorship, rather than competitive individualism. University links from the parish schools led to the professions rather than to commerce or industry, and many of the lads of parts returned as the next generation of ministers and teachers. Thus the parochial tradition was a rural affair, existing apart from the urban world which was the source of modernization and economic dynamism. It was the burgh schools, academies, and universities which were regenerated in the eighteenth century by Enlightenment ideals, science, and the demands of commerce, and these formed a middle-class educational sector to which neither the rural nor the urban poor had much access.

In a study of one French and one German region in this period, Maynes has spoken of the 'virtues of archaism': education was more developed in Baden than in southern France because of the survival of

---

[47] Stone, 'Literacy and Education', 80–1.

communal resources which were part of a semi-feudal rural structure.[48] Perhaps Scotland too displayed these virtues, with a parish school system funded locally from the produce of land, which worked well in stable and reasonably prosperous communities, but whose balance was easily disrupted by demographic change and by the advent of employment patterns incompatible with the traditional blend of work and schooling. Continental parallels also remind us that schools provided at parish level, supervised by the church and drawing on local financial resources, were to be found in many countries, nor was it unknown for Latin to be taught in such rural schools.[49] It was England which was out of step, since the Anglican Church did not see this as part of its duty. In many ways, as Houston argues, Scotland does not look exceptional in a European context, and it still depended on the legacy of 1696 at a time when many continental states were moving towards more centralized systems.

Yet it certainly had some points of superiority even when compared with continental countries. There was a uniform legal framework whose financial obligations on the landed class were regularly enforced, and which had actually produced a national system of schools. There were professional teachers, with permanent tenure and relatively high qualifications and social status, though this was itself an 'archaic' feature which depended on the lack of more attractive opportunities for educated men, and was coming under severe strain by the late eighteenth century. Educational progress was encouraged by an alliance of clergy, landowners, and urban intellectuals, and the kind of obscurantist hostility to education often found elsewhere was no longer thought respectable; it seems probable too that the model of literate culture was already becoming rooted in the popular mentality. For many Scots, education had become a point of pride as one of the features which distinguished their nation from England, and they looked to the parish schools as the model of progress and to Knox as the founder of the 'national' system. Reflections on this subject, coupled with enlightened interest in the problems of modernization and economic growth, were to shape educational debate as the problems of an expanding society made themselves apparent.

---

[48] M. J. Maynes, 'The Virtues of Archaism: The Political Economy of Schooling in Europe, 1750–1850', *Comparative Studies in Society and History*, 21 (1979), 611–25.
[49] Maynes, *Schooling*, 20; Furet and Ozouf, *Reading and Writing*, 71.

2

From the Enlightenment to the Victorian State

THE main argument of this chapter is that the Scottish élite derived from the parish school a concept of 'national' education which conditioned their response both to economic development in the eighteenth century and to the problems of an urban and industrial society in the nineteenth, eventually influencing the form taken by the modern state system. There was never a single Scottish view, for educational questions aroused many partisan interests. But certain common presuppositions can be identified. The first was belief in a unified system, originally instilled by the church's campaigns for orthodoxy, but later given secular form; unity should be both organizational, tying together the different levels of education, and ideological, helping to create a common culture. Second, the state should take a positive role in education, if only as the ally of the church. The parish school with its legal foundation and local financial endowment provided the model; some saw it as a literal model, which new schools ought to follow as far as modern conditions allowed, others were more concerned with the general principle of public support. A third principle, also derived from the parish schools, was that schools should not serve a single social class, but promote social integration, and a limited degree of social mobility, through their central position in the life of the community. A further idea, which perhaps implicitly underlay all these principles but was more deliberately stressed at some times than others, was that education was one of the sources of Scottish national identity, and that its internal cohesion and distinctive features needed to be preserved if Scotland was to retain its cultural independence within a political union which was itself fully accepted. This was often associated, even in the eighteenth century, with an idealized view of the Scottish educational past.

Elements of these ideas can be traced in the Scottish Enlightenment, among the clergy who expressed their views in the Statistical Account, and among the contending parties in the intense politico-religious battles of the early nineteenth century. By the 1830s the various principles of national education had been brought together and remodelled for nineteenth-century consumption, in a way which already relied on a historical 'myth' about the parish schools. But as this discourse developed, the schools themselves were acquiring minority status, along with the rural society which they served. Private enterprise, voluntary action, and religious dynamism were creating a very heterogeneous collection of schools: if a unified system was considered part of Scotland's educational inheritance, the reality seemed to be moving in the other direction. That this diversification was checked, and eventually reversed, was to be the work of the secular state. But the path from the old ideal of religious unity to the new one of democratic uniformity embodied in the 1872 Act was not simple.

In the first decades of the nineteenth century Scotland was a lively centre of educational thought and experiment, and radical ideas derived from the Enlightenment flourished especially in Edinburgh. But from the 1840s they fade away. Perhaps it was inevitable that once state intervention began it was the more conservative version of the national tradition put forward by the clergy which was preferred, and that radicalism had little place in the basic education offered to the masses. For behind the schooling movement lay fears of disorder and a desire to integrate the industrial work-force into society. To the 'notables', in Furet and Ozouf's words, the school 'was first and foremost an instrument of control, designed to moralize and discipline the masses'.[1] Nor was it unique, for this period saw a general movement to make social institutions more formal, hierarchical, bureaucratized, and systematic. As schooling became universal, it also became more uniform; curricula were standardized, and children were classified and subdivided—by age, by gender, by religious denomination, by social class, or by moral categories which separated the normal from the deviant. The increasing distinction of classes, as society became more complex and urbanized, posed a particular challenge to Scottish traditions which idealized the all-embracing parish school.

1. THE ENLIGHTENMENT

The concern of the church to bring religious instruction and literacy to the people had a natural social dimension, especially in the minds of the

---

[1] F. Furet and J. Ozouf, *Reading and Writing: Literacy in France from Calvin to Jules Ferry* (Cambridge, 1982), 120.

'Moderate' party who dominated the church from the 1750s. To spread a rational piety and to reinforce orthodoxy against the various forms of dissent was also to combat fanaticism, violence, intolerance, and superstition; to teach basic morality was also to promote obedience to parents and social authorities. Education was a modernizing, civilizing process which reinforced the social order, taught political loyalty, and created a work-force open to economic change. These were objectives on which clergy, landowners, and the growing intelligentsia of the cities could agree. There was thus no great gap between the views of the church and those of the thinkers today labelled collectively as the Scottish Enlightenment, many of whom were indeed themselves clergymen. Whatever the long-term implications of its doctrines, the Scottish Enlightenment (unlike that in France) was not an anticlerical or secularizing movement, and posed no challenge to the religious control of education.

Indeed, perhaps for that reason, it showed surprisingly little interest of any kind in educational questions, either theoretical or practical. There were no Scottish educational treatises to rival Rousseau's *Émile*, no proposals for national educational reform of the kind found at this time in many continental countries. Enlightenment theories were reflected most directly in élite education—in the organization and curricula of the universities and burgh schools—and hardly at all at the popular level. There is little doubt, however, that Scotland's historical experience promoted a broadly favourable view of popular education; here Scotland differed from France, where leading thinkers like Voltaire were distinctly hostile to educating the masses.[2] The Scottish thinkers, as recent historians have stressed, were inspired by a sense of society as a moral community sharing common values, and this may be seen as a secular version of the church's parochial ideal. In theoretical terms, their analysis of the development of societies from a backward to an advanced state was likely to emphasize education as a progressive force which could bring the masses to share in the process of improvement; more practically, education could be seen as a tool of economic progress in a small country which was richer in human than material resources.[3]

The fullest Enlightenment discussion of the subject was by Adam

[2] H. Chisick, *The Limits of Reform in the Enlightenment: Attitudes towards the Education of the Lower Classes in Eighteenth-Century France* (Princeton, NJ, 1981).

[3] See essays by D. J. Withrington and A. C. Chitnis in J. J. Carter and J. H. Pittock (eds.), *Aberdeen and the Enlightenment: Proceedings of a Conference Held at the University of Aberdeen* (Aberdeen, 1987); and, from a rather different point of view, G. Davie, *The Scottish Enlightenment and Other Essays* (Edinburgh, 1991).

Smith in *The Wealth of Nations* (1776). Smith asked how far education was a proper subject for government expenditure. He saw his age experiencing a fundamental shift from a closed agrarian society to an open 'commercial' one, in which social diversity and the free market would stimulate the spontaneous satisfaction of needs. Middle-class education could be left to itself, to be modernized by the force of parental demand. But for popular education, Smith recognized that demand was deficient and might need to be supplemented by public provision. The division of labour, the source of economic vitality in commercial societies, also had a negative side, confining the mental horizons of workers and dulling their intellects. If Scottish peasants and mechanics were more articulate and intelligent than English ones—and this was a common if stereotyped perception—it was because the division of labour had gone less far in Scotland. Further economic progress, therefore, might damage Scotland's existing advantage. Smith argued that state intervention might counteract this, and encourage basic education,

by establishing in every parish or district a little school, where children may be taught for a reward so moderate, that even a common labourer may afford it; the master being partly, but not wholly, paid by the public; because, if he was wholly, or even principally, paid by it, he would soon learn to neglect his business. In Scotland, the establishment of such parish schools has taught almost the whole common people to read, and a very great proportion of them to write and account.[4]

Thus the Scottish model was proposed for general adoption, as a compromise which avoided the evils attributed by Smith to educational 'endowments', which removed teachers altogether from market pressures. Smith was also prepared to go beyond Scottish practice with an element of compulsion—by imposing a literacy test, for example, before workers were admitted to a trade. The generalization of the three Rs would have wider social benefits, making the masses more moral and orderly, and basing support for the social order on rational assent rather than blind obedience. Thus the cost of education was one of the few objects which might legitimately 'be defrayed by the general contribution of the whole society'.[5]

Smith's arguments became standard ones, and are found in university lectures given at the end of the eighteenth century by men like

---

[4] A. Smith, *An Inquiry into the Nature and Causes of the Wealth of Nations*, World's Classics edn. (London, 1904), ii. 420–1.
[5] Ibid. 460.

John Millar at Glasgow and Dugald Stewart at Edinburgh—lectures which are a good guide to the ideas absorbed by the Scottish educated élite. Millar, a Whig of radical views, fitted Smith's argument about the dangers of the division of labour into a general historical picture of the progress of intellectual activity in Scotland since the Reformation. Education had diffused downwards to the common people; now this was threatened by the advent of a commercial society, which like the clerical tyrannies of old preferred a division between educated and uneducated classes. But it was 'the interest of the higher ranks to assist in cultivating the minds of the common people, and in restoring to them that knowledge which they may be said to have sacrificed to the general prosperity'. A 'liberal plan for the instruction of the lower orders' was thus called for, and the parish schools, though not without defects, provided a model.[6] Dugald Stewart was a more marked enthusiast for the parish schools:

In consequence of this national establishment, the means of a literary education, and of religious instruction, were in Scotland placed within reach of the lowest orders of the people, in a greater degree than in any other country of Europe; and the consequences have been everywhere favourable to their morals and industry, while the opportunity which has thus been afforded to gentlemen of moderate fortune, and to the clergy, to give an education to their children, at so easy a rate, in the elements of literary knowledge, has bestowed on this part of the United Kingdom a political importance, to which it was neither entitled from the fertility of its soil, nor by the number of its inhabitants.

Stewart was right to stress that the parish schools served middle-class interests as well as the common people, but he also thought that 'in consequence of the footing on which our parochial schools are established, there is scarcely a person of either sex to be met with who is not able to read, and very few who do not possess, to a certain degree, the accomplishments of writing and of cyphering'. The contrast between Scotland and England 'affords a decisive proof that, in such a state of society as ours, some interference on the part of government is indispensably necessary' to complete the revolution begun by the invention of printing, and Stewart looks forward to what might be accomplished in the new century by 'a government aiming systematically, and on enlightened principles, at the instruction and improvement of the multitude'.[7]

    [6] J. Millar, *An Historical View of the English Government* (London, 1803), iii. 87–9, 91–2; iv. 146–61.
    [7] W. Hamilton (ed.), *The Collected Works of Dugald Stewart*, i (Edinburgh, 1854), 511–12; ix (Edinburgh, 1856), 330–1.

2. THE OLD STATISTICAL ACCOUNT AND THE 1803 ACT

The views of the clergy in the Statistical Account are another guide to standard educated opinions. By the 1790s the case for popular education had to face a backlash caused by political reaction to the French Revolution. Once Britain was at war with France in 1793, radical ideas of all kinds came under suspicion, and the ability to read seemed less desirable if applied to Tom Paine rather than the Bible. The Church of Scotland shared in this reaction, and the General Assembly made new efforts to assert control over schools and enforce orthodoxy. In 1799 presbyteries were ordered to inspect all schools within their bounds, summon private teachers before them, and send an annual report to the Assembly. Although it took some years before the machinery of reports from presbyteries worked properly, this was the beginning of a new role for the General Assembly as a national co-ordinating body. But the attempt to squeeze out dissident teachers was only partly successful; presbyterial intervention in burghs was opposed by many town councils, and the civil courts were no longer willing to endorse the church's monopolistic pretensions.[8]

Like the Moderate leadership of the church, most of the contributors to the Statistical Account had no sympathy with social radicalism. But some of them were clearly alarmed that political prejudice might damage educational progress, and stressed in their reports that loyalty, morality, and respect for the social hierarchy were not threatened but reinforced by sound education. The view that 'Gothic ignorance forbodes nothing friendly either to private happiness or national improvement' was expressed, usually less pithily, by many a minister, sometimes with the support of international comparisons.

The good behaviour of the lower ranks in Scotland ... contrasted with the immoralities, crimes, and annual executions, of many of the same class, in the sister kingdom, can be ascribed to nothing so much as to the superior advantages, the former enjoy, of early education, and proper instruction, in the first principles of moral and religious duty. Deprive them of these, and they will soon become as great savages, as the most ignorant rabble of *London*, *Paris*, or *Birmingham*.[9]

---

[8] *Acts of the General Assembly of the Church of Scotland, MDCXXXVIII–MDCCCXLII* (Edinburgh, 1843), 870–4; A. Bain, *Patterns of Error: The Teacher and External Authority in Central Scotland, 1581–1861* (Edinburgh, 1989), 161–72.

[9] *OSA*, ii. 455 (Athelstaneford, East Lothian); vii. 77 (Cadder, Lanarkshire: this over-punctuated entry was written by the schoolmaster).

The advantages of education for economic development and modernization were also stressed. In a memorial asking for higher salaries in 1782, the parish teachers pointed out that without basic literacy 'the understanding can never be opened to the arts of civil life; the vigour of mind that prompts to discovery, to commerce, and to every improvement, must fail; and society itself must languish and decay'.[10] The need to improve salaries in order to attract better-qualified men was taken up vigorously in the Statistical Account, and was by far the commonest of the ministers' complaints. Under the 1696 Act, the maximum salary payable by the heritors was just over £11, and by the 1790s rising prices had condemned many teachers to a 'sort of genteel starving',[11] with total incomes of around £15–20. 'The want of proper schoolmasters', declared a West Lothian minister, 'is the principal cause of the ignorance, bigotry, and sectarism, which now prevails in many parts of this country. In former times, the commons of Scotland were justly accounted the most enlightened people of their station in Europe; but they will probably soon cease to deserve that honourable distinction', and 'it is only from the well informed and well educated part of the community, that candour, moderation, rational piety, and decency of manners can be expected.'[12] Some, like the minister of Duffus (Moray), castigated the meanness of the landed class: 'it seems the present generation of landholders wish to extirpate learning altogether, in order to introduce ignorance and slavery among the lower class of people, else they would give some encouragement to schoolmasters.'[13] The hostility to education of the 'affluent people' of today was contrasted with 'the conduct of Scotland, for at least an age after the Reformation'. The neglect of the teachers' condition threatened 'that taste for literature, that general knowledge, for which the Scotch were so deservedly celebrated, whilst the great mass of the people of the other nations of Europe were sunk in the most savage ignorance'.[14]

This was historical fantasy, though it shows that the doctrine of Scottish educational exceptionalism was already well established, along with its common accompaniment, laments that the golden age was in the past. What is perhaps most interesting about the Statistical Account is that schoolmasters' salaries became the starting-point for a theory about the functions of the parish school. Salaries needed to be adequate to attract men with a liberal education and gentlemanly habits. If

---

[10] Printed in *OSA* i. 193.   [11] *OSA* ii. 74 (Borthwick, Midlothian).
[12] *OSA* ii. 743 (Ecclesmachan).   [13] *OSA* xvi. 509.
[14] *OSA* v. 384 (Urr, Kirkcudbrightshire); vi. 364 (Kilwinning, Ayrshire).

university men disappeared from the parishes, so would the teaching of classics, and village schools would cease to be able either to attract the children of the local élite, or to germinate the seeds of talent and 'genius' among the poor. The various features of the system were thus interdependent. 'The institution of parochial schools', it was claimed, 'shows the wisdom and patriotism of our ancestors in a high degree. At these necessary and useful little seminaries of literary and religious knowledge, established by law in every parish, many have received the first principles of literature, who have become ornaments to their country, and blessings to mankind.' For schoolmasters, 'the Latin language ought ever to be held as an indispensable qualification, else youths of genius may lose the only opportunity of rising in the world'. For if inferior teachers are being recruited,

a thicker cloud of ignorance must be settling over the lower ranks of people, than that which covered their fathers. And while the reputation for learning, which Scotland has so long supported among the nations, must in a short time be lost, those numbers, who, by means of that mediocrity of literature acquired in the parish schools, rose from the lowest stations of life to *merit*, *wealth*, and *rank*, must be henceforth chained down, hopeless and inglorious, to the miserable sphere of their humble birth.[15]

The stereotype of the ambitious Scotsman, rising through merit and trained to conquer the world by the competitive rigours of the school, was already discernible. In adult life, he would be

pushed on to excellence in laudable pursuits by the same nerves which led him foremost in the youthful sport, and made him aspire at personal honour, or his master's applause, by rising *Dux* in the class through merit and industry. It might, therefore, be of great advantage to church and state, in a land where the road to eminence is open to all who will strive to attain it, were a man of a liberal and polished mind placed at the head of each of these nurseries of youth, qualified not only to teach children the alphabet, but to implant in their minds the seeds of virtue, and of that noble ambition which leads to preferment in the world, as at school, by personal worth and due submission to superiors.'[16]

As the last phrase reminds us, this ethic of individual ambition assumed the existence of a hierarchical society, in which talented individuals were discovered and advanced through the patronage of their social superiors. In practice, no doubt, reality fell short of the ideal. Nevertheless,

[15] *OSA* iii. 875 (Peebles); vii. 65 (Bothwell, Lanarkshire); xvi. 643 (St Andrews Lhanbryde, Moray).
[16] *OSA* iii. 623 (Roxburgh).

even in a decade of social reaction, there were plenty of Scottish ministers willing to proclaim that individual mobility was a beneficial part of the divinely sanctioned social order. Hence it is difficult to agree with R. A. Houston that 'provision of education for the poor in Scotland as in England was designed to prepare them for a preordained position in life, and not at all to provide an opportunity for social mobility'.[17] Ministers and intellectuals who had themselves risen in society through merit were naturally inclined to favour this process, to see intellectual ability as a source of social authority transcending the barriers of rank, and to argue for individual mobility as a social safety-valve. Alexander Christison, in a work of 1802 whose title—*The General Diffusion of Knowledge One Great Cause of the Prosperity of North Britain*—was a manifesto in itself, argued that education contributed to order because young men of 'genius' who escaped from the lower ranks (like himself) would especially appreciate the benefits of the existing system, and act as a conservative influence over others.[18]

The campaign for higher salaries was pursued by the clergy and by the teachers themselves, whose public status and connection with the church allowed them a collective professional voice. In 1802 the General Assembly once more stressed the teachers' role in combating subversion and contributing to 'the improvement, the good order, and the success of the people of Scotland'.[19] Their efforts were finally rewarded by an Act of Parliament of 1803, which doubled the statutory salary limits and overhauled the parish school system. The right to a schoolhouse and garden was now clearly defined, though the obligation on the heritors was limited, not very generously, to two rooms including the kitchen. The powers of heritors, ministers, and presbytery were reaffirmed, and the political fears of the time were expressed by confining powers over the school to heritors above a certain level of wealth. The act also allowed the parish salary to be divided to pay for 'side schools' in remote parts of the parish. But the law was still not extended to burghs, and the act did not deal with any type of school apart from the parochial. It was thus hardly an adequate response to the gathering problems of urban and industrial areas, where the field was left to voluntary action.

---

[17] R. A. Houston, *Scottish Literacy and the Scottish Identity: Illiteracy and Society in Scotland and Northern England, 1600–1800* (Cambridge, 1985), 231.

[18] A. Christison, *The General Diffusion of Knowledge One Great Cause of the Prosperity of North Britain* (Edinburgh, 1802), 7–10.

[19] *Acts of the General Assembly*, 891.

3. THE EARLY NINETEENTH CENTURY

It has been customary to see social reform in the early nineteenth century flowing from two great sources, the evangelical movement within the churches, and the more secular utilitarian doctrines which derived ultimately from the Enlightenment. Scotland had its own version of both these currents. Within the established church, evangelicals grew in strength and challenged the old order on church–state issues like the appointment of ministers by lay patrons. This struggle grew in intensity in the 1830s, and culminated with the Disruption of 1843, when the evangelical party led by Thomas Chalmers broke away to form the Free Church. The social implications of evangelicalism arose from its emphasis on internal spiritual life and personal salvation; evangelicals were affronted by religious ignorance among the common people, and reasserted the need for every individual to be able to read the Bible. They were inclined to attribute all social problems to the sinfulness of individuals, and to see church attendance, religious instruction, and Bible reading, along with the charity dispensed by the wealthy as part of their own religious duties, as the answer to poverty, crime, disorder, and intemperance. These feelings led evangelicals into a host of practical activities and organizations concerned with specific social problems as well as the direct promotion of religious faith at home and abroad. In time these activities were not confined to the evangelical party in the narrow sense, but became characteristic of the churches collectively.

The desire to change society by changing individuals was also a feature of utilitarian doctrines, which had affiliations with the Scottish Enlightenment, but reached Scotland in an updated form through the influence of Jeremy Bentham. Utilitarians believed in universal education as the instrument of human progress, and their 'environmentalist' psychology sought to achieve social harmony by moulding the individual character and personality from earliest childhood. These ideas, in a radical form, inspired Robert Owen's experiments at the factory settlement of New Lanark, after he entered into partnership with David Dale. It was in 1816 that he started his 'Institution for the Formation of Character', and published the full version of his *New View of Society*, which proclaimed (among much else) that 'the best governed state will be that which shall possess the best national system of education'.[20]

[20] R. Owen, *A New View of Society, and Other Writings*, Everyman edn. (London, 1927), 73.

In the short run, utilitarianism was more effective in the diluted, Whig-gish form represented by the *Edinburgh Review* of 1802, and by intel-lectuals of Scottish origin like James Mill and Henry Brougham. The *Edinburgh Review* frequently advocated Scottish practice as the answer to English problems, and the parish school system, praised for produc-ing a peaceful and unpauperized Scottish 'peasantry', was the model for English parliamentary bills in 1807 and 1820, the latter introduced by Brougham.

Both secular intellectuals and religious leaders like Chalmers even-tually called on the state to play a positive role in education. But in the first decades of the nineteenth century the emphasis was on voluntary effort, and reformers of all kinds were able to draw on a large reservoir of philanthropic good will. Among landowners, traditional paternalism was given a new stimulus. Among the growing middle class of the towns, the acceptance of charitable obligations became one of the marks of respectability and social status, and was one of the few outlets for public activity by women; much philanthropy was channelled through church membership, but there were also numerous voluntary organ-izations drawing on the middle classes for their funds and committee members. Among them were school committees and educational soci-eties, which were the characteristic form of action in the first two or three decades of the century. Most such societies remained local, usu-ally confined to one town; sometimes they proselytized for new meth-ods of education, but more often simply raised subscriptions and organized support for one or two schools. The first field for this type of activity was the Sunday school, whose original purpose was to impart basic literacy as much as religious instruction. In the anti-revolutionary 1790s the Sunday school movement became identified with political radicalism, and its expansion was checked when it was condemned by the General Assembly in 1799 as part of their war on unorthodoxy. Nevertheless Sabbath schools (as they were usually called in Scotland) continued to be supported by dissenting denominations, including non-Presbyterian ones like the Baptists and Congregationalists, and by lay benefactors. They were usually not associated directly with churches, but run by local Sabbath school societies or interdenominational committees.[21]

Sunday schools were imported from England. Peculiar to Scotland,

[21] C. G. Brown, 'The Sunday-School Movement in Scotland, 1780–1914', *SCHSR* 21 (1981–3), 3–26.

however, were the Gaelic school societies which sought to improve education in the highlands. The 1803 Act had not tackled the special problems of this region, and there was much dissatisfaction with the SSPCK, which was closely tied to the established church, and accused of ineffectiveness because of its emphasis on teaching in English. The influx of highland immigrants to the cities brought the problem of illiteracy home to the lowland bourgeoisie, and in 1811 a Society for the Support of Gaelic Schools was founded at Edinburgh. Similar societies appeared at Glasgow in 1812 and Inverness in 1818, and there were branches or 'auxiliaries' in other towns. The Gaelic school societies raised money in their home towns, and appointed and paid their own teachers; their schools were usually 'circulating' ones which moved on after an intensive literacy campaign in a selected district, aimed at adults as well as children. The Edinburgh society concentrated strictly on teaching Gaelic reading, and no more, with the Bible as the essential text. The Glasgow and Inverness societies, however, allowed the teaching of reading in English, writing, and arithmetic, and their schools developed on more orthodox lines. The Gaelic school societies generally had an evangelical motivation, but in 1824 the church responded with its own 'General Assembly' scheme, which planted yet more schools in the highlands with money raised through national appeals.[22] But much remained to be done: in 1826 the Inverness society published some *Moral Statistics of the Highlands and Islands*, which painted a gloomy picture of illiteracy and ignorance, and concluded that it was 'the might of Government only that can send forth the means effectually to enlighten the dark glens of our mountain land, and upraise its interesting and long neglected people to a full participation in that moral lustre which adorns the Scottish name'.[23]

A few years later, the General Assembly scheme was extended to the lowlands, for it was clear that these too were becoming missionary territory. The growing cities presented the special problem of coping with large numbers of children as cheaply as possible. The answer seemed for a time to be the 'monitorial' system, which allowed a single teacher to handle a large school through monitors, older pupils who transmitted basic skills to younger ones through a highly disciplined set

[22] D. Chambers, 'The Church of Scotland's Highlands and Islands Education Scheme, 1824–1843', *JEAH* 7/1 (1975), 8–17.
[23] *Moral Statistics of the Highlands and Islands of Scotland, Compiled from Returns Received by the Inverness Society for the Education of the Poor in the Highlands* (Inverness, 1826), 31–2.

of routines. Teachers had to be trained in these techniques, and the need for professional training—never felt by the old parish teachers, for whom university attendance was thought the touchstone of ability—now became the key to educational action. There were two rival monitorial systems, devised by Joseph Lancaster and Andrew Bell. Bell was of Scottish origin, and later left money for schools in Scotland, but he was an Anglican clergyman who had worked in India, and his 'Madras' system was taken up by the Church of England, while Lancaster's system was favoured in dissenting and utilitarian circles. In England and Wales, these systems were promoted by two national educational societies: Bell's by the National Society, founded in 1811, which was the educational arm of the Church of England, and Lancaster's by the British and Foreign Schools Society, founded as the Royal Lancasterian Society in 1808. The societies published manuals and reading-books, founded model schools, trained teachers in special colleges, gave advice and subsidies to schools throughout the country, and eventually became the channels through which state aid was administered. But they did not operate in Scotland. Lancasterian school societies appeared in Glasgow (1810), Edinburgh (1811), Aberdeen (1815), Dunfermline, and other towns, and the schools which they founded were to last for many years, but they did not develop into a national network. Nor did they have a particularly radical image, being supported by clergymen, employers, and other local notables as well as by Benthamite educational experts.

There was no need for an equivalent of the National Society in Scotland, where the established church already provided parish schools and worked through organs like the SSPCK. But there were many gaps in the cities, and these were to be filled by 'sessional' schools organized by local churches. In 1813, alarmed by political riots, the ministers and magistrates of Edinburgh created the Edinburgh Sessional School, a day-school supported jointly by several congregations. Later sessional schools were usually based on a single church and administered by its kirk session. Thomas Chalmers gave a new impulse to the movement when he took over a new parish in the east end of Glasgow in 1819, and founded schools there as part of a highly publicized experiment in the parish-centred solution of social problems. From the 1820s, sessional schools were at the centre of the church's efforts for urban education. Collections, appeals, and annual subscriptions provided the money, and much of the energy of the clergy went into organizing and superintending schools. City ministers came to be regarded as experts on education as on other social problems, and the day-school was usually only part of a network of philanthropic institutions which might also include Sabbath schools, evening classes, and 'district' or mission schools for the poor; for the sessional schools themselves often gave a superior education, with a well-qualified teacher, and they came to be seen as the urban equivalent of the parish school.

New schools demanded teachers trained in new methods, and especially in the testing if intellectually undemanding routines of elementary teaching. It was in the cities that formal teacher training developed. The first step was to send newly appointed teachers to a 'model' school for a few months to see new techniques in action. The SSPCK had long used this system. Now the original Edinburgh Sessional School was developed as a model school under the direction of John Wood, a philanthropic lawyer, and in 1826 the church began to use it regularly to train teachers for the General Assembly scheme. Wood had his own educational theory, known as the 'intellectual system', which encouraged teachers to use question-and-answer methods to promote intellectual understanding. Wood retained some features of the monitorial system, but reacted against its mechanical character, and insisted that trained adults were needed for effective teaching. Wood's better-known counterpart in Glasgow was David Stow, a businessman who became a disciple of Chalmers, and was influenced by the ideas of Pestalozzi, Owen, and other pioneers of a more humane approach to the teaching of young children. His earliest interest was in Sunday schools, but he then became a leading figure in the establishment of infant schools, another new idea of the age. The Glasgow Infant School Society was formed in 1826, and in 1828 Stow invited the English pioneer Samuel Wilderspin to visit Scotland. In the next few years infant schools run by local committees were opened in many Scottish towns, and in Edinburgh the Infant School Society of 1829 was a significant focus for educational activists. Later Stow took over one of Chalmers's schools for older children, and developed this and his infant school as centres for training teachers.[24] In 1836 he published a work on his 'training system' which attracted wide attention. Stow went further than Wood in rejecting monitorial methods, and emphasized the moral and religious influence of the individual teacher in shaping the child's personality.

As sessional schools expanded in the 1820s, the problems of urban

---

[24] P. McCann and F. A. Young, *Samuel Wilderspin and the Infant School Movement* (London, 1982), 107–25; S. Mechie, *The Church and Scottish Social Development, 1780–1870* (London, 1960), 140–6.

education came to the forefront, and the ability of purely voluntary methods to cope with them was increasingly questioned. This was a period of extremely rapid growth in the cities, and as immigrants flooded in from the countryside, the highlands, and (rather later) Ireland, the existing schools were overwhelmed. The growth of overcrowded working-class areas aroused acute alarm among the property-owning classes, who saw these as urban jungles impervious to religious and other civilizing influences, breeding-grounds for violence, disorder, and political radicalism. Incidents like the 'radical war', an outbreak of the Glasgow weavers in 1820, encouraged social panic. Historians of English education have commonly seen 'social control' as the dominant motive for the extension of working-class education at this time.[25] Some versions of this theory, which emphasize the desire to impose middle-class values on the workers and bend them to factory discipline, or which see religious motives as simply a front for social and political conservatism, may go too far. The evangelical impulses were sincere enough, and one should not discount the straightforward humanitarian desire to alleviate the pitiful ignorance and poverty of city children. But it is certainly true, and was indeed loudly proclaimed at the time, that education was expected to act as a moralizing agency, both through religious instruction and through the habits of obedience, order, punctuality, and self-control which were learnt from the disciplined pedagogy of the modern school. More generally, the argument that education was a prophylactic against crime and disorder became a standard justification for state action (since even in *laissez-faire* ideology the state had the function of maintaining order), and was kept alive into the 1850s by the Chartist movement and the continental revolutions of 1848.

Another reason for the heightening of educational concern in the 1820s was the publication of the first national educational statistics in 1819, the outcome of an inquiry started by Brougham. They were soon followed by others published by the church, and by further parliamentary inquiries. From the start, educational statistics were political weapons, and were cited selectively by rival parties. To some extent the 1819 figures were reassuring, as they suggested that Scotland still preserved its educational lead over England. But they also showed many

---

[25] The seminal discussion was R. Johnson, 'Educational Policy and Social Control in Early Victorian England', *Past and Present*, 49 (1970), 96–119. There are also suggestive essays in P. McCann (ed.), *Popular Education and Socialization in the Nineteenth Century* (London, 1977).

gaps in provision, and revealed how inadequate the old structure of the parish schools had become—they now accounted for only a third of the children at school.[26] Many of the other two-thirds were in 'private adventure' schools run for profit, and these schools probably played just as large a part as those sponsored by charities or churches in coping with the growth of demand in the towns. For conservatives this seemed a mixed blessing, as private teachers escaped supervision by the authorities. Thus one aspect of social control, and one motive for the extension of church activity, was the desire to bring children into schools which offered a guarantee of religious education, and where approved social values were taught by teachers trained in the new methods. In traditional communities, the established structure of church and school was a natural agency of social control; now the task was to create a substitute in the towns.

4. THE IDEAL OF NATIONAL EDUCATION

No one did more to promote this idea than Chalmers. As all commentators on his work have recognized, he aimed to reproduce in the city the paternalist social relationships of the country parish, maintaining social harmony and a sense of community by binding the social classes together around the parish church.[27] His most recent biographer, S. J. Brown, has called this the ideal of the 'godly commonwealth', and the appeal to a lost or idealized rural community, set against the harsh realities of the city, is a common (and natural) element in Scottish thought in the early nineteenth century. Chalmers's views on education were formed by analogy with the principle of church establishment. In the village, parish church and parish school went together; in the city too they must be based on the 'territorial' principle, supported by the state and serving the whole community within their district. When he opened his sessional schools in 1820, he called on the rich to let their children sit alongside others on the benches, so that as in the parish schools there should be 'an indiscriminate mingling of the children of all ranks and degrees in society'. This was a utopian vision in a city

[26] See discussion in Ch. 4.
[27] W. Hanna, *Memoirs of the Life and Writings of Thomas Chalmers* (Edinburgh, 1849–52), ii. 229.

where, as Chalmers himself acknowledged, residential segregation and class feeling were well developed, and in practice his schools were not designed for the really poor: one was for 'English' subjects and one for commercial ones, with fees of 2*s.* and 3*s.* per quarter respectively.[28]

In 1819 Chalmers had published a more general defence of the parish school model, and elaborated the case for the 'endowment' of education. He rejected the two extremes—providing free education for the poor through charity, or leaving them to pay for it themselves through the market—in favour of a 'medium' system, combining permanent endowment with moderate fees. This was the policy, he claimed, of the sixteenth-century reformers, and it had succeeded over the centuries in making education universal through custom and habit rather than compulsion. The problem was to recreate these habits in an urban context, where the roots of custom had been torn up. This could not happen unless the school was provided by some public agency, for Chalmers argued that, unlike material needs, intellectual and spiritual impulses did not arise spontaneously, but needed to be stimulated from above; supply must here precede demand, and only when education is already available can its value be appreciated. Thus Chalmers, in other matters a champion of *laissez-faire*, argued that it was not applicable to education, and criticized Adam Smith on these grounds (not entirely fairly, as we have seen). Endowment was also necessary, according to Chalmers, to realize the ideal of a school for all classes, for only a regular salary could attract well-qualified teachers; a school should be able to offer all that the middle classes needed, while keeping the fees low enough to exclude no one.[29]

These ideas were already present in the Statistical Account, itself given new currency in the 1820s when its originator, Sir John Sinclair, published a somewhat belated *Analysis*, discussing contemporary problems in the light of the parochial tradition.[30] Sinclair incorporated Chalmers's theory of the medium system into this work, and it was also cited with approval in the *Edinburgh Review* in 1827, when the Whig lawyer and intellectual Henry Cockburn warned that

---

[28] W. Hanna, *Memoirs of the Life and Writings of Thomas Chalmers* (Edinburgh, 1849–52), ii. 240; S. J. Brown, *Thomas Chalmers and the Godly Commonwealth in Scotland* (Oxford, 1982), 136–7.

[29] *The Works of Thomas Chalmers* (Glasgow, n.d.), xii. 193–206 (originally published 1819 as *Considerations on Parochial Schools*); T. Chalmers, *Church and College Establishments* (Edinburgh, 1848), 24 ff.

[30] J. Sinclair, *Analysis of the Statistical Account of Scotland* (London, 1826).

our ancient system of popular instruction is in an alarming condition, and that, if we really wish to make our parish schools continue to accomplish the purposes for which they were originally designed, we must cease to slumber over them with the half patriarchal half poetical dream, which is apt to come over us when we think of those rural seminaries—and must do something effectual to revive them.[31]

Chalmers's views were widely disseminated through his leading position in the church, and it was he more than anyone who recreated the parish school ideal for nineteenth-century purposes, and established it as the model for future development. For the Tory Chalmers or the moderate Whigs Sinclair and Cockburn, the ideal was a conservative one, designed to keep education in the hands of the traditional social and religious authorities, and to preserve old habits of deference. Cockburn argued that through the existing rural schools 'there has been diffused over the whole lower and middle regions of the community a remarkably steady air of piety, thoughtfulness, and virtuous pride', and reminded negligent heritors that 'it is they, beyond any other class of the community, who reap a direct patrimonial advantage from the orderly habits which are the results of parochial education'.[32]

Patriarchal idealization was taken to a more extreme level by the high Tories of *Blackwood's Magazine*, who insisted that all education was dangerous outside the control of the church.

Would you behold Scotland as she was—enter the country cottage of the as yet untainted *rural* labourer; you will see a frugal, industrious, and contented family, with few luxuries, but fewer wants—bound together by the strongest bonds of social affection, fearing God, and scrupulous in the discharge of every moral and religious duty; you will see the young at the village school, under the shadow of the neighbouring church, inhaling with their first breath the principles of devotion, and preparing to follow the simple innocent life of their forefathers, who repose in the neighbouring churchyard; . . . Such was, and, in many places, still is Scotland under the Church, the Schoolmaster, and the Bible.[33]

This idyll was contrasted with a lurid picture of crime, debauchery, and sedition in the manufacturing districts. A conservative social vision of the unchanging village community and of the role of the 'dominie' within it (as depicted, or rather caricatured, in several of Scott's novels) was to reappear in later years as part of 'kailyard' sentimentalism, but

---

[31] *Edinburgh Review*, 46 (1827), 111.   [32] Ibid. 110, 130.
[33] *Blackwood's Edinburgh Magazine*, 35 (1834), 246–7.

in the 1820s and 1830s it can be seen as one more testimony to the parish school ideal.

The chief targets of *Blackwood's* were the liberal and utilitarian reformers who looked to the state for action on social problems. Chalmers and Cockburn wanted the state to act in partnership with the church, while most of the intellectuals of the *Edinburgh Review* preferred a secular state acting independently. Yet this too was justified by an appeal to Scottish traditions: Chalmers's arguments against Adam Smith were widely echoed, and Scotland's educational superiority to England was ascribed to the state's support for the parish schools. Many of the Edinburgh literati envisaged a national system run on continental lines by a central ministry, and they were especially impressed by the French education law of 1833, which made a school mandatory in every parish, and which was itself based on a report on schools in Prussia by the philosopher Victor Cousin. These European developments attracted articles in the *Edinburgh Review* by the philosopher William Hamilton, who argued that 'all that Scotland enjoys of popular education above the other kingdoms of the British Empire, she owes to the State',[34] and by James Pillans, a noted educationist influenced by Bentham, who had been an enlightened reformer as rector of Edinburgh High School before becoming professor of Latin at Edinburgh. Also in the capital was a circle of radical reformers around the phrenologist George Combe, and it was his disciple James Simpson who produced in 1834 a plan for a centralized system of free, compulsory, and secular education, in which all classes and both sexes would be educated in common schools until the age of 14.[35]

By the 1830s, therefore, Scottish thinkers of various schools were coming to speak of a 'national' system of education, which would somehow extend the principles of the parochial tradition, which had served the nation so well since the Reformation, to meet the demands of a changing society. This did not necessarily mean a state system of the kind envisaged by Simpson, but it did imply that schools should be under some kind of common authority and ideological direction, and that there should be an organic link between the different levels of

[34] W. Hamilton, *Discussions on Philosophy and Literature, Education and University Reform* (London, 1852), 538. Cf. R. D. Anderson, 'Education and the State in Nineteenth-Century Scotland', *Economic History Review*, 2nd series, 36 (1983), 533.

[35] J. Simpson, *Necessity of Popular Education, as a National Object* (Edinburgh, 1834), 203 ff. Cf. his evidence in PP 1835, VII, *Report from the Select Committee on Education in England and Wales*, 121 ff.

education, serving to unify the national community. 'What is wanted', said Pillans,

is a well-digested and comprehensive scheme of popular instruction, organized upon one plan in its earlier stages, and diffusing its benefits equally and impartially over all. . . . Uniformity in the groundwork of the intellectual and moral habits of the people is thus secured, with that unity of feeling and nationality which contribute so much to individual happiness and general prosperity; and these blessings it is vain to expect in any other way than by Legislative interference.[36]

Pillans was actually speaking of his hopes for England, but cited Scotland and Germany as models. The implication was that Scotland already enjoyed unity of feeling, happiness, and prosperity. But once education did become a matter for legislative interference, the need for uniformity within the British state created new tensions between Scottish ideals and political reality.

5. THE ORIGINS OF STATE INTERVENTION

The 1832 Reform Act began a new era in Scottish politics, which had previously been narrowly oligarchic. The vote was given to the bourgeois élite, and the majority of the new Scottish MPs were Whigs or (as they were coming to be called) Liberals. The time seemed ripe for educational reform, and in 1833 Parliament approved an annual grant of £20,000 to assist school building in 'Great Britain'. In England this was divided between the National and British societies. In Scotland it was claimed by the church, and in 1834 the Liberal MP J. C. Colquhoun introduced a bill (the first attempt at Scottish educational legislation since 1803) to 'enlarge' the parochial system, by directing funds towards the endowment of teachers' salaries rather than to new building, for which there was less need in Scotland. Colquhoun attacked private schools, and wished education to be under the 'superintendence and moral agency' of the clergy.[37] The bill made no progress, though it did stimulate a new government inquiry into the state of schooling. Colquhoun was president of the Glasgow Educational Society, founded in 1834 as a political pressure group to promote the interests of the

---

[36] J. Pillans, *Contributions to the Cause of Education* (London, 1856), 152 (originally in *Edinburgh Review*, 1833).
[37] Hansard, 3rd series 24, 17 June 1834, 516.

established church, in which the evangelical party were now predominant. It was based on the old Infant School Society, and its joint secretaries were Stow and a young Chalmersite clergyman, George Lewis, who provided a manifesto under the arresting title *Scotland a Half-Educated Nation*. Lewis's aim was confessedly 'to shake the national satisfaction': he surveyed the latest statistical evidence, declared the existence of a crisis in the cities, and concluded that all the effort put into sessional schools and similar initiatives 'serves only to evince the entire impotency of the voluntary system to educate either an entire nation, or an entire city'. Following Chalmers, Lewis argued that 'in a national system, the Government must . . . have an eye to bring together all classes into the same school' in order to promote social harmony, and he added that it was now only the parish church and school which were distinctive to Scotland.

In these alone we survive as a nation—stand apart from and superior to England. These are the only remains we can show the stranger of the ancient excellence of our country—the only memorials of the wisdom and worth of bygone days. These are the only institutions around which linger Scottish feelings and attachments; in the support, extension, and improvement of which, may yet be rallied all the patriotism and piety of Scotland. . . . The evils of a century's neglect must now be remedied, that, refitted to the altered circumstances of our country, Scotland may again be crowned chief amongst the nations for wisdom, and knowledge, and righteousness.[38]

The campaign for state aid to church schools was part of a wider anti-voluntarist offensive conducted by Chalmers, which sought similar aid for building new churches. But this campaign was misjudged, as politicians would no longer accept the established church's claim to a monopoly of patriotism and piety. A Tory government might have been willing to accept Chalmers's vision of a church–state alliance, at least before Catholic emancipation in 1829 ended the era of the 'confessional' state and made religious liberty a common principle of politics. But the 1832 Reform Act began a period of Liberal dominance, and governments depended on dissenting support, in England as well as Scotland. The Scottish Central Board of Dissenters founded in 1834 proved an influential pressure group. The Church of Scotland was powerful enough to retain its existing positions, and to claim a special

---

[38] G. Lewis, *Scotland a Half-Educated Nation, both in the Quantity and Quality of her Educational Institutions* (Glasgow, 1834), 6, 44, 55, 75.

role as the church of the majority of the Scottish people, but its ambition to act as the sole educational arm of the state was disappointed.

There were some limited gains. The building grants—first paid in Scotland in 1834, and regularly from 1836—were at first confined to schools connected with the church, and mostly went to sessional schools in the cities or in large towns like Paisley and Greenock. Another small victory was the Highland Schools Act of 1838, which provided for new schools in certain highland parishes, and accepted the 'endowment' principle of paying a regular salary. But the most lasting achievement of the Glasgow Educational Society was a local one: the opening of the Glasgow 'Normal Seminary' for training teachers, which was based on Stow's training schools and directed by him. In the same year, 1837, Wood's training school at Edinburgh came under the control of the church's Education Committee, and in 1841 this committee also took over the Glasgow school as part of a deal with the government whereby the state provided an annual subsidy. Through these two 'normal' schools, the church now dominated the training of teachers, and its Education Committee, which also supervised the church's educational schemes and published an annual survey of the state of education based on reports from presbyteries, seemed to be emerging as a powerful national educational authority.

But this dominance was shattered in 1843 by the Disruption and the formation of the Free Church. Unlike the 'voluntarist' dissenters—most of whom combined to form the United Presbyterian Church in 1847—the Free Church continued to believe in the establishment principle, and saw itself as a kind of established church in exile. It therefore sought to reproduce the Church of Scotland's educational structure, with its own education committee, divinity colleges, normal schools (Stow headed the one in Glasgow), and day-schools supported by local congregations. To some extent this was to support teachers ejected from their posts because they had joined the Free Church, but the church's educational efforts soon took on a momentum of their own. Even before the Disruption, about a third of the Scottish population had rejected allegiance to the established church. Now there were three major Presbyterian churches, and the Church of Scotland attracted only 32 per cent of church-goers—in the cities it was only a fifth.[39] Thus its claim to be the national church could no longer be sustained, and the vision of

---

[39] C. G. Brown, *The Social History of Religion in Scotland since 1730* (London, 1987), 31, 61.

the godly commonwealth was shattered. Politically, the state was bound to respond to this situation by treating all denominations impartially.

While the Church of Scotland was united, its supervisory role in education had been so dominant that minority churches—dissenting, Episcopalian, and Roman Catholic—had not attempted to build up school networks of their own. The Disruption changed this, and coincided with changes in the state grant system which also encouraged denomination-alism. The early grants were given only for building new schools, but within a few years other small grants were introduced to encourage the adoption of new methods. In 1839 the Education Committee of the Privy Council (or Education Department) was set up to administer this expanding system, with Her Majesty's Inspectorate following in 1840. The new department was headed by the dynamic bureaucrat James Kay (later Kay-Shuttleworth), and when Parliament proved willing to spend more on education he devised a system of annual grants which could be claimed by all schools which met certain conditions, designed above all to increase the stock of trained teachers. Kay's ideas were embodied in Minutes of 1846, which applied to Scotland as to England and Wales, and these formed the basis of the so-called 'Privy Council system'. The regulations created a government teaching certificate, and teachers who passed it were paid an annual 'augmentation grant' to supplement their income. Certificated teachers received a further grant if they took on apprenticed 'pupil-teachers', boys and girls from the age of 13, who were themselves given a small state salary. The pupil-teachers taught school classes while also following a five-year programme of study; at the end of their apprenticeship they could compete for a 'Queen's Scholarship' which would pay for two years at a normal school, leading to the certificate examination. The normal colleges, though run by the church, and allowed to take private students, thus became dependent on state finance and Education Department regulations. The system as a whole concentrated financial aid on schools which used approved teach-ing methods, provided a cheap teaching force of adolescents to replace the unsatisfactory monitors, and promised to produce an increasing flow of qualified teachers who could take charge of schools. By quali-fying for state aid, schools acquired relative financial security, while the state retained a continuous power of supervision through the annual visits of its inspectors, and could use the grant regulations to enforce specific policies.

By 1849, when Kay-Shuttleworth retired, the state had established a permanent presence in education, with its own bureaucratic momentum, though within strict limits. Aid was given only to schools for the poor, as other classes were expected to look after themselves. It was meant to stimulate and support local and private effort, not to replace or weaken it: for a building grant, local resources had to provide half the cost, while annual grants could not exceed a third of a school's income, with fees and contributions making up the balance. Grants were not made to profit-making or 'adventure' schools, but only to local managers, usually connected with a church or an educational society. The system thus rested on a complex balance between public support and voluntary initiative, central and local funding. It was also designed to cope with the religious situation in England, where the state had to appear even-handed between Anglican and Nonconformist interests; the result was a 'denominational' system with rival empires of publicly funded schools. There was a similar outcome in Scotland. School grants were accepted by the Free Church in 1847 (building grants were particularly useful in its initial period of expansion), the inspectorate was divided on denominational lines, and subsidies went to the duplicate normal schools in Edinburgh and Glasgow. The United Presbyterian Church did not share in this bounty, although it did run schools, because its voluntarist principles forbade it to apply for state aid. But both Episcopalians and Roman Catholics welcomed the grants. The only disappointed suitors were secularists, who believed that religion should be the responsibility of parents rather than the school: the provision of religious instruction was a compulsory condition of grant, and a Secular School at Edinburgh founded by Combe and Simpson in 1848 was refused one. This collapsed after a few years, but a similar school at Glasgow founded in 1850 survived, finding a niche by serving the local Unitarians.[40]

The 1846 grant system was deeply unpopular among English voluntarists, who would have preferred the state to keep out of education altogether rather than entrench denominationalism. In 1847 the historian Thomas Macaulay, then an MP for Edinburgh (and a member of the Committee of Council on Education), deployed against the voluntarists, with characteristic vigour and over-simplification, Scottish arguments in favour of state action which went back at least to Dugald Stewart. England and Scotland, he claimed, provided almost perfect experimental conditions for testing a voluntary against a public system. One hundred and fifty years ago, England was wealthy and Scotland impoverished. Then came the 1696 Act.

---

[40] PP 1865, XVII, *Education Commission (Scotland), First Report*, 261.

The opulent and highly civilised nation leaves the education of the people to free competition. In the poor and half barbarous nation the education of the people is undertaken by the State. The result is that the first are last and the last first. The common people of Scotland . . . have passed the common people of England. . . . State education, tried under every disadvantage, has produced an improvement to which it would be difficult to find a parallel in any age or country. Such an experiment as this would be regarded as conclusive in surgery or chemistry, and ought, I think, to be regarded as equally conclusive in politics.

Macaulay appealed to the authority of Adam Smith and David Hume, as well as to the usual arguments about crime and disorder, to conclude that it was 'the right and the duty of the State to provide means of education for the common people'.[41]

The Victorian state had thus accepted by the 1840s that education was in its domain. Why then did it take another generation before the 1872 Act organized a comprehensive national system? One answer might be that Scottish opinion was ready for such a system, but that it was delayed by the subordination of Scottish interests to English ones in the Westminster system; that the 1872 Act had to wait on the resolution of England's problems in 1870. But this explanation would ignore the divisions within Scotland. The only practicable 'national' system before 1843 would have been one based on the Church of Scotland. That was already unacceptable to a large part of Scottish opinion, and became impossible after the Disruption. More profoundly, the parish school ideal put forward by Chalmers in his vision of the godly commonwealth reflected a culturally homogeneous, Presbyterian, rural Scotland which (if it had ever existed at all except as an ideal) was now receding into the past. The growth of Irish Catholic immigration posed a particular challenge to the idea of a single national culture. There were two further difficulties. One was that since the end of the eighteenth century numerous new schools of all kinds had grown up, especially in response to urban needs; they formed a powerful vested interest, reinforced by the boost given to denominational effort in 1846, and those who had invested money and effort in them were reluctant to give them up. Their relationship with the established parish schools, which themselves needed modernization, posed a complex problem for legislators. Second, the old 'national' ideal was a paternalistic one which was designed to entrench the rule of the old élites. This was becoming

---

[41] T. B. Macaulay, *The Miscellaneous Writings and Speeches of Lord Macaulay*, popular edn. (London, 1891), 735, 744. For the original debate, see Hansard, 3rd series 91, 19 Apr. 1847.

unacceptable both to the new middle class, who were the chief creators of the voluntary school system and who sought to control political life in the towns, and to the working class, whose own educational initiatives were modest, but who gained a voice with the advance of democracy in the 1860s. By that time, the control of education by middle-class kirk sessions or charitable committees itself seemed unsatisfactory, and the cause of national education was associated with the demand for elective local control.

Thus any new settlement would have to allow for religious diversity, reconcile voluntary effort and state action, extend the influence of local public opinion, and arrive at an acceptable definition of how Scotland's common culture could be defined in the modern world. That was unlikely to happen in the short run, as Scots did not agree on the place of religion in a 'national' system, and the Disruption made the Church of Scotland all the more determined to hold on to its remaining privileged positions. The problem could only be solved when religious passions died down, so that all or most of the churches were prepared to surrender their control. Once this degree of secularization was accepted, national unity could be re-established on the basis of common schools run by locally elected boards. Thus the thread of the community-based parish school tradition was rewoven. But the denominational system was probably an inevitable transitional stage, and it had its own rationale. The churches valued schools as a way of retaining their members' loyalty, training the young in their traditions, and evangelizing among the poor. The combination of state encouragement and competitive religious zeal was a powerful one, and between the 1840s and 1872 it was church schools, shaped to a common pattern by state grants, which came to provide the bulk of working-class education in the towns.

3

The Politics of Popular Education,
1850–1872

'EDUCATION will be right', wrote Henry Cockburn privately in 1846, 'exactly in proportion as secular sense and vigour are allowed to supersede clerical ignorance and intolerance.'[1] Many laymen agreed, and it can easily be argued that the modernization of the national system was delayed for twenty years simply by quarrels between the churches. However, the churches were organizations with much political influence, and the divisions in Scottish opinion ran deep. Between the two Reform Acts of 1832 and 1867, Scottish politics and party allegiances were dominated to an unusual degree by religion. The Established Church was identified with Conservatism, while the United Presbyterians and (less monolithically) the Free Church buttressed the dominant position of the Liberals, especially in the burghs. The churches learnt to mobilize a formidable apparatus of pamphlets, petitions, deputations, and public meetings, at both national and constituency level, which no MP could ignore—as Macaulay found when he was forced to resign his Edinburgh seat in 1856 because local activists disapproved of his support for Catholic educational interests in Ireland. As the years passed, laymen became increasingly impatient with the subordination of educational progress to the demands of an intransigent and quarrelsome clergy, but it took the widening of the franchise in 1867 to bring about decisive change.

1. THE PROBLEM OF NATIONAL EDUCATION

The campaign for legislative reform began in 1850 with the formation of the National Education Association, which had broadly based support in political and educational circles. Its objective was 'a general system of national education, on a sound and popular basis, and capable

[1] Letter to J. S. Blackie (professor at Aberdeen), in A. Bell (ed.), *Lord Cockburn: A Bicentenary Commemoration, 1779–1979* (Edinburgh, 1979), 83.

of communicating instruction to all classes of the community'.[2] 'National' was now often the shorthand term for 'non-denominational'. The NEA and subsequent reformers saw the proposed national system as a modernization of the parish school principle, which was sound in itself even if the parish schools themselves had been overtaken by economic and demographic development. The new version of the heritors and their assessments would be a school rate and a school committee elected by the ratepayers. These local committees would be able to take an impartial view of the needs of their district, eliminate overlapping and confusion, and found new schools where they were needed. Existing denominational schools, it was hoped, would be absorbed into the system, and would not need separate subsidies from the state. The parish schools might continue as a distinctive type, but the sectarian character which they had presented since the Disruption would be ended by abolishing presbyterial supervision and the religious test imposed on schoolmasters. The reform of the Poor Law in 1845, which had transferred responsibility from kirk sessions to locally elected parochial boards (though on a property-based franchise), seemed to provide a precedent.

But the educational problem was not solved so simply. The NEA itself fell victim to internal divisions, and soon faded out of the picture. There were to be twenty years of politico-religious warfare before the ideal of national education was realized. Scots liked to congratulate themselves that there was no 'religious difficulty' in Scotland of the type which divided Anglicans and Nonconformists in England, since the Presbyterian denominations differed on questions of church–state relations rather than on doctrine. The teaching of the Bible and the Shorter Catechism was a customary tradition on which, it seemed, all could agree. But Scottish ecclesiastics rose impressively to this challenge, and elaborated a set of difficulties of their own. The most contentious issue was what religious instruction should be given if schools were in the hands of a public authority rather than a church: how could it be both Christian and equally acceptable to all the shades of Christianity? Under a denominational system, parents were free to choose their school, and this problem did not arise. But if there were to be national schools supported by rates, and even more if education became compulsory, this became a difficult question. Most of the lay champions

[2] Resolutions cited in J. Kay-Shuttleworth, *Public Education as Affected by the Minutes of the Committee of Privy Council from 1846 to 1852* (London, 1853), 388. Cf. I. G. C. Hutchison, *A Political History of Scotland, 1832–1924: Parties, Elections and Issues* (Edinburgh, 1986), 71–2.

of national education wanted a 'secularist' solution, which would exclude religious instruction from the classroom, leaving it to be arranged privately by parents. The state would take a neutral stance, and the influence of ministers over schools would end. This was the initial position of the NEA. But it was never politically acceptable to the major churches, whose views were reinforced by their vested interest in the existing schools.

The position of the Church of Scotland was the simplest: preservation of the status quo. Control of the parish schools gave the church a continuing claim to a national role which it was quite unwilling to surrender, fearing this would lead inexorably to the disestablishment now being demanded by its ecclesiastical rivals. Unlike the Church of England, it would accept a 'conscience clause' allowing parents to withdraw their children from religious instruction; such a policy had long been customary, and in 1829, with highland conditions in mind, the General Assembly had specifically granted this right to Catholics. The church claimed that with this safeguard its schools already were 'national', not denominational; it agreed that there were educational deficiencies in the towns, but argued that these were exaggerated by the manipulation of alarmist statistics, and could be met by expansion within the existing framework without any need for legislation. These positions were endorsed by Conservative statesmen, speaking for landowners who regarded the parish schools as part of the established order and wanted to maintain their own grip on them as heritors, and for a wealthy middle class which had no desire to see the introduction of educational rates in towns, or the setting up of elected school authorities which might be dominated by radicals. And although the Conservatives were in a minority in Scotland, they could gain powerful parliamentary support by suggesting that any threat to the establishment in Scotland was a threat to the Anglican position in England, Wales, and Ireland.

The Established Church insisted that religious instruction should be guaranteed either by keeping schools under church control, or, if there was to be legislation, by direct legal prescription. At the other end of the spectrum, the United Presbyterians held a doctrinaire voluntarist position which rejected the right of the state to support or finance any religious teaching. They did not claim state grants for their own schools, but would oppose any legislation making religious instruction compulsory in publicly supported schools. Most UP members, unlike the more extreme English voluntarists, were not hostile to state education itself, and would welcome a national system if it could be reconciled with their principles; their leaders were thus the only churchmen to give full support to the NEA.

The Free Church had the most complex position, as it evolved from its early establishmentarianism to a more logical acceptance of its non-established status. Events had forced it into developing its own schools, but these soon became valued for their own sake, and in the early years the majority in the church, led by Robert Candlish, preferred to retain them, giving an absolute guarantee of religious education under ministerial control. The minority, including leaders like Thomas Guthrie, James Begg, and the journalist Hugh Miller, was prepared to accept a national system even at the price of secularism. Both sides laid claim to the legacy of Chalmers, who had died in 1847. Later the financial strain of maintaining its schools made the Free Church change its mind, and it became the main supporter of national legislation, seeking a compromise on religious instruction which would avert full-blooded secularism.[3] Many cross-currents remained, and for the political leaders of Scottish Liberalism who sought to further the 'national' cause the Free Church was an unpredictable and unreliable ally. To keep both Free and UP churches happy was difficult enough; to satisfy the Church of Scotland as well was almost impossible. Yet this was necessary if a national consensus was to be achieved, and politically desirable since the way Scottish business was conducted in the House of Commons made progress on legislation slow unless Scottish MPs of all parties were in accord.[4] Besides, the governments of the 1850s were mostly coalitions between Liberals and the 'Peelite' centre. There was thus a wide range of views to be appeased.

The secularist programme of the NEA inspired a private member's bill presented in 1850 by the Liberal MP Lord Melgund, but neither this nor a second attempt in 1851 succeeded. The Free Church was hostile to Melgund's bills.[5] But by 1854, when official legislation was proposed by the Lord Advocate, James Moncreiff, the Free Church had carried out its shift of policy, and was prominent at the public meetings

[3] D. J. Withrington, 'The Free Church Educational Scheme, 1843–50', *SCHSR* 15 (1963–5), 103–15; D. K. and C. J. Guthrie, *Autobiography of Thomas Guthrie, D.D., and Memoir by his Sons* (London, 1874–5), ii. 284–307.

[4] M. Fry, *Patronage and Principle: A Political History of Modern Scotland* (Aberdeen, 1987), 71–2.

[5] R. M. W. Cowan, *The Newspaper in Scotland: A Study of its First Expansion, 1815–1860* (Glasgow, 1946), 342–3.

which launched the campaign. Moncreiff was himself a Free Church-man, and a leading Whig lawyer. Achieving a settlement of the educational question, on terms which would appease religious factionalism and reconcile as many interests as possible, became a personal crusade for him, though he received only lukewarm support from his political chiefs. Moncreiff rejected a secularist solution, but in 1854 he began with the support of the UPs as well as the Free Church. This compromise soon fell apart, and it was the refusal of the voluntarists to accept even a minimal legal recognition of religious instruction which was the main cause of Moncreiff's failure. Since the Established Church was hostile from the start, his proposals came to be seen as expressing partisan Free Church interests rather than the national consensus which he sought.[6]

Introducing his bill in 1850, Melgund claimed that action was urgent because two-fifths of the children in Scotland, especially in Glasgow, were not receiving any education.[7] The same alarmist note was struck by Moncreiff in 1854. Education was no longer a matter of philanthropy or religious duty, he claimed, but 'a question of self-defence. If we do not encounter and overcome the ignorance of the people, the ignorance of the people will overwhelm us.' For despite our prosperity and civilization, there was growing up

in the very heart of our social system, in the very centre of our mighty cities, and at the very base and root of this immense community, what I do not err in terming a savage and barbarian race, tied to you by no sympathy, bound to your institutions by no common link. . . . We shall never deal with this question rightly except on the assumption that there exists at the very foundation of society a flood of deep, unfathomed, pestilential waters, which, unless prompt measures are taken, any upheaving of our social system may cause to burst their barriers, and sweep us and our boasted institutions to destruction.

The theme of education as a dam against the tides of crime and immorality was always a popular argument for state intervention, though perhaps becoming less convincing in the 1850s. Moncreiff also argued in the Chalmers tradition that voluntary effort had failed to meet the needs of the poor; he had no sympathy with the doctrinaire rejection of state action, appealing rather to the Scottish principle that 'the State has a duty to discharge in educating her citizens'. His aim was to extend and adapt the parochial tradition, and, as he put it in 1861, to 'depart

---

[6] Hutchison, *Political History*, 70–80 (the best account of this episode).
[7] Hansard, 3rd series 112, 19 June 1850, 77–8.

from the system of educational grants and revert to the good old Scotch system of having a truly national education in Scotland'.[8]

Moncreiff's bill, similar in outline to Melgund's, was the first of a series which extended to 1869. His programme changed little, and was marked by a spirit of compromise. In the parish schools, the religious test and presbyterial inspection would go; these were the minimum demands of the Free Church, and the first priority for Moncreiff, since denominationalism could only end when the Free Church was willing to give up its own schools. Control of the parish schools by the heritors would remain, but where new schools were needed there would be local committees with rating powers, which would eventually absorb the existing denominational schools. There would be a Board or Commission of Education in Edinburgh to establish the need for new schools, withdraw grants from unnecessary ones, and supervise the details of the new system, though it was not clear whether the Board would replace the Privy Council as the source of state aid or coexist with it. On religious instruction, Moncreiff's strategy was to conciliate the voluntarists by avoiding any legal prescription, while reassuring traditionalists with the argument that Scottish public opinion was so strongly in favour of religious instruction that its neglect was inconceivable. The preamble of the 1854 bill, though not its text, referred to the established practice of teaching religion in the parish schools. Moncreiff's national schools would be Presbyterian, but the rights of minorities would be safeguarded by a conscience clause, and this was held to justify the withdrawal of aid to denominational schools. Here Moncreiff's difficulties began: a conscience clause implied that there would in fact be religious instruction given by publicly salaried teachers, which alienated the voluntarists while failing to satisfy the Roman Catholic and Episcopalian minorities, who found Presbyterian-dominated schools unacceptable even with a conscience clause, and wanted their own schools to continue getting grants.

Thus the balancing act did not succeed. The Church of Scotland would not be satisfied with anything less than statutory force for the Shorter Catechism, and Conservative MPs launched an all-out attack on Moncreiff's 1854 bill, alleging that it dissolved the connection between education and religion, destroyed the venerable and efficient system of parish schools, gave no 'security' for religious instruction, and opened

---

[8] Ibid. 130, 23 Feb. 1854, 1152–4; 163, 25 June 1861, 1544. Cf. J. Moncreiff, *An Educational Retrospect* (Glasgow, 1886); W. H. Bain, '"Attacking the Citadel": James Moncreiff's Proposals to Reform Scottish Education, 1851–69', *SER*, 10/2 (1978), 5–14.

the way to secularism. These were the standard arguments, constantly repeated in later years. Agitation in favour of the bill was countered by political mobilization of the landed classes and other conservative forces, and public meetings and petitions on the education question reached a peak in 1854.[9] Within Parliament, the opposition played on fears that Scotland might set a precedent for attacking church schools in England, and the bill was lost by nine votes on the second reading. The Scottish MPs voted 36 to 14 in favour, with all the Liberals and all the burgh members giving their support.

The debate revealed that Moncreiff had been unwise to ignore the interests of Episcopalians and Catholics. Catholics might attend without difficulty in the highlands, but it was a different matter in the cities, where sectarian feelings ran high: there they had good reason to fear proselytism and popular anti-Romanism, and relied on their own schools to maintain the morale and identity of the (largely Irish) community. Besides, conscience clauses were rejected in principle by the Catholic clergy, who refused to distinguish between secular and religious instruction, and claimed that religion should infuse every branch of education. Catholics were not a powerful political force in Scotland, but there were plenty of Irish MPs to speak for them, while Episcopalian interests were watched over both by the landowners on the Whig wing of the Liberal party, and by Gladstone. Moncreiff tried to meet this difficulty with a clause allowing grants to continue for any schools which met certain standards of efficiency, but this only aroused the ire of the voluntarists, who could stir up trouble in their turn among the English and Welsh Nonconformists on the Liberal benches. When Moncreiff reintroduced his bill in 1855, he at first omitted this clause, and it passed its second reading in that form. At this stage, the Episcopalians were pacified by an assurance that Privy Council grants would continue independently of the new law.[10] But the clause was later reinserted as part of a political bargain with the Catholics, and defection by the voluntarists led to a reduced third-reading majority. This bill was finished off by a predictable defeat in the House of Lords.

After another effort in 1856, and an interlude of Conservative government, Moncreiff succeeded in 1861 with a limited measure confined to the parish schools. The Parochial and Burgh Schoolmasters Act

[9] J. D. Myers, 'Scottish Nationalism and the Antecedents of the 1872 Education Act', *SES* 4 (1972), 78–9.

[10] SRO AD 56 47/1, correspondence with Bishop Terrot and related documents, May 1855.

abolished the religious test, but to conciliate the Established Church parish schoolmasters still had to declare that their teaching would conform to the Scriptures and Shorter Catechism. This allowed Free Churchmen to be appointed, but kept the Presbyterian character of the schools. The Established presbyteries, however, lost their powers of discipline to the civil courts, and their function of examining newly appointed teachers was transferred to the universities. The general supervisory power of presbyteries was not formally abolished, and they continued to inspect Church of Scotland schools, but the only real power retained by the church was that the minister still acted with the heritors in making appointments. Other provisions brought the 1803 Act up to date, including an increase in salaries and a provision for 'retiring allowances' so that teachers did not have to stay at their posts even when incapacitated by age, sickness, or drink. But Moncreiff's attempt to enact the rest of his programme in 1862 met the usual fate.

2. THE REVISED CODE AND THE ARGYLL COMMISSION

At this point attention was diverted by the 'Revised Code' controversy. While attempts were being made to devise a legislative framework peculiar to Scotland, the Privy Council system common to Scotland and England was developing on its own lines, as the state subsidy steadily increased. In 1859 Robert Lowe was appointed to the recently created post of Vice-President of the Committee of Council—in effect, minister of education. He was the first politician to put a personal stamp on educational policy, a doctrinaire liberal hostile to any state intervention beyond helping the poor, and outspokenly unsympathetic towards Scottish traditions; his first priority was to curb rising costs to the taxpayer. In 1860 the grant regulations were brought together as a Code, and in 1862 Lowe's proposals were embodied in the Revised Code, the leading feature of which was 'payment by results'. The existing grants paid directly to teachers and pupil-teachers were replaced by grants paid to school managers, which depended on the number of pupils, their attendance record, and their performance at the annual inspection. The bulk of the grant would depend on tests in the 'three Rs'—reading, writing, and arithmetic—organized at six levels or Standards. The existing pupil-teacher and training systems were fitted into the new regulations, though with changes which threatened the finances of the training colleges (the term which was now replacing 'normal schools'). The

Revised Code had some progressive pedagogic features. It was designed to ensure that teachers gave equal attention to all their pupils, and the Standards encouraged the teaching of the basic subjects systematically and simultaneously; for it was still common for writing to be started later than reading. But the Code also encouraged mechanical cramming, to ensure the examination passes on which the teacher's fate hung, and discouraged any subjects outside Lowe's rigid definition of elementary education. It came under fierce attack south of the border, notably from champions of the previous system like Matthew Arnold and Kay-Shuttleworth.

In Scotland there were particular objections to the Revised Code. It was based on previous experience of capitation grants, which had been used in England but not Scotland, and on the recommendations of the Newcastle commission, reporting in 1861, which was confined to England and Wales. Scottish critics claimed that Scotland should have its own inquiry before changes were made. They objected to the failure to recognize higher subjects, which was seen as a threat to the university link, and complained that well-qualified teachers would be reduced to barren routine. (Lowe's answer to this was that in Scotland teachers were inclined to neglect the bulk of their children and concentrate on coaching the more promising lads.) They objected to Article Four, which laid down that grants were only 'to promote the education of children belonging to the classes who support themselves by manual labour'. This had been the principle since 1833, but in practice any Scottish school which was not obviously a middle-class one had been able to qualify; now the position of many schools on the grant list seemed threatened, there would be invidious inquiry into the parentage of individual children, and the tradition that schools were for all classes would be abandoned. The Code also ignored religious instruction, a feature welcomed by voluntarists but deplored by others.

Moncreiff's response to Lowe was to argue that money could be saved in Scotland by eliminating the wasteful competition between denominations. When the Revised Code was first debated in 1862, Scotland was exempted until the fate of Moncreiff's latest bill was decided, but when this failed it was expected to be enforced in 1863, until the protests of Scottish MPs secured a postponement. The Code was eventually introduced on 1 April 1864, but after further protests it was suspended in June, and the government conceded a royal commission on Scottish education headed by the Duke of Argyll. In fact the suspension of the Code applied only to 'payment by results': grants continued to be paid under the 'old Code' of 1860, but other aspects of the system like annual inspection according to the Standards went ahead. The full application of the Code was put off from year to year, first in anticipation of the Argyll report, then of comprehensive legislation, and it was not fully extended to Scotland until 1873.[11]

The Duke of Argyll was not an ornamental aristocrat, but a politician with active scientific interests. As a Liberal who was an Established churchman he was well placed to engineer a compromise, and he shared the Whiggish views of Moncreiff, who was himself a member of the commission: it is not surprising that its recommendations followed the lines of his earlier bills. But there were representatives of various parties and religious interests, and the commission carried out thorough and extensive inquiries, which produced much evidence for the historian as well as for contemporary political debate. Written and oral evidence was collected from educationists, clergymen, and interested laymen, a mass of statistics was compiled, and assistant commissioners made local investigations and wrote special reports on Glasgow, on the Hebrides or Western Isles, on the 'lowland country districts', and on 'burgh and middle class schools'; for the commission's remit was not confined to elementary schools.

This reflected current developments which were bringing the unity of Scotland's educational system into question. The traditional link between parish schools and universities was the symbol of this, and even though parish schools had no monopoly, as long as the universities kept the door open to their pupils a university education was accessible to anyone, including adults, who had the minimal knowledge needed to embark on the course. Now this seemed threatened from two directions, as the system moved towards stratification on class lines. On the one hand, the growth of purely elementary schools since the beginning of the century, especially for the urban working class, was creating a sector of education in which Latin and the graduate schoolmaster were unknown. On the other, there were strong pressures from the growing middle class for secondary and higher education to be developed on more specialized lines to meet their needs. The introduction of the word 'secondary', borrowed from the French and not in common use until the late 1860s, was a symptom of this. It replaced the term 'middle-class schools' which had been in vogue since about 1850; as this indicates,

[11] Cf. T. Wilson, 'A Reinterpretation of "Payment by Results" in Scotland, 1861–1872', in W. M. Humes and H. M. Paterson (eds.), *Scottish Culture and Scottish Education, 1800–1980* (Edinburgh, 1983), 93–114.

the underlying idea was not of a secondary stage following a primary one, but of secondary and elementary education as separate sectors with different clienteles.[12] The career demands of the middle classes, particularly the growth of professional qualifications and examinations and the need to compete on equal terms with the products of English education, gave a stimulus both to the expansion and overhaul of the burgh schools and to reform of the universities. A vocal reform party wanted the latter to raise their academic standards by introducing a rigorous entrance examination, which would raise the age of entry and squeeze out students not trained in proper secondary schools. Many secondary school headmasters naturally supported this programme, finding their own efforts undermined while the universities admitted students with rudimentary preparation. In the 1850s, university reform had more political appeal than school legislation, resulting in an important Act of Parliament in 1858. However, the detailed reforms which followed rejected radical solutions like an entrance examination; the curriculum was modernized, but the academic level of the first year remained low, preserving democratic access.[13]

But if one threat was warded off, the Revised Code with its disregard for higher subjects presented another, and there was a danger that legislation for a national system might abolish the parish schools as a recognizable category. Hostility between the parochial tradition and the new system of state funding had been developing for some years, one symptom being the foundation of the teachers' association, the Educational Institute of Scotland, in 1847. The founders of the EIS were mostly private and burgh schoolmasters, but it soon attracted the general body of qualified teachers, and its membership rose towards 2,000. The aim of the EIS was professional status for the teacher, on a level with the doctor or the lawyer. Initially it planned to award its own qualifications, taking the College of Preceptors founded in England in 1846 as a model, but it failed to persuade the government to give these official recognition. Instead the EIS claimed that all teachers should be graduates, asserted the unity of the profession from parish schoolmasters to university professors, and campaigned for university chairs and faculties of education. In its early years the EIS abstained from political

---

[12] 'Primary', also derived from France and adopted as early as 1833 by Pillans, was in common use by the 1860s as a synonym for 'elementary', but was not used in official documents.

[13] R. D. Anderson, *Education and Opportunity in Victorian Scotland: Schools and Universities* (Oxford, 1983), 27–69.

campaigning, to avoid sectarian divisions among its members, but it was inevitably hostile to the Revised Code, and indeed to the whole training system as it had developed since 1846, including the colleges. College-trained teachers, with no experience outside elementary schools, lacked the literary culture and professional ethos of the graduate, and undermined the status of the traditional teachers by accepting lower salaries. This was especially the case with women, who could not attend the universities, but were increasingly numerous among training-college graduates; no women were admitted to the EIS before 1872.

The Argyll commission heard much evidence about the relative merits of university and college training. It was hardly realistic, given the urgent needs of popular education, to dispense with the more cheaply trained elementary teachers, or with the professional expertise which the colleges alone taught. The commission thus gave firm support to the training system, though it was sympathetic to the idea that college students might also attend university classes. On other points, the commission gave more satisfaction to the traditionalists. Its statistical inquiries into university students' origins underlined the diversity of their schooling, and seemed to reinforce the case for the parish schools. In the commission's proposals these were to retain their identity, with their tradition safeguarded by a Board of Education for Scotland. More generally, the report declared in favour of 'the ancient theory of Scottish National Education', under which parish schools, burgh schools, and universities formed a single, organically linked system.[14]

The publication of the Argyll reports gave the signal for renewal of the agitation originally stimulated by the Revised Code. In 1868 a petition against the Code signed by 3,572 professors and teachers was presented to Parliament,[15] and the universities, led by Glasgow, also entered the lists. The universities were especially concerned at the threat to their recruitment if the parish schools no longer taught subjects like Latin and mathematics, and sought to ensure that a Scottish Board with university representatives was included in any legislation. They also acquired new champions when two Scottish university seats were created in 1868, with an electorate of graduates. Moncreiff was elected to one of these seats; his colleague was the scientist Lyon Playfair, already noted as a champion of technical education, who now became the

[14] Ibid. 106.
[15] J. Donaldson, *Addresses Delivered in the University of St. Andrews, from 1886 to 1910* (St Andrews, 1911), 469, 483–6.

chief spokesman, and perhaps myth-maker, for the parochial tradition. As he put it in 1869,

the spirit of John Knox, which still animates the Scotch people, demands that the old connection between the lower and higher education of the country should be preserved. Our Universities draw their main strength from the national schools of Scotland, and you must not cut them off from the roots. . . . the Universities of Scotland belong wholly to the people.[16]

Chalmers had invoked the spirit of Knox to support the alliance of church and state, Moncreiff to justify a national system standing above the denominations; now this creative myth was put to new use to resist the division of education into class compartments.

The first task of the Argyll commission was to pronounce on the view, held by Moncreiff and the reformers but contested by the Established Church, that there were major deficiencies in the existing elementary system. The commission conceded that 'the want of schools was not so great as had been generally supposed', and that numerically there were enough school places, but it argued that their quality left much to be desired. Inefficient and inadequate schools, it was claimed, were the main reason why parents kept their children at home or cut schooling short; private adventure schools and others outside the grant system were seen as falling short of modern standards. But how many children were escaping school altogether? Unfortunately the commission did not achieve full national coverage with its statistics, and the only urban area examined in detail was Glasgow, where conditions were held to 'furnish conclusive proof, that the voluntary system has hitherto proved utterly inadequate to effect the education of the masses of the population congregated in large towns'.[17] There is reason to believe that Glasgow was not typical, and that the commission exaggerated the number of unschooled children; nevertheless, it became an accepted fact in political debate that there were 92,000 such children in Scotland.

The commission's recommendations on elementary education appeared in 1867. Apart from some minor reservations, the report was unanimous, and to achieve this the actual proposals were more conservative than some of the observations in the body of the report. The Revised Code was pronounced sound, except for Article Four, and the policies of the Education Department and its inspectors were endorsed. The report came down decisively against denominationalism, and in

---

[16] Hansard, 3rd series 197, 12 July 1869, 1730.
[17] PP 1867, XXV, *Education Commission (Scotland), Second Report*, pp. xx, lvi.

favour of a national system for children of all classes and churches. Rational organization and central supervision were found lacking, and legislation was needed to ensure that local deficiencies were fully met. But the concrete proposals, embodied in a draft bill 'to extend and improve the parochial schools', envisaged a very gradual transition to the new system. There would be three types of national school: the parish schools, to be dubbed Old National, but otherwise left unchanged; Adopted schools, i.e. the existing denominational schools, which were to remain under church management; and New National schools run by school committees with rating powers, elected in rural districts and appointed by the town council in burghs. Both parish and Adopted schools could be transferred to school committees if the heritors or managers agreed, so that the schools would eventually coalesce into a single organization, but the time-scale for this was left open. The commission estimated that there were 3,000 parochial and certificated teachers, and that this number would need to be doubled: the expansion of 'New' schools was thus conceived on a large scale, and this was the most radical feature of the report. Conservatives, on the other hand, were satisfied by the preservation of the parish schools under the heritors, and by the commission's endorsement of the university link. On religious instruction, the report was silent, apart from providing for a conscience clause; but as in Moncreiff's bills, the implication was that national education would be essentially Presbyterian, and that grants to denominational schools which refused to enter the system would cease.[18] The special significance of the report was that the Church of Scotland representatives put their signatures to it. Though this did not prevent opposition to subsequent bills, a new level of consensus had been reached; ministers were usually able to work out compromises with the Scottish MPs, and it was the less controllable House of Lords which proved most obstructive. Between the Argyll report and the 1872 Act there were to be many legislative hurdles, and the act did not reflect the proposals of the report as closely as is sometimes supposed.

3. THE MAKING OF THE 1872 ACT

In 1867 a Conservative government was in office, and its reception of the Argyll report was hostile: any extension of rating was ruled out.[19]

---

[18] Ibid. pp. cliv, clxxiii–clxxxv, 88–106.
[19] Hansard, 3rd series 188, 21 June 1867, 321–38.

But in 1868 Gladstone was returned to power with an absolute majority, based on the extended franchise of 1867 which included the urban
working class. In Scotland, 53 of the 60 MPs elected were Liberals, and
they were perhaps emboldened by the new electorate to defy the middle-
class religious pressure groups. In 1869, Moncreiff introduced a bill
based closely on the Argyll recommendations. It began its career in the
Lords, where Argyll himself claimed that 'the parochial system in
Scotland was founded by John Knox, who laid down the principle,
which has never faded from the popular mind in Scotland, that it is the
duty and the function of the State to insist upon the education of the
people'; he appealed for sectarian rivalries to be buried in the national
cause. In the Commons, Moncreiff claimed that a national system was
desired by the whole of Scottish opinion, and that 'it is strongly the
view of Scotland that all the people should be, if possible, educated in
the same school. All ranks, all religions, should be so educated. That
was the old Scotch principle.'[20] He also tried to reassure critics of the
Revised Code that higher subjects were safe, and that the university
link would be preserved and extended. But in 1869 as in 1854–5,
Moncreiff ran into trouble with the government's voluntarist supporters,
since various hostile amendments inserted by the Lords included one to
continue denominational grants to Catholic schools; the 1869 bill passed
the Commons only in a mutilated and unsatisfactory form, and was
finally killed off by the Lords.

Moncreiff then left the scene to become a judge. His replacement
George Young was a man of more radical temperament, less committed
to conciliating conservative interests, especially the landowners.
Moncreiff's concern for the parish schools and the rights of heritors
seemed out of tune with the new urban Liberalism. In December 1869
Edinburgh town council passed a set of resolutions on education which
were taken up, and often adopted verbatim, by most of the larger burghs.
They called for a 'popular, unsectarian and undenominational system', for
a General Board of Education in Scotland based on representative bodies,
for burgh school committees chosen by town councils, and for an end
to denominational grants. They also wanted a 'compulsory clause'.[21]

[20] Hansard, 3rd series 194, 25 Feb. 1869, 296; 197, 12 July 1869, 1713.
[21] SRO AD 56 47/3, Resolutions of 14 December 1869. Similar resolutions in subsequent months, in AD 56 47/4, include town councils of Dunfermline, Galashiels, Perth,
Selkirk, Forfar, Kirkcaldy, Hamilton, Dumbarton, and Convention of Royal Burghs.
Edinburgh reiterated its resolutions in Dec. 1870. Glasgow and Aberdeen expressed
similar views in their own words.

Compulsory education was an idea rapidly gaining in public favour. Moncreiff had accepted it as an eventual aim, but had not included it in his bills, nor was it universally supported by professional educational opinion. Some of the witnesses before the Argyll commission had advocated it, usually in the form of an 'education test' imposed on children before they could be employed; this was the policy, for example, of the EIS. But the commission saw so many practical difficulties that it made no recommendation. During the 1869 debate, however, MPs from the cities sought to add compulsion to the bill.[22]

In 1870 the government concentrated on W. E. Forster's education bill for England and Wales, but in 1871 Young introduced a Scottish bill. This adopted some features of the English act, and further changes were to produce the Education (Scotland) Act of 1872. Young's bills included compulsory education. In 1871 it was to be a permissive power for school boards, as in England, but the 1872 Act imposed compulsion on all children between 5 and 13. This provision, which was not opposed by the Conservatives and attracted surprisingly little debate, put Scotland ahead of England. Young's second radical innovation was the system of school boards. Local committees had figured in national education schemes from the start, but there had been much debate about whether they should be uniform for burghs and parishes, and whether ministers or heritors should sit ex officio alongside elected members. There were fears, shared by many teachers, that boards of farmers, shopkeepers, and tradesmen would be interested only in utilitarian subjects, would be swayed by sectarian rivalries and political demagoguery, or would interfere oppressively in the day-to-day conduct of schools. Young cut through all this, and through the problem of marrying old and new schools which had made previous bills so complex, by creating a board for every burgh and parish, elected exclusively by the ratepayers, which was to take over the existing burgh and parish schools. The separate legal status of the parish schools was thus swept away, along with the powers of minister and heritors, the statutory salaries and life tenure of schoolmasters, and all other traces of the Acts of 1696, 1803, and 1861. The new school boards could levy rates, and borrow money to build their own schools; they were also to take over any existing schools which the churches and other managers wished to transfer, and within a few years most of the Presbyterian schools were either transferred or closed down.

[22] Hansard, 3rd series 198, 27 July 1869, 800–5.

It was politically impossible for Young to accept the Edinburgh programme's call for an end to denominational grants. These would continue for existing schools which wished to remain outside the board
system, and although building grants were withdrawn, new schools
could claim annual grants where the need for them was shown to exist.
In the long run, the only significant survivors were Episcopalian or
Catholic. With this exception—in Playfair's words the 'small parasites
of denominationalism which the Lord Advocate still allows to grow on
the national educational tree'[23]—the long-awaited goal of a national
system was achieved, and to have gained the co-operation of all the
churches was a notable political achievement. It contrasted with the
situation in England and Wales after 1870, where school boards were
only set up in areas where voluntary effort was shown to have failed,
and a powerful voluntary sector, predominantly Anglican, survived
alongside the board schools and in rivalry with them.

One contentious point in Young's plans was the Board of Education.
The 1872 Act created the Scotch Education Department, under a separate committee of the Privy Council, which took over all the Scottish
work of the Education Department, including the Code and the inspectorate. Young claimed that this made a local board of the type which
had appeared in Moncreiff's bills unnecessary. But the demand for a
board united radical liberals (provided it was 'popular', not appointed),
Playfair and the university party, and Conservatives who saw it as a
safeguard for church interests. Critics were sceptical about the independence of the SED, which would be based in London; according to
the Duke of Richmond, it would be no more than 'a room in Whitehall,
and the name "Scotland" painted over it'.[24] Young eventually conceded
this point, and the act set up a Board of Education in Edinburgh with
university representatives. But this was to be a temporary body of
government appointees supervising the transition to the new system,
not a permanent guardian of the parochial tradition. It was the SED, not
the Board, which issued the 'Scotch Code' which finally introduced
payment by results in 1873, and while in future all teachers in charge
of a school would have to hold the government certificate, there was no
provision for a supply of graduate teachers of the old type. There was
a vaguely worded clause (section 67), dating from the 1869 bill and
designed to pacify the universities, which enjoined the SED to keep up
traditional standards. But secondary education gained little from the

---

[23] Hansard, 3rd series 204, 27 Feb. 1871, 963.
[24] Ibid. 212, 5 July 1872, 692.

act. Burgh schools were transferred to school boards, and a limited number of them were designated as 'higher class' schools, which were to specialize in secondary subjects. But these were excluded from any funding by rates or taxes: Robert Lowe, now Chancellor of the Exchequer, was hostile on principle to state aid for middle-class education. In Scotland, however, support for such aid had grown during the 1860s as part of the debate on the meaning of a national system, and modest proposals for its extension had been made by Argyll. There was a clear contrast here between English and Scottish ideas of the state's role, and this debate was to continue after 1872.

Concern for these more purely educational issues meant that by 1872 religious controversy was muted, at least by earlier standards. Young's policy was to provide a conscience clause, but otherwise to say as little as possible about religious instruction, leaving it to school boards to determine; in Playfair's words, the act 'neither proscribes nor prescribes religion'.[25] One important change was that religion was excluded from inspection, and the previously denominational inspectorate was re-organized as a single corps. The Conservatives focused their criticism of the 1872 bill on religious instruction, and eventually succeeded (in the House of Lords) in inserting a reference to it in the preamble of the act, though this did not specify either the Bible or the Shorter Catechism. On the other hand, there was no clause like that in the English act which banned all catechisms and denominational 'formularies' in board schools: English school boards had to devise a non-denominational form of Christian teaching, but Scottish ones were free to continue Presbyterian instruction according to 'use and wont' (the customary phrase, though it was not in the act), and this was what in fact happened. Thus although in its long rearguard action the Church of Scotland had secured no stronger religious guarantees than it was offered in Moncreiff's 1854 bill, it could feel that something had been saved, and was now ready to compromise because its power to block change seemed to be crumbling. In the new political situation, secularism was much stronger, and was being promoted by Education Leagues active in Edinburgh and Glasgow. These were combated by a pro-religious Scottish Educational Association set up in November 1871 and supported by some Free Church as well as Church of Scotland ministers.[26] But after Gladstone's disestablishment of the Church of Ireland in 1869, the

[25] Ibid. 209, 7 Mar. 1872, 1582.
[26] Ibid. 211, 6 June 1872, 1313–14; T. Smith, *Memoirs of James Begg, D.D.* (Edinburgh, 1885–8), ii. 480–1; Hutchison, *Political History*, 120–1; SRO AD 56 47/5, Memorial of SEA, 1872.

Scottish church was disinclined to court the same fate by intransigence. Its influence in the new school boards could be considerable, especially in the countryside, and it still retained control of its training colleges.[27]

4. EDUCATION AND THE STATE

The details of religious and party disputes are necessary in order to explain the form which the 1872 Act took, but it arose from a wider context of debate which was not confined to Scotland. In the 1860s, educational issues were at the forefront of public discussion, and linked with questions of culture, science, democracy, and national strength. Scots might invoke John Knox to sanction state action, but the view that it was time for the state to supplement or supplant voluntary effort had come to dominate public opinion for other reasons. One was the grant of the franchise to workers; it was Lowe, during the debate over the 1867 Reform Act, who used the argument usually paraphrased as 'We must educate our masters'. This particular rhetoric was not heard in Scotland—perhaps the new masters were educated enough already— but there was certainly a feeling that a modern state needed both an educated citizenry and an educated work-force. Social problems persisted within Britain, underlined by the growth of trade unions, and politicians were becoming less inclined to accept that religious instruction was an all-purpose remedy, or to leave educational expansion to the churches; several decades of voluntary action did not seem to be mastering the problems of the great cities or eliminating the remaining bastions of illiteracy, and denominationalism had come to be seen as obstructing or distorting progress. The more faith was put in education as a panacea for political, economic, and social problems, the more urgent it seemed to bring it under secular control.

While dramatic events like the Paris Commune of 1871 reinforced fears of social disorder, a deep impression was also made by the military triumphs of Prussia in 1866 and 1870, which were held, like Germany's growing industrial strength, to rest on the foundation of compulsory education. As in the 1830s, Scots were very ready to look to the continent for models, and Playfair was particularly prominent among those who warned that British industry was losing its early

---

[27] Cf. D. J. Withrington, 'Towards a National System, 1867–72: The Last Years in the Struggle for a Scottish Education Act', *SES* 4 (1972), 107–24.

supremacy in the international economic struggle, and that both primary and technical education needed to be put on a more solid base. 'In the competition of nations, both in war and in peace,' said Playfair in 1870, 'their position for the future will depend upon the education of their peoples.'[28] And in this context the democratic claims for Scottish education seemed to have a new significance: in the debate on the Argyll report, the Liberal MP Mountstuart Grant Duff called for a system which

may give every boy of really superior ability, even if born in the depths of poverty, in every National school in Scotland, an opportunity of pushing his way from one grade of education to another, aided by the State, so that the country may not lose the chance of the services, in some form or other, of whatever talent is produced within her borders. Depend upon it, that, in the increasingly close competition between civilized nations, we shall need it all.[29]

In retrospect, the 1872 Act has commonly been seen as an inevitable stage in the transfer of education to state control, bringing order out of chaos: 'the time had clearly arrived for the institution of the "public" school.'[30] This remains the popular view. But it was not necessarily the view of contemporaries. The schools which had been aided by the state since the 1830s were already regarded as public, and the grant and inspection system imposed a high degree of centralization and uniformity. Compulsory education was, of course, a major extension of the state's intervention in private and family life. But the central state did not itself run schools after 1872 any more than before, and whatever bureaucratic potential may have lain in the SED, the immediate effect of the act was a shift of control from the churches and other voluntary bodies to local communities represented by the elected school boards. These became the recipients of grants under the Code, which gave the SED a decisive say in patterns of education, but the balance of their income came from rates (replacing the former voluntary contributions) and from school fees—for there was no move towards free education in 1872. This local devolution was partly a convenient solution to the problem of religious instruction, but also reflected the Liberal faith in public opinion and in local 'popular control' as the healthiest form of democracy. 'The policy of the Act', said Young in 1877,

[28] L. Playfair, *Subjects of Social Welfare* (London, 1889), 306.
[29] Hansard, 3rd series 188, 21 June 1867, 320.
[30] J. Scotland, 'The Centenary of the Education (Scotland) Act of 1872', *BJES* 20 (1972), 122.

is that the public schools of each school district shall be maintained and managed by the people of the district who are immediately interested in their welfare. . . . I must . . . emphatically protest against any proposal to subject school managers, whether school boards or others, to direct supervision or control by Government or other central authority.[31]

The creation of the SED was also a modest measure of Scottish administrative devolution. Some historians, however, have seen the 1872 Act as an Anglicizing measure. This line of thought began with Playfair, who complained that 'the three Bills of 1869, 1871, and 1872 are successive steps in the Anglicizing and lowering of Scotch elementary education',[32] and was continued by James Donaldson, later Principal of St Andrews University, who was active in the campaigns against the Revised Code as rector of Edinburgh High School. Donaldson argued that while Moncreiff's bills were 'peculiarly well adapted to the genius of the Scottish nation', the 1872 Act was based on the English model.[33] More recently, J. D. Myers has seen Moncreiff's bills as a lost opportunity to develop Scottish education on genuinely Scottish lines. There was a 'broad and powerful consensus' behind Melgund and Moncreiff, and the 1854 bill was defeated only by the power of English votes: an interpretation which underestimates both the solid positions which the Established Church retained in Scotland, and Melgund's and Moncreiff's difficulties with the Free Church and the voluntarists. The English can hardly be blamed, after all, for Scotland's religious divisions, and many historians would see the Disruption as the real turning-point, when Scotland lost the chance to preserve its cultural unity and to find distinctive solutions to social problems.

For Myers, the 1869 bill was 'the last distinctively Scottish educational reform measure of the period', and the 1872 Act was 'a further deterioration of Scotland's national culture and heritage'.[34] But Donald Withrington has stressed Young's authentic Scottish radicalism, and the relative conservatism of Moncreiff's proposals, which respected the interests of the landed class and would have preserved the parish schools as a separate sector. If the 1869 bill had gone through, it would have produced something very like the dual system of voluntary and board schools which was the outcome of the English act; the 1872 Act, by

---

[31] Speech reprinted in A. C. Sellar, *Manual of the Education Acts for Scotland* (7th edn., Edinburgh, 1879), 379–80.

[32] Hansard, 3rd series 209, 7 Mar. 1872, 1590.

[33] Donaldson, *Addresses*, 90, 466–9.

[34] Myers, 'Scottish Nationalism', 77, 87–8.

creating a single public system for all but non-Presbyterians, was closer to fulfilling the long-desired national ideal.[35] The 1872 Act naturally borrowed some features from the 1870 one, but in other ways went beyond it, and it was inevitable that a product of the 1870s would differ from proposals which originated over twenty years before.

From one point of view, the 1872 Act was a pragmatic adaptation of the legal framework to changes in the social context of education, and a practical solution to the awkward coexistence of the new state-funded schools and the old statutory sector. Educational efforts needed to be consolidated and rationalized in a way which would eliminate the remaining pockets of deficiency. The progress of secularization and urbanization also raised significant questions. The parish schools were maintained by a levy on landed property. That made sense when Scotland was predominantly a rural country, but in towns a rating system was needed if social burdens were to be borne fairly by all forms of wealth. The voluntary schools depended on charitable individuals and church members digging into their pockets, and public opinion made the wealthy feel this as an obligation; but a point might be reached, and probably was by the end of the 1860s, when the maintenance of ordinary schools (as distinct from special charitable causes) was seen as the natural responsibility of the state. The readiness of the churches to transfer their schools after 1872 suggests that voluntary funds were drying up, and that this was an obligation shed with some relief. It was not that religious belief itself or the social influence of the churches was in decline, but rather that the accepted boundaries between the spheres of action of church and state had shifted.

The churches were all the more willing to hand their schools over to the state because pedagogic progress required substantial capital investment, as the first generation of schools built in the 1830s or 1840s became obsolete. This was partly a matter of higher standards of hygiene and furnishing, on which the inspectors were increasingly insisting, and partly a matter of teaching methods. The voluntary system had produced numerous small schools, taught by single teachers in one large room. But as pupil-teachers and adult assistants became more numerous, the division of schools into separate classes was required, and only the school boards, with their public borrowing powers, had the resources to build the urban fortresses which dominate the popular image of Victorian schools. For an understanding of this, we need to

[35] Withrington, 'Towards a National System'.

look at the development of school provision in the period before 1872. We can then also ask whether the quarrels of politicians and churchmen seriously harmed the interests of working-class education by delaying more comprehensive state action, or whether working-class demand had a dynamic of its own which meant that popular education was already near to universal provision.

4

The Supply of Schools before 1872

HISTORIANS of Scottish education have been inclined to pass straight from the parish schools to the 1872 Act, neglecting the development of the 'privy council' system in the mid-nineteenth century, although it was in that period that effective education for the urban masses was really established. Not all features of the diverse system established before 1872 vanished overnight, and in the age before compulsory education the variety of schooling, as of literacy and patterns of attendance, has a special interest for the social historian. From the 1830s, it is also well documented. A new Statistical Account, based like the original on parish accounts by ministers, was published in 1845, and the same ministers contributed to annual reports by presbyteries which were collated by the Church of Scotland's Education Committee. The government inspectors appointed in 1840 also made their reports, published annually at some length by the Education Department, and large amounts of evidence were collected by the Argyll commission in the 1860s. Most of this evidence, of course, comes from middle-class observers with characteristic biases and assumptions, and their own political, religious, or bureaucratic axes to grind. It would be unwise to assume that statistical evidence was any more objective. Victorian statistics, despite their seeming precision, often rested on shaky foundations, and they were collected, published, and discussed with political motives in mind. None the less, they are an indispensable guide, and some of them allow us to formulate hypotheses about the longer-term development of Scottish education.

1. NUMBERS AND TYPES OF SCHOOL

Attempts were made from time to time to count the number of schools, along with the number of children in attendance. According to these surveys there were 3,633 schools in 1818 (almost certainly an underestimate), 5,042 in 1833–4, and 5,242 in 1851. The Argyll commission counted 4,451 schools in the rural two-thirds of the country, which suggested a total well over 5,000. In 1873–4 school boards were asked to survey all schools in their districts in order to estimate the number of new places needed, and found 4,819. By then small schools were already being closed as a result of the 1872 Act, and by 1877 there were only 4,078. It seems probable, therefore, that the number of schools reached a peak of up to 5,500 in the 1860s.[1] Table 4.1 shows the breakdown of schools and pupils according to type at three dates, though each inquiry used its own classification. The number of parochial schools was naturally limited by the number of parishes, and the main point to emerge from the table is the growth of schools run by the churches, reflecting the strength of voluntary and charitable effort. Growth in the number of schools did not simply reflect rising demand, but also new developments which created specialized types of school, such as the growth of separate education for girls, the expansion of children's employment in factories and mines, the creation through Irish migration of a large Roman Catholic community, the identification of new forms of social pathology for which schooling was seen as the cure, and the urge towards a more rigid stratification of social classes. But the most significant phenomenon was the rise of a state-aided sector of schools, headed by certificated teachers and using the officially approved pedagogic methods. Government inspectors and bodies like the Argyll commission tended to assume that these were the only efficient schools, and that progress lay in the elimination of their rivals; they were especially critical of small 'private adventure' schools with untrained teachers. Private adventure schools themselves varied in quality, and well-qualified schoolmasters could compete directly with parish and similar schools, and attract a clientele willing to pay high fees. In general, however, the effect of state subsidy was to drive out competition from private enterprise.

On this point there has been some historical controversy, especially around the views of E. G. West. West argued in relation to England that the 1870 Act was unnecessary because working-class educational needs were already met effectively through the market by a flourishing private sector. The expansion of education in response to industrialization was as rapid as might reasonably have been expected, and the country was well on the road to universal literacy. State intervention, in this view, had an essentially negative effect, checking the expansion of private schools and replacing free parental choice by bureaucratic

---

[1] For the sources of these statistics, see Appendix 1.

TABLE 4.1. *Classification of Schools and Pupils by Type of School*

1818. Select committee report

Type of school	Schools	Pupils	Pupils, %
Parochial	942	54,161	31
Endowed	212	10,177	6
Dames	257	5,560	3
Ordinary day-schools	2,222	106,627	60
Total day-schools	3,633	176,525	
Sunday schools	807	53,449	

1851. Educational census

Type of school	Schools	Pupils	Pupils, %
Burgh	88	10,326	3
Parochial	937	63,987	21
Church of Scotland	537	31,484	
Free Church	712	50,582	
United Presbyterian	61	4,768	
Episcopal	36	2,077	
Other Protestant	7	791	
Roman Catholic	32	3,509	
Total church schools	1,385	93,211	30
Endowed	491	32,901	11
Other 'public'	448	32,017	10
Private	1,893	78,000	25
Total	5,242	310,442	

1864. Argyll report

Type of school	Schools	Pupils	Pupils, %
Parochial	917	76,493	
Side	189	10,073	
Parliamentary	27	1,617	
Total Parochial	1,133	88,183	28
Church of Scotland	519	33,251	
Free Church	617	48,860	
Other Presbyterian	45	3,114	
Episcopal	74	6,202	
Roman Catholic	61	5,736	
Total church schools	1,316	97,163	31
Undenominational, etc.	1,092	92,166	29
Private adventure	910	35,283	11
Total	4,451	312,795	

Note: the Argyll figures cover only those (predominantly rural) areas for which detailed statistics were collected; they represent about two-thirds of the total.

Sources: see Appendix 1.

centralization. This argument, inspired by free-market ideology, has generally been contested by historians of English education. West also extended it to Scotland. He argued that the parish schools, on which the case for the effectiveness of state intervention in Scotland rested, only reached a third of the country (as indeed Table 4.1 shows), and that

the predominant number of Scottish children, in the large towns at least, received their schooling not from parochial schools but from competitive private fee-paying establishments. The question therefore arises: How far should the main credit for the superior progress in literacy be attributed not to the parochial schools but to the more widespread and more rapidly growing private schools?[2]

West's work is a valuable corrective to the uncritical habit of seeing the 1870 and 1872 Acts as monuments of progress. But his argument (about England as well as Scotland) is based on a fallacious contrast between state intervention and private enterprise, which ignores the intermediate stage of state-aided voluntary effort. Church schools with state subsidies were just as unfair competitors for private schools as rate-aided board schools were later, and many of the clergy were as hostile as government officials to private adventure schools. A true free market disappeared as soon as subsidies began in the 1830s, and all the evidence is that private schools aimed at the working class then began a steady decline. Even in 1818, by no means all the 'ordinary day-schools' were private schools, as West's argument rather misleadingly claims.[3] This was a catch-all category which included the society schools in the highlands and many other subscription and charity schools.[4] The 1851 figures were more discriminating, and reflected the contemporary habit of considering as 'public' any school which had a permanent 'endowment' or means of support such as a guaranteed salary or a schoolhouse, confining the term 'private' to teachers who depended entirely on fees. Private schools in this sense had 25 per cent of the market, but

---

[2] E. G. West, *Education and the Industrial Revolution* (London, 1975), 72.

[3] Ibid. 60–1; R. D. Anderson, 'Education and the State in Nineteenth-Century Scotland', *Economic History Review*, 2nd series, 36 (1983), 525–6; D. J. Withrington, 'Schooling, Literacy and Society', in T. M. Devine and R. Mitchison (eds.), *People and Society in Scotland, I: 1760–1830* (Edinburgh, 1988), 174–83.

[4] 'Subscription school' was a vague category which could cover charitable schools supported by annual collections rather than a fixed endowment, schools managed by committees of parents, or schools provided by employers.

not all were serving the working class, for these figures include schools of all levels.

It is not difficult to see why private schools declined. The extension of grants to schools which met the official criteria, especially after 1846, tended to drive out the smaller and less efficient schools, and to discredit teachers who did not use the new methods. Schools with higher fees might flourish, but the scales were weighted against those aiming at the ordinary working-class market. It was said in the 1840s that while a school charging 3*s*. to 6*s*. a quarter could survive, those which charged 2*s*. to 3*s*. were 'utterly valueless'. To make a living the teacher was forced to accept large numbers; it was estimated at Dundee that 'it requires 200 pupils to make a tolerable income to a teacher in a poor town district'.[5] A school with a building grant, on the other hand, could start off with superior accommodation, and once in receipt of an annual grant, fees only had to cover a third of the school expenditure: in the mid-1860s, total expenditure per pupil in state-aided schools averaged 26*s*. 1*d*., but the average fees paid by parents were 9*s*. 1*d*. Moreover, the pupil-teacher system allowed state-aided schools to exploit this cheap form of staffing to handle more pupils, and hence to collect more fees. When the Argyll commission surveyed the rural areas, it found that the average size of private adventure schools was 26, and of other unaided schools 45; but in state-aided schools there were 82 pupils per adult teacher, with pupil-teachers bringing the ratio down to 42.[6] Teachers thus had a strong incentive to sit for the certificate examination so that they could take a pupil-teacher, and to seek salaried posts or church sponsorship to qualify for a grant; connection with the Established or Free Church brought the additional prestige of presbyterial inspection. One movement taking place between the 1840s and the 1860s, therefore, was the conversion of private into 'public' schools; as the older generation of unqualified teachers died or retired, their schools vanished with them, and were replaced by permanent schools of the officially approved type, with teachers drawn from the new training colleges. This helps to explain why despite the expansion of denominationalism the total number of schools did not greatly increase. Some private adventure schools lingered on, but their poor quality was a subject of general agreement in official (and undoubtedly biased)

[5] PP 1845, XXXV, *Minutes of CCE, 1843–4*, 158; *Presbyterial and Parochial Reports on the State of Education in Scotland: Published by the General Assembly's Education Committee, 1842* (Edinburgh, 1843), 127.

[6] PP 1867, XXV, *Education Commission (Scotland), Second Report*, pp. clvii, 40–2.

quarters, from Kay-Shuttleworth in the 1850s, who saw them as 'an opprobrium to civilization', to the Argyll verdict that 'private adventure schools are almost invariably detrimental both to the health and education of all the children who attend them'.[7]

In 1870, about 2,000 schools received annual grants (compared with 1,000 in 1860), and they held some 40 per cent of the school population. But by no means all the schools outside the grant system were inferior ones. They might refuse state aid on grounds of principle (the United Presbyterians), or fail to qualify for it because their clientele was middle-class, or because they did not charge fees, as with many charitable foundations. Many parish schools, too, did not claim grants, partly for technical reasons (the heritors' assessments did not count towards the local voluntary contribution required by the rules),[8] partly because traditional schoolmasters were unwilling to seek the government teaching certificate. It was estimated in 1861 that only 20 per cent of the parish schools were state-aided, though by 1870 this had probably risen to 40–50 per cent.[9] SSPCK and Gaelic society schools in the highlands also received few grants, but in their case this was on grounds of quality. There was a bias in the system towards areas which were prosperous enough to produce voluntary contributions, and to sessional, Free Church, and similar schools rather than schools for the really poor. And despite the growth of the denominational system, the Church of Scotland got the lion's share of the grants, if only because parish and endowed schools, and any school not specifically denominational, came under its wing. In 1870 the Established Church claimed 1,251 schools and received £61,379 of a total of £106,500, compared with £36,179 for the Free Church (527 schools), £4,699 for the Episcopalians (90 schools), and £4,243 for the Catholics (65 schools).[10] The non-Presbyterian schools were now a significant group, though more geographically concentrated than others, with Catholic schools in the west, Edinburgh, and Dundee, and Episcopalian in Aberdeenshire, Kincardine, Angus, Perthshire, and Edinburgh.

[7] J. Kay-Shuttleworth, *Public Education as Affected by the Minutes of the Committee of Privy Council from 1846 to 1852* (London, 1853), 395; PP 1867, XXV, *Education Commission (Scotland), Report on the State of Education in the Country Districts of Scotland*, 107.

[8] Kay-Shuttleworth, *Public Education*, 371–6.

[9] PP 1861, XLIX, *Report of CCE, 1860–1*, 243.

[10] PP 1871, XXII, *Report of CCE, 1870–1*, p. clxi, and appendix 1, 1.

2. THE LOWLANDS

In the rural lowlands, the parish school remained at the centre of the system, and these schools, regulated by well-established customs, changed comparatively little. The condition of the schoolmasters improved significantly. In the 1790s their total incomes were said to average less than £20, but the 1803 Act fixed statutory salaries between £17 and £22; the range was raised to £26–34 in 1828, and £35–70 in 1861. Fees and other perquisites (it was still usual for teachers to act as session-clerk) remained an essential supplement, but by mid-century the total income of a parish schoolmaster was likely to be £70 or more; in non-parochial schools a total of £50 might be expected, in rural adventure schools only about £35. Since the endowed income of parish schools was used to attract masters of higher quality rather than to reduce fees, parish schools were not especially cheap. At the time of the Old Statistical Account, typical fees were 1s. 6d. per quarter for reading (though it could be 1s. in poorer areas), 2s. or 2s. 6d. for writing and arithmetic, 5s. for Latin. By the 1860s these sums had risen to 2s. for reading, 3s. 6d. for the three Rs, and between 5s. and 7s. 6d. for Latin and other advanced subjects. Quarterly fees remained the custom in parish schools, though elsewhere weekly payment became common, the average fee for the three Rs being 3d. or 4d. Parish schools still retained something of their comprehensive character: though by the 1860s the well-to-do 'seek now generally more aristocratic and less promiscuous schools for their children', it was still true that 'in small towns and villages, and in districts exclusively rural, the better schools are generally attended by a considerable number of scholars whose fathers are farmers, tradesmen, or professional men. The great majority of the parents, however, live by the sweat of their brows.'[11]

Parish schools remained accessible to the poor because the old obligation of kirk sessions to pay poor children's fees was transferred in 1845 to the new Poor Law authorities, the parochial boards. In some places there were charitable endowments which built special schools for the poor, as with the Philp charity in the Kirkcaldy district, but it was more common for endowments, or annual grants from landowners and philanthropists, to support the parish school by supplementing the

[11] PP 1865, XLII, *Report of CCE, 1864–5*, 273; PP 1860, LIV, *Report of CCE, 1859–60*, 258.

master's salary, sometimes in return for free places; the Milne bequest in Aberdeenshire, which added £20 to salaries in return for twenty-five places, was a substantial scheme of this kind; another was the Ferguson bequest, which added £10 to salaries in a large area of western Scotland. This kind of support could also be given on a subscription basis: in Ayrshire and Angus in the 1840s, with the encouragement of the church, the gentry subscribed to educational associations which distributed small sums to schools throughout the county.[12] The most celebrated endowment affecting parish schools was the Dick bequest, which supplemented the salaries of schoolmasters in the counties of Aberdeen, Banff, and Moray. They had to pass an examination of university standard, including Latin and Greek, and submit to regular inspection by the bequest's inspector. At first the grants were used to raise standards generally, but later it was the classics which were stressed, and the bequest reinforced the already close connection in the north-east between the parish schools and the universities of Aberdeen (King's College and Marischal College, not united until 1860), which offered a large number of competitive bursaries awarded through an examination based on Latin composition. In the 1860s 7 per cent of pupils were studying Latin in the Dick counties, compared with 4 per cent elsewhere. Nearly all the schoolmasters were Aberdeen graduates, and many of them had studied divinity and were hoping to qualify as ministers—a situation once common elsewhere, but by then unusual. The Dick payments were substantial, and brought the average income to over £122 in 1865.[13] The Dick bequest gave rural schools in the north-east a special character which lasted into the twentieth century.

The parish school retained a central position in the community even when other types of school expanded. The impression gained by comparing the Old Statistical Account with later sources is that, while the bare bones of schooling existed in the 1790s, much flesh was later put on the skeleton. New schools appeared to serve more remote areas, or acted as 'feeders' to the parish school. In the large parish of Melrose in 1834, for example, the parish school in the town was supplemented

---

[12] PP 1847, XLV, *Minutes of CCE, 1846*, 389; PP 1847–8, L, *Minutes of CCE, 1847–8*, 327.

[13] S. S. Laurie, *Report on Education in the Parochial Schools of the Counties of Aberdeen, Banff and Moray, Addressed to the Trustees of the Dick Bequest* (Edinburgh, 1865), 307–8, 340. Cf. M. Cruickshank, 'The Dick Bequest: The Effect of a Famous Nineteenth-Century Endowment on Parish Schools of North East Scotland', *History of Education Quarterly*, 5 (1965), 153–65.

in the surrounding villages by six 'considerable schools' with proper schoolhouses, and one endowed school; there were also

numerous other small schools among the remote onsteads and cottage groups, sometimes established by the teacher himself on a speculation, and sometimes by a number of families, who unite together and agree to hire a teacher, the usual rate being his board and lodging free, and his chance of scholars. . . . He is generally some pious old intelligent person in decayed circumstances, or a young aspirant after a higher school, who is gradually acquiring habits and attainments to fit him for more extensive usefulness. The whole system is working exceedingly well, and no additional schools are required.

The parish school itself was regarded as an 'upper seminary' for older pupils to study the higher branches of education.[14]

By the time of the New Statistical Account, schools taught by old people or young lads, once common everywhere, were mostly found in the borders, the south-west, or southern Lanarkshire, where shepherds and upland farmers led especially remote lives; even there, it was becoming difficult to find teachers 'willing to encounter this expatriation among the hills'.[15] Elsewhere, non-parochial schools were taking on a more settled form, with proper schoolhouses and salaried adult teachers. Apart from private adventure schools, they might have various origins. There were side schools under the 1803 Act supported by the parish. There were subscription or 'self-supporting' schools, set up by groups of parents and 'managed by local boards of working men and heads of families'.[16] There were General Assembly schools provided by the Church of Scotland, and similar schools belonging to other denominations, particularly the Free Church. While the latter often sited its churches as near to the rival Established edifice as possible, its schools seem to have been more prudently designed to complement the parish schools by serving a separate settlement.[17] In the rural lowlands denominational allegiance was less important in parents' choice than proximity, and they were likely to prefer 'that school where the three R's are most rapidly and efficiently taught, whoever keeps it'.[18]

One type which was everywhere expanding was the separate school

---

[14] *The New Statistical Account of Scotland* (Edinburgh, 1845) [hereafter *NSA*; counties are paginated separately within vols.], iii, Roxburghshire, 70.

[15] *NSA* iv, Kirkcudbrightshire, 142 (Minnigaff).

[16] PP 1867, XXV, *Report on the Country Districts*, 85.

[17] J. M. Beale, *A History of the Burgh and Parochial Schools of Fife* (n.p., 1983), 182.

[18] PP 1865, XVII, *Education Commission (Scotland), First Report*, 245 (evidence of T. Guthrie).

for girls. Mixed education had been the norm in Scotland, although girls were under-represented in the parish schools (36 per cent of their pupils in 1851). The parish school tradition was formed when expectations for girls were low, and although girls could and did study classics and mathematics,[19] they were debarred from the commercial and university careers which led on from the higher subjects. But while public opinion in the early nineteenth century clearly shifted in favour of full literacy for girls, this was accompanied by a growing feeling that 'girls should breathe the purer and gentler atmosphere of the female school, if the more womanly virtues are to live and grow'.[20] The authorities emphasized the teaching of sewing, and by 1860 the Education Department was insisting on this as a condition of grant. This was partly to prepare girls for their role as wives and mothers, but also to help them earn a living. Hence the name 'female industrial schools' which was generally applied to working-class girls' schools in the mid-nineteenth century (which should not be confused with the semi-penal 'industrial' schools discussed later). Needlework required a female teacher, and the 1861 Act authorized heritors to pay a separate salary to a schoolmistress.

Sometimes mistresses taught girls or infants within mixed schools, sometimes they had schools of their own. There were schools which took girls through the whole of their school career, and segregation of the sexes was especially common in charitable foundations. But many of the 'female' schools were a modernized version of the dame school, teaching younger boys along with girls, and sending their older pupils on to the regular school. At the time of the New Statistical Account, traditional dame schools were still numerous: Arbroath had ten of them, 'intended chiefly for beginners, taught by elderly women in the more humble walks of life', and at Cullen (Banffshire) the minister thought 'these humble seminaries . . . highly deserving of encouragement, were it for nothing more, than their utility in relieving mothers of much trouble during the day, and keeping their children out of harm's way'.[21] But by the 1860s it could be said that 'the *dame* is being gradually superseded by the certificated mistress, fully equipped to give girls a thorough education', and that 'the process of detaching the girls to separate schools, and putting them under the charge of mistresses, is

[19] L. Moore, 'Invisible Scholars: Girls Learning Latin and Mathematics in the Elementary Public Schools of Scotland before 1872', *History of Education*, 13 (1984), 121–37.
[20] Laurie, *Report on Education*, 189.
[21] *NSA* xi, Forfarshire, 102; xiii, Banffshire, 349.

going on pretty rapidly'.[22] It was in schools of this kind that most female graduates of the training colleges could expect posts, and it was practically unknown for a woman to be in charge of a mixed school: 'in Scotland, *mixed schools under a master* are the normal type. A mistress is seldom entrusted with the charge of boys above eight or nine years of age.'[23]

Founding and supervising girls' schools became a favourite activity for the ladies of church congregations and the wives of employers and landowners. In Ayrshire in the 1840s, 'female schools of industry are numerous throughout the county, and may be found in almost every parish. They are commonly promoted, superintended, and aided by committees of ladies, whose patronage is always essential to their success.'[24] At Kilmarnock, while the gentlemen of a subscribers' committee patronized a free school for neglected and factory children, the ladies had a school of industry teaching reading, needlework, and stocking-knitting to twenty-five girls.[25] At Collessie in Fife, the female school was 'a neat and well adapted building in the cottage style . . . erected at the expense of the Melville family, and partly endowed'.[26] It was normal for aristocratic ladies to maintain such schools near their mansions: the Duchess of Roxburghe had one at Kelso, the Duchess of Atholl at Dunkeld, Lady Galloway at Cumloden, Lady Huntly at Aboyne. Sometimes these aristocratic efforts went beyond girls' schools. At Dalkeith the Duke of Buccleuch maintained two Episcopal schools, the boys providing the choir for his private chapel, while at Huntly a picturesque complex of four schools built by the Duchess of Gordon formed an ornamental approach to Huntly Lodge.[27]

One inspector in the 1840s drew a parallel between the patriarchal motives of landed and industrial employers.

Landowners, and other proprietors, more especially those of the larger manufactories and mines, are often found to provide for the education of the people engaged in their service. They may be supposed to do so from different views. The relation of superiority in which they stand, may be felt to have its duties in regard to the moral condition of their dependents [*sic*]; and assuredly

[22] PP 1863, XLVII, *Report of CCE, 1862–3*, 160; PP 1865, XVII, *Education Commission (Scotland), First Report*, 18 (evidence of John Gordon).

[23] PP 1865, XLII, *Report of CCE, 1864–5*, 258.

[24] PP 1847, XLV, *Minutes of CCE, 1846*, 398.

[25] *NSA* v, Ayrshire, 559, and cf. 470 (Stevenston).   [26] *NSA* ix. 36.

[27] PP 1854, LII, *Minutes of CCE, 1853–4*, vol. 2, 1055–6; *NSA* xii. 1043–4 (the parish school, a Church of Scotland sessional school, an infant school, and a sewing school for girls).

that condition, of whatever complexion it may be, reflects on all connected with it by any opportunities of influence. The labour of the intelligent workman may be considered as somewhat more productive than that of others; and with many it may be a point of good ambition to establish on their possessions the ornament of an instructed and moral peasantry.[28]

Motives of this kind, along with the remoteness of many mills and collieries, encouraged paternalistic employers to provide schools along with housing, churches, or shops. Now factory legislation, which made it compulsory for working children below a certain age to combine work and schooling, gave a further incentive. The first effective Factory Act was in 1833; children below 13 had to attend school for at least two hours daily. In 1844 this was raised to three hours (two-and-a-half in the winter), which had to be completed before 6 p.m.—under the 1833 Act children usually had their classes in the evening, and arrived too tired to learn. This was called the 'half-time' system, although much more time was spent at work than at school. There were obvious advantages for employers in having works schools under their own control. They could be used as an instrument of social discipline, and schoolmasters appointed by the employer could be relied on to teach the right moral lessons and not to stir up trouble. At Catrine in Ayrshire, a community entirely dependent on a cotton mill, the half-time system was used long before it became compulsory. In the 1790s the company maintained a schoolhouse, and paid the master a salary of £15. As well as a day-school, he taught the factory children between 7 and 9 p.m., with the help of an assistant who worked by day as a clerk in the mill; on Sunday the teachers catechized the children and accompanied them to church. By the time of the New Statistical Account, the master, still paid by the company, was teaching half-timers during the day and older children at night. At Stanley in Perthshire, where cotton mills employed 1,000 people, the company paid a teacher who knew Latin, Greek, and French.[29] This was hardly typical, but factory schools usually got good reports from inspectors. Teachers were relatively well paid, though they worked hard for it: at Lochwinnoch (Renfrewshire) in 1836, the works teacher had to teach sixty ordinary pupils by day, thirty working children who left the mill at 6 p.m. for their daily class under the 1833 Act, and yet another sixty older children who arrived at 8 o'clock for an evening class.[30] Evening classes in works schools may sometimes have

---

[28] PP 1845, XXXV, *Minutes of CCE, 1843–4*, 170.
[29] *OSA* vi. 567–8 (Sorn); *NSA*, v, Ayrshire, 145; x, 446 (Auchtergaven).
[30] *NSA* vii, Renfrewshire, 107.

had an element of technical training, but like Sunday schools they were mainly used by adolescents for catching up on the basics.

The early Factory Acts applied only to textile mills, but by the 1860s they had been extended to most large works. Half-time schools were most commonly found in cotton-manufacturing areas like Renfrewshire and Dumbartonshire, and in the linen and jute towns of the east like Arbroath, Forfar, and Dundee, where they were to survive longest. In larger towns, manufacturers sometimes set up joint schools, but the Argyll commission found only one in Glasgow, and in Scotland only 1 per cent of factory employees were half-timers, compared with 9 per cent in England.[31] The Glasgow employers, it was said, preferred not to employ children under 13, and this was true of most manufacturing industries. Apart from textiles, the chief employer of children was coal-mining, and the Mines Acts of 1842 and 1860 tried to protect education by banning work below a fixed age, and making children produce certificates of literacy. Thus the colliery schools provided by most coal-owners were ordinary day-schools rather than half-time schools, as were the 'iron works schools' which were equally common in areas like Lanarkshire, Ayrshire, West Lothian, and Stirlingshire. At Coatbridge, the Baird company of Gartsherrie were noted for their schools, built in the 1840s; the famous Carron ironworks near Falkirk, on the other hand, did not provide any until the 1860s.[32] A few other companies, like the Caledonian Railway at Carstairs Junction, also built schools for their employees. These efforts were not as philanthropic as might appear, for parents (and sometimes all workers, whether parents or not) paid for them by a compulsory deduction from their wages, normally 2*d.* a week.[33]

3. THE HIGHLANDS

In the rural lowlands, the gaps in the parish school system were mostly filled by mid-century; there were complaints, indeed, that denominational rivalry caused over-provision. The quality of schools might vary,

[31] PP 1867, XXV, *Education Commission (Scotland), Report on the State of Education in Glasgow*, 114–18.

[32] D. Bremner, *The Industries of Scotland: Their Rise, Progress and Present Condition* (1869: repr. Newton Abbot, 1969), 40, 47. Cf. J. Gordon, 'On the State of Education among the Mining Population of Lanarkshire', *Transactions of the National Association for the Promotion of Social Science*, 1860, 370–9.

[33] PP 1867, XXV, *Report on the Country Districts*, 79.

but the Argyll commission acknowledged that the remaining problems of illiteracy and non-attendance were not to be explained by a shortage of school places. It was a different matter in the highlands, and the commission's special report on the Hebrides, written by Alexander Nicolson, a young Gaelic-speaking lawyer, painted a dark picture of poverty and ignorance. This report, a document of considerable literary power, was confined to the Western Isles, but there were similar conditions in parts of the mainland. The fundamental problem was poverty, for neither the parish system nor voluntary effort could work well without a foundation of local resources. Highland schools found it difficult to qualify for state grants, and their disadvantages interacted in a way which made it almost impossible to break through into the new world of state-sponsored pedagogy. Nicolson's most telling complaint was that though among the poorest inhabitants of the British Isles, the highlanders failed to benefit from state aid which was supposedly directed at the poor. It was 'a system that gives least help to those that need it most'.[34]

Highland parish schools had long struggled with very adverse conditions, and neither the side schools of 1803 nor the parliamentary schools of 1838 solved the problem of large parishes and difficult communications. Parishes often had absentee landlords who left their factors to manage the school, and the highlands lacked a large middle class whose cultural influence could filter down and whose wealth could support educational philanthropy. Voluntary contributions were thus in short supply, and so was fee income. Sometimes parents paid in kind, by supplying the schoolmaster with peat or labouring on his croft, but even when they could afford fees they became accustomed to not paying them. Free education became deep-rooted through the charitable character of the Gaelic societies, and by denominational competition after 1843. The habit of free education was deplored by orthodox educationists because it was thought to discourage regular attendance, but it also meant that parish teachers had to live on the bare statutory salary, and that private teachers could hardly survive at all. It was difficult to attract qualified men to highland schools, and without them it was impossible to take pupil-teachers and attract an annual grant. Many schools also failed the hurdle of the Code's accommodation standards, and even parish schools could be primitive in aspect. At Torosay

---

[34] PP 1867, XXV, *Education Commission (Scotland), Report on the State of Education in the Hebrides*, 21.

(Mull) in 1843, the heritors divided the salary to provide four schools, but under the 1803 Act this exempted them from building a school-house, and

there is not a proper parochial school-house in the whole parish. The children in the depth of winter are often up to the ancles [*sic*] in water, and frequently the teaching of them is interrupted altogether, when the ill-thatched hovels allotted to them as school-houses are stripped bare by high winds.[35]

Earth floors and thatched roofs conformed to the usual building type in the Hebrides, but not to the regulations laid down in London.

In the more prosperous parts of the highlands, parents could club together to found extra schools. At Latheron (Caithness) in 1840, a huge parish with more than eighteen schools, private teachers

are selected from the most talented and promising of the scholars in attendance at the parish school, where they are again to be found in attendance how soon their own schools close in the beginning of summer. Here they spend the summer and harvest in revising their former studies, and adding as much as possible to their stock of already acquired knowledge. By these means they return with fresh vigour and increased resources to their former stations in winter. Thus they continue to advance in the higher branches of education, until qualified for the Society or even parochial schools . . . so that the district schools are a kind of nurseries for the more advanced seminaries, which in their turn liberally repay the debt they have incurred.

Some of these 'district teachers' had even reached the university.[36] A less enthusiastic report in 1833 noted that many adventure schools were conducted by 'a boy, or an aged female, a retired soldier, an innkeeper, or a fisherman', while according to the presbytery of Kintyre in 1841 'many of the private teachers are incapable of communicating know-ledge, and others have none to communicate'.[37] The employment of such teachers and the organization of subscription schools shows that the spirit of self-help was not lacking in the highlands, but also that conditions lingered there which were becoming obsolete elsewhere.

[35] *NSA* vii, Argyll, 294. For similar conditions on Mull in the 1860s, see PP 1867, XXV, *Report on the Hebrides*, 55.
[36] *NSA* xiv, Inverness-shire, 113; xv, Caithness, 110.
[37] *Educational Statistics of the Highlands and Islands of Scotland: Prepared by the General Assembly's Education Committee, from Returns made by the Parochial Minis-ters* (Edinburgh, 1833), 18; *Report on the Returns from Presbyteries on the State of Schools in the Year 1841, by the General Assembly's Education Committee* (Edinburgh, n.d.), 52.

The Gaelic school societies provided a new voluntary impulse based on funds raised in the lowlands. In the nineteeenth century, the SSPCK began to live on past glories. Its schools remained where they had been originally planted, mostly in the southern and eastern highlands, and failed to follow the moving educational frontier. After 1811 the new societies took up the baton, but eventually public interest waned and subscription income fell. The Edinburgh society reached its peak around 1830, although it continued to operate into the 1880s, still concentrating on Gaelic reading and itinerating its schools from one 'station' to another. But the Inverness society handed its schools over to the General Assembly around 1840, and the Glasgow one disappeared in 1851.[38] The church's General Assembly schools became the most effective supplement to the parish schools, offering a full range of education and introducing teachers trained in the new methods at Edinburgh or Glasgow. These methods then percolated through local schools: at Jemimaville in Easter Ross, the General Assembly school in 1836 was

certainly one of the most efficient and best taught seminaries in the north. The intellectual system has been adopted, and with great success. Many young men taught at this school are now the teachers of subscription schools through the country, very much to the satisfaction of their employers.[39]

The Disruption gave a new impulse to highland education. Much of the region transferred its allegiance to the Free Church, overwhelmingly so in the Western Isles. Denominational rivalry could be bitter, fuelled by the support of landlords for the Establishment, and in the northern counties—Ross-shire, Sutherland, and Caithness—Free Church ministers were known to refuse the sacrament to parents who did not use their own schools. Parish and Free Church schools thus competed for scanty resources. In compensation, religious rivalry stimulated a revival of the Gaelic school movement and drew in new contributions from lowland congregations. The original (Edinburgh) Gaelic School Society passed into the hands of Free Churchmen, but in 1846 the Established Church formed a Ladies' Gaelic School Association, which followed the current trend to supporting separate schools for girls. The Free Church in turn began its Ladies' Association in 1850, which by the 1860s had some fifty-five schools, not confined to girls. There was

---

[38] C. W. J. Withers, *Gaelic Scotland: The Transformation of a Culture Region* (London, 1988), 152; A. W. Harding, 'Gaelic Schools in Northern Perthshire, 1823–1849', *TGSI* 52 (1980–2), 1–19.

[39] *NSA* xiv, Ross & Cromarty, 50–1 (Kirkmichael).

a separate Free Church Ladies' Association in Glasgow, which specialized in schools for the Catholic communities of the Western Isles. For
the survival of indigenous Catholicism was an additional complication
of highland education. The communities in the eastern highlands, in
Moray, Strathspey, and Braemar, were able to finance their own schools,
but in the west resources were lacking, and it had been the custom for
Catholics to use the parish schools. If Protestant sources are to be
believed, their religious convictions were respected and harmony was
maintained. The Free Church Ladies' Associations used a distinctive
system. The salaried teachers were young men who taught in the summer, but were supported at a university in the winter, when they handed
the school to a substitute, usually a local youth. The aim was to increase the supply both of education and of Free Church ministers. This
combination of teaching and study was not unknown in the lowlands—
it was sanctioned, for example, by the Dick bequest—but its adoption
at this late period shows how hard-pressed the resources of the churches
were. Finding and keeping trained teachers, especially Gaelic-speaking
ones, was a persistent problem, and once they qualified highlanders
could easily find more comfortable posts than those on offer back home.

Even so, the evidence suggests that by the 1860s a great many gaps
had been filled, and that the more intractable problems had retreated
westwards. Nicolson found 226 schools in the Western Isles, but only
33 received government grants, and among the 286 teachers there were
only 47 certificated adults and 10 pupil-teachers. These schools were
provided by no fewer than thirteen different agencies, many controlled
by committees in Edinburgh or Glasgow, and Nicolson stressed the
urgent need for some supervising authority to rationalize these small,
poorly organized schools. The Free Church ran 111 of them, and had
49 per cent of the pupils (97 per cent in Lewis). Only 19 per cent were
in the 42 parochial schools (26 parish, 6 side, 10 parliamentary). The
Free Church schools included 47 belonging to the two Ladies' Associations. There were 30 schools of the original Gaelic School Society, 10
of the Church of Scotland Ladies' Association, and 29 General Assembly schools. But the SSPCK had only 17, and these were the least
efficient of all, showing 'a certain rusticity of character in their whole
equipment and style of teaching'; only one earned a government grant.[40]
Seventy-four per cent of the pupils—91 per cent in Lewis—paid no
fees, and whereas in the lowlands the rule of thumb was that a third of

---

[40] PP 1867, XXV, *Report on the Hebrides*, 24, 74 ff., 83, 108, 122, 176.

a school's income came from fees and another third from the government grant, in the Hebrides fees contributed only 9 per cent and grants 14 per cent; heritors' assessments and endowments provided 16 per cent, but this left 62 per cent to come from voluntary subscriptions, mostly raised outside the region.[41] What was needed, concluded Nicolson, was not more schools, but better buildings, higher salaries, more qualified teachers, and 'a strict and uniform, but not too inflexible, system of government, combining local representation with central control'.[42]

4. THE CITIES

The failure of the grant system to reach the poorest children was common to the highlands and the big cities, but in other respects they could hardly be more different. In urban Scotland, society presented a complex hierarchy of wealth and status, and the larger the town, the more the subtleties of class distinction and residential segregation were reflected in the ecology of its schools. In larger towns the burgh schools were out of reach of the working class by the 1860s, as town councils reorganized and rebuilt them to meet the new demand for secondary education, and ceased to provide separate 'English' schools. As day-schools with moderate fees, however, they were often accessible to the growing middle stratum of shopkeepers, small traders, and clerical workers, who sought an education directed to practical and commercial needs. This was a market which could also be successfully served by private teachers. This class in turn overlapped with the reasonably prosperous élite of skilled workers and artisans, for whom education was a mark of respectable status and a means of self-help. The gap between these families and the poorer working class was a large one, and it was probably the former who benefited most from sessional schools and others aided by the state. The original Edinburgh sessional school of 1813 had been directed towards the poor, but later foundations were intended to take pupils 'as well from the industrious classes of the community, as from the indigent and idle', and 'to assimilate, as far as possible, the Sessional to the parochial schools of the national establishment'.[43] The title 'parish school' was often used, and the

---

[41] PP 1867, XXV, *Report on the Hebrides*, 105, 179–80 (figures total 101% after rounding up).

[42] Ibid. 134.   [43] PP 1850, XLIV, *Minutes of CCE, 1848–50*, vol. 2, 549–50.

Chalmers model implied that the school would try to appeal to a wide social spectrum.

Schools of the sessional type in Perth were established, unusually, by the town council, which carried out an educational survey in 1834 and found 'great deficiency'; a public appeal raised £200, and the council added another £200, thus qualifying for a government building grant of £400, which allowed places to be provided for 400 scholars, to be taught on Wood's system.[44] More typical was the action of St Stephen's church in Edinburgh, where the parishioners raised £800 to qualify for a building grant. Once built, the school cost £130 a year to run, raised by an annual collection. This was a wealthy New Town parish adjoining the poorer district of Stockbridge, ideal conditions for the voluntary system; where local resources were scantier, it might not work so well.[45] But sessional schools soon spread to all the larger towns. At Dundee, where Chalmers's disciple George Lewis became a parish minister active in social questions, the first opened in 1832, and by 1842 there were eight, educating 1,629 children, while sixty-five adventure and subscription schools between them taught 3,688.[46] At Aberdeen, where the local pioneer was the Revd A. L. Gordon, there were ten sessional schools by 1842 with 983 pupils, and the clergy were celebrating their success. Ten years before, they claimed, the poor depended entirely on adventure schools, mostly wretched affairs conducted by broken-down tradesmen and the like; but the vigorous extension of the 'parochial system' had driven out all but a few, and 'the complete and speedy extinction of adventure schools for the lower orders might be hailed as a benefit to the cause of education.'[47] But as Allan MacLaren has shown, the superior teaching of the Aberdeen sessional schools soon began to appeal to shopkeepers and artisans, and kirk sessions opened separate 'district' schools for the poor.[48] This upward drift of sessional schools was common; they tried to appoint well-qualified masters who could teach Latin, and often charged relatively high fees, paid by the quarter

---

[44] *NSA* x. 123–4. Because these schools were not connected with a church, they appear to have received their grant through the English National Society.

[45] House of Lords Sessional Papers, PP 1845, XIX, *Report from the Select Committee Appointed to Inquire into ... the Parochial Schoolmasters in Scotland*, 90–1 (evidence of the Revd W. Muir).

[46] *Presbyterial and Parochial Reports, 1842*, 54–5.

[47] Ibid. 133–4; PP 1842, XXXIII, *Minutes of CCE, 1841–2*, 214, 224. Cf. *NSA* xii. 41–2.

[48] A. A. MacLaren, *Religion and Social Class: The Disruption Years in Aberdeen* (London, 1974), 145–9.

rather than the week. At Greenock the Highlanders' Academy, built
with a government grant in the 1830s, soon attracted 'a considerable
number of the children of families in the middle ranks';[49] in Glasgow
St Enoch's sessional school, in Edinburgh Dr Andrew Thomson's school
(founded as St George's sessional, but later taken over by the Free
Church) established a high reputation. In several towns, indeed, the
Free Church developed 'grammar schools' as rivals to the burgh schools,
and the practising schools attached to their Glasgow training college
included a model 'middle class' or 'intermediate' school.[50]

The United Presbyterians were also active in the respectable segment
of the market. In the 1860s they had two schools in the Anderston
district of Glasgow, which was dominated by foundries and engineering works; those who stayed on beyond eleven or twelve, 'although the
children of mechanics and skilled workmen, went mostly to offices
instead of following their father's occupation, this being looked on as
a rise in social position', and one of the UP schools, charging 4d.–6d.
a week, attracted

the higher orders of the neighbourhood, being the children of shopkeepers,
master-builders, cap-manufacturers, engineers, foremen of different works. The
high fees attract a better class. For though not so strongly as among merchants,
professional men, and our upper classes in the west end, the caste feeling does
exist to a considerable extent in Anderston among those who are in easy circumstances of the shopkeeper and foreman class. They prefer a school with high
fees, as being more 'genteel'.[51]

The other school charged only 2d. to 4d., and this was more typical of
the grant-aided urban 'schools where a working man may command a
sound education for his children at a moderate expense'.[52]

Many churches ran both a sessional school, likely to be used by the
working-class members of its own congregation, and a district or 'mission' school planted in a slum area and designed to reclaim those 'who
were dropping out of the pale of the Christian Church and the habits of
Christianized society'.[53] The way had been shown by Chalmers: after
he moved from Glasgow to Edinburgh, he founded a school in the West
Port, a poor district where it was claimed that only a third of the

[49] *NSA* vii, Renfrewshire, 465.
[50] PP 1867, XXV, *Report on Glasgow*, 76, and cf. 5–7, 140, 154–6.
[51] Ibid. 54–5.
[52] PP 1857, sess. 2, XXXIII, *Minutes of CCE, 1856–7*, 667.   [53] Ibid. 667.

children were at school. Opened in 1844, this developed into a complex which included a day-school, a girls' sewing school, evening classes for both sexes, an infant school, and a library and reading-room. There were also Sabbath schools attached to Chalmers's church, but these were kept separate in order to play down the denominational side. These schools were an impressive example of evangelical energy, and Chalmers's territorial idea was copied later, especially by the Free Church. But they really expressed the charity of the rich towards the poor, rather than class harmony within an urban community.[54] In mission schools the typical charge was a penny a week, which was often waived. They did not range much beyond the three Rs, attendance was irregular, and few older children stayed on. Churches were sometimes accused of starving these schools in favour of their sessional schools, and were tempted to overcrowd the classrooms to maximize income. Financial resources and teaching standards were usually inadequate to attract a government grant: in 1865, 41 of 46 sessional schools in Glasgow had grants, but only one of the 25 mission schools.[55]

It was at the mission rather than the sessional level that most Roman Catholic schools operated, for the growing Catholic community contained few members of the working-class élite. Irish immigration did not begin on a large scale until after 1800, but by 1831 Glasgow had over 35,000 Irish Catholics; the inflow reached its peak after the Irish famine of 1846. The earliest Catholic schools were provided by a Catholic Schools Society of 1817 supported by Protestant churches and employers. Catholic-run schools began to expand in the 1830s, but their future only became secure after 1848 when state grants began, and when both male and female religious orders arrived to take over the teaching. By 1872 ten parishes in Glasgow maintained twenty-two schools, with about 6,000 pupils, and there were schools in all the cities and in the towns of the industrial west. Catholic schools usually charged a penny a week, but were recognized as well taught, and were able to earn grants. There were separate schools for boys and girls, but otherwise they resembled those of other churches; pupil-teachers were used, but there was as yet no Catholic training college in Scotland, and few

[54] S. J. Brown, 'The Disruption and Urban Poverty: Thomas Chalmers and the West Port Operation in Edinburgh, 1844–47', *SCHSR* 20 (1978–80), 65–89; id., 'Thomas Chalmers and the Communal Ideal in Victorian Scotland', in T. C. Smout (ed.), *Victorian Values: A Joint Symposium of the Royal Society of Edinburgh and the British Academy, December 1990* (Oxford, 1992), 61–80.

[55] PP 1867, XXV, *Report on Glasgow*, 7–8, 13–14, 30, and *Second Report*, map opposite p. xlvi.

openings for adult lay teachers.[56] In attaching schools to their churches, Catholics were only following the common pattern, although management was more exclusively in the hands of the clergy than in the Presbyterian churches. But for the Catholic community the schools had a special role in expressing and maintaining their religious and ethnic identity, and as a bond of solidarity in a harsh social environment. The price paid was that Catholic children were kept apart from others, and the scanty resources of the schools and their emphasis on basic education made it more difficult for individuals to escape from the working-class ghetto than if they had enjoyed free access to the general range of schools. Catholic schools were used only by Catholics, and did not allow exemption from religious instruction. Episcopalian schools similarly insisted on teaching the Church of England catechism, but with less justification, for the Argyll commission discovered that only a minority of their pupils were Episcopalian. In the cities Episcopalian schools seem to have been of the mission rather than the sessional type, but they had a significant role on the educational scene. In 1855 the Episcopal Church founded a small training college for men in Edinburgh, converted to a college for women in 1867.

It might be thought that free schools supported by endowments would cater for the poorest children of all. But this was not necessarily the case, either because there were special conditions of admission, or because the prestige of the foundation attracted able teachers and made a school place a sought-after privilege. This was the case with the half-dozen residential hospitals in Edinburgh. Some of these were designed for middle-class children who had suffered family misfortune, others were purely orphanages; but the oldest and grandest of them, George Heriot's, drew most of its boys from the artisan class. Fatherlessness was a condition of entry, but the pupils were not taken in until they were 8, and then stayed for about six years. The boys in the hospital ended up in skilled trades, offices, and in a few cases at the university. But the wealth of the Heriot trust also impelled it, under a special Act of Parliament of 1836, to open a dozen day-schools. These 'outdoor' schools were free, and thus could not get state grants, but they were generally recognized as superior, and used by the respectable working classes. In Glasgow there were no residential hospitals, but there were more than a dozen free day-schools, mostly founded at various times by individuals whose names they carried: Alexander's, Wilson's, and Allan

---

[56] M. Skinnider, 'Catholic Elementary Education in Glasgow, 1818–1918', in T. R. Bone (ed.), *Studies in the History of Scottish Education, 1872–1939* (London, 1967), 13–70.

Glen's were among the best-known. Alexander's, in the east end, was 'a formidable antagonist to private adventure schools for the poorest classes, and to mission schools', but most of the Glasgow schools, like the Heriot's schools, attracted 'the children of respectable labouring people', and the best of them were on the level of sessional schools. This use of endowed funds offended against the educational orthodoxy of the 1860s: free education offered to those who could afford to pay fees was held to 'pauperize' the recipients, and it was found shocking that the Glasgow working class felt they were 'entitled to enjoy' these bequests.[57] The reform of such endowments and the future use of the funds was to prove a controversial issue after 1872.

True paupers had their children's education attended to by the Poor Law authorities. In England there were separate workhouse schools, which were a significant part of the public sector. In Scotland there were a few schools within poorhouses, but the general practice was to send pauper children to ordinary schools. The authorities were likely to choose the cheapest school, and take the children away as soon as they had mastered the three Rs, but at least the stigma of segregation was avoided. In a special category were the industrial or 'ragged' schools for the destitute, the subject of a well-publicized movement in the 1840s. The two Scottish pioneers were Sheriff Watson at Aberdeen, who opened his first industrial school in 1841, and the Revd Thomas Guthrie, a leading figure in the Free Church, noted especially for his interest in working-class housing. Guthrie launched three schools in Edinburgh in 1847 (for boys, girls, and younger children), along with a *Plea for Ragged Schools*, which aroused much attention. Guthrie's aim was to rescue children who ran wild on the streets and to save them from falling into crime, and like Watson he sought to attract them by providing meals (hence they were called 'feeding schools'). The children went home at night, but were kept for a long day, and taught 'industrial' crafts like tailoring and bootmaking for boys, and sewing and domestic work for girls, as well as the three Rs. A Glasgow Industrial School Society began work in 1847, while in Edinburgh Guthrie's insistence on a Protestant education for all children led to a rival United Industrial School with separate religious instruction for Protestant and Catholic children—a rare Scottish example of the secularist principle in action.[58]

---

[57] PP 1867, XXV, *Report on Glasgow*, 14, 91.
[58] A. G. Ralston, 'The Development of Reformatory and Industrial Schools in Scotland, 1832–1872', *SESH* 8 (1988), 40–55; P. Mackie, 'The Foundation of the United Industrial School of Edinburgh: "A Bold Experiment"', *Innes Review*, 39 (1988), 133–50.

Reformers like Watson and Guthrie were inclined to see poverty and crime as part of the same phenomenon. Watson had encouraged magistrates to use his schools for vagrant and criminal children, and the Scottish schools were eventually absorbed into a national system of industrial and 'reformatory' schools defined by acts of 1854 and 1866, and supervised by the Home Office. Reformatories (which had precursors called 'houses of refuge') were for children and young people convicted of crimes; industrial schools were for vagrants, younger convicted children, or children neglected by their parents. But even in the latter, most children arrived on a magistrates' warrant; the schools became residential, and moved from the philanthropic to the penal sphere. They were not a negligible sector of education: in the 1860s Glasgow alone had four reformatory and four industrial schools (including the Buchanan Institution, a large endowment of 1859), and the total for Scotland was about twenty, including several under Catholic direction. They were mostly in industrial towns, but some, like those at Campbeltown, Rothesay, and Stranraer, relied on the reforming virtues of fresh air and agricultural labour. There were also training-ships for boys in the Tay and Clyde estuaries.

All the urban schools discussed above were supported by some sort of endowment, subscription, or government grant, and they do not exhaust the list. The early Lancasterian schools in Edinburgh, Glasgow, and Aberdeen survived into the 1860s, and Lancaster's rival Andrew Bell left money for schools for the poor in Aberdeen, Inverness, Edinburgh, Leith, and Glasgow, as well as founding the Madras Academy at St Andrews, which served as an elementary school for the town as well as a secondary school. It is not surprising, therefore, that private adventure schools for the poor declined. Various sources make it clear both that these schools were meeting a large part of the demand in the early nineteenth century, and that they were later 'swallowed up' by their rivals.[59] In Glasgow, the Old Statistical Account found over sixty private schools, alongside a number of charity schools.[60] The 1818 survey found about eighty private schools, with 7,200 pupils, and provision for the poor was thought adequate.[61] By 1837 the balance was shifting, with the presbytery of Glasgow reporting 72 wholly or partly endowed schools and 74 'mere private schools', and by 1857 it had moved decisively against the private sector. In that year a survey by the

[59] PP 1867, XXV, *Report on Glasgow*, 9.   [60] *OSA* vii. 324.
[61] PP 1819, IX, *A Digest of Parochial Returns made to the Select Committee Appointed to Inquire into the Education of the Poor*, vol. 3, 1387–8.

North British Daily Mail found 28,463 pupils in 213 schools, of which only 23, with 6 per cent of the pupils, were private schools for the working class, though there were 44 'higher class' private schools. Of the remaining 146 schools, 101 were run by the churches, including 13 Roman Catholic schools, and these contained 55 per cent of the pupils. Only 61 of the 213 schools, however, were state-aided.[62] A few years later the Argyll inquiry made similar findings: 35,565 pupils were distributed between the following types of school: sessional 12,560, 'mission' 4,469, Episcopal 948, Roman Catholic 2,795, private adventure 6,838, others (including charitable) 7,955. This meant that 58 per cent were being educated by the churches, and 19 per cent by private schools—but as in 1857 the majority of these were serving the middle class.[63]

In the working-class districts of Glasgow the share of adventure schools was more like a tenth, and they were at the bottom of the market. Teachers survived by taking young children and feeding them into other schools, by providing a child-minding service for working mothers, or by charging such low fees that they could only scrape a wretched existence by cramming children into basements and tenement rooms. Some combined teaching with another job or keeping a shop. ('When trade prospers, the birch is abandoned', said the presbytery of Dundee in 1840.[64]) These unqualified teachers and unsuitable premises attracted universal condemnation. According to the 1857 newspaper survey, they presented 'extraordinary scenes of wretchedness, stench, and disorder', while the Argyll report contained vivid descriptions of hopelessly inefficient schools—many of them clearly serving the Irish community—which were held to justify the conclusion that 'the sooner private adventure schools for the lowest classes cease to exist the better'.[65] E. G. West's contention that 'the predominant number' of children in the large towns were being educated in private schools therefore seems unsustainable. More soundly based historically is the work of Phil Gardner, who produces much English evidence to show that private schools for the working class were more widespread than has been supposed before the 1870 Act and survived it for some years.

---

[62] *NSA* vi. 921; R. Somers, *Results of an Inquiry into the State of Schools and Education in Glasgow* (Glasgow, 1857), 16–17.

[63] PP 1867, XXV, *Report on Glasgow*, 132. Cf. Table 5.7 below.

[64] *Report of the Committee of the General Assembly for Increasing the Means of Education in Scotland . . . May 1840* (Edinburgh, 1840), Report on the Returns from Presbyteries, 39.

[65] Somers, *Results of an Inquiry*, 16; PP 1867, XXV, *Report on Glasgow*, 56.

Parents often preferred these schools to those offered by the churches because of their flexible hours, their practical curriculum, and their absence of religious and moral indoctrination. Further research may uncover similar evidence for Scotland, but that available at present seems to suggest that only parents who could pay fees at the top of the working-class scale had access to private education of any quality; perhaps the private schools had less appeal because the competing Scottish churches themselves offered a wider range and choice than their English counterparts.[66]

Observers could conclude that in the towns as in the highlands the grant system was not bringing aid to the poorest. While sessional schools prospered, those which charged lower fees struggled to survive, and some of the most deserving schools could not qualify for a grant at all. The Argyll report on Glasgow found that in the relatively prosperous districts north of the Clyde 25 per cent of all children were in state-aided schools, while on the poorer south side this fell to 10 per cent; the average for rural areas was 41 per cent.[67] Thus state intervention, supposedly introduced to help those who could not help themselves, did not seem to be reaching the really poor. The main achievement of the grant system, it may be argued, was to provide schools of real quality at moderate fees for those in the countryside who needed an alternative to the parochial school, and for the skilled working class and lower middle class in the towns. By the end of the 1860s, partnership between the state and voluntary action was probably reaching the limits of its potential, especially as churches and philanthropic subscribers began to rebel against financial burdens which were increasingly felt to belong to the state alone. It was easy to point to the anomalies and gaps in the system—overprovision through denominational rivalries, underprovision through the lack of local resources—and to feel that the great diversity of local management, for schools which differed little in their teaching and internal arrangements, should give way to a more uniform and rational system. Democrats could also point out that nearly all schools were in the hands of local notables and property-owners, whether these were heritors, the clergy and kirk sessions, employers, landlords, or those who sat on the multifarious charitable committees. School boards might introduce popular control, and return some power to parents, though through indirect electoral means rather than the exercise of

---

[66] P. Gardner, *The Lost Elementary Schools of Victorian England: The People's Education* (London, 1984). For post-1872 evidence on this question, see Ch. 9 below.

[67] PP 1867, XXV, *Report on Glasgow*, 138; ibid., *Second Report*, appendix, 39.

market choice. The 1872 Act was to sweep away both ancient parish schools and the denominational system. Yet the latter had put down its own roots in its thirty years of operation, and many older habits were to survive for at least a generation after 1872.

5

Literacy and School Attendance

CHAPTER 4 was about the supply of schools, which reflected the priorities of élites. This one is about demand, and involves trying to see what families sought from schooling and how they used it, as well as estimating the extent of literacy and school attendance. Although literacy was not acquired only through formal schooling, the nineteenth century saw an increasing trend towards standardization and uniformity, reflecting a deeper movement of 'institutionalization', as the school supplemented or replaced the family as the publicly approved agency of socialization. In Scotland contemporaries were perhaps especially inclined to use school attendance as a criterion of progress. The ideal of the parish school had a powerful grip on the Scottish mind, and the fact that traditional habits of education were not transferred to cities and new industrial communities, or adopted by the industrial working class, created a sense of national degeneration which might underestimate what was actually being achieved in difficult conditions, or how far Scotland still compared favourably with other countries. Since the ideal of a universally literate community existed, it was used as the standard against which deficiencies should be measured, and it is difficult for the historian to avoid sharing the language of progress and backwardness.

The general argument of this chapter is that by 1872 both literacy and attendance were at a high level, and that where national averages fell short this usually reflected localized problems, in the highlands, the big cities, and some heavily industrialized areas. Here there were children who did not attend school at all, and who did not learn to read. In the rural lowlands and in most towns, literacy was all but complete, and hardly any children escaped contact of some sort with the school. But nineteenth-century evidence suggests that this was a comparatively recent achievement, and regional disparities in the lowlands can still be traced in the statistics. The picture in rural areas seems to be one of steady progress from modest standards to higher ones, with no golden age in the past to which Scots needed to look back with regret. The highlands presented special problems, but there too movement was in the direction of improvement, and conditions resembled those in the lowlands a few generations before. But even in the rural lowlands, patterns of attendance were flexible and irregular, allowing education to be combined with an early start to work, and forming a customary system which might be resistant to new ideas about full-time schooling. Pressures for children to leave school were always strong, and where the balance tipped in their favour education suffered. This was the rationale behind compulsory education, state intervention being invoked to give universality a final shove.

1. THE NATIONAL PICTURE

As we saw in Chapter 1, R. A. Houston estimated that literacy, defined as the ability to sign one's name, stood at only 65 per cent for men in the lowlands in 1750, and 15 per cent for women. Not until 1855 did compulsory registration of marriages produce reliable statistics, and the national average then was 89 per cent for men and 77 per cent for women (compared with 70 and 59 per cent for England and Wales in the same year). Clearly much had changed in a hundred years, but it is impossible to say whether the national average improved continuously, or whether there was a phase of decline caused by industrialization and population growth, which was at its most rapid in Scotland between 1801 and 1831.[1] For England, Roger Schofield has argued from local parish registers that the literacy of married couples showed no dramatic increase between 1750 and 1840, though women's literacy did grow rather more than men's.[2] For both England and France, it has been shown that industrialization created a distinction between 'traditional' towns, where literacy was higher than in the surrounding countryside, and factory towns where it was lower.[3] No studies of this point have been made for Scotland, and the materials for doing so are not readily available, but Smout suggests that 'the almost universal and intelligent literacy of the Lowlands . . . must have reached its height at some point

---

[1] M. Flinn (ed.), *Scottish Population History from the 17th Century to the 1930s* (Cambridge, 1977), 302.

[2] R. S. Schofield, 'Dimensions of Illiteracy in England, 1750–1850', in H. J. Graff (ed.), *Literacy and Social Development in the West: A Reader* (Cambridge, 1981), 201–13.

[3] F. Furet and J. Ozouf, *Reading and Writing: Literacy in France from Calvin to Jules Ferry* (Cambridge, 1982), 197–232; M. Sanderson, *Education, Economic Change and Society in England, 1780–1870* (London, 1983), 9–16.

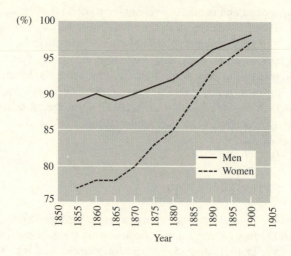

Fɪɢ 5.1.   Literacy of Brides and Bridegrooms, 1855–1900

about the middle of the eighteenth century, and then slowly declined as a higher proportion of Scots came to live in the ill-provided towns.'[4]

Figure 5.1 shows how literacy developed at five-year intervals from 1855 to 1900, though these national averages concealed local variations which will be looked at later.[5] Since people got married in their mid-twenties, the figures reflect the state of education about fifteen years before. There was little change down to 1865, but a steady rise after that, which might be linked with the growth of state aid to schools in the 1840s. The 1872 Act, on the other hand, had no perceptible effect on a process already well under way; the first generation subject to compulsory education would be coming into the statistics in 1885 or 1890. The graph shows that throughout the period the rate of growth was steeper for women than for men, and suggests that a change in attitudes to the schooling of girls, or at least towards teaching them to write, was a fundamental phenomenon of these years. And if Houston's estimate for eighteenth-century women's literacy is anything like correct, this change must have started well before 1855.

This general picture of growth is confirmed by estimates of the number

[4] T. C. Smout, *A History of the Scottish People, 1560–1830*, paperback edn. (n.p., 1972), 450.
[5] Unless otherwise stated, the sources for all tables, figures, and maps are shown in Appendix 1; tables with Roman numbers are part of that appendix.

TABLE 5.1. *School Attendance, 1818–1871*

Year	Source	Type of measure	Total pupils	Girls as % of boys	Pupils per 1,000 population
1818	Select committee	Pupils on roll	176,525		84
1833–4	Parliamentary return	Average attendance	236,325	70	100
1851	Education census	Attendance on census day	310,442	79	108
1864	Argyll report	Pupils on roll	418,367		137
1873	School board returns	Pupils on roll	515,353		153
1851	General census	Scholars aged 0–15	407,322	90	141
1861	General census	Scholars aged 0–15	448,054	93	146
1871	General census	Scholars aged 0–15	552,020	95	164

of children attending schools. These were collected on different bases, and each had its own deficiencies. One problem was that before education became compulsory there was a large gap between children 'on the roll' of a school and those in attendance on a particular day, which varied significantly between summer and winter. Estimates of 'average attendance' are probably the best indication of effective schooling, but they depended on guesswork. Another difficulty is that officials tended only to count children in full-time attendance at day-schools, while parents who were asked about their children's attendance (as they were in censuses) were likely to count evening classes or Sunday schools as a valid form of education. Since parents were also unlikely to admit that their children were neglected, or working illegally, censuses probably give too favourable a picture of effective schooling, while other types of survey may underestimate it.

Table 5.1 therefore shows the results of the general censuses as a separate series from those of other inquiries, including the special educational census of 1851 which was based on returns from schools rather than households. As well as the total numbers, it shows girls' attendance as a percentage of boys', and the number of pupils per thousand total population, a standard measure for comparing educational achievement.

This ratio shows that attendance was growing in real terms, but also suggests, as with the literacy statistics, that growth was faster after 1850 than before. The 1818 figures are the least reliable, however, and probably too low; the table leaves open the question whether in the early nineteenth century the growth of population outran the capacity of the educational system to respond. As we shall see later, it was certainly doing so in some industrial areas. In the 1850s and 1860s, when population growth was slower and when the efforts of church and state in providing schools were being consolidated, there was more chance to catch up. Even so, much of the growth was due to more attendance by girls, and probably to longer attendance by those who had already acquired the educational habit, as well as to the bringing in of previously unschooled social strata.

The ratio of scholars to total population was a crude measure of progress, but it was generally used at the time as a way of comparing countries or localities. Its significance really depended on the age structure of the population and on what was considered a reasonable length of attendance. In the 1820s and 1830s, to have one in eight or nine of the population at school (equivalent to 111–125 per thousand) was the standard aimed at, and was achieved in countries like Prussia, Holland, and Switzerland where education was thought particularly advanced. The 1818 survey, though falling short of this, showed that Scotland was ahead of England. But by 1833 this was less clear: one in ten in Scotland, one in eleven in England and Wales. The 1851 education census produced 'on the roll' figures of one in 7.8 for Scotland and one in 8.5 for England and Wales, and its publication in 1854 was seized on by opponents of Moncreiff's bill to show that no new intervention was needed. International comparisons for 1850 show that the Scottish attendance figure of 108 per thousand was ahead of France (90), but behind Switzerland (140) and Germany (160).[6] By the 1860s, the international target figure was one in six (167 per thousand). The Argyll commission, whose statistical inquiries were seriously impaired by their failure to collect data for any large town except Glasgow, discovered one in 6.5 children on the roll in the rural two-thirds of the country which was properly surveyed, though their national estimate of 418,367 corresponds to a figure of one in 7.3. These ratios seemed near enough to those in Prussia, where education was compulsory, to justify the

---

[6] A. Green, *Education and State Formation: The Rise of Education Systems in England, France and the USA* (London, 1990), 14–15.

argument that where efficient schools were provided, Scottish school attendance could be brought close to the ideal without compulsion.[7]

A more satisfactory measure was the percentage of an age-group attending school. Censuses made it possible to state this, but at first only in quinquennial groups. In 1861, for example, 64 per cent of children between 5 and 15 were described as 'scholars'. But since few children stayed at school for ten years, the value of this information was limited. As E. G. West has pointed out, this method of calculation had a fundamental ambiguity which often misled contemporaries, or was exploited by them to make unjustified claims.[8] To say that 64 per cent of a ten-year age-group were at school might mean, at one extreme, that 64 per cent of the children attended school for ten years and 36 per cent did not attend at all, or at the other, that every child went to school for 6.4 years. The truth obviously lay between the extremes, but in using this measure of 'deficiency' propagandists often interpreted it in the first sense and exaggerated the number of children escaping education entirely.

Thus Lord Melgund, introducing his 1850 bill, estimated that there were 321,000 children at school and 500,000 of school age. This left 180,000, or 36 per cent, who were 'left quite uneducated'.[9] Kay-Shuttleworth in 1853 came to the same conclusion by equally crude calculations: he put scholars at 225,000 (surely a gross underestimate: he simply multiplied an estimated 4,500 schools by an average size of fifty), and the age-group at 358,848 (an eighth of the total population). Thus the deficiency was 37 per cent, and Kay-Shuttleworth concluded that 'from the accounts given of the condition of juvenile depravity in the large towns, and of the destitution of the Highlands, little doubt can be entertained that barely two-thirds of the children who ought to be at school are in attendance on any School in Scotland.'[10]

Similarly, the Argyll commission used the very unrealistic age-group 3–15 as a basis for asserting that in Glasgow 'little more than one-third of the children of school-age are now attending school'; only the most persevering reader would discover that if the age-group 5–13 was used, nearly two-thirds of Glasgow children were on a school roll. Nationally,

---

[7] PP 1867, XXV, *Education Commission (Scotland), Second Report*, pp. xix, cxxix–cxxx, 1–3.

[8] E. G. West, *Education and the Industrial Revolution* (London, 1975), 8–10.

[9] Hansard, 3rd series 112, 19 June 1850, 78.

[10] J. Kay-Shuttleworth, *Public Education as Affected by the Minutes of the Committee of Privy Council from 1846 to 1852* (London, 1853), 371.

the commission's total of 418,367 was related by them to an estimated 5–13 age-group of 510,382 (one in six of the population). The difference of 92,000 was the figure for unschooled children which was so much cited in political debate.[11] Whether valid or not, it was only 18 per cent of the age-group. Yet the view that on the eve of 1872 a third of all Scottish children were escaping schooling, perhaps based on a confused misreading of the Argyll report, has appeared in several reputable works.[12]

Fortunately a more precise source is available. The 1871 census asked how many children at each age 'were in regular attendance at school, or were in receipt of education at home under tutors or governesses'.[13] This revealed that for the age-group from 5 to 12, to which compulsion was to apply after 1872,[14] the overall attendance was 80 per cent for boys and 78 per cent for girls, not so far from the Argyll estimate of 18 per cent deficiency. Eighty per cent was a high figure by contemporary standards, though perhaps lower than in Prussia or France at the same period.[15] Especially interesting are the patterns of attendance by age, which are shown from 3 to 18 in Figure 5.2. Few went to school below the age of 5—fewer than in England. At 5, about half were sent to school, but attendance was most regular between 6 and 12. Nearly three-quarters seem to have stayed for as long as this, but the peak age was 9 (92 per cent of boys, 89 per cent of girls). After that attendance fell steadily, and steeply after 12. These figures of course include middle-class children, and it is notable how few stayed beyond 15 or 16. While at the lower ages girls' attendance usually lagged behind that of boys, this evened out later—presumably because there was more pressure on boys to leave school for work.

As in other censuses, questions put to parents may exaggerate effective attendance, and the national averages may conceal a more complex

[11] PP 1867, XXV, *Second Report*, pp. lv, cxxix–cxxx, clxxiii–iv; cf. ibid., *Education Commission (Scotland), Report on the State of Education in Glasgow*, 126–7, 130.

[12] Notably J. Scotland, *The History of Scottish Education* (London, 1969), i. 359.

[13] PP 1872, LXVIII, *Eighth Decennial Census of the Population of Scotland taken 3d April 1871*, vol. 1, p. x. This applied only to children from 5 to 12; for older children the figures are presumably derived, as in other censuses, from occupational description as 'scholars'.

[14] This was usually expressed as 'between 5 and 13', i.e. children could leave on their thirteenth birthday. In this chapter, reference is to actual ages. For the original figures for 1871, and those for later years showing the impact of compulsory education, see Tables 9.2 and 9.3.

[15] M. J. Maynes, *Schooling in Western Europe: A Social History* (Albany, NY, 1985), 134.

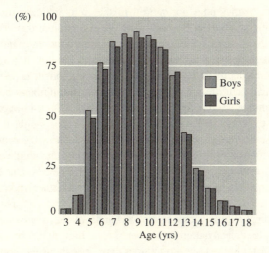

Fɪɢ 5.2. School Attendance by Age, 1871: Scotland

pattern of using schools for short but overlapping periods. One interpretation of the figures would be that while half the children stayed for the full eight years from 5 to 12, there was a minimum or 'core' attendance of about four years, between 6 or 7 and 10 or 11, which even poorer parents attempted to secure. The Argyll commission estimated average attendance in rural areas at four-and-a-half years, and declared that 'it will be prudent to assume, in framing a scheme of National Education, that the majority of scholars will leave the day-school at ten or eleven'.[16] But most children who went to school at all were likely to be there at 8 or 9, and the maximum attendance levels reached then suggest that, as a national average, no more than 10 per cent escaped schooling altogether.

2. REGIONAL VARIATIONS

The Argyll report on the 'lowland country districts' distinguished three zones of development. In the southern counties, including Midlothian and Ayr, 'nearly all the native population can read with ease, and the majority can write, but the Irish settlers are in great ignorance, and, as

[16] PP 1867, XXV, *Second Report*, pp. xxv, cxix.

a rule, can neither read nor write.' In the 'midland' counties—Perth, Stirling, Fife, and the north-east—'with the exception of the older people, and many from among the fishing population, the great majority of the industrious poor can read, and some proportion can write; but there is a considerable number who are not sufficiently educated as to be able either to read or write with pleasure.' Finally, in the north 'there is still great ignorance among the Highland crofters and fishermen'.[17] This excluded the Western Isles, where Nicolson's report made it clear that illiteracy was even greater, and one could argue with the report's geographical breakdown, since other evidence suggests that Perth, Fife, Banff, or Caithness hardly fell below 'southern' levels. But the report shows how even in the 1860s full literacy was either incomplete, or seen as a recent acquisition, and points to the many factors—poverty, local custom, religion, occupation, the labour market—which interacted to shape attendance patterns.

Maps 5.1 and 5.2 show school attendance per thousand population in 1818 and 1851.[18] They too suggest the existence of three zones in the lowlands: the borders and south-east, the area of highest attendance; the rest of the southern and central lowlands; and the north-east, which in 1818 had figures closer to the highlands. By 1851 the ratio had risen throughout the rural counties, and the difference between them had narrowed, the change in the north-east being especially striking. The figure in Aberdeenshire, for example, rose from 66 to 121. In the highlands improvement was slower, but here the figures were distorted by the use of county divisions: the west highlands and Western Isles, undoubtedly the most backward areas, brought down the averages for Inverness-shire and Ross-shire. Argyll was more advanced than the counties to its north, while Caithness reached 'lowland' standards; so did Orkney, though this is concealed in these maps because the statistics combine it with Shetland, where school attendance was low. Finally, the maps show the problems of the industrial areas. In Dumbartonshire, Renfrewshire, and Lanarkshire, the heartland of the new industries, attendance actually fell between 1818 and 1851, while other industrial and mining counties like Ayrshire, Stirling, West Lothian, Selkirk, and Angus stood out from the rural counties which they adjoined.

Another index of change was the gap between boys and girls. Maps 5.3 and 5.4 show attendance by girls as a percentage of attendance by

[17] PP 1867, XXV, *Education Commission (Scotland), Report on the State of Education in the Country Districts of Scotland*, 5.
[18] For the figures on which they (and Maps 5.7–8) are based, see Table II.

boys for 1833–4 and 1851. Again the different rural zones are apparent, as is the rapid catching up by the north-east and the highlands: here the percentages were in the 50s in 1833–4, compared with a Scottish average of 70, but in the 70s by 1851. The striking feature of the 1851 map, however, is the gap between rural areas as such and industrial ones, where the percentage was in the 80s. This was not necessarily because of more advanced attitudes in the latter, but because both boys and girls left school early under the pressure of work. This comes out from Maps 5.5 and 5.6, which show attendance between 5 and 12 according to the 1871 census.[19] By this time the gap between boys and girls, so striking in the 1830s, was in most cases below 5 per cent. In Clackmannan, Stirlingshire, and West Lothian there were more girls at school than boys, probably because these were mining counties where boys left early to go down the pit. Comparing these maps with Maps 5.1 and 5.2, the differences between the lowland zones had now been flattened out. Orkney, Caithness, and even Sutherland fitted the lowland pattern, though the western highlands did not. The industrialized counties of the west, however, stood out from the rest, and the map shows something of an east/west division overlaying the rural/industrial one, since the figures for eastern industrial counties like Fife and Midlothian were among the highest.

Maps 5.5 and 5.6 can also be compared with Maps 5.7 and 5.8, which show the literacy figures for marriages between 1861 and 1870. The disparities between regions, and between men and women, are greater than in the 1871 attendances, as one would expect from figures reflecting the educational situation around 1850. But there is a broad correspondence between literacy in the 1860s and attendances in both 1851 (Map 5.2) and 1871. By 1871 male literacy reached 99 per cent in Peebles and Selkirk, and was over 95 in most lowland counties; in Dumbarton, Renfrew, and Lanark it was between 83 and 85, and in the highlands it fell to 64–5 in Inverness and Ross. For women, rates were around 70 in the western industrial counties, only 53 per cent in Inverness and 49 per cent in Ross. These figures were published as part of the 1871 census, and the original table also distinguished between towns, the countryside, and 'insular districts', and gave separate figures for Edinburgh and Glasgow. The results are shown in Table 5.2. Another variable was religious denomination, and Table 5.3 shows the striking disparity between Roman Catholic marriages and others. Clearly a

---

[19] For the actual figures, see Table 5.4 below.

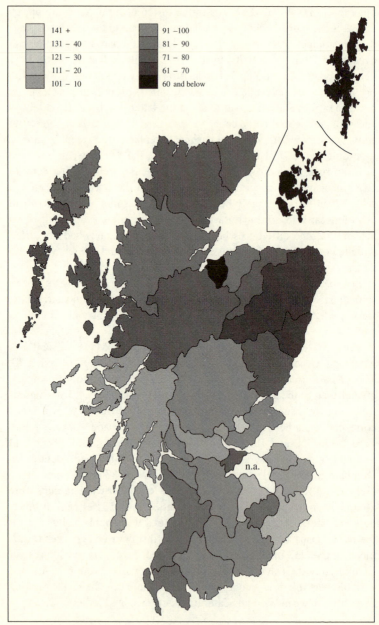

MAP 5.1.   School Attendance per Thousand Population, 1818

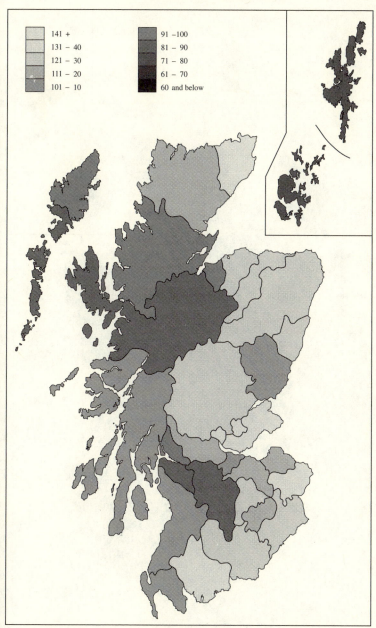

MAP 5.2. School Attendance per Thousand Population, 1851

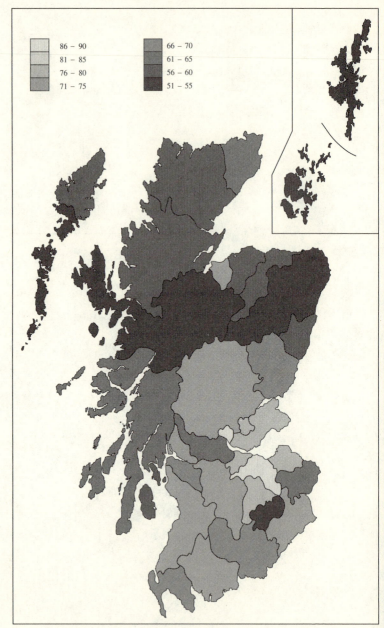

MAP 5.3.   Attendance: Girls as Percentage of Boys, 1833–4

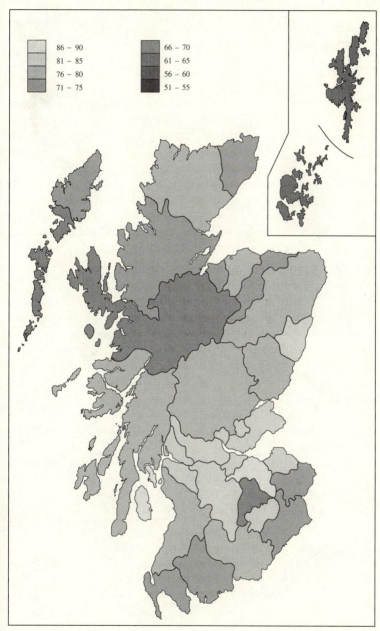

MAP 5.4. Attendance: Girls as Percentage of Boys, 1851

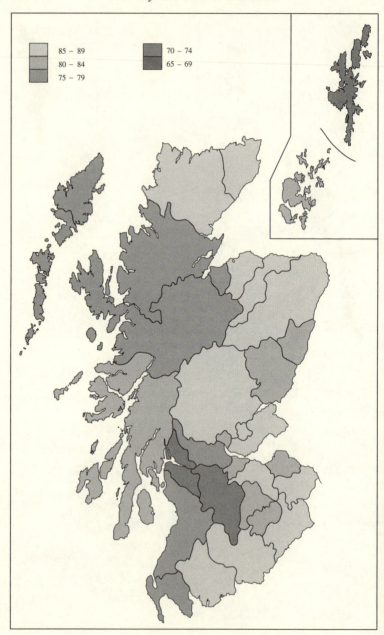

MAP 5.5.   School Attendance of Boys, 5–12, 1871 (%)

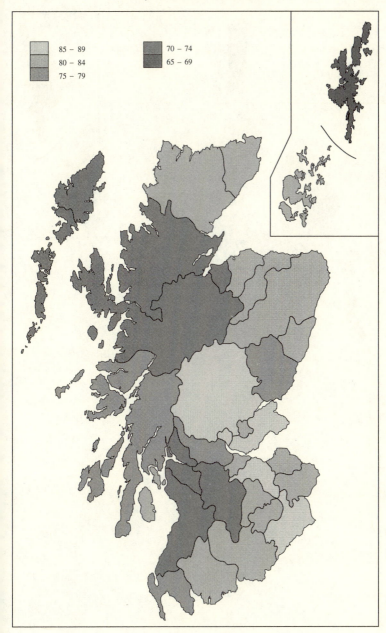

85 – 89	70 – 74
80 – 84	65 – 69
75 – 79	

MAP 5.6. School Attendance of Girls, 5–12, 1871 (%)

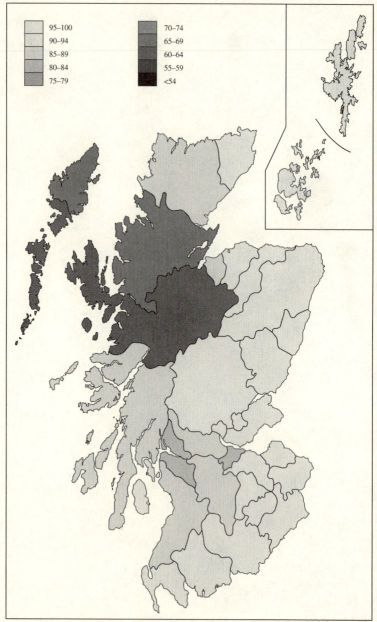

MAP 5.7.   Male Literacy: Bridegrooms Able to Sign, 1861–70 (%)

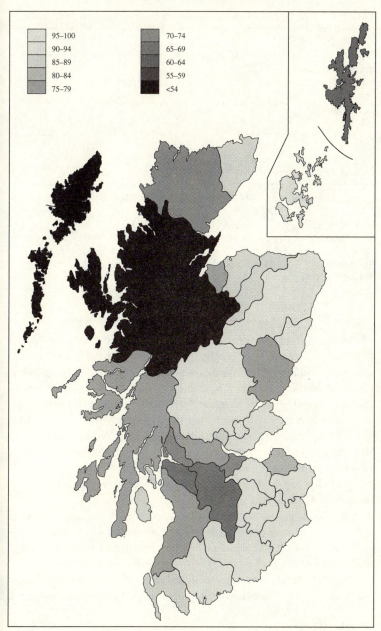

MAP 5.8. Female Literacy: Brides Able to Sign, 1861–70 (%)

TABLE 5.2. *Literacy of Married Couples by Type of District, 1861–1870*

	Men, %	Women, %
Insular districts	75	61
Mainland rural districts	92	85
Town districts	88	75
Edinburgh	96	91
Glasgow	84	67

TABLE 5.3. *Literacy of Married Couples by Denomination, 1869*

	No. of marriages	Men, %	Women, %
Church of Scotland	9,761	93	83
Free Church	5,095	93	84
United Presbyterian	3,277	96	88
Episcopalian	450	90	79
Roman Catholic	2,043	54	38
Others	1,393	94	82

substantial part of the illiteracy in Scotland can be explained by the presence of Catholic Irish immigrants, who were numerous in Dundee and West Lothian as well as the western counties. This also explains why Wigtownshire, which had a high population of Irish labourers, differed from other rural counties.[20] The Irish did not bring a tradition of universal literacy with them, and their problems were compounded by poverty, large families, concentration in unskilled and casual employment, and reluctance to use Protestant schools. As recent migrants they were at the receiving end of industrialization, whose effects are therefore difficult to distinguish from the more purely cultural consequences of Catholicism.

In the Old Statistical Account, direct comments on literacy were rare. But in the new one, and in a government inquiry of 1833–4, ministers were asked to assess it, distinguishing between children below 15 and adults. This evidence tends to confirm the hypothesis that the achievement of full literacy was something within memory. Over large areas, adults as well as children were reported wholly literate, except for a

[20] D. M. Mason, 'School Attendance in Nineteenth-Century Scotland', *Economic History Review*, 2nd series, 38 (1985), 276–81.

few elderly women or immigrants. Here school attendance was enforced by public opinion: 'it would be reckoned a great reproach to any parent if he neglected to send his children to school at the proper age' and illiteracy was 'felt as a degradation'.[21] In one Angus parish in the 1830s, 'the man who could not read' was pointed out as a curiosity.[22] But even in otherwise favoured areas a distinction was drawn between Scots and Irish. Rural Ayrshire and Wigtownshire provided many examples; at Portpatrick in 1838, in a population of 1,991, of whom 421 were Irish-born, 83 persons over 15 could not read and 383 could not write.[23]

In those lowland counties where progress was more recent, a distinction was often made between the generations. Among the older people, most could read, but substantial numbers, especially of women, could not write. One Kirkcudbrightshire schoolmaster was to testify in the 1860s that 'the elder women are generally not so well educated in writing. Of half a century ago, or more, I have often heard them say, *their* acquiring writing was carefully prohibited.'[24] In 1842 it was reported from Aberdeenshire that 'education is more valued by all classes than formerly, and in nothing is this more clearly seen than in the additional number of girls which is now to be found in all the schools'.[25] Sources from that period often give the impression that the current generation was the first to be taught writing as a matter of course, and that it was still a precarious skill. Typical comments were: 'A considerable proportion of the poorer children are taught writing, but for such a short time, that, although almost all can sign their names, yet many of them write very indifferently'; 'All persons in the parish, of proper age, can read, and almost all write a little'; 'There is perhaps not an individual in the parish above the age of ten who cannot read; and the rising generation are in the course of being taught to write.'[26] Even so, according to the 1851 census, while 86 per cent of the boys at school were currently learning to read, and 87 per cent of the girls, for writing the figures were 61 and 52 per cent.[27] By the 1860s, it was taken for

[21] *NSA* ii, Haddingtonshire, 170 (Yester); v, Ayrshire, 412 (Barr).

[22] D. K. and C. J. Guthrie, *Autobiography of Thomas Guthrie, D.D., and Memoir by his Sons* (London, 1874–5), i. 129–30.

[23] *NSA* iv, Wigtownshire, 143–4, 158–9.

[24] PP 1867, XXV, *Report on the Country Districts*, 182.

[25] *NSA* xii. 798 (Birse).

[26] *Report of the Committee of the General Assembly for Increasing the Means of Education in Scotland . . . May 1839* (Edinburgh, 1839), 43 (Pettinain, Lanarkshire); *NSA* xiii, Banffshire, 109 (Mortlach); *NSA* xi, Kincardineshire, 168 (Glenbervie).

[27] PP 1854, LIX, *Census of Great Britain, 1851, Religious Worship, and Education: Scotland, Report and Tables*, 42–3 (table E).

granted in the rural lowlands that boys and girls would learn both skills, but observers still remarked on the extent of adult illiteracy, a true census of which, commented one inspector, would 'sadly shock one of the national feelings of many a patriotic Scotchman'.[28]

Whatever the situation in the lowlands, it was generally agreed that the highlands were worse. In 1826 the Inverness school society published its *Moral Statistics of the Highlands and Islands*, which gave very high estimates of illiteracy; Donald Withrington has argued that they were overestimates,[29] and when the General Assembly carried out its own survey of the highlands and northern isles in 1833 it came up with lower figures. These estimated school attendance at one in 9.5 of the population (which was relatively high), but claimed that 83,397 persons over 6 in a population of 504,955 were unable to read either Gaelic or English (though this, of course, included children who were still learning), and that at least three times as many were unable to write. Both these surveys showed that generalization about the highlands was misleading, and that the worst conditions were in the west. In 1833 illiteracy was high in Ross-shire and the synod of Glenelg (Skye, the Western Isles, and the mainland areas opposite Skye), lower but still significant in Argyll, Sutherland, and Caithness, and almost non-existent in Orkney and Shetland.[30] In the western highlands, ministers replying to surveys usually reported that illiteracy was high among both adults and the rising generation, and did not think it worth distinguishing between ability to read and write.

But elsewhere in the highlands in the 1830s and 1840s, conditions were similar to the less developed parts of the lowlands. In most of Caithness, Orkney, Easter Ross, eastern Inverness-shire, Strathspey, and the southern parts of Argyll, nearly all children learned to read and write, most adults were also literate except that some women could not write, and complete illiteracy was confined to the aged, who were 'dying fast away'.[31] But school provision was under more strain than in the wealthier lowlands, and there were black spots like the town of Thurso.[32] In parishes which lagged behind, the distinctions between adults and children, reading and writing, and men and women were still significant.

---

[28] PP 1860, LIV, *Report of CCE, 1859–60*, 259.

[29] D. J. Withrington, 'Schooling, Literacy and Society', in T. M. Devine and R. Mitchison (eds.), *People and Society in Scotland, I: 1760–1830* (Edinburgh, 1988), 181–3.

[30] *Educational Statistics of the Highlands and Islands of Scotland* (Edinburgh, 1833), 6–7, 13, 28–9.

[31] *NSA* xiv, Inverness-shire, 114 (Moy). 　　　[32] *NSA* xv, Caithness, 11.

At Kilchoman on Islay, 'the young people are all taught to read,—the boys to write and figure.' In Urquhart and Glenmoriston (Inverness-shire), education was said to be so much valued that in a few years there should be few or none unable to read the Bible—a modest enough claim. At Canisbay (Caithness), 'all between six and fifteen years of age can read, but the females are not commonly taught to write. There are none upwards of fifteen years of age who cannot read, except a very few aged individuals.' At Walls (Shetland), 'though not more than a twelfth part of the population attend school at one time, and very often a much smaller number, yet the whole of the young people learn to read their Bibles with tolerable accuracy. A considerable number also learn to write, but seldom before they are grown up,—the parents considering that they discharge their duty sufficiently when they afford them the means of learning to read.'[33] Shetland provides an interesting example of how high literacy (at least for men) could coexist with what all reports agreed were inadequate schools and low school attendance. More often, in the highlands, relatively abundant provision of schools failed to stimulate a thirst for education.

In 1860 an inspector reported that education in the Western Isles 'is still very low; but that depth of ignorance, when few could read and still fewer could write, no longer exists'.[34] Yet Nicolson's report for the Argyll commission still found much backwardness. Pupils on the roll of schools formed one in 6.6 of the population, which was as high as in the rural lowlands. But average attendance was only one in nine, and achievement was limited by irregular attendance, summer desertion, impoverished schools, and ill-qualified schoolmasters. Nicolson found that at any one time only 49 per cent of the pupils were learning to write, compared with 65 per cent in the lowlands. Gaelic society schools might still teach only reading, and girls' schools still sacrificed writing to practical work. In one such school, Lady Dunmore's embroidery school in Harris, out of twenty-six girls only sixteen could read and three write.[35] Most parents, thought Nicolson, were content when 'their children have gone through a three or four years' curriculum of inter-mittent attendance, with a resulting ability to flounder more or less blindly through a piece of English reading, and perhaps to scrawl an

---

[33] *NSA* vii, Argyll, 657; xiv, Inverness-shire, 50; xv, Caithness, 32, and Shetland, 22.
[34] PP 1860, LIV, *Report of CCE, 1859–60*, 271.
[35] PP 1867, XXV, *Education Commission (Scotland), Report on the State of Education in the Hebrides*, 27, 114, 122, 174–5.

ungrammatical letter with infinite labour'.[36] He also studied marital signatures, and found that in 1862 only 52 per cent of the bridegrooms and 35 per cent of the brides in the Hebrides signed their names. Adult illiteracy varied from island to island: of the main islands, Islay was the most advanced, Skye in between, and Lewis and Harris the least literate. In Islay, among adults over 15, 68 per cent of males could read and write, 19 per cent could read only, and 13 per cent neither; for women the figures were 37, 37, and 25. In Skye, 69 per cent of males could read, but only 47 per cent of men and 12 per cent of women could write. In Carloway, a sample district of Lewis, 60 per cent of adult men could read Gaelic, 26 per cent could read English, and 27 per cent could write; almost as many women could read Gaelic (58 per cent), but only 5 per cent could read English and 3 per cent write.[37] This suggests that the Gaelic schools had an impact on Gaelic literacy, but that for women in particular education was thought complete once the Bible could be read in the native tongue.

3. THE 1871 CENSUS AND PATTERNS OF ATTENDANCE

The 1871 census included data about attendance by annual age-group for every parish, and the totals for counties are shown in Table 5.4.[38] The general pattern conformed to the national average, with attendance reaching a peak at the age of 8 or 9, and girls achieving slightly lower levels. But there were significant variations in the length and concentration of attendance. In 'advanced' lowland counties like Roxburgh, Dumfries, Berwick, Perth, Aberdeen, Banff, and Moray, attendances were uniformly high between 6 and 12, for the most part staying above 80 per cent, and fell off fairly quickly thereafter. In the highlands, there was a quite different pattern, with children slower to start school, but then staying on longer. Whereas the Scottish average attendance was 40–1 per cent at 13 and 22–3 per cent at 14, in counties like Ross and Cromarty and Inverness, where attendance at the peak was no more than 88 per cent, some 60 per cent of children were still in school at

[36] PP 1867, XXV, *Education Commission (Scotland), Report on the State of Education in the Hebrides*, 98.

[37] Ibid. 14–15, 68–9, 122, 192, 194–5.

[38] The right-hand column corresponds to Maps 5.5–6. The regional divisions are those used in Flinn, *Scottish Population History*. For an earlier discussion of these data, see R. D. Anderson, 'Education and the State in Nineteenth-Century Scotland', *Economic History Review*, 2nd series, 36 (1983), 530–1.

TABLE 5.4. *School Attendance by Age, Counties, 1871*

% attending at age		5	6	7	8	9	10	11	12	13	14	5–12
Far North												
Caithness	Boys	55	80	87	93	93	94	93	89	69	44	85
	Girls	54	80	83	90	93	91	92	92	68	45	84
Orkney	Boys	50	70	81	92	91	93	93	88	59	35	82
	Girls	54	70	77	85	91	92	90	82	54	30	80
Shetland	Boys	36	51	64	76	80	86	82	78	48	21	70
	Girls	34	55	64	72	73	80	73	65	41	11	65
Highlands												
Argyll	Boys	44	70	83	88	92	91	90	86	63	37	80
	Girls	45	63	81	87	89	89	92	83	57	32	79
Bute	Boys	47	76	89	95	90	92	87	81	45	29	82
	Girls	44	72	89	93	92	90	86	77	42	18	80
Inverness	Boys	54	69	78	85	85	87	86	84	66	43	78
	Girls	52	64	77	76	79	82	83	78	57	35	74
Ross and	Boys	45	61	76	85	86	87	88	87	71	42	77
Cromarty	Girls	43	60	73	77	84	83	84	79	61	36	73
Sutherland	Boys	60	74	85	86	97	92	95	91	56	36	85
	Girls	54	70	81	86	88	91	92	86	50	29	82
North-east												
Aberdeen	Boys	65	85	92	95	95	93	88	75	47	25	86
	Girls	63	81	89	94	93	92	87	79	45	26	84
Banff	Boys	66	84	91	94	93	93	92	83	52	34	87
	Girls	60	84	87	89	91	89	86	79	53	33	83
Kincardine	Boys	58	83	92	92	95	94	86	75	50	27	84
	Girls	57	74	89	90	92	91	81	70	42	23	80
Moray	Boys	66	85	90	94	92	93	90	80	57	34	86
	Girls	60	78	87	91	91	90	88	82	58	41	83
Nairn	Boys	54	75	79	85	94	92	85	75	57	28	79
	Girls	38	68	78	74	84	87	86	69	54	26	71
Eastern lowlands												
Angus	Boys	67	84	89	92	91	88	79	65	33	18	82
	Girls	63	80	86	89	88	82	75	58	26	13	78
Clackmannan	Boys	65	89	95	94	97	90	81	58	31	21	84
	Girls	71	89	93	93	94	89	82	66	31	16	85

TABLE 5.4. *Continued*

% attending at age		5	6	7	8	9	10	11	12	13	14	5–12
East Lothian	Boys	58	77	91	93	95	92	88	76	44	20	83
	Girls	53	75	87	91	92	92	89	80	50	22	82
Fife	Boys	69	88	93	96	96	96	90	75	44	25	88
	Girls	64	88	93	95	94	92	86	72	32	16	85
Kinross	Boys	59	87	94	95	98	92	85	74	47	24	85
	Girls	56	81	94	96	96	94	83	73	47	25	84
Midlothian ˙	Boys	60	84	92	94	95	93	88	76	46	25	85
	Girls	57	81	91	94	94	93	90	81	50	27	85
Perth	Boys	70	85	95	96	95	94	89	79	49	32	88
	Girls	65	85	91	94	95	92	88	80	50	25	86
Stirling	Boys	54	80	89	94	91	89	78	60	28	13	79
	Girls	52	75	86	91	92	87	83	71	39	19	79
West Lothian	Boys	62	84	93	94	95	93	84	63	28	13	84
	Girls	59	80	90	94	93	92	87	80	44	19	84
Western lowlands												
Ayr	Boys	39	74	88	93	94	89	80	60	34	18	76
	Girls	36	70	85	89	89	85	78	65	32	17	74
Dumbarton	Boys	38	69	84	86	88	83	74	61	41	28	72
	Girls	35	67	80	85	85	80	73	61	35	19	70
Lanark	Boys	37	66	82	87	89	85	77	57	28	13	72
	Girls	34	62	77	85	85	85	78	66	32	16	71
Renfrew	Boys	42	71	84	88	89	85	78	61	31	16	74
	Girls	37	66	80	85	88	84	77	62	29	16	72
Borders												
Berwick	Boys	52	80	93	95	97	97	93	86	61	32	86
	Girls	52	76	88	93	95	95	90	83	53	18	84
Dumfries	Boys	56	80	94	96	95	95	93	83	55	31	86
	Girls	56	80	89	94	94	92	89	82	48	26	84
Kirkcudbright	Boys	54	78	91	96	95	96	91	84	61	30	85
	Girls	50	74	89	92	94	93	90	86	48	29	83
Peebles	Boys	44	75	91	98	99	97	94	79	55	26	84
	Girls	43	68	91	91	95	95	88	73	42	13	80
Roxburgh	Boys	55	85	94	97	97	98	93	87	53	29	88
	Girls	47	75	92	95	94	97	93	83	44	25	85

TABLE 5.4. *Continued*

% attending at age		5	6	7	8	9	10	11	12	13	14	5–12
Selkirk	Boys	40	75	92	94	97	95	94	81	31	17	83
	Girls	41	71	88	92	99	95	91	82	27	15	82
Wigtown	Boys	45	69	82	87	90	89	87	78	52	28	78
	Girls	40	66	80	87	86	85	84	78	49	26	76
SCOTLAND	Boys	52	76	87	91	92	90	84	70	41	23	80
	Girls	48	73	84	89	89	88	83	72	40	22	78

13, 40 per cent at 14, and (though this is not shown in the table) 30 per cent at 15. Caithness and Orkney combined this with high levels of standard attendance. This appears to reflect a pattern of short full-time schooling followed by several years of winter attendance, which was typical of the highlands and was probably once normal in the lowlands. Even in the rural lowlands, most counties in 1871 had over 40 per cent of their children still at school at 13—beyond what was to become the compulsory school age. But regional custom seems to have differed in the starting age, with 60 per cent or more being sent at 5 in the north-east and eastern lowlands, but 50 per cent or fewer in the borders. Lowest of all (apart from Shetland) were the industrial counties of the west, which displayed late starting, early leaving, and levels of peak attendance which rose above 90 per cent only in Ayrshire.

Statistics of this kind obviously conceal very complex patterns. When parents said that their child was attending school 'regularly', they might not count summer absence, which was a persistent problem for administrators. The Revised Code insisted on a minimum attendance of 200 days a year, but it was said that even in areas of high attendance only about half the children attained this norm.[39] What parents sought from the school system did not necessarily conform to the official definition of its purpose provided that literacy was achieved, and 'archaic' habits survived. 'A labouring man', it was reported from Ayrshire in the 1830s, 'cannot afford to send to school at one and the same time all his children who are at an age for attending it. But he gives a year's schooling

[39] *Report of the Committee of the General Assembly for Increasing the Means of Education in Scotland . . . 1863* (Edinburgh, 1863), Abstract of Reports of Presbyteries, p. iv; S. S. Laurie, *Report on Education in the Parochial Schools of the Counties of Aberdeen, Banff and Moray* (Edinburgh, 1865), 341, 347.

to one, and then a year's schooling to another, and then revives the education of the first by an additional quarter for him; and so on with the others, till the whole of his children are enabled to read tolerably well, and do accounts'; and it was common to report that 'children of a numerous family get a quarter or two at school in rotation,—sometimes even that two of them go alternately each day or meeting.'[40] Educational experts were reluctant to admit that fees were a disincentive to attendance, and there was no call for their abolition before 1872. Yet the weekly fee in a parish school was about 3*d*., at a time when unskilled workers were paid 10*s*. or less, and skilled ones about 15*s*. With a large family, fees could soon prove a strain, and it was observed in 1870 that younger children were often kept longer at school because their parents were better off once their older siblings were working.[41] The real economic cost of full-time attendance lay not in the fees, however, but in forgoing the child's wages, which could be 2*s*. a week on the farm, 3*s*. or more in a factory.[42]

In the late 1860s child employment in agriculture was investigated by a royal commission, whose findings are consistent with the census data. They reported that children began school at 6 or 7; those from better-off families were likely to attend continuously until 13 or 14, but the children of labourers gave up full-time schooling once the three Rs had been mastered and they were old enough to get paid summer work, which was from 9 onwards. Thereafter they were sent to school only in the winter, and the scholastic winter, unlike the climatic one, was short. Children left school in April, and did not return until November, or even January, so that it might be only one full quarter which was taken. After a few years of this partial attendance, children would leave school for good, at 14 in the lowlands, 15 or 16 in the highlands. Adolescents might come back for a quarter or two once they were earning enough to pay their own fees, and many schoolmasters ran evening classes for these students; 'sometimes they do this when they are anxious to improve themselves in order to get some special appointment, such as a clerk's place or a place on a railroad.'[43]

---

[40] *NSA* v, Ayrshire, 390 (Dailly); xi, Kincardineshire, 149 (Laurencekirk).

[41] PP 1870, XIII, *Commission on Employment in Agriculture, Fourth Report*, 11.

[42] I. Levitt and C. Smout, *The State of the Scottish Working-Class in 1843* (Edinburgh, 1979), 84–9, 114–19; cf. PP 1867, XXV, *Education Commission (Scotland), Second Report*, pp. clvii-clxi.

[43] PP 1870, XIII, *Commission on the Employment of Children, Young Persons, and Women in Agriculture (1867), Fourth Report*, 9; cf. PP 1867, XXV, *Education Commission (Scotland), Second Report*, pp. cxiv–cxv.

No doubt both attendance and literacy varied with the rural social hierarchy, but evidence on this is fragmentary. Certain groups like miners and fishermen were renowned for their 'wildness' and recalcitrance to education, while others like shepherds were known for their attachment to it even when they lived in remote settlements. Among the rural population, 'small village tradesmen' and wage-earning labourers and farm servants were thought more likely to keep their children at school than weavers, crofters, or small independent farmers, who needed their children's labour in the family economy.[44] This may account for the relative backwardness of the north-east in the early nineteenth century, for this was a region where many smallholdings existed alongside the large farms; since these peasant farmers were in progressive decline, it may also explain why school attendance there improved. In the same way, the division between advanced and backward areas of the highlands corresponded broadly to the difference between 'farming' and 'crofting' districts.[45] In areas dominated by large farmers, children would only be taken from school when paid employment was available.

The agricultural employment commission found the desire for education general among the labourers. 'We just keep our children at school till they are educated,' they were told by a Midlothian hind's wife. 'It's all we've got to give them, poor things, and we do what we can to make them scholars.' But they also found parents 'glad to get them away to work as soon as they can write, and read the Bible, and do a little counting', and concluded that there was 'a large minority, even among the native Scotch children in the rural districts, growing up with very imperfect education, and for the practical purposes of life with none at all'.[46] Like many observers in the 1860s, they thought that rural children's work was on the increase, and threatening the level of school attendance. Watching animals was the traditional and almost universal task given to boys, and at harvest time all hands were required in the fields. But there were now new kinds of work outside the harvest period: hoeing and thinning turnips, gathering whelks or mussels, and bark peeling for tanneries were among those frequently mentioned. And there was always pressure on girls to stay at home to help their mothers in the house and dairy, or to look after younger children.

[44] PP 1867, XXV, *Report on the Country Districts*, 7–13.
[45] I. Carter, *Farmlife in Northeast Scotland, 1840–1914: The Poor Man's Country* (Edinburgh, 1979); T. M. Devine, *The Great Highland Famine: Hunger, Emigration and the Scottish Highlands in the Nineteenth Century* (Edinburgh, 1988).
[46] PP 1870, XIII, *Commission on Employment in Agriculture, Fourth Report*, 8, 11, and section S, p. 69 (comma inserted for clarity).

This led the commission to consider compulsory education, and they found widespread support for it among ministers, landowners, teachers, and even farming employers, either as a legal obligation, or in the form of an education test before children were allowed to work. Most of the assistant commissioners who carried out local inquiries favoured limited compulsion—one proposal, which recognized the strength of existing habits, was for eight months compulsory schooling each year between 6 and 10, and four months between 10 and 13—but the commission itself made no recommendation.[47] This caution was shared by the Argyll commission, which thought opposition to compulsion still too strong, and put its faith in a gradual process of enlightenment. It argued that poor attendance was not due to lack of schools or economic constraints, but to the 'apathy' and 'indifference' of parents. 'The demand for the education of their children corresponds to the state of education of the parents', and

the further and deeper it penetrates through the lower strata of society, its influence will extend more widely. People will in time begin to appreciate its real value; as they grow up themselves well taught to read and write, they will learn to insist upon their children following in their footsteps.[48]

There was sociological insight as well as political expediency behind this remark about family mentalities: school attendance was a consequence of literacy as much as a cause. But if sure but slow progress put the target of universal attendance within sight in the rural lowlands, this was not always the case elsewhere.

4. FACTORIES, TOWNS, AND THE WORKING CLASS

The patterns of rural education respected the seasonal rhythms of agriculture, and allowed the acquisition of literacy to be combined with the early demands of labour. They were compatible with artisan industry, where children contributed to family work-tasks as on the farm, but not with the factory system or with the conditions of labour in large towns, where leaving school meant an irrevocable choice of full-time work for long hours. When children could take jobs as early as 8, traditions which depended on prolonged part-time attendance until 13

[47] PP 1870, XIII, *Commission on Employment in Agriculture, Fourth Report*, 13–14.
[48] PP 1867, XXV, *Report on the Country Districts*, 13, 37.

or 14 collapsed, and the habit of learning writing later than reading meant that only partial literacy might be acquired; even reading was a skill which might be lost if it was not solidly grounded and regularly exercised. The factory laws could be seen as an attempt to transfer the tradition of part-time continuation to a new context, as could evening classes and Sunday schools. But much work escaped this legislation, and in towns the community pressures which impelled rural parents to do the best for their children were difficult to re-establish.

The 1830s and 1840s were decades when the system was coming under particular strain. First, this was when weaving in the textile industries, especially cotton, shifted decisively to factories. Handloom weaving survived in specialized or luxury branches, but these were years of crisis for the ordinary weavers, whose numbers had expanded along with mechanized spinning, but who now faced unemployment and poverty wages. Second, it was after 1830 that the iron industry of Lanarkshire expanded spectacularly with the adoption of the hot-blast process and the simultaneous exploitation of coal and local iron ore. Rural parishes were swamped by the growth of mines, blast-furnaces, and workers' housing, and in towns like Coatbridge, Airdrie, and Motherwell the existing social infrastructure proved hopelessly inadequate. And third, although the general population increase was slowing down, Irish immigration was not, and it accelerated after the famine of 1846. Immigrants—from the highlands as well as Ireland—naturally settled where work was most abundant, and these were the areas already suffering from the strains of expansion.

It was the textile mills which first attracted the attention of legislators, and there were a number of surveys of literacy among their workers. The early factories often had an imported or immigrant work-force, and there was little continuity with the educational habits of the Scottish countryside, or between the new working class and the old. Factory work itself did not require literate skills, except for a handful of clerks and foremen. Yet surveys usually discovered that most factory workers could read, though far fewer could write. The inquiry which preceded the 1834 Factory Act concluded that 96 per cent of Scottish mill-workers of all ages could read, but only 53 per cent could write; in England the figures were 86 and 43 per cent. The same survey included an 'educational census' of the Grandholm linen mills, near Aberdeen, which is summarized in Table 5.5. Of the 1,119 workers, only 28 per cent could read and write, 45 per cent could read only, and 27 per cent were totally illiterate. Of the lowlanders, 21 per cent were illiterate, compared with

TABLE 5.5. *Education of Workers at Grandholm Mills, 1833*

	Type of labour				
	Heckling	Spinning	Weaving	Mechanics	Total
Origins of workers					
Lowlands	134	557	168	41	900
Highlands	30	48	34	5	117
Ireland	2	23	66	1	92
Other	8	0	1	1	10
Extent of literacy					
Read and write	117	77	69	46	309
Read only	38	349	116	0	503
Neither	19	202	84	2	307
Origins of 307 illiterate workers					
Lowlands	17	147	25	0	189
Highlands	2	32	12	2	48
Ireland	0	23	47	0	70

Source: PP 1834, XX, *Factories Inquiry Commission, Supplementary Report, Part I*, 89.

41 per cent of the highlanders and 76 per cent of the Irish. About 60 per cent of the workers in this mill were women, although the 'mechanics' were obviously all men, as well as being mostly lowlanders and nearly all literate.[49] The fact that in the general survey 96 per cent could read has been used to argue that industrialization was not having a deleterious impact on education.[50] But the statistics have to be seen in their contemporary context, and 53 per cent able to write was a low figure at a time when girls as well as boys were being taught this skill in the rural lowlands. At Grandholm mills, 21 per cent of the lowland workers could not even read, which suggests that mill-workers were distinctly disadvantaged by comparison with the population at large— and also perhaps that the inquiry's national estimate of 96 per cent needs to be treated sceptically.

[49] PP 1834, XX, *Factories Inquiry Commission, Supplementary Report of the Central Board . . . Part I*, 35, 42, 89; cf. R. K. Webb, 'Literacy among the Working Classes in Nineteenth Century Scotland', *SHR* 33 (1954), 108.
[50] West, *Education and the Industrial Revolution*, 68.

Thus conditions in the industrial regions seemed to be slipping back a generation. That was certainly the view of ministers in the 1830s and 1840s, who insisted particularly on the inability of struggling families to pay fees. The worst reports came from large towns in the west, and from areas with coal-mines and distressed handloom weavers, a pattern similar to that in England at the same period.[51] In normal conditions, the contact of rural weavers with towns was a stimulus to education, as at Kilbarchan near Paisley: 'The necessity of being able to write . . . is strongly impressed on them, by a constant intercourse of all ages and both sexes, with the warehouses whence work is to be obtained.'[52] But in Ayrshire in 1847 it was the 'manufacturing workmen', especially the weavers, who were said to make least use of schools. Attendance was better among miners since the recent Mines Act, and better still in agriculture; but 'it is in towns where the schools are found to be attended, in general, with the greatest regularity and for the longest period'. At Tarbolton in 1842, 'during the last ten years, there has been a gradual diminution of the proportion of the population attending school. Boys are now at the loom, or go down the coal-pit, when ten or eleven years of age. Girls at even a more tender age earn their subsistence at needle-work.' In the Newmilns–Darvel area, 'the education in the manufacturing villages is sadly defective. This arises solely from want, not of the will, but of the means on the part of the parents to educate their children. Nothing can exceed the anxiety of the parents in this respect, but they can neither spare their children's work nor their wages.' At Dalserf (Lanarkshire), children were removed from school to 'employ them at the weaving-loom and tambouring-frame before they have been even taught to read perfectly. Any deficiency of this kind is in general afterwards supplied by attendance on week day evening and Sabbath schools.' But although all learnt to read, 'writing is by no means so common a qualification.'[53] A survey of school-leavers in Ayrshire in 1846 showed that in a sample of 4,360 from 52 schools, 360 left unable to write with ease, 640 unable to write at all, and 774 without having learnt arithmetic. At Sanquhar (Dumfriesshire), a parish of 3,268 souls whose industries included the Wanlockhead lead-mines, a carpet factory, and handloom weaving, only two people over 15 could not read, but 350 could not

---

[51] W. B. Stephens, 'Literacy in England, Scotland, and Wales, 1500–1900', *History of Education Quarterly*, 30 (1990), 564.

[52] *NSA* vii, Renfrewshire, 381.

[53] PP 1847, XLV, *Minutes of CCE, 1846*, 387; *NSA* v, Ayrshire, 763 (Tarbolton), 852 (Loudoun), and cf. 188–9 (Galston), 237 (Dalry); *NSA* vi. 759.

write.[54] And at Dundee in 1832–3, where many schools were connected with the mills, it was thought that reading was nearly universal, but not writing: 'many in our public works [factories] are entirely ignorant of it.'[55]

As the factory acts took effect, children covered by them were probably better off than those in unregulated trades, or from poor families depending on unskilled and casual labour. At Paisley in the 1830s, 'of the families employed in factories, a greater proportion of the children are attending school than of the families of weavers or labourers, and this goes far to demonstrate the wisdom of some clauses in the Factory Bill.' In the same town in 1840, the presbytery reported that 'the inadequate remuneration, especially to the private teacher, is highly detrimental to the cause of education. . . . the people, in general, cannot afford higher wages [school fees], and many of them are not able to pay even the present inadequate sum for the education of their children', a situation which the presbytery thought general in western Scotland; they added that evening classes were a 'sorry substitute' for proper schooling, in an area where children were put to work at 7 or even 6. When free schools were opened for the unemployed in Paisley during the trade crisis of 1842, they attracted over 3,000 pupils—proof, argued the clergy, of a latent but unsatisfied demand.[56] In Paisley, Greenock, Glasgow, and Dundee in the 1830s the ratio of pupils to population was reckoned to be one in twelve or thirteen. It was evidence of this kind, combined with a general sense of urban crisis, which lay behind the campaigns for sessional schools and state subsidies.

The Children's Employment Commission which reported in 1842–3 covered both factories and mines, and shocked public opinion with its descriptions of very young children working underground. In the east of Scotland, it was reported, miners' children left school at 9, if they went at all. Of 3,836 children and young persons examined,

only 866 *pretend* to write their names, out of which number I might venture to affirm that it would require a well-practised eye to decipher even 150, and of

---

[54] PP 1847, XLV, *Minutes of CCE, 1846*, 392–4; *NSA* iv, Dumfriesshire, 312.

[55] *NSA* xi, Forfarshire, 46.

[56] PP 1837, XLVII, *Education Enquiry, Abstract of the Answers and Returns made Pursuant to an Address of the House of Commons, dated 9th July 1834*, 631; *Report on the Returns from Presbyteries Regarding the Examination of Schools in the Year 1840, by the General Assembly's Education Committee* (Edinburgh, 1840), 23, 28; *Presbyterial and Parochial Reports on the State of Education in Scotland: Published by the General Assembly's Education Committee, 1842* (Edinburgh, 1843), 27.

those whose names are tolerably legible, I believe that not a couple of dozen could be found to write a dozen consecutive lines on any given subject capable of being read and understood.[57]

The Mines Act of 1842 forbade the employment of boys under 10, and girls of any age, but had no schooling requirement. A second act of 1860 raised the minimum age to 12 in principle, but allowed boys between 10 and 12 to be employed if they were either attending school twice a week, or could produce a certificate showing that they could read and write. Such procedures were easily abused, as complaisant teachers bent the rules for parents, or even accepted bribes; this was said to be one reason why private schools were preferred to state-aided ones.

No doubt there was much change between the 1840s and the 1860s, but much was still found amiss in industrial areas. A survey in one Lanarkshire mining district in 1862 claimed that while 94 per cent of working people could 'read easy narratives', only 60 per cent could sign their names. At Annbank (Ayrshire), the Argyll assistant commissioner descended a pit and interviewed thirteen boys. Six could read and write, but the other seven had not been to school, and only one of them could read a little. At Penicuik, a voluntary education test before employment was applied at one paper mill, whose employees were mostly literate, but at another

it had to be given up. So many had to be rejected that the paper-works were in danger of coming to a standstill, and now there is no test. Mr. —— [the employer] considered that this was due to the unsatisfactory condition of the education in the village. Too much time was given to Latin, French, and fancy work, and not enough to useful education.[58]

And among factory employees in Bridgeton, Glasgow, 94 per cent of men could read and 92 per cent write, but while 92 per cent of the women could read, only 58 per cent could write. These figures were supplied by the employers, and the investigators thought them improbably high, given the conditions in the district's schools. By contrast with the commission's favourable view of rural education, it considered that the factory acts had failed, and that only a change of attitudes by parents could alter the situation: 'in Glasgow, the contest is so severe

---

[57] PP 1842, XVI, *Children's Employment Commission, Appendix to First Report, Mines, Part I*, 399.
[58] PP 1863, XLVII, *Report of CCE, 1862–3*, 147; PP 1867, XXV, *Report on the Country Districts*, 26–8.

between education and money-making, that by common consent it results in education going to the wall.'[59]

Table 5.6 gives school attendance profiles from the 1871 census for the twenty largest towns in order of size, the population threshold being about 15,000. For Glasgow, there are separate figures for the city, for Govan (which included middle-class suburbs in the west and south-west), and for the Barony parish (a working-class and industrial area in the east). The main point made by the table is the contrast between 'traditional' towns, with Inverness at their head (probably helped by its attraction for boarders from all over the highlands), and industrial ones, with Airdrie at the bottom. While most of the towns had higher attendance figures than the counties of which they were part (see Table 5.4), the relationship was reversed in the cases of Glasgow, Dundee, Greenock, Dunfermline, and Airdrie. Three other points may be made. First, as with the county figures, the contrast between industrial and traditional towns is overlaid by one between east and west, with industrial or semi-industrial towns like Arbroath, Montrose, Dunfermline, and Perth having higher attendance levels than western equivalents like Kilmarnock or Ayr. This is especially striking in the early years of education: 62–6 per cent were attending at age 5 in Dundee, only 30–4 per cent in Glasgow. Second, the impact of industry on education is shown by the percentages still at school between 12 and 14. These were lower overall in the industrial towns, and varied according to sex: in textile towns where most juvenile employment was for girls, it was the boys who stayed on (Dundee, Paisley, Dunfermline, Arbroath); in the big cities, and in areas of heavy industry or mining, it was the girls (Glasgow, Edinburgh, Aberdeen, Greenock, Leith, Airdrie, Coatbridge, Falkirk, Hamilton, Stirling). Dunfermline on the one hand, Coatbridge on the other, demonstrate this especially clearly. Finally, the table shows that by 1871 there was no general urban educational crisis. The figures for Edinburgh and Aberdeen were higher than in almost any rural county. But there were serious problems in Glasgow, where attendance levels reached maxima of 88 per cent for boys and 85 per cent for girls, and rose and fell around the peak much more sharply than in other large towns. Perhaps 15 per cent of the city's children were getting no effective schooling. The Argyll estimate of one-third was an exaggeration; it may have made sense for Glasgow if quality was also taken into account, but the extrapolation of this figure to other towns was certainly unjustifiable.

[59] PP 1867, XXV, *Report on Glasgow*, 109, 121.

TABLE 5.6. *School Attendance by Age, Towns, 1871*

% attending at age		5	6	7	8	9	10	11	12	13	14	5–12
Glasgow:	Boys	34	62	79	86	88	85	77	60	28	12	71
City	Girls	30	62	74	85	84	84	79	67	31	15	70
Glasgow:	Boys	46	75	91	92	95	92	84	66	34	20	79
Govan	Girls	41	69	85	93	92	91	84	73	37	22	77
Glasgow:	Boys	36	63	81	86	89	86	82	65	44	23	73
Barony	Girls	31	59	76	84	83	78	74	63	37	19	68
Edinburgh	Boys	62	86	93	94	96	94	89	78	49	28	86
	Girls	59	82	91	94	94	94	91	83	53	30	86
Dundee	Boys	66	80	84	88	86	81	72	53	26	13	77
	Girls	62	77	82	85	83	75	67	48	17	8	73
Aberdeen	Boys	75	91	94	95	94	92	86	70	44	25	87
	Girls	75	88	92	94	94	94	87	81	42	27	88
Greenock	Boys	39	60	83	86	89	86	79	67	40	17	72
	Girls	35	63	78	82	89	85	84	73	50	28	72
Paisley	Boys	48	75	86	89	90	86	81	60	28	16	76
	Girls	42	72	81	89	89	85	77	54	17	11	74
Leith	Boys	63	84	90	91	93	92	89	78	50	23	84
	Girls	62	84	90	95	93	94	90	81	54	25	86
Perth	Boys	76	89	98	94	92	96	93	82	48	33	90
	Girls	71	87	90	91	94	93	91	81	51	26	87
Kilmarnock	Boys	31	74	88	97	95	91	85	68	30	15	77
	Girls	34	71	87	90	90	86	77	63	27	17	74
Dunfermline	Boys	69	85	94	96	97	97	90	71	35	14	87
	Girls	58	87	93	94	96	94	84	63	17	8	83
Airdrie	Boys	36	65	81	86	87	78	71	44	23	10	68
	Girls	31	63	74	83	80	83	72	60	25	11	68
Arbroath	Boys	66	88	93	93	94	94	81	63	31	14	84
	Girls	63	85	92	93	87	83	79	53	23	11	80
Ayr	Boys	54	81	86	88	95	90	85	75	49	31	82
	Girls	48	77	87	87	88	90	83	72	47	24	79
Inverness	Boys	80	90	97	98	97	97	94	93	75	57	93
	Girls	71	85	93	93	91	96	92	89	69	50	86
Coatbridge	Boys	45	67	80	86	84	84	65	45	19	9	69
	Girls	42	66	84	85	86	85	75	65	38	23	72

TABLE 5.6. *Continued*

% attending at age		5	6	7	8	9	10	11	12	13	14	5–12
Falkirk	Boys	43	80	89	94	89	91	85	69	29	11	79
	Girls	45	73	83	89	91	86	90	74	46	19	78
Hamilton	Boys	36	69	85	89	91	89	70	50	30	11	72
	Girls	37	61	79	89	84	85	76	72	32	19	73
Montrose	Boys	82	90	96	97	97	96	81	76	32	12	89
	Girls	77	93	98	95	95	88	88	71	37	20	88
Dumfries	Boys	64	86	96	97	94	91	94	79	53	22	87
	Girls	59	87	89	99	96	90	90	82	36	27	86
Stirling	Boys	66	85	93	91	91	89	85	69	44	16	84
	Girls	59	80	88	92	95	89	86	75	47	27	83

The problems of Glasgow had attracted comment since the days of Chalmers and Stow, especially those of the central slum area, much of which was demolished after 1866 under the City Improvements scheme. In Blackfriars in the 1830s, 'the greater part of the children are only taught to read, and from the poverty of the parents very few remain long enough at school to learn to do that perfectly'.[60] In 1846, the town council sponsored an inquiry into educational destitution conducted by Sunday-school teachers, and public concern was kept alive by such works as the Revd Robert Buchanan's *The Schoolmaster in the Wynds* (1850), which described conditions in the Tron parish, where the poorest families lived in intensely overcrowded housing. In 1857, the reporters of the *North British Daily Mail* conducted another survey, which also identified the Tron as the worst area. The overall pupil/population ratio for the city was one in 14, and in the best district one in 7, but in the Tron it was one in 34. Calton and Bridgeton, the factory districts in the east end, had one in 18 and 22 respectively. This careful survey concluded that most workers' children attended for three years or less, and left at 10 or 11. Those who stayed that long 'have acquired the art of reading with fluency, can write a little, may be considerably advanced in simple arithmetic, and have become acquainted with many facts in geography and history'. But there were also many who left at 8 or 9, and partial or complete illiteracy was common. The root of the

---

[60] PP 1837, XLVII, *Education Enquiry . . . 1834*, 489.

problem was the easy availability of work, for 'every branch of skilled labour, as well as our shops and warehouses, offer employment to little boys who can read and scrawl their names. For a still less educated class, there are the factories, the bleachfields, the tobacco-works, and a host of minor manufactures.'[61]

Both the Argyll report and the 1871 census treated the registration districts of Glasgow separately, and Table 5.7 illustrates some of the differences. The pupil/population ratio had improved to one in 9.6, but this ranged from one in 6.6 in the middle-class Blythswood district to one in 13.2 in Tradeston. The 1871 census shows a somewhat different pattern, but there were still significant variations in overall attendance (columns 7–8), at the peak age of 9 (columns 9–10, giving some indication of how many escaped schooling altogether), and in those still at school at 12 (columns 11–12). It is significant that, apart from High Church, more girls than boys stayed on even in the textile districts, illustrating the pull of casual and industrial work for boys. The 1871 figures also show the low levels in Clyde, the central district which included Tron parish. Columns 1 to 4 illustrate the under-provision of grant-earning schools on the south side (Hutchesontown was the district including the Gorbals), and the concentration of private schools in Blythswood and Tradeston, the latter having a substantial lower-middle-class population.

Many of the poorest children, according to the Argyll report, still left early to work 'as errand boys and girls, in tobacco-works, and as vendors of newspapers or lucifer-matches, and other articles offered for sale upon the streets'. Other children were 'running wild' because of the 'apathy and dissolute habits' of their parents. Catholic children were especially likely to escape education: in some districts, it was thought, over half. One priest reported that though most of the parents could read, few could write, and they were impatient to get their children to work once basic reading had been acquired.[62] The 'tobacco boys' of Glasgow and Edinburgh were a notorious example of juvenile labour drawn from the poorest class. They started work around 8, and were discarded after a few years. An official inquiry in 1864 found that of 655 tobacco boys in Glasgow 218 were totally illiterate, 310 could read only, 46 could read and write, and only 81 had all three Rs. Many

---

[61] R. Buchanan, *The Schoolmaster in the Wynds: or, How to Educate the Masses* (3rd edn., Glasgow, 1850); R. Somers, *Results of an Inquiry into the State of Schools and Education in Glasgow* (Glasgow, 1857), 5, 8, 10–12.

[62] PP 1867, XXV, *Report on Glasgow*, 35, 48–9, 80, 157–9.

TABLE 5.7. *Variations between Districts in Glasgow*

District	Argyll report						1871 census: % attendance					
	Number of schools			% pupils in		Pupil/population ratio : one in	Ages 5–12		At age 9		At age 12	
	Total	Grant-aided	Private adventure	Private adventure	Roman Catholic		B	G	B	G	B	G
	(1)	(2)	(3)	(4)	(5)	(6)	(7)	(8)	(9)	(10)	(11)	(12)
Middle class												
Blythswood	29	4	22	49	0	6.6	78	75	93	89	71	78
Old central areas												
Central	36	10	8	8	9	7.1	74	72	87	86	63	68
Clyde	10	7	2	5	0	11.3	64	65	80	79	48	65
Mixed central/industrial												
High Church	24	9	6	11	0	9.8	66	62	86	78	60	55
Textile areas												
Bridgeton	19	8	8	19	20	12.3	66	62	85	77	54	62
Calton	18	6	6	14	17	8.9	70	69	85	80	58	66
Heavy and general industry												
Milton	21	8	6	9	12	8.1	71	71	85	86	53	67
Anderston	17	7	7	13	8	10.2	74	74	92	92	64	70
South side												
Tradeston	24	1	19	56	0	13.2	74	72	93	87	68	76
Hutchesontown	11	3	4	20	12	12.3	71	68	89	85	58	66
Glasgow total	209	63	88	19	8	9.6	71	69	88	84	60	67

had not been to school at all. There was an evening 'tobacco boys' school' at Edinburgh which dated from 1820, and the Glasgow manufacturers followed suit in 1862. But less than half the children attended. The Argyll commission declared that few of their parents 'care a rush for schools or education', and that dead-end jobs of this kind produced 'hopelessly ignorant and uneducated men and women' who became the next generation of uncaring parents.[63]

The tobacco boys of Glasgow were no great advertisement for Scottish education, but nor were they typical of the working class. The evidence cited has concentrated on crisis areas, but it shows that most factory workers could at least read. Even among the tobacco boys, 67 per cent could do this, and this gives us a kind of rock-bottom measure of illiteracy, as do the figures for the literacy of criminals which propagandists were fond of citing to show that education would reduce the crime rate. Even at this desperate social level, Scotland retained its superiority over England: nearly 90 per cent of the Scots convicts transported to New South Wales in the early nineteenth century were literate.[64] R. K. Webb, in an extensive survey of the evidence for working-class literacy, concluded that absolute inability to read could reach 30 per cent in the worst milieux, with many more able to read only imperfectly. He suggested that 'on balance, one could expect the general average of the urban working classes to fall somewhere between two-thirds and three-quarters literate'.[65] This depends on the definition of literacy (and of the working class), but for the eve of 1872 it would seem an over-pessimistic conclusion. The evidence presented in this chapter, even after the prejudices of middle-class observers have been allowed for, leaves little doubt that there were stubborn areas of illiteracy in industrial and urban Scotland, but there were also many working-class families, perhaps the majority, who had long passed the literacy threshold.

Over the centuries the line between those who were completely literate and the rest moved steadily down the social hierarchy. By the mid nineteenth century it ran through the working class itself: the divide between well- and ill-educated workers was as sharp as the line of educational privilege which separated workers generally from the middle

---

[63] PP 1867, XXV, *Report on Glasgow*, 37–9; PP 1865, XX, *Children's Employment Commission (1862), Fourth Report*, 80.

[64] S. Nicholas, 'Literacy and the Industrial Revolution', in G. Tortella (ed.), *Education and Economic Development since the Industrial Revolution* (Valencia, 1990), 56.

[65] Webb, 'Literacy among the Working Classes', 102–5, 109–14.

classes. Within the working class, one can perhaps distinguish four groups. First, the élite of artisans and skilled rural workers, whose literacy was secure and who had some sort of access to its cultural rewards; it was from this group that the 'lads of parts' who found their way to a university were most likely to be drawn. Second, there was the broad respectable mass, who had an adequate if crude basic education; they achieved full literacy, but on the basis of four or five years of schooling, not the eight which the 1872 Act was to prescribe. This kind of education had long been available in the countryside, and its consolidation in the towns was perhaps the chief achievement of the 1830–70 period. Third, there were those who were too poor or too casually employed to afford the fees of the better schools, and had to make do with a scrambled and interrupted education, perhaps made up through Sunday schools or evening classes; they certainly learnt to read, and normally by the 1860s to write as well, though not with much facility, and not always including girls. Finally, there were those who escaped schooling altogether, who were a significant number in Glasgow and some industrial areas, but non-existent in other parts of the lowlands. When contemporaries talked about the 'residuum' which the 1872 Act was intended to bring in, they were thinking of both these last two groups, for the quality and effectiveness of education mattered as well as mere attendance.

5. CONCLUSIONS

No conclusion on literacy and school attendance makes much sense as a generalization about Scotland. For the rural lowlands, the argument has been that there was a process of gradual improvement, with regions which had formerly been at different stages of development converging to common standards. There is little evidence of any phase of decline, and the nineteenth-century evidence seems broadly compatible with Houston's pessimistic interpretation of the pre-industrial period. Three points illustrated in this chapter may perhaps be emphasized. One is that children stayed at school for longer than the common picture of Victorian Britain suggests. In 1871 one-fifth of those aged 14—two years beyond the leaving age to be established in 1872—were still receiving education. But as the surprisingly high attendance levels in the highlands show, this might be a sign of prolonged and intermittent rather than advanced education. The second point (and probably the one of most interest to general historians of literacy) is the persistence until well into the nineteenth century of reading literacy unaccompanied by the ability to write. The children of the 1840s were often described as the first generation who automatically learnt to write; by the 1860s inability to write was the main criterion of educational backwardness. This gap must surely have been much greater in the eighteenth century, so that Houston's estimates based on signatures need to be revised upwards if literacy is defined as the ability to read. The third point is the move towards educational equality between men and women, of which teaching writing to girls was a part. Houston's figures for female signatures before 1750 show that there was a long way to go, and the process can be seen under way in the early nineteenth century; it was not fully reflected in literacy figures until its end, but by 1871 girls were staying at school almost as long as boys, and in some places longer. This revolution in expectations still awaits historical explanation.

The evidence does not justify the extreme picture of educational destitution on the eve of 1872 which some contemporaries painted, but nor does it permit an over-optimistic view. Even in the 1860s, after all, 31 per cent of women in Lanarkshire and Renfrewshire were signing the marriage register with a mark. It seems likely that the failure of schooling to overcome the effects of industrialization was at its worst in the decades before 1850, and that there was a steady recovery thereafter. Whether the working class would have been better served if a national system had been introduced to replace denominationalism in the 1850s is difficult to say. The real constraint was what the state was prepared to pay, but the argument of Moncreiff and others that the grant system led to maldistribution of resources and failed to tackle the black spots was plausible. Education may have been expanding because the literate part of the population sought a longer and more elaborate schooling, while the less literate areas and occupational groups remained stubbornly untouched. This was the rationale behind compulsion. The situation in the west highlands was an obvious example, but once education was regarded as a matter of national prosperity and citizen's rights, it was difficult also to see why 77 per cent of 11-year-old boys should be at school in Glasgow and 86 per cent in Aberdeen, or 67 per cent of 11-year-old girls in Dundee and 91 per cent in Edinburgh. The use of compulsion to iron out such differences had a moral as well as a political dimension.

At the beginning of the nineteenth century, the parish school provided Scottish education with its ideal. But its success in achieving universal or near-universal literacy and its hopes of future progress depended on conditions which only fully existed in the rural lowlands, and not always there: a prosperous community, vigilant landowners and clergy, economic and social conditions which gave families an incentive to acquire basic skills, the pressure of community opinion, a well-established parish school. Where any of these conditions were absent, the state of schooling and literacy could easily revert to an earlier phase, marked by the gaps between reading and writing and between boys and girls. Even after two centuries of the church's campaign for mass education, it still rested on a fragile balance of forces which was easily disturbed, and which (despite Chalmers's vision) it was impossible to recreate in the cities. Furthermore, in rural areas the achievement of literacy had not relied exclusively on full-time schooling, but also on intermittent attendance and the exploitation of winter leisure time. The industrial revolution introduced new patterns of full-time employment which cut schooling off much earlier. Evening classes, or the part-time attendance of the factory acts, proved an unsatisfactory substitute for full-time schooling. Those who controlled the provision of schools, and in due course the state, responded to this with a new set of emphases: on formal schooling as the key to literacy, on a standard curriculum designed to instil the three Rs as rapidly as possible, on the full-time day-school as the chosen instrument of policy, and eventually on compulsion with a fixed leaving age. The elementary school which emerged from this process was moulded by the demands of an industrial, urban population, and was to become the universal type after 1872.

6

Education, Culture, and Democracy

DAVID VINCENT has recently published a book on literacy and popular culture in England which ranges with great richness over the cultural and social consequences of education.[1] The materials hardly yet exist for such a study of Scotland, desirable though it would be given the special position of education in Scottish life. This chapter, in a book which is mainly concerned with the development of educational institutions, looks selectively at what the experience of elementary education meant and what it might lead to. The first section discusses the development of educational techniques and of the curriculum. The relationship of education to modernization and economic development is touched on with reference to the fate of the Gaelic language. In Scotland, much discussion focused on education as a means of individual mobility and on the link between schools and universities; this is examined with a later chapter on developments after 1872 in mind. But there was another tradition of individual advancement which relied on self-education rather than formal schooling; associated especially with artisans, it was not easily reproduced in the conditions of industrial society, but by 1872 it was being transmuted into a system of adult and technical education.

1. CURRICULUM AND CULTURE

In 1857 James Pillans looked back to the rural schools which he had seen thirty years before.

The master's business was almost universally—for there were some honourable exceptions—to meet daily with some fifty, sixty, or seventy children; to keep them together for two or three hours at a time, in a tolerable state of noisy subordination, which was prevented from breaking out into deafening clamour or open rebellion only by the constant fear and frequent application of the lash; to call up successively the different classes into which they were clumsily

[1] D. Vincent, *Literacy and Popular Culture: England 1750–1914* (Cambridge, 1989).

arranged, and to hear, it may be with conscientious attention, each pupil drawl out his portion of a lesson, the sense of which it was never attempted—and from the nature of what was read, it would have been impossible—to make him comprehend; while all the rest of the school, except that individual and his master, were either practising or meditating mischief, or, what is worse than either, in a state of absolute idleness.[2]

What Pillans described was the 'individual' system of teaching where pupils came up in turn to recite a lesson, read, or show what they had written. At the other end of the spectrum was the 'simultaneous' system where the teacher gave a collective lesson to a relatively homogeneous class of children. But this implied large schools graded by age and a staff of experienced teachers, conditions which rarely existed in rural schools, and depended on resources which in the early nineteenth century were seldom available. Thus changes in educational technique consisted principally of attempts to introduce a simultaneous element into schools conducted by a single adult teacher. Pillans himself when rector of Edinburgh High School abolished corporal punishment and experimented with the monitorial system. He championed professional training, and campaigned for chairs of 'paideutics' at the universities. These were not established until the 1870s, but the normal colleges began to turn out a corps of teachers trained in the new techniques of school management.

The Lancasterian and Madras monitorial systems were the first of these, and the Lancasterian schools established in Scottish towns could handle several hundred pupils. They were taught in a single large room, with groups at different stages of progress clustering around the monitors, and the master presiding over this application of the division of labour. Thomas Markus has described the system as 'a central invention of Enlightenment ideology applied in an industrial context', and has examined the architectural history of these early schools—for each system made its own demands for floor plans and furnishing. Like prisons and factories, they represented a desire to regulate, systematize, and supervise human activities characteristic of the Benthamite phase of social thought.[3]

---

[2] *Transactions of the National Association for the Promotion of Social Science*, 1857, 204.

[3] T. A. Markus, 'The School as Machine: Working Class Scottish Education and the Glasgow Normal Seminary', in T. A. Markus (ed.), *Order in Space and Society: Architectural Form and its Context in the Scottish Enlightenment* (Edinburgh, 1982), 201–61. Cf. D. Hamilton, *Towards a Theory of Schooling* (London, 1989), 75–96.

It was this mechanical aspect, as well as the obvious deficiencies of the inexperienced monitors, which stimulated the innovations of Wood and Stow. The essential principle of both Wood's 'intellectual' or 'interrogatory' and Stow's 'training' systems was that children must understand what they learn, instead of being stuffed with facts or drilled in unthinking routines. That required an experienced teacher, and limited the effective size of schools. Stow, the more influential of the two through his work at the Glasgow Normal Seminary, gave a central place to simultaneous teaching of the whole school, using a 'gallery' or tiered floor. The three Rs would be taught in small groups, as in other schools, but the teacher would give gallery lessons in religious instruction and elementary science. For Stow the moral, religious, and intellectual aspects of education were inseparable. The playground was an essential part of the regime, but widely disseminated engravings from Stow's manuals showing children at play have made his system appear more relaxed than it was: the teacher was expected to study the children's conduct in the playground, and correct their moral faults in the subsequent lesson. Stow's work is permeated by the characteristic Chalmersite emphasis on moralization and the rescue of the 'sinking classes', and on the school as the remedy for crime and urban disorder.[4]

Owen's experiments at New Lanark, with their stress on music and dancing, were more libertarian, but although some features survived Owen's departure they cannot be said to have influenced other Scottish schools. The New Statistical Account reported complacently that the pupils 'receive instruction in the ordinary branches, more suitable to their rank of life than the ornamental accomplishments to which, under a former management, an exclusive attention had been paid'.[5] The ideas of Stow and Wood, on the other hand, were converted into routines by the normal colleges. They were seen as a single approach, whose adoption could be reported with pride, as at Comrie parish school, where 'the modern improvements of the Normal and Sessional School of Edinburgh, and the training school of Glasgow, have been introduced with success'.[6] Saunders's claim that under the new methods 'the parish school became a fiercely equalitarian, competitive and argumentative democracy' takes a somewhat romantic view of their intellectual

---

[4] D. Stow, *The Training System, Moral Training School, and Normal Seminary or College* (9th edn., London, 1853).

[5] *NSA* vi. 27. Cf. I. Donnachie and G. Hewitt, *Historic New Lanark: The Dale and Owen Industrial Community since 1785* (Edinburgh, 1993), 96–107, 131–3, 149–51.

[6] *NSA* x. 592.

potential,[7] and their more expensive or impractical aspects were dropped. Neither Stow's teaching of science, nor the elaborate fittings of his playground, seem to have been widely adopted, and the gallery was usually confined to the teaching of infants. Nor was Stow's renunciation of corporal punishment much imitated: the tawse remained the symbol of the Scottish schoolmaster.

Perhaps this was understandable when order had to be kept in a single large schoolroom. Some masters, it was said in 1847, 'give lessons daily in ten or twelve different branches, and to pupils in all stages of progress'.[8] Skilful teaching depended on classifying them into groups (usually five or six, according to their progress in reading), and arranging a timetable so that the teacher could attend to each group in turn for fifteen or twenty minutes. By the 1860s the leading authority was Simon S. Laurie, secretary of the Church of Scotland Education Committee, and inspector for the Dick bequest. It was not easy, he wrote, 'to teach, on the average, four subjects to each of sixty or eighty children, of different ages and of different stages of progress, within five hours'. The answer lay in a carefully structured routine:

the words 'Classification' and 'Time-table' sum up the whole of organization. The extent to which each group is brought into immediate personal contact with the teacher depends on the relation which the numbers taught bear to the teaching power, and on the master's skill in multiplying his presence. An average attendance of seventy gives quite as large a school as ought to be attempted single-handed.[9]

Laurie provided a model timetable for a school of sixty, divided into six classes, which could be handled by a single teacher with the help of a monitor.[10] As the master taught one group, the others were reading, preparing lessons, copying, or writing under the monitor's supervision. Apart from religion, the three Rs, and music (customary in parish schools, where children were taught the unaccompanied psalm-singing which the master led on Sunday in his role as precentor), the only extra subject in Laurie's timetable was a little geography. Latin and mathematics would be taught, if required, before the school opened at ten, and

---

[7] L. J. Saunders, *Scottish Democracy, 1815–1840: The Social and Intellectual Background* (Edinburgh, 1950), 293.

[8] PP 1847, XLV, *Minutes of CCE, 1846*, 399.

[9] S. S. Laurie, *Report on Education in the Parochial Schools of the Counties of Aberdeen, Banff and Moray* (Edinburgh, 1865), 146, 149–50.

[10] Ibid. 290–1. A similar timetable is in PP 1867, XXV, *Education Commission (Scotland), Report on the State of Education in the Country Districts of Scotland*, 154.

grammar after it closed at four. The only relief from this routine was that schools did not open on Saturday.

Seventy was not an unusual size for a parish school, and Stow thought eighty the maximum for any school. The introduction of pupil-teachers, however, introduced new possibilities, especially in the towns. More could be entrusted to them than to monitors (though the latter continued to be used for subsidiary tasks), and a master working with pupil-teachers could adopt more flexible methods. By 1859, an inspector contrasting conditions with twenty years before could write that 'instead of *one* master painfully conscious of his inability to overtake a tithe of what he feels should be done, we have now, if not a teacher for each branch, at least, such a division of labour as leaves little to be desired in this respect.'[11] This change had an effect on school buildings. Rural schools, and early schools in towns, consisted of a single large schoolroom. But now one or more small classrooms were added, which could be used for the specialized teaching of groups, for infants, or for sewing classes for girls. As more adult assistants became available, at first chiefly female, subdivision could be taken further. But even in the 1860s trained teachers were in short supply, and most training-college graduates could expect to take charge of a school as their first appointment. School managers could not afford more than one adult salary, and most of the denominational schools financed by the Code were small ones with a single qualified teacher. Education expanded through the cellular multiplication of rival schools, not through comprehensive provision for all the children of a district.

There were some exceptions. Endowed schools might be rich enough to pay several salaries, and in Catholic schools the religious orders provided adult teachers influenced by continental traditions of class teaching. By the 1860s, larger schools were appearing in the cities. The biggest in Glasgow was St Enoch's sessional, where the Argyll commission found over 1,200 pupils, taught by a headmaster, eight assistants, and twelve pupil-teachers. There were four separate departments: infants (5 to 8), juvenile (8 to 12), senior, and a 'supplementary' school for poorer children; for the main school had established a high reputation, and was used by the independent working and shopkeeping classes. In 1870 St Enoch's had 1,030 children, Gorbals East Free Church school 928, St Andrew's Roman Catholic 823, St Mary's (Calton) Roman

---

[11] PP 1859, sess. 1, XXI, Part 1, *Report of CCE, 1858–9*, 259. Cf. PP 1850, XLIV, *Minutes of CCE, 1848–50*, vol. 2, 558–61 on methods used in sessional schools.

Catholic 749, the Highland Society's school 725, the 'model' or practising schools of the two training colleges over 600 each.[12] The development of schools like these, housed in large free-standing buildings
similar to those later built by school boards, underlined the archaic
character of the many small schools surviving from the early days of
expansion, installed in tenement buildings or one-room halls.

A powerful incentive to the 'classification' recommended by Laurie
was the Revised Code and its Standards. The Standards did not apply
to children under 6, and did not necessarily correspond to classes; it
was for the teacher to decide which children should be presented for
examination at each level. But once a child had been presented for one
Standard, it had to take the subsequent one the next year. Moreover,
children had to be presented simultaneously in all three subjects, for the
Code was intended to enforce the teaching of writing alongside reading.
Here custom in Scotland still lagged behind, and in the first examinations under the Revised Code, Scotland performed significantly less
well in writing than England.[13] This was partly a matter of furnishings
and equipment: writing required desks or tables instead of benches, and
slates, copy-books, pens, and paper. Hence the higher fees traditionally
charged. Laurie, who like all experts insisted on the integrated teaching
of the three Rs, recommended replacing separate subject fees by a
single consolidated fee. 'By such an arrangement,' he observed, 'the
power of objecting to this or that particular subject being taught to their
children would be taken out of the hands of ignorant parents.'[14] None
the less, the Argyll commission found that 'the tradition and custom in
the Scotch schools has been to teach nothing but reading and the Catechism for the first two or three years of a child's school life'.[15]

The standards required by the Code were not especially high. In
reading, the tests ranged from 'narrative in monosyllables' (Standard I)
to 'a short ordinary paragraph in a newspaper, or other modern narrative' (VI). In writing, they emphasized dictation, to test spelling as well
as penmanship. In arithmetic, the Standards covered the four rules,
fractions, money, and weights and measures. Apart from these, geography and grammar were the only subjects taught at all widely. In a

[12] PP 1867, XXV, *Education Commission (Scotland), Report on the State of Education
in Glasgow*, 154–6, and cf. 62–3; PP 1871, XXII, *Report of CCE, 1870–1*, list of
schools.

[13] PP 1865, XLII, *Report of CCE, 1864–5*, p. viii.

[14] Laurie, *Report on Education*, 334.

[15] PP 1867, XXV, *Report on the Country Districts*, 137, and cf. 160.

sample of rural schools examined by the Argyll commission, the percentages studying individual subjects were: reading 98, writing 65,
arithmetic 57, geography 33, and English grammar 30. History claimed
11 per cent, but Latin only 3 per cent, and Greek 0.2.[16]

These were the 'secular' subjects. Religious instruction, which was
the same in all Presbyterian schools, was more distinctively Scottish
than the three Rs. Study of the Bible began with the New Testament,
but soon moved on to the Old, which gave more scope for memorizing
the details of sacred history and geography. Children were also expected to memorize the Shorter Catechism. With 107 articles, this
document was short only by comparison with the Larger Catechism
(there was also an unofficial 'Mother's Catechism' for the very young).
The elevated language of its first article—'What is the chief end of
man? Man's chief end is to glorify God and to enjoy him for ever'—
was not sustained throughout, but the Catechism did provide lessons in
clear expression and deductive reasoning as it elaborated on the Christian scheme of sin and redemption, the Ten Commandments, and the
Lord's Prayer. Unlike its Church of England equivalent, the Shorter
Catechism did not instruct children to do their duty in the state of life
to which it should please God to call them, but it did extend the fifth
commandment to include 'the preserving the honour, and performing
the duties, belonging to every one in their several places and relations,
as superiors, inferiors, or equals'. Religious instruction was the basis of
such political or social ideology as the schools inculcated, for strategies
of social control relied on the straightforward belief that reading the
Bible, learning the Catechism, and absorbing copy-book precepts would
transform the child's moral nature.

The Shorter Catechism, learnt by successive generations since the
seventeenth century, was commonly held to have formed the national
character and the 'metaphysical' cast of the Scottish mind. Since most
children did not go beyond the three Rs to encounter any sort of poetry
or literature, religious instruction could be seen as the only component
with a cultural dimension, and the Bible was the only coherent literary
text studied at school. This was particularly significant because the
reformed church had from the start adopted English rather than Scots
as the language of its documents, and it was the 1611 Authorized Version
of the Bible which was used. There was therefore a tension between the

---

[16] Ibid., *Education Commission (Scotland), Statistical Report on the State of Education in the Lowland Country Districts of Scotland,* 14–17.

formal language of the school and the Scots used by children at home, and indeed by the schoolmaster in ordinary conversation. Such tensions were commonplace in nineteenth-century Europe, as official languages were enforced as part of policies of national integration, and they were particularly acute when written culture itself was still contending with oral tradition as a means of socializing individuals and transmitting communal values. Nevertheless, William Donaldson has argued in his studies of the north-east that literacy did not lead to the rapid elimination of Scots, but in the new conditions of the nineteenth century stimulated vernacular literature through the flourishing local press.[17]

The clash of cultures was of course most dramatic in the Gaelic-speaking highlands, and it was there that the modernizing role of education was most apparent. In 1826 the Inverness School Society enthused at length about its advantages:

The universal diffusion of a right education should be ardently promoted by patriots and politicians, because the universal intelligence of the people is the best safeguard of social order, of freedom, and of peace; because it is the stimulus of enterprise,—the creative source of public wealth,—the most stable foundation of political greatness and glory;—and because our present imperfect progress in it is the distinction to which we mainly owe our proud rank among the nations. Men of learning and taste should cherish it, because the elements of education are the instruments which can bring into full action that boundless extent of genius and of intellectual endowment, which Providence has scattered so profusely and so impartially among every rank of men; they are the paths by which the Newtons, and the 'mute inglorious Miltons' of the hamlet may reach the heights of usefulness and of fame: and philanthropists should strive to advance it, because it presents the means most easy and most effectual, to meliorate the condition of mankind,—to soften their manners,—to refine their pleasures,—to multiply their comforts,—and to extirpate their most baneful and degrading vices.[18]

Thus order and political loyalty, social mobility and economic development were complementary aims. Many lowlanders were inclined to blame the backwardness of the highlands on the people's indifference and lack of enterprise, which were too often seen as inherently Celtic characteristics. More careful observers thought that the highlanders had

[17] W. Donaldson, *Popular Literature in Victorian Scotland* (Aberdeen, 1986). Cf. id., 'Popular Literature: The Press, the People, and the Vernacular Revival', in D. Gifford (ed.), *The History of Scottish Literature*, iii: *The Nineteenth Century* (Aberdeen, 1988), 203–15; D. J. Withrington, 'Scots in Education: A Historical Retrospect', in J. D. McClure (ed.), *The Scots Language in Education* (Aberdeen, n.d.).
[18] *Moral Statistics of the Highlands and Islands of Scotland* (Inverness, 1826), 34–5.

a real desire for education, but were trapped in a vicious circle. 'The Highlanders are ignorant merely because they are poor', said the General Assembly in 1833; but poverty was self-perpetuating, for 'by ignorance they are unqualified for the enterprise that carries on the progress of society, and by the limited and simple industry to which they are confined, they contribute little to the national resources.' Education was the key to stimulating individual ambition, and as the church's Education Committee put it in 1837, 'this ambition of individuals is not only useful to the community, by the examples it affords, of energy and enterprise, but is uniformly accompanied with a reputable moral deportment.'[19]

This meant education in English, and while attitudes towards Gaelic softened and most schools in Gaelic areas began by teaching Gaelic reading, the declared aim of all parties was to hasten the acquisition of English. In the SSPCK schools, even in the 1860s, no Gaelic reading was allowed except from the Bible; the language was not used as a medium of teaching, or taught as a subject. It was the language of the Bible and the pulpit, but (unlike Welsh) it did not have a press or a prose literature attuned to the contemporary world. As the presbytery of Abernethy (Inverness-shire) put it in 1840,

with rare exceptions, the majority of those who are educated at our Highland country schools never from choice peruse an English book; and hence the vast body of information on religious, moral, and scientific subjects that is open to the Lowlander is entirely shut up to the Highlander, and the English language, capable of conveying knowledge of the highest kind and upon every subject, is to him a dead language.

This was 'an evil which cannot be effectually remedied till the Gaelic becomes totally extinct as a spoken language. As a step towards the consummation of this event, so devoutly to be wished, let the use of the Gaelic be banished from the schools.'[20] Nicolson, in his Argyll report on the Hebrides, took a similar view, arguing that 'the general ignorance of the English language constitutes a special and powerful obstacle to the progress of improvement in the district', and that 'reading,

---

[19] *Educational Statistics of the Highlands and Islands of Scotland: Prepared by the General Assembly's Education Committee, from Returns made by the Parochial Ministers* (Edinburgh, 1833), 12–13, 16; *Report of the Committee of the General Assembly for Increasing the Means of Education in Scotland, Particularly in the Highlands and Islands . . . 1837* (Edinburgh, 1837), 18.

[20] *Report of the Committee of the General Assembly for Increasing the Means of Education in Scotland . . . 1840* (Edinburgh, 1840), Report on Returns from Presbyteries, 47.

writing, and arithmetic will not satisfy hunger or clothe nakedness. But they will increase the power and the facilities for overcoming the circumstances which cause these miseries.'[21] This was the orthodox position of school inspectors, highland ministers, and the highland educated classes. But while in the eighteenth century the government had positively promoted education as an engine of economic development, in the nineteenth the churches and Gaelic school societies were left to struggle alone. Even the prolonged crisis caused from 1846 by the failure of the potato harvest did not evoke any special action.

The place of Gaelic in education has been well covered by scholars, notably Victor Durkacz and C. W. J. Withers, who agree on the broad picture: Gaelic was handicapped by its legacy of hostility, but the societies—Durkacz especially stresses the work of the Edinburgh school society—succeeded in the nineteenth century in creating widespread Gaelic literacy, even if this was confined mainly to religious reading.[22] For a generation or so, English and Gaelic literacy coexisted, and while monolingualism, poverty, and inadequate education seemed to go together in the Western Isles, which were eventually to be Gaelic's last redoubt, the language did not retreat from the southern and eastern highlands until well after effective schools had been established there. Education in English was not necessarily fatal to Gaelic, and some scholars have argued that the work of the Gaelic societies formed a promising development which might have established a stable bilingualism, until cut off by the 1872 Act.[23] This is not entirely convincing, given the societies' own emphasis on Gaelic as an aid to learning English, though it is certainly true that the state system, even before 1872, gave little encouragement. Under the 1846 regulations, a small special grant was made for a time to Gaelic-speaking teachers, but this was withdrawn by the time of the Revised Code, under which children of all ages had to be questioned in English. The pupil-teacher, certificate, and training-college examinations were also of course in English, though the training colleges did have some church-supported scholarships for highland students. Given more sympathetic official attitudes, Gaelic might have survived more effectively. But Withers and Durkacz

[21] PP 1867, XXV, *Education Commission (Scotland), Report on the State of Education in the Hebrides*, 132–3.

[22] V. E. Durkacz, *The Decline of the Celtic Languages: A Study of Linguistic and Cultural Conflict in Scotland, Wales and Ireland from the Reformation to the Twentieth Century* (Edinburgh, 1983), 96–153, 158–64; C. W. J. Withers, *Gaelic in Scotland, 1698–1981: The Geographical History of a Language* (Edinburgh, 1984), 116–60, 258–61.

[23] e.g. M. Macleod, 'Gaelic in Highland Education', *TGSI* 43 (1960–3), 320.

argue that the real problem lay with attitudes within the highlands, both among the English-oriented élite and among a people long exposed to their views. It was generally reported that parents themselves wanted their children taught in English, and the perception that this was the key to individual advancement was an integral part of the awakening interest in literacy. Once literacy in English became general, the speaking of Gaelic rarely lasted more than a generation or two, this being part of the complex of changes by which highland society was remodelled to suit the needs of a centralized state and a market economy.

2. EDUCATION AND SOCIAL MOBILITY

The highlands show how basic literacy could itself be a transforming force. But in most of Scotland this frontier had long been passed, and the 'democratic' implications of education could be measured by how long children stayed at school, how far they studied advanced subjects, and whether the school led on to wider opportunities. The aspect of this which attracted most attention was the teaching of Latin in the parish schools, and the ability of talented boys to pass directly from them to the university. Because the maintenance of this link was vital to the welfare of the universities themselves, it came under scrutiny whenever university reform was on the agenda. In the 1820s, a royal commission found that 585 out of 841 parishes had schoolmasters (parish or private) who had attended a university, and who could therefore teach the classics. In the 1860s, the Argyll commission investigated the backgrounds of university students in detail, and claimed that over half had been educated at parish schools; the statistical basis of this can be questioned, but it was used to justify the universities' campaign to ensure that the bills of 1869–72 preserved traditional standards. The Argyll inquiry also found that over 20 per cent of the students came from the working class, and propagandists like Playfair were inclined to conflate these findings, and to assume that the parish schools were the main channel of educational democracy. In fact, the figures showed that most working-class students were older than middle-class ones, and came after a period of work and self-education, not straight from school.[24] An

[24] This question is discussed at length in R. D. Anderson, *Education and Opportunity in Victorian Scotland: Schools and Universities* (Oxford, 1983), 103–61. For student recruitment in the 1860s, see also id., *The Student Community at Aberdeen, 1860–1939* (Aberdeen, 1988), 6–11, 135–9.

example was Alexander Macdonald, the miners' leader and MP, born in 1821, who left school at 8 to work as a miner, and later paid his way through Glasgow University by returning to the pit every summer.[25] Moreover, even though Playfair's claim that there were 500 working men or sons of working men in the universities was probably correct, they have to be set against an elementary school population of half a million.[26] The channels of mobility remained narrow, and were far more open to artisans and skilled workers than to the really poor.

All the same, the openness of the universities was genuine, and was sustained by their relatively low fees and modest life-style, the absence of an entrance examination, and the existence of numerous bursaries. These features may have benefited the middle as much as the working classes, but as long as the parish school link was formally maintained, the open character of the universities was guaranteed. Its defenders could always point to individual cases of poor boys sent up to university by their local dominie, and Latin had a symbolic as well as a practical value as 'the means whereby alone the poorer youth of the country can rise to those positions for which their ability and character fit them'.[27] National pride could be echoed even in the sober pages of an inspector's report: 'The Scotch poor have enjoyed, and have not abused, the boon of higher education for all who could profit by it. In England nothing short of genius will lift a boy from the National school to the University. In Scotland good useful ability, prudence, and hard work are the only requisites.' Writing in 1872, this inspector urged that traditional opportunities should be recognized, and that the new Code should be framed 'with Scotch knowledge and sympathy'.[28] After the 1872 Act, these were to be controversial matters.

It was still true in the 1860s that most parish schoolmasters could teach Latin and mathematics to the level needed for university entry. Indeed, the prestige of Latin was such that it was studied by many male pupil-teachers, and was on the training-college curriculum. But whether teachers were called on to use it depended on local conditions. At one time, parish schools were used for their convenience by many farmers and local professional men, but this habit was in decline even in the

[25] J. M. Bellamy and J. Saville, *Dictionary of Labour Biography*, i (London, 1972).

[26] Address of 1870, reprinted in L. Playfair, *Subjects of Social Welfare* (London, 1889), 300.

[27] *Report of the Committee of the General Assembly for Increasing the Means of Education in Scotland . . . 1859* (Edinburgh, 1859), 65.

[28] PP 1872, XXII, *Report of CCE, 1871–2*, 100 (J. Kerr).

1790s. 'Some time ago it was the practice of the better sort of farmers here, to send their sons to the school a few years to learn Latin', it was reported from Perthshire at that time; 'but very little Latin is now taught in this part of the country; and such as destine their sons for the learned professions, generally send them to towns and grammar-schools.'[29] This process accelerated in the nineteenth century, and by the 1860s middle-class parents who cared about careers and examinations would normally send their sons to burgh schools, which as yet had no scholarship links with local elementary schools. The growing prestige of urban secondary education also undermined the old habit of parish schoolmasters taking boarders. The remaining middle-class clientele for the parish schools was described by the Argyll report: 'in those of the old-fashioned parish schools which we visited, we found, not unfrequently, a class of three or four boys in Latin, two of them, perhaps, the minister's sons, and one the teacher's.'[30] Parish schools remained important for university entry in the highlands, where there were few towns, and in the north-east, where it was sustained by the Dick bequest and the Aberdeen university bursaries. But even there, Laurie noted that those who stayed on and studied Latin were mostly 'the sons of small farmers, tradesmen, or ministers', and he thought the classics in long-term decline, as railways both made movement easier, and offered 'the clever sons of peasants, small farmers, and petty tradesmen, remunerative occupation as attractive to the common mind as the Ministry'.[31] The old cycle of recruitment which linked parish schools and universities belonged to a rural world of restricted opportunity, and in more advanced areas like Berwickshire it could be reported in the 1840s that 'Latin seems almost banished from our parish schools in this county'.[32]

But if the classics were declining, schools could still promote social mobility in two ways: by the development of 'higher' subjects of a more modern kind, and through the pupil-teacher system. In large towns, schools followed the social hierarchy, and those who sought something more than elementary education found it by paying higher fees. Elsewhere, schools could still offer a mixture of subjects, and attract a diverse clientele. Where parents could afford to keep their children on, it was reported in 1860, they 'are generally well educated, not only in

---

[29] *OSA* xii. 245 (Clunie).
[30] PP 1867, XXV, *Report on the Country Districts*, 133.
[31] Laurie, *Report on Education*, 124, 307.
[32] *NSA* ii, Berwickshire, 163 (Hutton).

common branches, but often in middle class branches, so as to be fitted to enter the university or any of the commercial employments of life'.[33] Another inspector reported in 1869 that about a fifth of his schools, in the west and south-west, gave an education 'comprising languages (Latin and French), a little geometry and algebra, in some instances a little Greek, a portion of English history, some notions of English literature and of physical science'.[34] The Argyll report thought that once village tradesmen had seen the value of practical subjects like writing and bookkeeping, they also developed a demand for 'the higher and more ornamental branches of education; for French, music, drawing, and the more elaborate kinds of needlework and knitting'.[35] Parish schools were thus beginning to offer a quasi-secondary education suited to the expanding lower middle class, a need left unsatisfied by the existing network of burgh schools.

One example of how a knowledge of languages and a love of learning could be acquired in local schools was James Murray, the son of a village tailor in the borders, born in 1837. Murray left school at 14, and like many before established himself in teaching without any formal training. Success led to a move to London, and though Murray never attended a university he became famous as the creator of the *Oxford English Dictionary*.[36] A few years later, he might have become a pupil-teacher, for this became a very significant channel of social mobility, open both to the working class and to women. It was the path trodden by Ramsay MacDonald, born in 1866 at Lossiemouth. Staying at school until 18, he acquired 'an education superior to that of any Labour leader of his generation', and was later to recall it with sentimental pride.[37] MacDonald did not carry on to the training college, but even those who failed the examination could get teaching posts, as 'ex-PTs', or benefit in other careers from their prolonged education.

Elementary teaching was a job with security and prestige, if not very well paid, and most recruits came from the skilled working or lower middle classes. The college training course opened up new opportunities. Once in Glasgow or Edinburgh, male students had a chance to

---

[33] PP 1860, LIV, *Report of CCE, 1859–60*, 258.

[34] PP 1868–9, XX, *Report of CCE, 1868–9*, 340, and cf. 356–60. See also PP 1870, XXII, *Report of CCE, 1869–70*, 376, 379.

[35] PP 1867, XXV, *Report on the Country Districts*, 12.

[36] K. M. E. Murray, *Caught in the Web of Words: James A. H. Murray and the 'Oxford English Dictionary'* (2nd edn., Oxford, 1979), 3–26.

[37] D. Marquand, *Ramsay MacDonald* (London, 1977), 12; cf. his reminiscences in W. Barclay, *The Schools and Schoolmasters of Banffshire* (Banff, 1925), 306–8.

attend university classes, and might continue part-time study in their first post. By the 1860s the Education Department felt that so many college students were finding jobs outside teaching that they were departing from their proper mission and becoming 'little universities'; the Revised Code cut back their numbers and funding.[38] For women, the colleges were especially important while they were excluded from the universities, and since teaching was one of the few careers open to middle-class women the training colleges had fee-paying private students alongside the scholarship-holders. But the prestige of the classically trained parish teacher made the feminization of the profession slower than in England. The 1871 census showed that 49 per cent of the 12,192 Scottish teachers of all kinds were female, compared with 74 per cent in England, and many qualified Scottish women had to go south to find posts.[39]

3. SELF-HELP AND TECHNICAL EDUCATION

So far we have been discussing the effects of formal schooling. But there was always an alternative tradition of self-education and informal learning, which was strongest among skilled workers and artisans like joiners, shoemakers, masons, and tailors. Weavers were noted for their interest in literature and culture: the weaver poets of Paisley and Renfrewshire were especially celebrated, and in Dunfermline weaving supported a radical popular culture which was experienced by the young Andrew Carnegie in the 1840s.[40] This self-educated culture was damaged by the collapse of handloom weaving,[41] but throughout Scotland one could find men who, starting from a very imperfect education, read and discussed books on religion, history, philosophy, or science; usually they stayed in their original occupations, but sometimes they went on to become writers or self-taught naturalists. The best-known example is Hugh Miller, born in 1802, who grew up in this atmosphere in Cromarty. His family would have made sacrifices to send him to a university, but he decided that 'the only school in which I could properly

---

[38] Evidence of R. Lingen, Kay-Shuttleworth's successor, in PP 1865, XVII, *Education Commission (Scotland), First Report*, 326.

[39] H. Corr, 'An Exploration into Scottish Education', in W. H. Fraser and R. J. Morris (eds.), *People and Society in Scotland, II: 1830–1914* (Edinburgh, 1990), 303.

[40] A. Carnegie, *Autobiography of Andrew Carnegie* (London, 1920), 1–19.

[41] N. Murray, *The Scottish Hand Loom Weavers, 1790–1850: A Social History* (Edinburgh, 1978), 161–4.

be taught was that world-wide school which awaited me, in which Toil and Hardship are the severe but noble teachers'. He was a working stonemason before becoming a geologist, journalist, and Free Church notable, and compared the practical intelligence of workers favourably with the academic education of the 'university-taught lads' among his childhood friends.[42]

But could an essentially artisan tradition be transmitted to the new industrial working class? Here more formal institutions of part-time education might be needed, and they were likely to operate at a more elementary intellectual level. The most important unofficial institutions, though for children rather than adults, were undoubtedly the Sunday schools, which expanded in striking fashion from the 1830s. By 1871 there were over 350,000 scholars, which means that they must have reached most working-class children. In the early years they had concentrated on basic literacy, but were now turning to a more purely religious approach, as control shifted after the Disruption from non-denominational societies to individual church congregations. In the 1840s, factory inquiries found that Sunday schools were refusing to teach secular subjects and only admitting children who could already read. Perhaps it was different in Glasgow, for we also learn that in 1851 children unable to read formed 18 per cent of the total entering Sunday schools there, and that this had fallen to 6 per cent by 1870.[43] Their older function was now passing to evening classes of various kinds, some attached to day-schools (in which case they could benefit from state subsidy), some to churches, some run by charities which specialized in this work. These classes were largely filled with working-class adolescents who had recently left school and were still trying to master the basic subjects. In Glasgow in the 1860s, there were also special classes for adults between 18 and 25, and a quarter of those attending were completely illiterate: yet more evidence of how education was cut short by the pressure of full-time work.[44]

A more ambitious programme of adult education was that of the Mechanics' Institutes. Their prehistory starts in 1796, when Anderson's Institution was founded at Glasgow under the will of John Anderson,

---

[42] H. Miller, *My Schools and Schoolmasters, or the Story of my Education* (Edinburgh, 1907), 141, 367.

[43] C. G. Brown, 'The Sunday-School Movement in Scotland, 1780–1914', *SCHSR* 21 (1981–3), 15–16, 23–4; PP 1843, XIII, *Children's Employment Commission, Second Report*, 154, 174.

[44] PP 1867, XXV, *Report on Glasgow*, 111–12, 142–9. Cf. T. Kelly, *A History of Adult Education in Great Britain* (Liverpool, 1962), 155–7.

a professor at the university. Anderson intended his institution to be a rival university, but it was not until 1828 that it had a wide enough spread of subjects (including medicine) to adopt this title. The early lectures were mainly in physics and chemistry, and though the professors were part-timers, the institution attracted some distinguished men. They gave evening lectures aimed at a relatively sophisticated and well-off audience. But George Birkbeck, who was professor in 1799–1804 before leaving to become a pioneer of adult education in London, started a separate 'mechanics' class', and in 1823 this split off to become the Glasgow Mechanics' Institution. It was the first to use this name (which was more common in Scotland than 'Institute'), but had a precursor in the School of Arts at Edinburgh, founded in 1821 by Leonard Horner, one of the Whig circle based on the *Edinburgh Review*. At Edinburgh control remained firmly in the hands of the wealthy subscribers, while at Glasgow the members themselves were in charge; but both aimed at teaching 'mechanics'—skilled workers in industry—to understand the scientific principles underlying their work, with the hope that this would make them more efficient as well as more enlightened. The movement caught on, and in the 1820s Mechanics' Institutions or Schools of Arts were established in most towns. A short-lived Scottish Union of Literary and Mechanics' Institutions was set up in 1848, and by 1851 there were said to be 55 institutions with 12,554 members.[45] Their fortunes, however, were very mixed. After the initial enthusiasm, many ran into financial difficulties or closed. They survived as buildings for lectures or recreation, but very few had regular educational courses. Neither the Dundee nor the Greenock institutes, though they were situated in large industrial towns, succeeded in keeping classes going.[46] The former, indeed, collapsed in 1849. The main legacy of the institutes was their libraries: these, or separate 'mechanics' libraries' as at Edinburgh and Perth, often formed the basis of municipal libraries, which were authorized by an act of 1853. Town councils were slow to take action, however, and only four towns 'adopted' the act before 1872. It was not until the 1890s, usually with grants from Andrew Carnegie, that most towns acquired their public libraries.[47]

---

[45] J. W. Hudson, *The History of Adult Education* (London, 1851), pp. vi–vii, 184.

[46] R. M. Smith, *A Page of Local History: Being a Record of the Origin and Progress of Greenock Mechanics' Library and Institution* (Greenock, 1904); J. V. Smith, *The Watt Institution, Dundee, 1824–49* (Dundee, 1978).

[47] W. R. Aitken, *A History of the Public Library Movement in Scotland to 1955* (Glasgow, 1971), 303–11, 349.

The only institutions with permanent classes were Glasgow (both Anderson's University and the Mechanics' Institution), Aberdeen, and Edinburgh, where the School of Arts was described in 1851 as 'the only establishment in Britain deserving the title of a "People's College" '.[48] These evening classes were based on science, but also covered subjects like drawing, English, or French, and awarded diplomas to students who pursued a systematic course. Even their champions admitted that they were no longer reaching 'mechanics', but their clientele remained a 'popular' one which included skilled workers as well as clerks, teachers, and students.[49] In their urban setting, they could play a new role in promoting lads of parts. At Glasgow, David Livingstone (b. 1813) started his medical studies at Anderson's at the age of 23 after leaving school at 10 and educating himself while working in a cotton mill. At Aberdeen, the Mechanics' Institution was an important stimulus to Alexander Bain, who left school at 11 and worked as a handloom weaver before going to Marischal College, eventually becoming a leading philosopher and professor at Aberdeen University.[50] At the Mechanics' Institution, Bain was part of a 'mutual instruction class' where young men debated and read papers, and this was a movement which spread to the countryside. At Carluke in Lanarkshire in the 1840s there was a 'Useful Knowledge Society' with forty-four members, weekly lectures, and a library, and in Aberdeenshire a flourishing network of village 'mutual improvement societies' began in the same decade.[51]

The spirit of self-improvement was thus abroad, and it is no coincidence that Samuel Smiles, author of the celebrated Victorian guide to success in life *Self Help*, spent his early career in Haddington, which had one of the earliest schools of arts (1823), and which was the centre of the 'itinerating libraries' founded in 1817 by Samuel Brown to serve the surrounding villages.[52] Smiles later wrote biographies of Telford and Watt, and it was James Watt who became the patron saint of the

[48] Hudson, *History of Adult Education*, 75.

[49] Ibid. 31–9, 58–62, 74–81, 86–7; A. H. Sexton, *The First Technical College: A Sketch of the History of 'the Andersonian' and the Institutions Descended from it, 1796–1894* (London, 1894); *NSA* vi. 179–82 (Glasgow) and xii. 47–8 (Aberdeen).

[50] A. Bain, *Autobiography* (London, 1904); G. M. Fraser, *Aberdeen Mechanics' Institute: A Record of Civic and Educational Progress* (Aberdeen, 1912), 15–19.

[51] *NSA* vi. 594; I. R. Carter, 'The Mutual Improvement Movement in North-East Scotland in the Nineteenth Century', *Aberdeen University Review*, 46 (1975–6), 383–92; R. H. Smith, *An Aberdeenshire Village Propaganda Forty Years Ago* (Edinburgh, 1889).

[52] J. M. Simpson, 'Three East Lothian Pioneers of Adult Education', *Transactions of the East Lothian Antiquarian and Field Naturalists' Society*, 13 (1972), 43–60.

mechanics' institutes. When he died in 1819, there were various moves to commemorate him, one being the Watt Institution at Dundee, set up 'for instructing young tradesmen and others in art and science,—that, like him whose name it bears, they might be stimulated to pursue the honourable course of improvement'.[53] At Glasgow Mechanics' Institution, 'a colossal statue of James Watt is placed on the pediment of the building, by a subscription of one shilling from each student in successive years'.[54] This was erected in the 1820s. In 1851, the Edinburgh School of Arts changed its name to the Watt Institution, and erected its own statue of 'the great practical philosopher', to commemorate his name 'among a class of men to which he himself originally belonged'.[55] Yet another statue was installed in the Hunterian Museum at Glasgow University, and a painting by William Stewart shows two artisans gazing reverently at it and at a model of Watt's steam-engine.[56] At Dundee, and possibly elsewhere, there was an annual celebration on Watt's birthday.[57] This cult was perhaps a curious one for working men, for Watt was, in Smiles's words, 'emphatically well-born'.[58] His father was a leading citizen of Greenock, and Watt's early career as an instrument-maker was an example of downward rather than upward mobility. What was commemorated was partly his perseverance in adversity, partly his success as a businessman, but above all his work as an inventor in demonstrating the transforming power of technology.

Technical education was a new concept of the 1850s and 1860s, and one sponsored by the state. Despite some experiments in agricultural education in the 1840s, attempts to introduce vocational training into ordinary schools had never come to anything, apart from the needlework taught to girls. Even the works schools set up by employers were confined to general education. It was from quite a different angle, the teaching of industrial design, that the government first intervened in this sphere, on the grounds that in the age of mass production workers needed artistic training if British products were to retain their supremacy. A central school of design opened in London in 1837, and provincial ones followed, reaching Glasgow in 1844 and Paisley in 1848. The textile industry was their main target, and the local management committees were dominated by calico printers at Glasgow, shawl manufacturers at

---

[53] *NSA* xi, Forfarshire, 47.   [54] *NSA* vi. 181.

[55] PP 1854, XXVIII, *First Report of the Department of Science and Art*, 397; Hudson, *History of Adult Education*, 79.

[56] Glasgow, Hunterian Art Gallery.   [57] Smith, *Watt Institution*, 30.

[58] S. Smiles, *Lives of Boulton and Watt* (London, 1865), 79.

Paisley.[59] The Great Exhibition of 1851 gave a new impulse to this movement by demonstrating the artistic superiority of continental wares, and was followed in 1852 by the creation of a Department of Practical Art under the Board of Trade. Its presiding genius was Henry Cole, one of the organizers of the Exhibition and an ally of Prince Albert. Cole sought to extend aesthetic education 'with the view of laying the foundation for correct judgment, both in the consumer and the producer of manufactures'.[60] In 1853 the department widened its scope to become the Department of Science and Art, and in 1856 it was put under the Committee of Council on Education. The scientific side was run by Lyon Playfair, until he left for the chemistry chair at Edinburgh in 1858.

The early schools of design were directly financed by the government, and ran into many controversies. Local industrialists often felt, as at Paisley, that they did not pay enough attention to practical needs.[61] The policy of the DSA was not to found new schools of this kind, but to encourage locally run schools of art, subsidized indirectly through grants. New schools were established permanently (there were others which did not last) at Aberdeen (1853, based on the Mechanics' Institution), Dundee, Stirling, Edinburgh (1858), Perth, Inverness, Kilmarnock, and Leith. One of their duties was to organize art education in local elementary schools, and to provide courses for schoolteachers. Like the Mechanics' Institutes, they were soon diverted from their original target. In their evening classes, clerks and teachers were to be found as well as designers, engravers, pattern-makers, and similar skilled artisans. They also had day classes attended by students from the middle classes, including both the sons of manufacturers and many of 'no occupation', especially women. Most of the students were under 20, and these schools were really tapping an unsatisfied demand both for artistic education of a general kind, and for a practical education at the secondary level. The conflict between fine and applied art was especially apparent at Edinburgh, where the new school had formerly been the Trustees' Academy, run since 1760 by the Board of Manufactures and the home of a highly regarded school of painting. Its subordination to the DSA regulations which stressed stereotyped drawing exercises and ornamental design was unwelcome.[62]

---

[59] PP 1852–3, LIV, *First Report of the Department of Practical Art*, 95, 98.
[60] Ibid. 2.   [61] Q. Bell, *The Schools of Design* (London, 1963), 130–3.
[62] L. Errington, *Master Class: Robert Scott Lauder and his Pupils* (Edinburgh, 1983), 34–7.

The DSA built up a complex of museums and colleges at South Kensington, and its system of grants, prizes, and scholarships became a significant force in the educational world. It also founded the Industrial Museum in Edinburgh, linked with a chair of technology at the university, though the latter did not survive the death of the first incumbent. On the science side, the DSA grants were at first rather disorganized, and Aberdeen Mechanics' Institution was one of the few Scottish beneficiaries; in 1859 its 'school of science' had 99 students, and the teachers included James Clerk Maxwell, then a professor at Marischal College.[63] The only specialized science institutions encouraged by the government were schools of navigation to prepare young men for certificates in the mercantile marine, and Scotland acquired three of these, at Leith, Aberdeen, and Glasgow, in 1855–7. In 1859, the science grants were reorganized on a system which provided the model for Lowe's 'payment by results'. Prospective science teachers sat an examination for a departmental certificate, and could then give courses which qualified for grants according to their pupils' examination success. Grants were meant to go only to the 'industrial classes', defined as those with incomes under £100 p.a. In 1865 a similar scheme extended drawing grants from the schools of art to any teacher who qualified. The courses subsidized by the DSA were either evening classes intended mainly for workers, or classes in ordinary elementary and secondary schools, especially in drawing.

The Scottish response was at first slow. In 1869 there were only 28 science centres in Scotland compared with 354 in England and 132 in Ireland. In the next few years they expanded rapidly, so that by 1872 there were 119.[64] They included bodies like Anderson's University and the Mechanics' Institution in Glasgow, but there was no necessary connection with industry, and many science classes were in ordinary schools. Aberdeenshire alone had 37: this was because university graduates, who were numerous among teachers in the north-east, did not have to take the special DSA examination in order to qualify for grants. Teaching elementary science did not require practical or vocational work, and was thus a relatively easy way of gaining extra income for teachers and schools. The system did something to encourage general science education, but by the end of the 1860s there was a feeling that it was missing the mark where 'technical' education was concerned.

[63] PP 1860, XXIV, *7th Report of DSA*, 36.
[64] PP 1868–9, XXIII, *16th Report of DSA*, p. vii; PP 1873, XXVIII, *20th Report of DSA*, pp. ix, 41, 133 ff.

The DSA owed its origins to the 1851 Exhibition. It was another international exhibition, at Paris in 1867, which revived fears of industrial rivalry, and started a new movement for technical education in which Playfair was especially prominent. A conference on the subject, bringing together industrialists and educationists, was held at Edinburgh in 1868. In 1870 Playfair gave an address which defined technical schools as those which offered 'to teach the workmen, the foremen, and the managers the scientific principles lying at the base of their industries', the formula used fifty years before by the founders of Edinburgh School of Arts. Playfair asked why Britain was

the only leading State in Europe that is neglecting the higher education of the working classes, and of those men above them whose duty it is to superintend their labour. . . . science must be joined to practice in the advancing competition of the world, in order that a nation may retain the strength and energy of manhood.

Scotland 'is asleep and is dreaming of her past glories', but 'it was not by dwelling on the past that John Knox laid the basis of prosperity for his country.'[65] The response to this call will be examined in Chapter 11.

[65] Playfair, *Subjects of Social Welfare*, 317, 328, 335–6.

7

Educational Politics after 1872

THE 1872 Education Act was not the beginning of state education in Scotland, but the culmination of a long process of public intervention. It had decisive effects none the less. One was to introduce two new actors onto the educational stage, the school boards and the SED. The teachers might be considered a third, and there was now a confident secular and professionalized educational world able to attack pedagogic questions with a new spirit. The act also removed religious issues from national educational politics, and here Scotland differed from England, where the dual school-board and voluntary system caused continuing tension and demanded further legislation, as a result of which school boards disappeared in 1902. Scotland had no need for legislation of this scope, nor did it see major commissions of inquiry corresponding to the Cross report of 1888 on the workings of the elementary system or the Bryce report of 1895 on secondary schools, both important sources of evidence for the historian. The Parker committee, which reported in 1888, was a minor equivalent.

Much of Scottish education developed on similar lines to England; innovations sometimes happened first in one country, sometimes in the other, but the common political system and the need to equalize expenditure meant that they could not diverge very far. The most significant differences were in secondary education, where state aid began in Scotland in 1892, ten years before England, and where the structure of the system created a fundamentally different debate. The relationship of SED and school boards also reflected the distinct political culture of Scotland. The SED was a more powerful and directive body than its English equivalent, making Scottish education more uniform and centralized. This was partly due to the compactness of a small country and the weakness of the voluntary sector, partly because the SED took over the 'national' tradition which was developed by Scottish Presbyterianism and which we have seen as a shaping force in nineteenth-century debate. The same tradition made the comprehensive organization of education under school boards seem natural to Scottish opinion, and they expressed the strong local spirit which many observers have seen, in the absence of a Scottish state, as characteristic of nineteenth-century Scotland. In R. J. Morris's words, 'Scotland had a higher regard for community and locality as a basis for action than the English' and 'a sense of the value of the individual operating in the moral framework of small communities'.[1] Individualist rather than collectivist, and still rooted in the authority of local notables, this spirit was part of the liberalism to which Scotland long remained faithful.

1. SCHOOL BOARDS

Directly elected school boards were a feature of the Scottish scene for over forty years. While in England they were only set up where voluntary schools were thought inadequate, in Scotland every parish and sizeable town had one, making a total of about 980 (the number declined over the years with amalgamations). Some were very small, and the 1872 Act reproduced one of the weaknesses of the parish school system by retaining the boundaries of the old parishes, which often (like their names) bore little relation to modern patterns of settlement. In Glasgow, the Glasgow board covered only the old municipality, while the growing suburbs were served by the large and active Govan board, or by smaller ones like Maryhill, Springburn, Cathcart, and Eastwood. (Maryhill and Springburn amalgamated with Glasgow in 1911.) Edinburgh and Leith also had separate boards. Boards were elected every three years, on a relatively broad franchise: occupiers of property worth £4 per annum, including women. In the cities this was wider than the municipal franchise, which was confined to those who actually paid rates. In rural parishes, it was wider than the parliamentary franchise until the Third Reform Act of 1884, but narrower afterwards, as agricultural labourers might have the parliamentary but not the school board vote. These differences could have political significance, but in 1908 the franchise was assimilated to that for other local bodies. A special feature of the school boards, copied from the English Act of 1870, was the 'cumulative vote', a crude form of proportional representation designed to give places to religious minorities. Voters had as many votes as there were seats on the board, and could concentrate them on a single candidate. The cumulative vote regularly produced two or three Roman Catholic members (usually priests) in the cities and

---

[1] R. J. Morris, 'Victorian Values in Scotland and England', in T. C. Smout (ed.), *Victorian Values: A Joint Symposium of the Royal Society of Edinburgh and the British Academy, December 1990* (Oxford, 1992), 41, 45.

in smaller towns in the west; in Edinburgh, Episcopalians were also numerous enough to use this device. Catholics and Episcopalians had their own schools outside school-board control, but used their position to protect their interests and to prevent discrimination in matters such as the enforcement of attendance, where board powers extended to all parents. The system also allowed contests to be avoided by sharing the seats amicably between the various local parties and interests.

In 1903, when school boards were threatened with abolition, an MP praised them as 'a system of representative and popular management by those who were intimately acquainted with the wants of the various localities'.[2] The evidence suggests, however, that their 'popular' character was limited, and that those elected were often the same kind of local notables as had governed education before 1872. In the countryside, landowners lost their power as heritors, but could still dominate school boards through their factors and tenants, and any laird who took an interest had little difficulty in becoming chairman. Deference remained strong, and some landowners were still willing to build schools as appurtenances of their estates; in 1890 Lord Leven donated a school costing £900 to Ferness, Nairnshire.[3] More commonly it was ministers who were most prominent on rural boards (with three main denominations, there was no shortage), the balance being made up by farmers and shopkeepers. In 1873, a quarter of the newly elected board members were ministers of religion.[4] It is possible that by the early twentieth century rural boards were becoming more democratic—it was claimed in 1905 that they were composed largely of parents and of 'working men such as the grieve and the small crofter'[5]—but local studies are so far lacking. Apart from some episodes in the highlands, the boards do not seem to have become centres of demagogic or radical agitation, as opponents of popular control before 1872 had feared.

Urban school boards are better documented, though only Glasgow has attracted a full-scale study, by James Roxburgh. It was not necessarily typical, for while in the west of Scotland the boards were dominated by businessmen, in the east clergymen and (in the early years) university professors had more influence. In the 1870s both Edinburgh and Aberdeen had professors as chairmen, and on the Aberdeen board

---

[2] Hansard, 4th series 123, 18 June 1903, 1339 (T. Shaw).

[3] *EN* 2 Aug. 1890, 521.

[4] A. J. Belford, *Centenary Handbook of the Educational Institute of Scotland* (Edinburgh, 1946), 150. Belford does not give a source for this.

[5] Hansard, 4th series 145, 8 May 1905, 1226.

elected in 1879 five of the fifteen members were professors, at the university or the Free Church divinity college; in the 1890s the Free Church professor James Robertson contested the chairmanship with the Unitarian minister Alexander Webster. At Leith, the Revd David Kilpatrick was chairman for over twenty-five years. The Dundee board was also dominated by ministers, and did not elect a lay chairman until 1906; school board affairs did not attract the jute barons.

According to the clerk of Glasgow school board, 'it has become almost a proverb in Scotland that the men with the best chance to get into the school board are those that have either a kirk or a work; that is to say, either a clergyman or an employer of labour.'[6] In 1877 the *Educational News* contrasted the first chairmen of the Glasgow and Edinburgh boards: 'The one represented "business." The other represented "culture." '[7] The cultural representative was Henry Calderwood, United Presbyterian professor at Edinburgh University and prominent Liberal. The businessman was Alexander Whitelaw, leading partner in the Baird iron company of Gartsherrie (which also determined educational affairs in Coatbridge), and he was the first of a number of wealthy businessmen who dominated the Glasgow board: John Neilson Cuthbertson (produce broker, and long-serving chairman), Michael Connal (warehouseman and ironbroker), and William Mitchell (calico printer). All had a strong religious inspiration, and saw school board work as only part of their religious and charitable activity. Mitchell, for example, who headed the Glasgow board's attendance committee for many years, was also interested in juvenile delinquency and founded the East Park children's homes. In more purely industrial towns, employers took the lead. The first chairman at Govan was the shipbuilder Alexander Stephen, who gave £1,000 for scholarships so that local children could go to Glasgow University.[8] At Paisley, the Coats family had a long association with the school board, as with other educational activities in the town; the first chairman, Thomas Coats, contributed £1,000 to building each of the board's first five schools. At Kirkcaldy, the linoleum manufacturer Michael Nairn spent £10,000 on building a new High School to mark his chairmanship.[9] Thus within a new framework older paternalist attitudes continued.

---

[6] PP 1884–5, XI, *Report from the Select Committee on School Board Elections (Voting)*, 160.

[7] *EN* 28 Apr. 1877, 208. Cf. J. M. Roxburgh, *The School Board of Glasgow, 1873–1919* (London, 1971), 20–8.

[8] *EN* 27 June 1885, 419–22.   [9] *EN* 3 June 1893, 373.

Callum Brown has argued, with special reference to Glasgow, that by the 1890s evangelical businessmen were beginning to withdraw from school boards because they thought their religious efforts had failed, and that 'educational ideology shifted towards welfarism under social-ist and Christian socialist influence'.[10] This was certainly a period when the wealthy élite began to lose interest in local affairs and leave them to small businessmen or professional men, but we lack data about the changing composition of school boards. One symptom of change was the election of educational experts with their roots in the world of schools: David Ross, rector of the Church of Scotland Training Col-lege, was elected at Glasgow in 1894; at Edinburgh Alexander Mackay, the editor of the EIS journal the *Educational News*, was elected as an 'education' candidate in 1897,[11] and his successor S. M. Murray, who had moved from a headmastership under the board to become full-time secretary of the EIS, was elected in 1906.

From the start, the wide electorate encouraged the emergence of 'working men's' or ratepayer candidates. What the working man was deemed to want was low rates and low school fees, and economy was the watchword of ratepayer campaigns—an interest shared by shop-keepers and small property-owners and businessmen. Candidates at-tacked extravagant buildings, high teachers' salaries, and expenditure on secondary schools for the middle class; these views were linked at the national level with campaigns for free education. Thus while wealthy municipal leaders were often prepared to spend public money lavishly for reasons of civic prestige, those lower down the social scale had a narrower and more grudging view. At Dunfermline, for example, a meeting called in 1879 by a committee of working men denounced the extravagance of the school board and called for the most rigid economy; three candidates were elected.[12] In the 1880s, school board elections were taken up by trades councils. They were unsuccessful in Edinburgh and initially in Glasgow, but at Aberdeen the trades council got six candidates elected in 1885, and was allowed a share of the carve-up in years when contests were avoided.[13] Later there was a similar

---

[10] C. G. Brown, *The Social History of Religion in Scotland since 1730* (London, 1987), 177, and cf. 200.

[11] *EN* 10 Apr. 1897, 258–9.

[12] *EN* 15 Mar. 1879, 149; 23 Aug. 1879, 432–3.

[13] M. Fry, *Patronage and Principle: A Political History of Modern Scotland* (Aber-deen, 1987), 86; K. D. Buckley, *Trade Unionism in Aberdeen, 1878 to 1900* (Edinburgh, 1955), 96, 120–8.

arrangement at Glasgow. These candidates, not necessarily working men themselves, were usually linked with electoral committees on the radical wing of the Liberal party, like the conference of 'ward Liberals' at Kilmarnock which endorsed five candidates pledged to economy, or the Kinning Park Working-Men's Parliamentary and Municipal Reform Association, which adopted its own candidates to campaign against high rates and to challenge the municipal clique which had hitherto fixed the elections in Govan.[14] Both these examples are from 1885. Many elections in these decades were fought on the issue of 'economy', and a victory of the economy party was often marked by a reduction in teachers' salary scales. After 1900, as working-class representation began to pass into Labour hands, especially in Glasgow, more positive policies were adopted, such as the provision of hot meals for poor children, though it was the state rather the ratepayer which was expected to pay the bill. But in 1918 there were still only 120 Labour members of school boards in Scotland.[15]

Women were eligible both to vote for school boards (if they were independent occupiers of property) and to be elected. At the first elections in 1873, women formed a quarter of the electorate in Edinburgh, a fifth in other large towns. Seventeen women were elected, the best-known being Flora Stevenson at Edinburgh, who was to serve until her death in 1905, becoming chairman in 1900.[16] Women members were never numerous: despite attempts by the suffrage movement to encourage candidates, there were still only 76 in 1906, though this was proportionately more than in England and Wales, where there were 370 women on boards when they were abolished in 1902.[17] Women became a recognized element on urban boards, and there are signs that female voters used the cumulative vote in their favour. At Edinburgh in 1882, for example, the two women candidates came second and third in the poll (after the sole Episcopalian) with almost identical votes, and while all the male candidates were labelled by religious denomination, the women were not.[18] Women's special status was also acknowledged (as with Roman Catholics and Episcopalians) by selecting another woman

[14] *EN* 24 Jan. 1885, 76; 14 Mar. 1885, 178.

[15] *EN* 18 Jan. 1918, 39. For the memoirs of a Glasgow Labour school board member, see W. M. Haddow, *My Seventy Years* (Glasgow, n.d. [*c*.1943]).

[16] Parliamentary Return in PP 1873, LII; slightly different figures in PP 1874, XX, *First Annual Report of the Board of Education for Scotland*, p. viii.

[17] *EN* 12 Feb. 1909, 146; P. Hollis, *Ladies Elect: Women in English Local Government, 1865–1914* (Oxford, 1987), 130, 486.

[18] *EN* 1 Apr. 1882, 206.

to succeed those who died or resigned; vacancies on school boards were filled by co-option, not by-elections.

Most women members came from the upper middle class, and were leisured spinsters or widows, involved in a wide range of social and charitable activities and in the general women's movement, including both suffragism and the campaign for entry to the Scottish universities. Both Flora Stevenson and Phoebe Blyth, elected with her in 1873, fitted into this pattern. As Helen Corr has pointed out, several of the early members were champions of cookery teaching in schools, which was being promoted as a special field of female expertise. Grace Paterson and Mary Barlas, elected as the first women members at Glasgow in 1885, were both involved in this cause, Paterson being principal of one of the two cookery schools in the city; Margaret Black, who headed the other one, was elected in 1891.[19] At Paisley, a prominent early member was Jane Arthur, who was an activist in women's causes, including the suffrage movement.[20] But she was also the wife of a leading business-man, and so represented another kind of woman member: the female relations of local notables, whether landowners or industrial employers. For women as for men, old forms of paternalism merged into new ones of public service. Indeed, since women had been active in school management before 1872, through church congregations as well as philanthropy, it could be argued that the election of women to school boards compensated rather meagrely for the loss of an important role. Under the school board regime, separate girls' schools and their ladies' committees disappeared, as did charities like the ladies' Gaelic school societies.

When two women members of Govan school board resigned in 1886—they included Mrs Pearce, wife of the local shipbuilding magnate and MP—they hoped they would be replaced by women, as this 'would strengthen the hands of the lady teachers in the schools, and possibly secure for the girls a course of instruction in those domestic arts which were of more help towards securing happy homes than any amount of mere book knowledge'.[21] It was inevitable that women members would take a special interest in girls' subjects like needlework, and in the

---

[19] H. Corr, '"Home-Rule" in Scotland: The Teaching of Housework in Schools, 1872–1914', in J. Fewell and F. Paterson (eds.), *Girls in their Prime: Scottish Education Revisited* (Edinburgh, 1990), 43.

[20] A. Slaven and S. Checkland (eds.), *Dictionary of Scottish Business Biography, 1860–1960* (Aberdeen, 1986–90), ii. 337–9.

[21] *EN* 13 Nov. 1886, 812.

welfare side of school board work. Flora Stevenson ran a charity which
provided meals for poor children, Jane Arthur was noted both for her
interest in needlework and for the promotion of day nurseries. There
are also signs that women continued to be involved in school management below board level. At Edinburgh and Paisley in the 1880s there
were 'lady visitors' attached to each school to supervise needlework,
and when HM Inspector examined domestic work at Coatbridge in
1881 the event was attended by 'a large representation of the ladies of
Coatbridge'.[22] After 1900, when issues like meals and medical inspection came to the fore, women members came especially into their own.

The powers of school boards were strictly defined by law and by the
annual Code, which was used by the SED to penalize deficiencies,
reward innovation, and enforce a common curriculum. The parliamentary grant, distributed after an annual inspection of each school, was an
essential source of income along with rates and (until the 1890s) school
fees. In curricular matters school boards had little real freedom. They
were also bound to enforce attendance and to provide places for all
children of school age. For twenty years after 1872, building new schools
was their dominant task, and although many former church schools
passed into their hands these were usually so small or old-fashioned
that they had to be replaced. But there were some areas of policy where
boards had more discretion. One was religious instruction, deliberately
devolved to boards by the 1872 Act, and in the early years still contentious. Another was the relation between elementary and secondary
education. Unlike English school boards, Scottish ones usually controlled the historic burgh school of their town. The level of fees at these
middle-class schools, the development of alternative forms of 'higher
grade' education more closely linked with the elementary schools, and
the organization of the links between the different types of school could
all be controversial issues, involving class and community feeling.

Boards also had considerable freedom in the employment of teachers. There was no national salary scale, and—apart from the 'old
parochials' appointed before 1872—no security of tenure. The generosity of school boards varied, and personal or sectarian considerations
could influence policy. The larger urban boards, though vulnerable to
the campaigns of economizers, generally tried to attract well-qualified
teachers and to create some kind of promotion structure. Smaller ones
were more easily tempted to pay low salaries and to dismiss teachers

[22] *EN* 3 Jan. 1880, 14; 10 Jan. 1880, 28–30; 4 June 1881, 350.

for arbitrary reasons. The defence of teachers against such pressures, and the improvement of tenure, was the first priority of the EIS after 1872. Some small rural boards were notorious for their treatment of teachers, and ministers, used to having the teacher under their thumb before 1872, could be especially tyrannical. In 1882, after a dismissal case at Leswalt in Wigtownshire which attracted national attention, the law was changed to give teachers some legal safeguards, but it was not until 1908 that they acquired a right of appeal to the SED.

2. THE SED

Until 1885 the charge that the Scotch Education Department was only a name on a door had some truth. The English and Scottish Codes at first differed only in detail, and the two departments had the same central bureaucracy—although the secretary between 1870 and 1884, Francis Sandford, was the son of a Glasgow professor, and had some familiarity with Scottish conditions. Only the inspectors were based in Scotland. The SED had to share its power both with the Department of Science and Art, which continued to administer technical education from South Kensington, and initially with the Board of Education in Edinburgh created by the 1872 Act. This board, which included two university principals, supervised the setting up of school boards, the first surveys of educational deficiency, and the transfer of church schools. It also developed its own views on the curriculum, being particularly concerned to preserve the parish school tradition of teaching Latin, and it came into public conflict with the SED. But it was a temporary body, and despite patriotic campaigns for its retention it disappeared in 1878.[23]

Similar campaigns led to the creation of the Scottish Office in 1885, and the transfer of the SED to its supervision; the officials moved across Whitehall to Dover House. This transfer went against the recommendations of a Select Committee in 1884 for a new ministry of education covering both England and Scotland, and was opposed by many educationists, including Playfair, on the grounds that Scottish education would carry less political weight as part of the rather miscellaneous responsibilities of the Secretary for Scotland. In practice the SED became a small but powerful and creative department. Above all, it

---

[23] B. Lenman and J. Stocks, 'The Beginnings of State Education in Scotland, 1872–1885', *SES* 4 (1972), 93–106.

acquired a formidable permanent head in Henry Craik, who was its secretary until 1904. Craik was the son of a Glasgow minister, and (like Sandford) was educated at Glasgow University and Balliol College, Oxford. He had spent his whole career in the Education Department's London office. Most Scottish Secretaries, preoccupied with more urgent problems, were prepared to allow Craik his head, and parliamentary control was also weak. Legislation by statute was only needed for the extension of compulsory attendance, as in 1878, 1883, and 1901. One of the most significant changes, the abolition of fees, was the by-product of legislation on local government. Changes in the Code were laid before Parliament annually, but they were often of a technical character which only experts could grasp, and Craik was able to carry out important changes incrementally. His most striking achievement was to give the SED a central role, quite unanticipated by the 1872 Act, in the development of secondary education. The main limitation on specifically Scottish policies, backed up no doubt by Treasury control behind the scenes, was the need for 'equivalence' between Scottish and English expenditure. Under the 'Goschen formula', the revenues allocated to Scotland were supposed to be eleven-eightieths of those used for the same purpose in England and Wales. As we shall see, there were occasions when this could be exploited to put Scotland ahead of England.

Craik had a higher profile than most civil servants. In 1885 he published an article supporting a 'British' ministry of education,[24] and there were three editions, the first in 1884, of his book *The State in its Relation to Education*, an exposition of the development of educational policy in England and Scotland; it appeared in a series, 'The English Citizen: his Rights and Responsibilities', which Craik himself edited. His personal contribution to policy was openly acknowledged, usually in fulsome terms, by ministers and MPs, and he sat on several committees of inquiry as a full member. When he retired, he was elected as a Unionist to one of the Scottish university seats, and took an active and partisan role in politics. His influence was at its height between 1895 and 1903, during the Unionist tenure of the Scottish Office by Lord Balfour of Burleigh. Balfour was one of the few Scottish Secretaries to have a real interest in education, and the two men worked closely together. It was not surprising that Liberal MPs became restive at Craik's influence, and in the 1900s there was much criticism of the arbitrary

[24] *Fortnightly Review*, NS 37 (1885), 476–90.

and 'despotic' power of the department. By the time the Liberals came to power in 1905, Craik had retired. His successor John Struthers, though a strong personality with a clearly identifiable educational strategy, was politically more self-effacing.

The development of educational expertise outside the official world was limited. Two university chairs of education were founded in 1876, at Edinburgh (filled by S. S. Laurie) and St Andrews, but the SED resisted their attempts to develop a role in teacher training. Most school boards had no full-time officials; local bankers or solicitors acted as clerk and treasurer. The clerks of the larger urban boards, however, were significant local figures and achieved some influence of their own. They participated in meetings of the Conference of School Board Clerks, a British organization, and founded a Scottish Association of School Board Clerks and Treasurers in 1895. The school attendance officers and even the janitors had their own organizations. All these avoided controversial matters, but the larger boards frequently exchanged information and held *ad hoc* conferences on current issues. In 1897 a Scottish School Boards Association was formed to act as a political pressure group, but the diverging interests of urban and rural boards made it difficult for them to speak with one voice. The most significant educational organization was undoubtedly the Educational Institute of Scotland.

3. TEACHERS AND THE EIS

Before 1872 the EIS had chiefly represented burgh and parish teachers, and the teachers' sense of professionalism was weakened by their allegiance to rival churches. Now the teachers could see themselves as public servants, and the EIS launched two important initiatives. One was a weekly newspaper, the *Educational News*, which began in 1876 and became the main forum for Scottish educational debate. The other was an annual congress, held at the New Year from 1875 and rotating between Scottish towns. This was aimed at general public opinion, and devoted to wider educational issues rather than professional concerns. The speakers and platform guests included MPs, civic dignitaries, school board chairmen, business leaders, and experts on the questions of the day, and the teachers' pride and confidence in their new social status was reflected in a round of dinners and receptions. At local level, the EIS branches also discussed policy issues as well as organizing social events and outings. 'No one now dreams of looking to the Churches for educational guidance,' boasted the *Educational News* in 1888. 'By common consent the work is left to the Institute.'[25] It was certainly true that the educational authority of the churches disappeared rapidly after 1872. Debates in the General Assemblies were usually confined to their residual responsibility for the training colleges and, apart from the occasional school board chairman, clergymen ceased to make any mark on educational debate.

The evolution of the EIS reflected change in the teaching profession itself, which became larger, feminized, and more highly qualified. After 1872 the Established and Free churches each opened an extra college at Aberdeen, initially for women only, while SED regulations encouraged men at the Glasgow and Edinburgh colleges to combine some university courses with their college training. Some universities wanted a direct share in professional training, a claim at first resisted by the SED, but conceded in 1895, after women had been admitted to the universities; all except Edinburgh joined this 'Queen's Student' scheme, which supplemented the traditional recruitment of 'Queen's Scholars' through the pupil-teacher system. In 1907 the state took over the six Presbyterian colleges (there were also small Episcopalian and Catholic ones, for women only), and university and college training were integrated; pupil-teachers were replaced by 'junior students', who were no longer used as part of the teaching force. These changes are illustrated in Table 7.1. One notable feature is the rapid raising of qualifications in the 1900s: the SED was within sight of excluding uncertificated teachers altogether, and by 1914 40 per cent of male teachers, but only 8 per cent of women, were graduates. This rising status was to some extent reflected in salaries, but not as much as teachers might have hoped, and the gap between men's and women's salaries was hardly narrowed. Women were a third of the profession in 1870, two-thirds by the 1900s, but they remained concentrated in the lower ranks, partly because they usually left on marriage, partly because of the tradition of graduate teachers, which made school boards reluctant to appoint female heads. After 1872 public schools were normally mixed, and women teachers, like lady managers, might regret the disappearance of separate girls' schools.

While the old-style EIS activist was a university man who appreciated classical quotations in speeches and articles, the new one was a

---

[25] *EN* 11 Aug. 1888, 555.

TABLE 7.1. *Teachers in Public Schools, 1870–1914*

	Number	% women	Average salary (£) Men	Women
1870				
Certificated teachers	2,486	33	110	55
Pupil-teachers	3,227	41		
Total teachers	5,713			
Training-college students	503	59		
1880				
Certificated teachers	5,330	41	139	71
Pupil-teachers	4,582	62		
Stipendiary monitors	70			
Uncertificated assistants	554			
Total teachers	10,536			
Training-college students	892	63		
1899				
Principal teachers	3,535	35	171	79
Certificated assistants	6,841	72	110	68
Uncertificated assistants	2,371	93		
Pupil-teachers	4,111	81		
Total teachers	16,858			
Graduates	838	0		
Training-college students	1,112	72		
Queen's Students	65	42		
1914				
Certificated teachers	20,248	74		
Principals		42	192	98
Assistants		82	142	85
Uncertificated assistants	552	91		
Pupil-teachers	24	96		
Total teachers	20,824			
Graduates	3,350	36		
Training-college students	2,570	80		

Sources: PP 1871, XXII, *CCE Report*, pp. clxii, 339; PP 1881, XXXIV, *CCES Report, 1880–1*, PP. viii, xxi, xxiii, 82, 88–9, 91; PP 1900, XXIV, *CCES Report, 1899–1900*, 40–1, 409–12, 593, 643, 657; *SED Reports, 1914–15*, Statistics of Day Schools, 105–6, 108, Training of Teachers, 48.

product of the training colleges and marked by the distinctive ethos of the elementary school. Perhaps the most significant change was the rise of 'class' teaching. Before 1872 most qualified teachers could expect to run their own school, but changes in methods and the building of large urban schools led to the rise of the adult assistant, whose chances of promotion were limited; a majority were women, but male assistants were more likely to resent their status. By 1890 there was tension between the rank and file and the old leadership, and the assistant teachers were founding their own local associations. In 1896 these came together as the Scottish Assistant (later Class) Teachers' Association, with 3,232 members, of whom 1,952 were in Glasgow; the EIS itself had only 1,000 members in the city.[26] However, the EIS succeeded in absorbing their demands, and the Class Teachers' Association (or Federation, as it was also called) became a linked organization and a pressure group within the EIS rather than a rival. One result was that membership of the EIS expanded. There were only 1,232 members in 1876, and 1,808 in 1879, though the *Educational News* claimed a circulation of 3,000.[27] In the 1880s EIS membership climbed towards 3,000, and by the mid-1890s it was about 4,000. Thereafter it rose more rapidly, to 6,345 in 1903 (the year when the EIS first appointed a full-time secretary), over 8,000 in 1905, 13,000 in 1912, and 14,000 in 1914, about 70 per cent of those eligible. This expansion naturally meant a greater role for women. They were first admitted in the 1870s, but there were still only 200 female members in 1878.[28] As time passed they claimed more local and national offices, and a distinctive role in meetings and congresses. A Ladies' Committee was set up in the 1890s, but women members of the General Committee, a woman vice-president, and a woman EIS President (Elizabeth Fish) were not elected until 1899, 1905, and 1913 respectively.[29]

The class teachers were only one of a set of specialist or subject groups, several of which gave distinct opportunities to women: infant teachers, sewing mistresses, domestic science teachers all had local or national associations which began in the 1880s and 1890s. Other bodies like the Scottish Modern Languages Association (1896) and the Classical Association of Scotland (1902) were patronized by secondary

---

[26] *EN* 27 June 1896, 427–8.

[27] *EN* 27 Sept. 1879, 506. The *EN* is also the source for later figures.

[28] *EN* 26 Oct. 1878, 522.

[29] According to Belford, *Centenary Handbook*, 180, a woman was elected to the General Committee in 1874, but this was an isolated case.

teachers and university professors.[30] In the early years of the EIS, these men were also kept within the fold; professors filled the presidential chair on several occasions. But the interests of elementary and secondary teachers were increasingly divergent. An Association of Higher Class Public Schoolmasters founded in 1874 was joint organizer of the first New Year congresses, but became defunct in 1878. Its place was taken in 1886 by the Association of Teachers in the Secondary Schools of Scotland. Disagreements about educational policy made its relations with the EIS acrimonious, and from this time onwards the EIS was essentially an elementary teachers' organization, until the different grades were reunified in 1917.

4. POLITICS AND RELIGION

The EIS aspired to influence policy, but its relations with the SED were not close. Since there were no national salary scales, it had no negotiating role, and the political system did not encourage officials like Craik to deal directly with pressure groups. Parliament was still at the centre of decision-making, and the commonest form of political action was constituency pressure on MPs. By the 1890s the EIS had learnt to play this game, and was active at general elections in seeking pledges from candidates on issues like tenure and pensions. The most formal type of action, much used by school boards, was the deputation to London, which was introduced to the Secretary for Scotland by sympathetic MPs, and submitted its case in speeches backed up by written memoranda. This largely superseded the mass petitions and public meetings favoured before 1872. The centrality of Parliament meant that certain MPs—and peers like Balfour of Burleigh—acquired a reputation as educational specialists. Most of them were Liberals, partly because education, as an instrument of social progress, was seen as a distinctively Liberal cause, but also because, as in the 1850s and 1860s, the sharpest policy divisions were within the Liberal party.

The achievement of the 1872 Act was to take religion out of national educational politics, probably to the relief of most MPs. The two remaining religious issues, whose impact was local rather than national, were religious instruction and the position of Catholic and Episcopalian

---

[30] See special issue of *EN* on teachers' organizations, 21 Oct. 1910.

schools. Under the 1872 Act, existing denominational schools continued to receive state aid, and new ones could qualify for annual grants if a demand for them was shown to exist. In practice, this meant that the SED authorized Catholic schools wherever there was a significant Catholic community. But it was much more difficult for Episcopalians to prove such a need: they did not form cohesive communities, many of the pupils in their schools were not from Episcopalian families, and school boards were likely to object to a rival school which threatened their own finances. At Ardchattan in Argyll, the school board maintained a protest for several years in the 1890s, resigning *en masse* and being re-elected several times, after the SED had rather unwisely authorized a small Episcopalian school. The number of these schools remained around 70 in the 1880s and 1890s, but had fallen to 53 by 1918 (see Table IV in Appendix 1).

Catholic schools, on the other hand, grew from 65 to 226. They retained a solid working-class constituency in the industrial and mining areas, and Italian and Polish immigration brought in a new clientele. By 1914 Catholic schools held about an eighth of all Scottish pupils, but the proportion was a fifth in Glasgow, and a third or more in Coatbridge, Motherwell, and other Lanarkshire strongholds. Since there were no building grants for denominational schools after 1872, maintaining this separate system demanded many sacrifices from the Catholic community. Without wealthy benefactors, much of the capital cost fell on contributions and collections by the faithful. But contrary to the impression given in some heroic accounts, the state's annual grants covered most of the running costs, and were increased in 1897 as a by-product of legislation introduced to help English voluntary schools. Like board schools, Catholic schools were regulated by the Code, and on the secular side of education had little to distinguish them. The teaching body was increasingly laicized, but Catholic teachers remained underpaid and underqualified compared with those employed by school boards, and there was a heavy reliance on pupil-teachers; not until 1894 was a training college, for women only, opened in Glasgow by the Sisters of Notre Dame.

The denominational schools remained apart from the national system. Catholic and Episcopal teachers had their own organizations, and if any of them joined the EIS they made no impact on its proceedings. As long as religious instruction was part of a teacher's duties, non-Presbyterians were unlikely to be found in board schools: the Episcopalians complained that their training-college graduates had to go to

England to find jobs,[31] and it was taken for granted that most school boards would not employ Catholics. It was rare for Catholic priests (who ran their schools with little lay participation) to appear at general educational meetings, and their presence as elected members of school boards was not always welcome. Boards sometimes contained ranting Protestant ministers who specialized in insulting Catholics, and there were laymen of the same kind, like the Free Church industrialist William Kidston at Glasgow, who was praised for his 'stout-hearted Protestantism' at a meeting in 1879 which called for Catholics to be banned from membership of school boards.[32] The west of Scotland, especially towns like Coatbridge and Motherwell, was the stronghold of sectarianism. Hostility between Catholic and Protestant pupils was a familiar part of street life: in 1878, a priest at Motherwell complained that children

were in the habit of insulting him when passing the schools by shouting, 'To hell with the Pope,' 'Holy water,' &c. He had been recently insulted opposite one of the schools when in company of clerical friends; the children gathering round them as if they were perambulating showmen, and hooting in the hearing of the teacher and of Her Majesty's Inspector.[33]

In 1879 this priest, Dr Glancy, got himself elected to the school board, where he could do something to prevent such scenes. But sectarianism was still alive at Motherwell in 1912, when the board dismissed a teacher who had become a Catholic convert, a case which attracted national attention.

The 1872 Act left school boards free to determine their own form of religious instruction, and the old battles were refought in the early board elections. On one side 'use and wont'—the Bible and the Shorter Catechism—were backed by the Church of Scotland, the Free Church, and many United Presbyterians, and formed a rallying-point for urban Conservatism.[34] On the other, outright secularism was rare, though at Aberdeen the philosopher Alexander Bain, disciple of Comte and John Stuart Mill, won an isolated seat.[35] But there was a modified secularism based on simple Bible reading without any dogmatic commentary, as enforced by law in English board schools, and recommended by a

[31] PP 1888, XLI, *Third Report of the Committee Appointed to Inquire into Certain Questions Relating to Education in Scotland*, 21–2.
[32] *EN* 22 Nov. 1879, 605–6.   [33] *EN* 7 Dec. 1878, 602.
[34] I. G. C. Hutchison, *A Political History of Scotland, 1832–1924: Parties, Elections and Issues* (Edinburgh, 1986), 120–5.
[35] A. Bain, *Autobiography* (London, 1904), 315.

Scottish National Education League formed for the 1873 elections.[36] Its proponents argued that neutral religious instruction combined with the conscience clause would obviate the need for denominational schools, though this argument was never likely to convince Catholics, who claimed with some justice that the public system in Scotland was essentially Presbyterian. A survey in 1874 found that out of 2,452 schools, 78 (run by seventeen school boards) taught the Bible without the Shorter Catechism, and 218 (forty-two boards) excluded both.[37] Aberdeen excluded the Shorter Catechism as part of a compromise between Presbyterians and Episcopalians, and adopted the curriculum of the London school board. At Dundee, the Catechism was taught in schools taken over from churches, but not in new ones.[38] But Edinburgh and Glasgow, the latter the least disposed of the big cities to religious liberalism, were both strongholds of use and wont, where religious instruction took up the first forty minutes of every school day.[39] In country parishes the presence of ministers on the boards kept the Catechism alive. In towns the issue flared up politically from time to time—'there were two things that filled our madhouses—whisky and the Shorter Catechism', declared a Leith member in 1891[40]—and in the 1890s secularism was taken up by the labour movement. The Catechism generally survived until 1918, though perhaps taught with decreasing conviction as liberal theology undermined the old certainties; an interdenominational committee tried to refurbish it in 1907 by devising a simplified version more suitable for children.

5. THE HIGHLAND QUESTION

Another issue which caught fire in the 1880s was the state of education in the highlands, particularly the Western Isles. The 1872 Act left champions of the Gaelic language dissatisfied, but more urgent was the financial state of some highland school boards. As before 1872, the system depended on local contributions (now in the form of rates) matching central ones, and it broke down where poverty was widespread. The act allowed some extra grants in highland counties, but

---

[36] Hutchison, *Political History*, 133, 140; Roxburgh, *School Board of Glasgow*, 16.
[37] *EN* 15 Jan. 1881, 45–7, based on D. Mackinnon (ed.), *School Board Directory and Educational Year-Book for 1874* (Edinburgh, 1874), which may be an unreliable guide.
[38] Bain, *Autobiography*, 315; *EN* 14 June 1879, 305; 16 Aug. 1879, 422.
[39] *EN* 17 Nov. 1877, 566 (Edinburgh); 24 Nov. 1888, 819 (Glasgow).
[40] *EN* 18 July 1891, 480.

these were inadequate for the extensive building programmes which were needed. Highland school boards often lacked the legacy of a sound parish school, and were forced by geography to provide many small schools. Those transferred by the churches, the SSPCK, or the Gaelic school societies were usually in poor shape and needed replacing. Building was expensive because of the rigid constructional standards of the SED, especially on islands where stone, timber, and skilled crafts-men had to be brought from the mainland.[41] In the Western Isles the long-established habit of remitting fees also weakened school board finances. The result was that, while the average school rate in the low-lands was 4*d*. or 5*d*. in the pound, some highland parishes were charg-ing 1*s*. 6*d*., 2*s*., or even more; the highest rates were in impoverished Lewis, where the impossibility of payment made the boards effectively bankrupt.[42] The problem merged into the more general grievances of crofters about poverty and the land question, which led in the 1880s to eruptions of violence and to the appointment of the Napier commission on crofting, which reported in 1884.

Alexander Nicolson, author of the Argyll report on the Hebrides, was a member of this commission, and probably wrote its educational sec-tion. Although twenty years had seen marked progress in the condition of buildings, the quality of teaching, and attendance, the heavy financial burdens were said to be turning the people against the benefits of edu-cation. The shortages of secondary education and of Gaelic-speaking teachers were also underlined. The Napier report was especially critical of the inflexible attitudes of the SED, and recommended a series of financial concessions to help the crofting counties.[43] The SED was stung by this criticism, and commissioned Craik (not yet Secretary) to pre-pare a special report on the highlands. Craik attacked the validity of the Napier commission's evidence, and blamed poor attendance on the 'apathy' of parents and the failure of school boards to enforce the compulsory laws. If they did this, and charged proper fees, their finan-cial problems would not have arisen. Craik was more sympathetic on the question of secondary education, and recommended special grants to attract graduate teachers to selected schools. These grants, along with limited encouragement for Gaelic, were incorporated into the

---

[41] For the problems in Orkney and Shetland, see special report in PP 1874, XX, *First Annual Report of the Board of Education for Scotland*, 94 ff.
[42] PP 1878, XXX, *Fifth Annual Report of the Board of Education for Scotland*, 501 ff.
[43] PP 1884, XXXII, *Report of Her Majesty's Commissioners of Inquiry into the Con-dition of the Crofters and Cottars in the Highlands and Islands of Scotland*, 66–81.

'Highland Minute' of 1885. There were also extra grants for general support, but these had to be earned through improved attendance.[44] This rather grudging response to highland grievances was incorporated into the Code, and the new grants became permanent. But boards continued to complain that they were 'the victims of a rigid and frigid imperial red-tapeism', and the EIS held special conferences on the question at Oban in 1887 and Portree in 1888.[45] The finances of school boards were further undermined by campaigns for non-payment of rates which were part of the continuing crofter protest, and in 1888 bankrupt boards had to be baled out by further special grants, in return for which they had to accept the tutelage of an inspector. Thirteen boards accepted these grants, which continued for some years.[46]

One problem of highland school boards was dominance by landlords and factors, who acted in a high-handed way impossible in the low-lands. On Lewis, for example, the 'chamberlain' or factor was chairman of all four school boards, and attempted to rescue their finances by adding fines to the rents of tenants whose children's poor attendance caused the loss of government grants.[47] Tension was exacerbated by the Free Church allegiance of most of the highland population. It existed in another form in Barra and South Uist, where the population was mostly Catholic but the school boards, dominated by the landowner, Lady Cathcart, refused to appoint Catholic teachers. The Napier commission's advice was that 'the remedy lies in the hands of the ratepayers at any ensuing election of the Boards', but the tenants feared reprisals if they provoked a contested election.[48] In 1888 the advice was taken, and both parishes elected a Catholic majority, though the Barra election was invalidated after legal action by Lady Cathcart.[49] Once the bitterness of these events died down, Catholic religious instruction was introduced, as the 1872 Act allowed, and was pointed to as an example of Scottish tolerance. But such tolerance had not been much in evidence in the highlands of the 1880s, when teachers could be dismissed by landlord-dominated boards for their political activities, as at Alness

[44] PP 1884–5, XXVI, *Report on Highland Schools by Henry Craik, Esq., LL.D.*; Minute of 30 Apr. 1885 in PP 1884–5, XXVI, *CCES Report, 1884–5*, 84–7.

[45] *EN* 30 Apr. 1887, 317; 10 Sept. 1887, 620–3; 11 Aug. 1888, 552–4.

[46] PP 1889, XXXII, *CCES Report, 1888–9*, 102–3; PP 1890, XXXI, *CCES Report, 1889–90*, pp. xvii–xviii.

[47] Hansard, 3rd series 270, 16 June 1882, 1402–3.

[48] PP 1884, XXXII, *Report into the Condition of the Crofters*, 71, and cf. appendix A, 97–101.

[49] *EN* 18 Feb. 1888, 119; 21 Apr. 1888, 281–2; 19 May 1888, 356; 17 Nov. 1888, 808.

in Easter Ross, or for the reverse reason when triumphant crofters themselves won an election, as at Rousay in Orkney;[50] on Barra, the first
action of the Catholic board was to sack the Protestant teacher.

6. CONTROVERSIES OVER SECONDARY EDUCATION

'Government has done a wise and noble work in organising the elementary education of the country for the benefit of the working classes, the
possessors of so much political power,' said a secondary schoolmaster
in 1876; 'but it still remains for it to organise the secondary education
for the sake of the classes immediately above them, their employers
and natural leaders.'[51] The view that the state had a duty to organize
middle-class education was general in Scotland, but not in England,
and had not prevailed in the 1872 Act, which transferred burgh schools
to school boards, but forbade expenditure on them from the rates. In
these circumstances, attention turned in both countries to using the
funds locked up in charitable endowments to provide a network of
secondary schools. In England there was an important Act of Parliament in 1869, which embarked on the reform of decayed grammar
schools. Scotland also had an Endowed Institutions Act in 1869, but
this was a limited affair. It did not create a body of commissioners like
the English act, and its powers expired after a few years; its only
significant result was the remodelling of the middle-class schools run
in Edinburgh by the Merchant Company. In 1872, Scottish critics were
pacified by setting up a commission of inquiry on endowed schools
headed by Sir Edward Colebrooke. This surveyed the endowments in
detail, and its final report in 1875 recommended further legislation.[52]
S. S. Laurie, who was secretary of the Colebrooke commission, founded
an Association for the Promotion of Secondary Education in Scotland
in 1876 to push for the implementation of the report. In 1878 there were
two Acts of Parliament, one easing the financial restrictions on higher
class schools, the other setting up a royal commission on endowments,
headed by Moncreiff, which had the power to draw up reform schemes,
though only with the consent of the endowed bodies themselves. This

[50] *EN* 30 Oct. 1886, 772–3; 4 Dec. 1886, 864–5; 11 Dec. 1886, 877.
[51] *EN* 30 Dec. 1876, 666 (Alexander Martin, Aberdeen Grammar School).
[52] This and the following paragraphs summarize a story told in more detail in R. D.
Anderson, *Education and Opportunity in Victorian Scotland: Schools and Universities*
(Oxford, 1983), ch. 5.

was replaced in 1882 by a further commission under Balfour of Burleigh, which had compulsory powers, and which sat until the end of 1889, carrying out a complete overhaul of endowments at both elementary and secondary level. These reforms had some highly controversial features, and the Educational Endowments Act of 1882 was the most bitterly contested piece of legislation after 1872. The conflict was largely within the Liberal party, a division no longer based on religion, but related to the different electoral clienteles to which the party attempted to appeal. The creation of state-supported secondary schooling was a cause which had wide middle-class backing, especially perhaps among those who did not yet aspire to membership of the university-educated élite. But this might conflict with working-class interests, unless (as was not yet really the case) a direct path for the able could be created from the elementary to the secondary school. The invocation of John Knox and the traditions of the parish school by both sides gave the debate a special emotional resonance.

While the promotion of secondary schools was one issue, another was the maintenance of 'higher' teaching, especially of Latin, within ordinary schools. This had already been at stake in the Revised Code dispute, and was now taken up vigorously by the temporary Board of Education, which included the influential Principal of Edinburgh University, Alexander Grant. At this stage, there seemed no incompatibility between campaigning to preserve the parish tradition in rural schools and calling for a new network of urban secondary schools, and men like Grant and Laurie did both. But by the 1880s it was clear that two rival ideals were crystallizing, secondary and elementary. On the secondary side were spokesmen for university interests, secondary school teachers and their Association founded in 1886, and politicians, both Conservative like Balfour of Burleigh and from the orthodox or 'Gladstonian' wing of the Liberal party like Colebrooke and C. S. Parker. They saw school reform as a way of raising academic standards in the universities, through a higher school leaving age and a university entrance examination. If this programme was carried out, boys educated in rural schools would no longer have direct access to the universities, and true secondary education would be concentrated in the towns. On the other side were those who argued that the road to the universities and the professions should remain open to all by retaining higher subjects in as many schools as possible, and preferably within each parish as tradition prescribed. The parochial tradition was not just a survival to be cherished, but a blueprint for future development. This view, supported chiefly by the EIS and its mouthpiece the *Educational News*, but also by politicians on the Radical wing of Liberalism, saw the different types of education as 'organically' linked, while the secondary education party wanted a 'graded' system in which only selected children from elementary schools would be admitted to secondary schools. Thus it became impossible to separate the discussion of middle-class education from wider questions of democracy and opportunity, whose ideological and practical implications will be explored further in Chapter 10.

Some aspects of endowments reform were uncontroversial, and in Scotland, unlike England, the process was not complicated by religious disputes. In the case of endowments for elementary schools, the principle adopted was that since school boards now had a statutory responsibility for all children, it was inappropriate for charities to run their own schools. Schools were either closed down or transferred to the boards, and the money tied up in the endowments was used for scholarships, grants for school improvement, and other ancillary purposes. The SSPCK, for example, gave up its remaining schools, and was transformed into the Highlands and Islands Educational Trust, and in most towns the smaller endowments were combined into a similar trust. Endowments without their own schools, like the Dick bequest, were less affected. A second and more controversial principle was that since school boards had rating powers, charitable funds should not be allowed to 'relieve the rates' by supporting free education. Free education itself was frowned on by orthodox Liberals as a form of indiscriminate charity which 'pauperized' its recipients, but their critics claimed that endowments should retain their original purpose of helping the poor. Controversy reached its highest pitch over a third feature, the reorganization of large foundations to form modern secondary schools, including the abolition of the residential system in hospitals. The new schools were inevitably designed for the middle class, and the endowment funds were used to provide a limited number of scholarships awarded competitively on principles of merit. Critics claimed that this amounted to 'spoliation' of the poor, and the confiscation of working-class rights by the middle classes; scholarships, while in theory awarded by merit, would in practice go to those who had the right background of family ambition and culture. The most bitterly fought case was George Heriot's in Edinburgh, where the transformation of a free residential hospital for the working class into a fee-paying day-school was finally imposed in 1885. It did not help that the Heriot's outdoor schools, which were also free, were simultaneously handed over to the school board. The founder of these schools in the 1830s, the veteran Radical Duncan McLaren, was an MP until 1881, and continued to champion free education. In Glasgow, the closing of charity schools and the diversion of their funds into two educational trusts was similarly condemned by James Caldwell, who became an MP in 1886. The defence of free education and of the alleged rights of the poor thus became a talisman of Radical Liberalism.

A further irritant was the development by Glasgow and Govan school boards of 'higher grade' schools, which taught advanced subjects for higher fees. These were designed partly to give opportunities to able children completing elementary education, but also to serve middle-class families who could not afford the more traditional schools, including 'higher class' schools like Glasgow High School which were now under school board control, or who did not seek full classical education. In the eyes of Caldwell, and other MPs who sat for Glasgow working-class constituencies like Charles Cameron and G. O. Trevelyan, this was using rates paid by the hard-pressed working man to subsidize those who should be paying economic fees. These men were hostile even to the modest expenditure on higher class schools allowed by the 1878 Act.[53] Disputes over secondary education were referred to the Parker committee, originally set up to discuss teacher training; it included Craik, who was now developing a policy within the SED which gave priority to raising academic standards. The symbol of this was the school Leaving Certificate introduced in 1888, based on classics and mathematics, and open only to endowed and higher class schools. For as the Balfour commission worked its way through local schemes, it too insisted that reformed secondary schools should have a university orientation. Endowed and higher class schools came to be seen as a single group, but one more sharply separated than before from elementary schools and their higher grade extensions.

## 7. THE ABOLITION OF FEES, TECHNICAL EDUCATION, AND ADMINISTRATIVE AREAS	.

Free education had not been foreseen in the 1872 Act, and educationists supported fees because they brought in extra resources and encouraged

---

[53] Hansard, 3rd series 242, 9 Aug. 1878 (McLaren, Cameron).

regular attendance. Their abolition eventually came about because there was a political demand for it, to satisfy which the parties began to outbid each other, and which can be related to the extension of the franchise in 1884.[54] Free education had originally been a demand confined to radicals and working men's representatives. It was voiced in Parliament in 1877 by McLaren, citing the Heriot's schools as a model. In 1878 an association to campaign for it was formed at Greenock. In 1880 McLaren, Cameron, and others introduced a private members' bill, and when this was resubmitted in 1881 it provoked considerable debate. Reactions were generally hostile; the EIS, for example, thought the abolition of fee income would lead to cuts in teachers' salaries. These bills would have given permissive powers to school boards, but no extra funds, and free education was not politically practicable without a new source of revenue to supplement the rates, and to compensate denominational schools for their loss of income.[55]

The issue then slumbered until revived at the level of high politics by the radical leader Joseph Chamberlain. In 1885 he made free education part of the 'unauthorized programme' which sought to push the Liberal party to the left and to appeal to the new electorate. Gladstone reluctantly accepted this, but his return to power in 1886 was followed by the split in the Liberal party over Irish home rule and the installation of Salisbury's Conservative government. It was under the Conservative banner, therefore, that free education was introduced: since the state of public opinion seemed to make it inevitable, they were anxious for a settlement which would give favourable terms to the voluntary schools, especially in England. Free education, observed the president of the EIS, 'from being the dream of a few, and the faith of perhaps fewer, has suddenly assumed portentous dimensions, divided political parties into rival factions, estranged personal friends, and . . . been discussed with bitterness and animosity'.[56] But the more it was discussed, the more it seemed to appeal to Scottish opinion. By 1888 it had become 'a good electoral card' in school board elections.[57] It was not on the agenda of the Parker committee which reported in that year, but Parker was later to claim that it

---

[54] For the general politics of the issue, see G. Sutherland, *Policy-Making in Elementary Education, 1870–1895* (Oxford, 1973), 163–90, 283–309.

[55] Hansard, 3rd series 235, 12 July 1877, 1219–20; *EN* 28 Dec. 1878, 643; 21 Aug. 1880, 479, 484; 20 Nov. 1880, 694–5; 22 Jan. 1881, 73; 28 May 1881, 340–1.

[56] *EN* 2 Jan. 1886, 7 (D. Ross).   [57] *EN* 31 Mar. 1888, 232.

took its origin from popular demand in Scotland, rendered irresistible by the new franchise. . . . Scotch electors, seeing plainly how much as parents they had to gain from it, declared in favour of the new policy, and left politicians to invent reasons for the change. . . . On both sides of the House, almost at the same moment, it was discovered that Scotch electoral opinion demanded free education.[58]

The mechanism which allowed this, and some other important changes, was a series of laws on local government finance, which avoided unpopular increases in local rates by allocating certain nationally collected taxes to local purposes. Scotland received its 'equivalent' under these laws, but did not have to use the money in the same way as England. It was pressure from MPs, notably W. A. Hunter of Aberdeen, which ensured that money from probate duties which became available in 1889 was used to make education free. The 'probate grant', and subsequent allocations of the same kind, were incorporated by Craik into the Code. Free education was introduced in the compulsory Standards (I to V) in 1890, for all pupils between 5 and 14 in 1891, for all between 3 and 15 in 1894. For most Scottish children, 1890 was the effective date, a year earlier than in England. The fee grant was also payable to the denominational schools, and these too became free. School boards were allowed to retain fees in higher grade schools, though this was controversial: it was opposed by Cameron and Caldwell, who argued that

free education must be free all round; all classes of the community must stand on an equal footing in all schools. . . . the schools in Scotland, at the time of the Reformation, were established on the principle of perfect social equality, which was continued down to 1872, when the Act was passed.[59]

When G. O. Trevelyan was Scottish Secretary between 1892 and 1895, he tried to act against these fee-paying schools. But they survived, and one effect of the abolition of fees was to underline the distinction between elementary and secondary or quasi-secondary education.

The legislation which made free education possible also created elected county councils, in 1889, and provided new grants for technical education. As will be shown in Chapter 11, concern for technical and scientific education built up during the 1870s and 1880s. A Technical Schools (Scotland) Act of 1887 authorized school boards to provide such schools, but provided no extra money. At that time, there were still no elected

[58] *EN* 24 May 1890, 345.
[59] Hansard, 3rd series 338, 22 July 1889, 1012 (Caldwell).

authorities above the parish or burgh level, which also hampered the expansion of secondary education, as burgh school boards were unwilling to subsidize schools which served a wide rural area. The creation of county councils seemed to open the way to larger educational units, and the introduction of county committees for 'intermediate' education in Wales in 1889 was a model which attracted many in Scotland. In 1890, further changes in local government finance provided funds to be used for technical education, and these were allocated not to school boards, but to county and burgh councils. This was known officially as the Residue Grant, unofficially as 'whisky money', since it came from duties on drink. In 1891, education was made free in England; there was an 'equivalent' sum for Scotland, but since fees had already been abolished this was available for other purposes, and pressure from Scottish MPs, influenced by the recommendations of the Parker committee, ensured that most of it went to secondary schools. This was the Equivalent Grant, and it proved politically controversial. Craik wished to use it to build up the higher class and endowed schools, hitherto starved of public money, while the free education party—Cameron, Caldwell, and Trevelyan—were against any sort of subsidy to the middle classes. Most Liberal MPs thought the money should be widely spread to encourage secondary education in higher grade and rural schools. The compromise achieved in 1892, after the Liberals returned to power, was that most of the grant was handed over to county Secondary Education Committees, which had joint membership from local authorities and school boards. Glasgow, Edinburgh, Aberdeen, Dundee, Govan, and Leith had their own committees. The grants were based on population, and the committees had a good deal of freedom to draw up their own schemes.[60] This settlement, by spreading state funds among the different types of school, paved the way for a reconciliation of the elementary and secondary ideals of development, and the divisions which were so acute in the 1880s began to disappear.

However, there was now an extremely confused administrative situation, with four sources from which secondary and technical education (often seen at this time as two aspects of the same need) might draw funds: the SED, via the Code; the Department of Science and Art; the 'whisky money' administered by local authorities; and the secondary education committees. The use of the whisky money was especially

---

[60] For the detailed politics of this question, see Anderson, *Education and Opportunity*, 210–15.

criticized: several county councils developed coherent schemes of technical education, but the burghs, many of which were very small, either used the money to reduce rates instead of spending it (as the law allowed), or dissipated it in small sums. Craik tried to counteract this by encouraging local authorities and secondary education committees to pool their funds in common schemes, and the Scottish Association for the Promotion of Technical and Secondary Education, a body founded in 1893 which attracted a wide array of politicians and educationists, spent most of its energy campaigning for greater co-ordination and for the unification of authorities. Developments in England gave a fresh impetus in 1895, when the Bryce commission recommended the creation of a new ministry of education, incorporating the DSA. This took place in 1899 with the creation of the Board of Education, and was followed in 1902 by the abolition of school boards and the transfer of education to county and county borough councils. This reform of local administration did not happen in Scotland, though developments since 1889 seemed to point in the same direction. But in 1898 the DSA's Scottish work was transferred to the SED, and this allowed Craik to embark on a new policy of unified development. The political story will be taken up in Chapter 12, after various aspects of the system created in and after 1872 have been explored in more detail.

8

Making Citizens

NATIONAL educational systems based on compulsory attendance were to be found in all advanced countries in the late nineteenth century. The importance attached to them arose from the consolidation of the nation-state, the introduction of political democracy with its demand for loyal citizens, and the desire for peaceful integration of the new urban masses created by industrialization. This chapter will look at some of the ideological justifications for popular education put forward in Scotland in this period, and at their practical manifestations in the school curriculum and in the social tasks which the school was increasingly expected to perform. Most of these ideas were expressed in a 'British' context, and perhaps the most common general theme was an awareness of Britain's international position, and the need to use education to strengthen the economy and to exploit the country's human resources. It was generally accepted that to provide education was now the duty of the state; in return citizens had a duty of loyalty, which it was one of the functions of the school to instil. The religious arguments about morality and social control prevalent before 1872 gave way to more secular ones in which notions of efficiency, national strength, and citizenship provided the rhetorical commonplaces.

Historians of Europe in this period have spoken of 'social imperialism' as a strategy by which governments offered prosperity and social protection to workers in return for loyalty to a centralized, expansionist state and its governing élites. In the case of Britain, they have identified a 'national efficiency' movement which was especially strong after the shock caused by Britain's difficulties in the Boer War of 1899–1902, and which was stimulated by the growing strength of Germany, seen both as a model to be imitated and as a potential rival for economic and political supremacy.[1] In the 'struggle for survival' posited by the social Darwinist vocabulary of the age, Britain's institutions needed to be overhauled and its sources of strength organized by the state. The

---

[1] See G. R. Searle, *The Quest for National Efficiency: A Study in British Politics and Political Thought, 1899–1914* (Oxford, 1971).

national efficiency movement was part of a reaction against classic *laissez-faire* liberalism of which imperialist and protectionist Tories, progressive 'new Liberals', and collectivist socialists each had their own versions. These historical interpretations, stressing the integrative or conservative purposes of educational reform, have tended to supersede older ones which saw it in terms of social progress and democratic idealism. They also lay the emphasis on political motivation and the conscious manipulation of policy by élites. A more structural approach would see education reflecting and reproducing the class and gender divisions of society through a diffuse process determined by a 'discourse' of accepted concepts which defined the limits within which alternatives could be discussed. However, these approaches should not be allowed to obscure the fact that actual changes in education depended on conventional political conflict and on the balance between rival ideals.

Ideas about the social function of education, and its role in regulating and disciplining an industrial society, embraced a variety of concerns. One was the acuteness of social problems in the big cities, as the industrial and urban working class became a majority of the nation. From the 1880s, as socialism and trade-unionism became significant forces, the problems of urban poverty, slum housing, crime, public health, unemployment, and casual labour came to the forefront of discussion. Once the whole population was passing through the public school, it was natural to see education as an instrument of social reform and welfare. This was often linked with ideas about 'physical deterioration' and racial degeneration, given a scientific aura both by social Darwinism and by the new prestige of medicine. The Scottish cities, notably Glasgow and Dundee, provided ample evidence of these problems, and as in the days of Chalmers education was seen as a key to their solution.

The need to act on working-class youth was further related to the concept of 'adolescence', popularized in the book of that title published by the American psychologist Stanley Hall in 1904. As Harry Hendrick has shown, the way of thinking which it represented can be traced back to the 1880s. Compulsory education gave the state some influence over the values of even the poorest children, but they left school all too soon, and if the benefits of education were not to be lost its moral and socializing effects must somehow be prolonged. There was a particularly dangerous period between leaving school and getting a permanent job, since many employers did not take on children under 14, or for some craft apprenticeships 16. The casual employment of youths in dead-end work was blamed for long-term unemployment; it was thought to undermine regular habits of work, and was blamed for 'loafing', hooliganism (the subject of a moral panic in these years), and other adolescent evils. There were therefore calls to raise the school leaving age, and to organize evening or 'continuation' classes, perhaps with compulsory attendance. But adolescents might also be reached through sport, youth work, or uniformed movements. The expansion of such initiatives was in some ways a new version of social control, reflecting 'the exercise of power and influence by the professional middle class and its circle, as they came into contact with working-class adolescents' and sought to reinforce the family, or if need be provide a substitute for it, as a source of social discipline.[2] By the early twentieth century it can also be seen as a response to the growth of working-class leisure, attempting to divert youthful attention away from such bugbears of schoolteachers and social moralists as professional football, comic papers, and the cinema.

The final theme is political integration and the exclusive loyalty now demanded by the nation-state. In many European states, most obviously Germany and Italy, the formation of a new nation gave the school a vital role in merging older regional identities into a new national consciousness and in creating political allegiances. But even in older centralized states like France, the school bore a heavy ideological burden in this period, as the place where young citizens learnt the political principles of the French Revolution, a 'civic' morality to replace religion, an approved version of the nation's history, and faith in science and progress.[3] The classic statement of the 'moral' role of education was made by Émile Durkheim in the 1900s. The function of the school was to create in the child attachment to a wider group. The three main groups were the family, the *patrie*, and humanity at large, but of these the fatherland, or state, now had primacy. 'The centre of gravity of moral life, which once resided in the family, is tending more and more to shift. The family becomes a secondary organism of the State.' 'Humanity' admittedly represented the highest moral ideals, but since there was as yet no supranational organism to which loyalty could be taught, the nation-state had to stand in for it. Thus it was to the *patrie* above

---

[2] H. Hendrick, *Images of Youth: Age, Class, and the Male Youth Problem, 1880–1920* (Oxford, 1990), 9.

[3] See E. Weber, *Peasants into Frenchmen: The Modernization of Rural France, 1870–1914* (London, 1977), 303–38.

all that the school should teach attachment, and this was the cause of 'the primordial importance of the role which is assumed today by the school in the moral formation of the country'.[4] For Durkheim, the French Republic stood for the supreme ethical values of liberty and justice. For the British, the Empire had a similar role as the bearer of progress and civilization, and it was particularly important to Scots as an organism which could subsume English and Scottish loyalties in a common, higher patriotism.

In Scotland one can identify three styles of educational discourse. One was the congratulatory mode. Every year there were more children in school, higher attendance, better-qualified teachers, a fuller and more flexible curriculum, wider educational opportunities. This mode naturally prevailed in the reports of the SED, which always contrasted current progress with the situation inherited in 1872, and were claiming by 1914 that the country's educational organization was virtually complete. A second mode of discourse judged current deficiencies, or justified desirable changes, by an appeal to Scotland's traditions of democracy, generally idealized in the form of the parish school. But a third rhetoric was that of efficiency and international competition, and these themes pervaded the public discussion of education long before 'national efficiency' was at its height. The 1872 Act itself, after all, reflected a new belief in the duties of the state, and the idea of efficiency was later applied to four fields of action. One was technical education, the subject of intensive discussion from the 1880s onwards, and one where the German example loomed especially large. Another was the need to link elementary and secondary education: if the intellectual resources of the population were to be fully exploited, talent must be sought out and scientifically selected. Equality of opportunity, a phrase invented in this period, provided a new way of thinking about a traditional Scottish ideal, and the historical development of Scottish schools meant that both the debate and the policies which flowed from it had a character unique to Scotland. These two themes will be taken up in Chapters 10 and 11. Two others will be discussed in the present chapter: the relation between education and social welfare, and the use of the school curriculum to create citizens. In order to make this comprehensible, this is also the chapter in which the general development of the curriculum after 1872 will be discussed.

---

[4] É. Durkheim, *L'Éducation morale* (new edn., Paris, 1963), 62–7.

1. EDUCATIONAL IDEOLOGY IN SCOTLAND

Durkheim's starting-point was the search for social solidarity in an age when religion was on the decline. Callum Brown has argued that we should not exaggerate the secularization of nineteenth-century Scotland, and it is true that the influence of the clergy kept religion to the fore in school boards, at least until the 1890s; a school attendance committee chastising a parent for neglecting to send a child to school could look very like a kirk session.[5] Within the schools, a religious atmosphere and Christian culture continued to prevail. Religious instruction occupied part of every day, and the teachers, trained in colleges still controlled by the churches, were almost all church attenders who took it for granted (unlike their French counterparts) that Christianity should be the basis of morality, and that every child should be familiar with the Bible, which was at the very least 'a compendium of practical ethics'.[6] Religious and ethical priorities were stressed in the books and essays of Laurie, which were standard fare in the training colleges. Teachers might be anticlerical in resenting the intrusion of clergymen and denominational rivalries in school affairs, but they were not anti-religious. The classroom continued to stress familiar virtues, and few would have quarrelled with the section on discipline in the Code which required that

all reasonable care is taken . . . to bring up the children in habits of punctuality, of good manners and language, of cleanliness and neatness, and also to impress upon the children the importance of cheerful obedience to duty, of consideration and respect for others, and of honour and truthfulness in word and act.[7]

Nevertheless, things had changed since the time when teachers worked under the direct authority of ministers, congregational committees, employers, or landowners. School board control meant that the moral aims of education had to be more formally and subtly defined. Moreover, religion was no longer a part of the curriculum financed and inspected by the state, and any attempts by the SED and its inspectors to define the purpose of popular education had to avoid explicit religious statements. Before 1872 it was possible to rely for the moralizing effects of schooling on ecclesiastical control, the character of the teacher, and the transforming powers of the Bible; afterwards, when attendance was

---

[5] C. G. Brown, *The Social History of Religion in Scotland since 1730* (London, 1987), 197–200.

[6] *EN* 4 Mar. 1882, 141.   [7] Cited from 1878 Code.

longer and more regular, and basic literacy ceased to be the over-whelming priority, attention could turn instead to the content of the secular curriculum.

In the 1870s, official justifications of education were often of a well-worn kind. The correlation between education and the decline of crime was still frequently asserted, as was its role in defusing social tensions by acting as a safety-valve for mobility. The 1872 Act, wrote one inspector, 'lays the foundation of higher intelligence in the lower orders, and must in time greatly diminish pauperism and crime, by elevating the sentiments and tastes of the people'.[8] Outside official circles, it was champions of technical education who were the first to use the vocabulary of efficiency. Lyon Playfair had declared in 1870 that 'the great object before us is to establish an efficient organisation of public intellect',[9] and a favourite theme was that Scotland, as a country without fertile natural resources, depended on the exploitation of its 'brain power'. In 1885, in a rectorial address at St Andrews, Lord Reay said that

the chief wealth of Scotland consists in the natural resources of Scottish brains. The development of brain-power on a wide scale is what a Scottish statesman has to look to. . . . Development of more brain-power in Scotland means increased national efficiency and less danger from democratic ignorance.[10]

Reay was a Scottish peer and an intimate of Lord Rosebery, the leading Scottish statesman, whose group of 'Liberal Imperialists' were to be champions of national efficiency in the 1900s.[11] They included the Scottish MP Richard Haldane, who was very active in educational affairs in England, and who was a particular admirer of Germany and its institutions. But belief in a strong state was not confined to Liberals. In many ways it came more naturally to Conservatives, with their belief in authority and national military strength. If they had opposed the extension of state action before 1872, that was because of their link with the Church of Scotland; afterwards the 'established' tradition in secularized form emphasized national unity and the formation of common ways of thinking, and both Balfour of Burleigh and Craik saw the expansion of state action in education as a natural and creative force.

---

[8] PP 1876, XXV, *CCES Report, 1875–6*, 132 (A. Dey).

[9] L. Playfair, *Subjects of Social Welfare* (London, 1889), 305.

[10] Quoted in R. D. Anderson, *Education and Opportunity in Victorian Scotland: Schools and Universities* (Oxford, 1983), 269.

[11] M. Fry, *Patronage and Principle: A Political History of Modern Scotland* (Aberdeen, 1987), 114.

Haldane was deeply influenced by the German philosophic idealism derived from Hegel, which stressed the 'ethical' role of the state and the way in which the citizen was bound to it by concepts of duty and service. By the 1900s, mainly through the influence of the philosopher T. H. Green at Oxford, these ideas had a strong presence in Scottish universities, where important chairs were held by men like Henry Jones (philosophy, Glasgow), Richard Lodge (history, Edinburgh), or H. J. C. Grierson (English, Aberdeen and Edinburgh). Grierson declared in 1895 that 'the welfare of the State was intimately bound up with the efficiency of its citizens in every calling they pursued', Jones in 1899 that 'the battle for existence amongst nations is becoming more and more a battle between ideas'.[12] The prevalence of this way of thinking in the 1900s is illustrated by Alexander Darroch, who succeeded Laurie in 1903 as professor of education at Edinburgh and Scotland's chief academic educationist. For Laurie, education was about developing the character and moral sense of the individual; he believed passionately that the primary school as much as the secondary should be a place of liberal and humanistic education, from which utilitarian concerns were excluded.[13] For Darroch, who entitled a collection of his papers *Education and the New Utilitarianism*, it was about preparing citizens for the service of the state. His book *The Children* of 1907 sought 'to emphasise that the aim of all education is to secure the social efficiency of the future members of the State, and that this involves an endeavour to secure the physical, the economic, and the ethical efficiency of the children of the nation'. This language, and admiration for a state on German lines which acted 'to develop the national capacities and to perfect the national life',[14] ran through Darroch's writing.

2. SCHOOLS AND SOCIAL WELFARE

By Darroch's time state action was being extended to the feeding and medical inspection of schoolchildren, and compulsory 'continuation' classes for school-leavers were much discussed. But social welfare activities in schools, and attempts to extend social discipline to

---

[12] *EN* 2 Nov. 1895, 738; 6 May 1899, 311. Cf. Hendrick, *Images of Youth*, 234 ff.

[13] See e.g. address of 1888 reprinted in S. S. Laurie, *The Training of Teachers and Methods of Instruction: Selected Papers* (Cambridge, 1901), 137–53.

[14] A. Darroch, *The Children: Some Educational Problems* (London, 1907), p. v; *Education and the New Utilitarianism, and other Educational Addresses* (London, 1914), 120.

adolescents, had been the subject of voluntary action for many years. Some of this went back before 1872, but the act stimulated it by diverting philanthropic funds and energies, particularly those of the churches, away from the simple provision of schools. Sunday schools, now devoted exclusively to religious education, were an obvious example. They reached their peak in the 1890s, and were part of the experience of most working-class children: in 1891 there were 487,365 children on the rolls, about 70 per cent of the number in elementary day-schools.[15] By the 1880s youth clubs, temperance and sporting organizations, and societies for the welfare of apprentices or young domestic servants were part of a network of institutions directed at adolescents. Not surprisingly, Glasgow was a particular breeding-ground, two notable results being the foundation of the Boys' Brigade in 1883 by the Free Churchman William Smith, and of Celtic Football Club in 1888 by the Marist Brother Wilfred, the latter designed originally to raise money for the feeding of poor Catholic schoolchildren.[16]

While these activities took place outside the school, within it particular emphasis was put on drill and physical education. According to one inspector in 1875,

State or imperial action is now becoming a larger factor with us; and in controlling the education of the country it finds a field to which no one can dispute its title in elevating the condition of the multitude, not merely through the spread of intelligence but also by direct culture of its moral sentiments, tastes, and habits.

Moral training was needed as an antidote to crime, intemperance, and the decline of the family. Military drill, he thought,

is a capital auxiliary to moral discipline, and on that ground alone should find a corner on the time-table of all large schools, and especially of those where the children are disorderly and barbarous by habit and instinct. . . . It is, I suppose, admitted that the physique of the working classes in this part [Renfrewshire] is degenerating, and that it is desirable to educate a nation vigorous in body as well as in mind.[17]

[15] C. G. Brown, 'The Sunday-School Movement in Scotland, 1780–1914', *SCHSR* 21 (1981–3), 23–4; cf. Brown, *Social History*, 85–6, and his 'Religion, Class and Church Growth' in W. H. Fraser and R. J. Morris (eds.), *People and Society in Scotland*, ii: *1830–1914* (Edinburgh, 1990), 326–31.

[16] See W. H. Fraser, 'Developments in Leisure', in Fraser and Morris, *People and Society*, 250–6. Cf. J. Springhall, B. Fraser, and M. Hoare, *Sure and Stedfast: A History of the Boys' Brigade, 1883 to 1983* (London, 1983), 28–45.

[17] PP 1876, XXV, *CCES Report, 1875–6*, 161, 163 (D. Ross).

Much was expected of drill, and it was promoted as an answer to intellectual 'over-pressure', which medical experts blamed for physical degeneration. Initially, military drill was favoured, and it was taught by ex-soldiers, who were often the school janitors. Its advocates claimed that it 'gave young lads a fine deportment and general bearing in their walk',[18] but there were also drawbacks. Some radicals on school boards attacked drill as a manifestation of militarism—'the creator of a warlike and barbarous spirit, utterly repugnant to the ideas of Mr. Cobden'— while others were alarmed by the colourful language of the drill ser-geants: it was 'objected to by both teachers and parents for reasons similar to a prejudice against parrots that had been at sea'.[19] Military drill was supplemented by 'musical drill', gymnastics, and eventually by team games as the fashion for these filtered down from middle-class schools. By the 1890s wide virtues were being claimed for physical training. According to the *Educational News*,

The habit of acting in concert, of strict obedience to the word of command, of deference to authority, of military precision, all contribute to the formation of a character, in which sense of duty, *esprit de corps*, respect for authority, and affection for, and loyalty to, school, are conspicuous. Surely it is reasonable to hope that pupils imbued with such a spirit will go out into the world well prepared to play their part as good citizens, looking upon the world as a big school, in which petty selfish interests must be subordinated to the general good, sympathising with the joys and sufferings of their fellow-men, and ac-tuated by that true independence which is the result of duty well done.[20]

In 1895 the Code made PT or drill compulsory, but ten years before that Edinburgh school board had taken a lead by fitting up a gymna-sium in every school, and having its pupil-teachers professionally trained.[21] In 1889 an Aberdeen solicitor and sports enthusiast, George Cruden, established a physical training college which acquired a near-monopoly in courses for teachers, until the Carnegie trust at Dunferm-line opened its full-time College of Hygiene and Physical Training in 1905. Swimming was also popular in the towns, usually in public baths, and there were inter-school swimming competitions in the 1890s in Edinburgh, Govan, and no doubt elsewhere. Similar competitions and leagues indicate that football was also played in many elementary

---

[18] *EN* 13 Nov. 1886, 812 (member of Motherwell school board).
[19] PP 1882, XXV, *CCES Report, 1881–2*, 156; PP 1899, XXVI, *CCES Report, 1898–9*, 488 (referring to 20 years before).
[20] *EN* 19 Mar. 1892, 197–8.
[21] *EN* 26 Jan. 1884, 77; 21 Feb. 1885, 132; 20 June 1885, 403–5.

schools, though this development was delayed both by the expense of acquiring fields, and by the teachers' suspicion of professional football as a mass entertainment.

Craik was a particular enthusiast for military drill; as an MP he was to support compulsory military training for boys. In 1900, after the outbreak of the Boer War, the SED issued a significant circular on physical exercise in schools. Such exercises, especially drill, were

pre-eminently useful in developing those habits of comradeship, of responsibility, and of individual resource, which are of supreme importance, not only to the nation as a whole, but to the individual pupil. Indirectly they bring the individual into contact with the principles which lie at the foundation of national defence, and they bring home to him his duties and responsibilities as a citizen of the Empire, while at the same time giving him an opportunity of strengthening and developing his physical powers, and rendering him more fit for his ordinary employment. Whatever form the military service of our country may hereafter assume, it is evident that the strength and security of the Empire as a whole, as well as that of every individual citizen, must depend upon the extent to which the moral elements of responsibility, duty, and readiness of judgment, along with the physical capacities, may be developed. . . . Attention to physical training becomes all the more urgent owing to the tendency of population to gather to the larger towns, where the opportunities for physical exercises are necessarily restricted.[22]

War recruiting revealed to an alarmed nation the poor physical state of the urban working class, and led in 1902 to a royal commission on physical training in Scotland, headed by Lord Mansfield, which preceded the better-known English committee on 'physical deterioration'. It included Craik himself, the president of the Boys' Brigade (J. Carfrae Alston), and an Aberdeen medical professor, Alexander Ogston, as well as several interested MPs. These included the Liberal Unionist Thomas Cochrane, who trailed his own views on 'physical education in relation to a democratic army' in advance of the report:

One of the blots in our educational system is that boys are practically freed from all restraining influences on reaching the age of 14. It cannot be denied that the next few years, from 14 up till 18 or 19, are the most critical in the lives of all as moulding the future of an individual; and any organisation that would . . . connect these years with the school life would have a far-reaching effect for good.

[22] PP 1900, XXIV, *CCES Report, 1899–1900*, 263.

For Cochrane the ideal organization would be a cadet corps for school-leavers.[23] The Mansfield commission looked at all levels of education, and its witnesses included a parade of secondary school rectors who were enthusiasts for team games, uniformed organizations, and military training.[24] Some inspectors, elementary headmasters, and school board members shared these enthusiasms, but Craik's circular had also revived opposition to militarism on school boards like Dundee and Glasgow, and his belief in military drill was not widely shared. The commission's report pointed to the inadequacy of physical training at the elementary level, and recommended its systematic development, including organized games. Military drill was not specifically recommended, though cadet corps and the Boys' Brigade were seen as valuable auxiliaries to the work of the school. The main significance of the report, however, was its revelations about the physical condition of Scottish city children. It commissioned reports on Edinburgh and Aberdeen, and these were followed up in the next few years by other official and unofficial inquiries.[25]

The 1903 report thus emphasized the case for medical inspection in schools, a cause which attracted all-party support, and turned the spotlight on environmental factors like housing and nutrition. At a time when concepts of social reform were under intense discussion, child welfare became accepted as a field where educational and social remedies had to be combined. The important Children Act of 1908, and other legislation of the period on juvenile employment, delinquency, cruelty to children, and mental and physical handicap, applied to both Scotland and England, and gave new responsibilities to school boards. Medical inspection of schoolchildren was embodied in a Scottish education bill of 1904, but this did not reach the statute-book. Powers to provide for crippled, epileptic, and 'defective' children were given in 1906, and boards began to appoint medical officers and inspect children even before the 1908 Education Act gave general powers of inspection—though not of treatment until the law was extended in 1913. Although the powers were permissive, there was strong pressure from the SED to appoint full-time medical and nursing staff, and by 1914 the

---

[23] *EN* 31 Jan. 1903, 87.

[24] R. Anderson, 'Secondary Schools and Scottish Society in the Nineteenth Century', *Past and Present*, 109 (1985), 199–201.

[25] I. Thomson, 'The Origins of Physical Education in State Schools', *SER* 10/2 (1978), 15–24; PP 1903, XXX, *Report of the Royal Commission on Physical Training (Scotland)*, i. 15–19, 35–6.

medical services developed by the larger boards extended to dental and ophthalmic clinics and a range of special schools, both for the handicapped and for specific conditions like tuberculosis or skin disease. One new idea of the time for delicate children was the 'open air' school, where the classroom was opened up to the elements; but its propagandists admitted that in Scotland 'climate had to be contended against', and Scottish experiments with this kill-or-cure treatment were cautious.[26] Its main champion was Mrs Leslie Mackenzie, a member of Edinburgh school board, whose husband was the medical member of the Local Government Board and the man whose evidence had done most to influence the Mansfield report. In 1912 Mackenzie prepared the first annual report on the medical inspection of schoolchildren, after which the SED acquired its own Medical Officer.

Medical inspection was relatively uncontroversial because it was an innovation where the state had no rivals. The same was not true of school meals, which were already part of a cluster of charitable activity centred around public schools, extending also to clothes, boots, and fresh-air holidays. Much of this work was originally intended to encourage regular attendance, as in the days of the ragged schools, but compassion was also stimulated by the greater visibility of ill-clad and half-starved children once schooling became compulsory, and by the growing view that the health and physique of the working classes was a matter of national concern. These activities were essentially a female preserve. Some of the early experiments with meals were in rural areas. In Aberdeenshire, Lady Aberdeen organized a scheme on the Haddo estates, and they were fairly widespread in the east of Scotland.[27] Describing a scheme at Farnell in Angus, an MP observed that 'the meal which was supplied to the scholars would, perhaps, appear to English Members something almost contemptible; but in Scotland their ideas on the subject were plainer and less ambitious, and they considered a bowl of soup not a bad dinner. The bowl of good soup was all that was given'—without even bread. The children paid a halfpenny a day and the older girls helped with the cooking.[28] The menu at Aberdeen in 1905 also fell short of the gastronomic standards of the House of Commons: 'The bill of fare is varied each day as follows:—Monday,

---

[26] *EN* 27 Nov. 1908, 1359.

[27] *EN* 15 Mar. 1884, 182; 24 Jan. 1885, 77; PP 1884–5, XXVI, *CCES Report, 1884–5*, 175–6.

[28] Hansard, 3rd series 283, 17 Aug. 1883, 1028 (J. A. Campbell); cf. *EN* 15 Nov. 1884, 754–5.

broth; Tuesday, fish soup; Wednesday, potato soup; Thursday, lentil soup; Friday, vegetable soup.'[29]

In the larger towns, 'penny dinners' were a well-established institution by the 1880s. At Glasgow, the Poor Children's Dinner Table Society went back to the 1860s; at Edinburgh, Flora Stevenson ran the Association for the Feeding and Clothing of Destitute Children; in Dundee, the poorest children were given free dinners, others penny tickets to be used in cafés. However, these schemes normally operated only between January and March, the cooking and eating facilities were makeshift, and while school boards co-operated closely with the charities and ladies' committees which raised the money, they were not allowed to support them out of their own funds. In the eyes of the *Educational News*, that would be 'too socialistic in its tendencies to be quite safe'.[30] The public provision of meals was indeed a demand of the labour movement, on school boards and nationally, and this made it controversial. Its opponents—who included both Craik and Flora Stevenson—argued that to depart from the voluntary principle would undermine parental responsibility, and it was not until 1908 that school boards acquired limited powers to provide clothing and school meals. At Edinburgh the board organized the service on a large scale with central kitchens and motor vans to distribute the food, but it still worked in co-operation with the existing charities; although the *Educational News* could declare by 1912 that 'the bogey of the loosening of the bonds of parental responsibility has been laid', the move from voluntary to collective action was very cautious.[31]

A further area of welfare, which remained in the voluntary sector, was the provision of day nurseries and kindergartens, partly to help working mothers, partly to rescue the children of the slums. Edinburgh pioneered the 'free kindergarten' in the 1900s, one of them maintained voluntarily by the students at the Training College, and the movement later spread to Glasgow. Even for three-year-olds, motives of national efficiency were invoked: '"You cannot breed an imperial race in the slums," says Earl Roberts. The falling birth-rate demands our care of every little child born to the State.'[32] The development of out-of-school 'play centres'—hailed as a 'patriotic work' and a means of training citizens—was also started in Edinburgh.[33] In 1917 the SED made a

---

[29] *EN* 11 Feb. 1905, 113.   [30] *EN* 7 Dec. 1889, 839.
[31] *EN* 5 Jan. 1912, 4.   [32] *EN* 25 Feb. 1910, 198.
[33] *EN* 9 Dec. 1910, 1286; 23 Dec. 1910, 1323.

grant allowing school boards to open play centres, and the Education Act of 1918 included nursery education for the first time among the duties of education authorities.

3. THE ELEMENTARY CURRICULUM

The content of the curriculum was determined, with limited scope for local variation, by the ever-changing annual Code. The temporary Board of Education had a hand in drafting the first Scottish Code of 1873, and some concessions were made to Scottish conditions.[34] But payment by results, suspended since 1864, was now put into operation. The subjects taught fell into three main categories. The three Rs were taught according to the six Standards, corresponding approximately to ages 7 to 12, and here payment depended directly on the examination of individual children at the inspector's annual visit. The Code also included history and geography in the three top Standards. Second, there were subjects which were taught to most children, but outside the framework of the Standards: religious instruction, needlework for girls, music (which usually meant singing), and drawing, financed for most of the period before 1898 by the Department of Science and Art rather than the SED. Third, there were 'specific subjects' for older children, which went beyond the standard curriculum, and where the grants again depended on individual performance.

Specific subjects had a particular significance in Scotland because the board schools included many former parish, sessional, or burgh schools which had taught advanced subjects. If this teaching was fitted into the specific subject mould, it could be supported by government grants. Each specific subject had a three-year programme, and although they could be started in Standard IV, they were also suitable for older children who stayed on after Standard VI. Specific subjects were among the points of dissension between the SED and the Board of Education. The latter demanded a four-year syllabus based on the 'university subjects'—Latin, Greek, and mathematics—along with English literature, French, and German; or failing that, wanted these subjects distinguished by higher grants. It accused the SED of neglecting Section 67 of the 1872 Act, which required it to maintain the standards of the old parish schools. The SED argued in response that specific subjects provided

[34] PP 1874, XX, *First Annual Report of the Board of Education for Scotland*, 75 ff.

adequately for 'higher' education where it was needed, but that teachers should not be diverted by the cultivation of star pupils away from giving sound elementary education. The SED refused to give a privileged place to university subjects, and insisted on introducing domestic economy for girls and a range of elementary sciences: physical geography, mechanics, chemistry, 'animal physiology', light and heat, magnetism and electricity, and botany. This made a total of fourteen. Critics continued to complain that the same grant could be earned for factual subjects crammed from textbooks as for more testing ones like Latin or mathematics, and even inspectors' reports were sceptical about their educational value. In practice, the specific subjects usually chosen were those which teachers felt equipped to cope with. In 1880, for example, the most popular subjects were English literature (33,910 candidates examined), domestic economy (22,256), physical geography (12,871), Latin (5,293), animal physiology (5,209), French (2,608), mathematics (2,388), and magnetism and electricity (1,112); the numbers for the other science subjects, and for Greek and German, were very small. These choices represented 50,881 individual pupils, but only 2,578 reached the third year.[35] At a time when there were over 400,000 children in the schools, specific subjects were a relatively minor part of school work, although numbers increased every year, and were proportionately higher than in England.

The Code was always widely criticized for its inflexibility, its encouragement of mechanical methods, its bias against the traditional higher subjects, and the strain placed on teachers when their reputation depended on a single day's examination performance. There was little change down to 1885, but from 1886 Craik introduced a series of changes which culminated in 1890 in the abolition of individual examination on the Standards. Although similar reforms were carried out in England at much the same time, Craik gained personal kudos for meeting the long-standing grievances of Scottish teachers, and his initiatives were all the more striking because they coincided with the abolition of fees.[36] Craik's policy was to allow more freedom and flexibility for teachers and inspectors, to remove some of the tension from annual inspections, and to shift to capitation grants based on attendance and a broad assessment of the quality and atmosphere of the school. Individual examination was retained in specific subjects, but Craik reduced

---

[35] PP 1881, XXXIV, *CCES Report, 1880–1*, 98–9.
[36] See e.g. *EN* 1 Mar. 1890, 153–4; Hansard, 3rd series 348, 7 Aug. 1890.

the list of these by transferring most of them to a new category of generally taught 'class subjects', of which schools were to select two or three. They included English literature, history, geography, and elementary science, which replaced the former range of specialized scientific topics. A reduced list of specific subjects, including the classical and modern languages, survived until 1899, when the Code was entirely recast, and the Standards themselves disappeared. Craik also moved away from the detailed prescription of curricula and encouraged schools to submit their own schemes related to local conditions; but the effects of this were limited, the habit of uniformity being now deeply ingrained, and teachers continued to think in terms of the Standards long after they had been officially abolished.

The original Code reflected the state of education before 1872, when the three Rs were the first priority and other subjects could be seen as marginal luxuries. But as attendance became more regular and prolonged, the standard curriculum could take on more specialized features. One aspect was the development of domestic subjects for girls to supplement the traditional concentration on needlework. The main innovation after 1872 was cookery, while 'domestic economy' as a specific subject added general household management; this was compulsory for girls who took any specific subject. In the 1890s laundrywork and dairying were added as grant-earning specialities, but even cookery lessons were slow to spread given the expense of equipping special classrooms. It was only after 1900 that domestic subjects really became established. They had a vocational purpose at a time when domestic service was the largest single outlet for girls leaving school, but also naturally reflected the 'separate spheres' view of women's role in society; working-class women, like middle-class ones, were expected to sustain the family by providing an attractive and comfortable home, and from an efficiency perspective women needed to be trained in hygiene and nutrition so that they could bring up a fit generation of young citizens. But as Helen Corr and Lindy Moore show in recent studies of this subject, the cause of domestic subjects, far from being imposed by male authority, was championed by middle-class feminists, who sought 'to secure an independent power base from men by stressing the special virtues which women could offer in public education and in the home'.[37] Domestic subjects were seen as a form of technical

---

[37] H. Corr, '"Home-Rule" in Scotland: The Teaching of Housework in Schools, 1872–1914', in J. Fewell and F. Paterson (eds.), *Girls in their Prime: Scottish Education Revisited* (Edinburgh, 1990), 48.

education, and required a new form of expert training run by women. Schools of cookery were founded privately in the 1870s in Edinburgh, Glasgow, and Dundee, with later additions at Aberdeen and Elgin. They supplied itinerant teachers for schools in their areas, and gave teaching qualifications which were recognized by the SED; later they developed into fully-fledged colleges of domestic science. But the introduction of domestic subjects into the curriculum met resistance from working-class parents, who thought that girls should learn them from their mothers, and resented the intrusion of the school into family affairs; Moore has also argued that in Scotland there was a strong tradition of academic education for girls, which made the educational world generally unreceptive to domestic training, and prevented it from being as successful as in England.[38]

It was true that domestic subjects diverted girls from more academic ones, particularly at the specific subject level. But while girls studied cookery or needlework, non-academic subjects were also found to occupy the time of the boys. At different times military drill and swimming lessons filled this role, though physical exercise was soon extended to girls as well. There were also male vocational specialities like agriculture and navigation. But these were never widely popular, and the standard male equivalent of cookery came to be 'manual training', first encouraged in the 1890 Code, and promoted to a class subject in 1895. It had an ideology borrowed from the Swedish *Slöjd* movement, Anglicized to Sloyd. Manual or 'hand and eye' training was seen as an element in education running through from the kindergarten (also being promoted at this time) to the technical evening class, and giving a general training in practical ability distinct from the skills of particular trades. 'It should not only be a training for hand and eye,' said the SED in 1895, 'but should cultivate the intelligence of the children, and accustom them to observation, exactness, practical judgment, and forethought, and so develop perseverance and self-reliance.'[39] This owed much to John Struthers, then a senior inspector, who was president of the Sloyd Association of Scotland, also known as the Educational Handwork Association, founded in 1892. The Association had the support of various influential figures, held regular congresses, and

---

[38] L. Moore, 'Educating for the "Woman's Sphere": Domestic Training versus Intellectual Discipline', in E. Breitenbach and E. Gordon (eds.), *Out of Bounds: Women in Scottish Society, 1800–1945* (Edinburgh, 1992), 10–41.
[39] PP 1895, XXX, *CCES Report, 1894–5*, 163. Cf. 445 ff., special report by Struthers on Sloyd and Kindergarten Occupations.

published a periodical, *Hand and Eye*. It organized teachers' courses in Scotland, and sent teachers to be trained at the movement's bases in Sweden and Germany. For younger children manual training included clay modelling and 'cardboard work', but woodwork was the main subject taught, and this was for boys. By the 1900s, the larger school boards had specialized manual training staff holding certificates issued by the Sloyd Association. But while the SED made serious efforts to introduce practical training, attempts to make science a part of general education were less successful. When the specific subjects in science were abolished in 1886, elementary science became a class subject, but it was later downgraded, and regarded like manual training as a male equivalent of domestic science. The SED would not allow it to be taught without proper equipment, and in 1900 only forty-two schools took up this option.[40] In the general curriculum it was replaced by nature study, a 'softer' subject which could be regarded as suitable for girls, and which did not require much equipment beyond jamjars. One liberating aspect of nature study was that it encouraged excursions into the countryside, though in the cities 'nature' was interpreted widely to include visits to factories and gasworks.

In 1892 Craik consolidated his changes by introducing a Merit Certificate to stimulate and reward the completion of elementary education. It could be both a recommendation for employers, and a way of identifying the minority fitted for further study: 'a means of selecting, by a test in subjects which all alike have an opportunity of learning, those pupils for whose advantage it is that time should be spent in giving them higher education'.[41] The Merit Certificate originally required a minimum age of 13, passes in two class subjects and all three stages of one specific subject, and a certificate of 'character and conduct' from the teacher. This proved over-ambitious, and only about 2,000 certificates a year were awarded; in 1898 the age was reduced to 12, and the specific subject requirement cut out. The new certificate, redefined as 'the natural goal of every pupil in an Elementary School', was equivalent to completing Standard V.[42] Even so, by no means all children were able to reach this standard by the age of 12, or even 14. For those who did, and who completed Standard VI, elementary schools still offered no coherent advanced curriculum.

[40] PP 1900, XXIV, *Report of CCES, 1899–1900*, 425.
[41] PP 1890–1, XXX, *Report of CCES, 1890–1*, pp. xxx–xxxi.
[42] PP 1898, XXVIII, *Report of CCES, 1897–8*, pp. xxxv, 149.

The modest targets set for the Merit Certificate should warn us against exaggerating the cultural influence of elementary education. Since 1872, attendance had become more regular and the qualifications of the teaching staff had improved, but early leaving and large classes weakened the impact of education. Formal literacy was virtually complete by 1900, but experience later in the twentieth century suggests that the statistics concealed much functional illiteracy, and for most children a little history, geography, and English literature (especially poetry) were all that was added to the three Rs. By 1899 the list of basic subjects was complete, and attention turned (as we shall see in Chapter 10) to the curriculum of over-12s. The 1900s did see the publication of a series of SED memoranda on the teaching of individual subjects, which were not unduly prescriptive and encouraged teachers to experiment with their own methods. Much had changed since the days of payment by results. Yet, generally speaking, Scottish education remained classroom-bound, and was not noted for its openness to new ideas. It produced only one radical thinker, A. S. Neill, a son of the schoolhouse whose *A Dominie's Log* (1916) was based on his experience as a rural teacher, and attacked the aridity and stereotyping of the education which he was forced to dispense to the children of agricultural labourers. The book was serialized in the *Educational News*, and attracted considerable attention; Neill's child-centred views would probably not have got far in any state system, but it was significant that he had to go to England to put them into practice.

Whether or not Scotland's 'bookish' educational culture explains its pedagogic conservatism, one can also point to two practical reasons. First, the late age at which most children started school meant that kindergarten methods, from which 'progressive' ideas tended to flow upwards, had little impact in Scotland. The ideas of Pestalozzi and Froebel were still discussed in the late nineteenth century as radical innovations, and those of Maria Montessori in the 1900s seem to have made few converts. Second, Scottish educational policy was made by the SED, which was more resistant than the new Board of Education in England to the influence of educational experts. Neither the office of educational inquiries headed by Michael Sadler, an important channel for the introduction of ideas from abroad, nor the Consultative Committee set up in 1899 to represent the general educational world, had equivalents in Scotland. Craik and Struthers remained firmly in charge, and their mentality was essentially bureaucratic.

4. UNIONISM, HISTORY, AND GAELIC

Several recent analyses have emphasized that for the Scottish élite in the years before 1914 nationalism was not the opposite of unionism but fused with it.[43] The business and professional classes benefited from the union and from the British Empire, and secondary and higher education were remoulded to ensure that Scots won prizes in the wider British arena, but this did not detract from pride in Scotland's distinctive cultural inheritance. The national attitudes of the masses have been less studied, but their British loyalties were clearly in place well before 1872, and it would be implausible to claim that the state needed to use education to destroy local loyalties or to bring peasants out of rural isolation. What one can observe, however, is the way in which unionist attitudes were reflected in the curriculum, and especially in the teaching of history, the most 'political' subject, and one where Scottish susceptibilities were sometimes offended. The British Empire was especially important because it was seen as a kind of synthesis of English and Scottish histories. As one minister put it, during a discussion of history textbooks by Dunblane school board,

> the present Union, rather than former differences, ought to be its main subject of instruction to the youth of our land. . . . our main object of historical teaching is to make enlightened and loyal citizens, not of Scotland or of England of the past, but of the British Empire of to-day.[44]

Much the same view emerged from a history of modern Scotland published by Craik in 1901—not a school textbook, but perhaps aimed at teachers—and from Craik's view of those 'epochs where education really was instrumental in working national regeneration'. One such was

> the development of the Scottish parish school in the middle of the eighteenth century, when Scotland was seeking a place in the sun for herself, determined to find a place amongst the greater nations, developing from being merely a poor country with hardly any commerce, and living under a burden of poverty,

---

[43] Fry, *Patronage and Principle*, 109–18; D. McCrone, *Understanding Scotland: The Sociology of a Stateless Nation* (London, 1992), 126–33; R. J. Morris, 'Victorian Values in Scotland and England', in T. C. Smout (ed.), *Victorian Values: A Joint Symposium of the Royal Society of Edinburgh and the British Academy, December 1990* (Oxford, 1992), 38, 45.
[44] *EN* 25 Jan. 1907, 82 (A. Ritchie).

into one which was within a generation or two to take a prominent place in Colonial work, and in the development of our Empire generally.[45]

Education and the union together had given Scotland its chance to share in the progress of civilization.

One aspect of the relationship between Scotland and England was administrative, and there was controversy over the Board of Education and the transfer of the SED to the Secretary for Scotland. The EIS took the 'anti-Scottish' line on the latter, and its president declared that

we are one nation and one profession whether we are Scotchmen, Englishmen, or Irishmen, and the sooner distinctions which entail disqualifications and disadvantages are for ever effaced the sooner will this grand British Empire become united in heart and soul, and yet more great, glorious and free.[46]

But not all EIS members agreed, and the leadership of the Institute was criticized for taking such a strong line on the issue. In Parliament, most Liberals were for the Scottish solution, but Playfair joined Balfour of Burleigh in opposing it, arguing that 'no country can less afford than Scotland to narrow the ambition of its educated classes or to parochialize its institutions'.[47] Parochialism and sentimentality were always the main charges against those who argued for a distinctive Scottish identity, along with the brisk historical view put by the *Educational News* that 'until Scotland was united to England it was one of the poorest and most wretched countries in Europe. Since the Union it has flourished, and become rich and prosperous.'[48] Such views were not imposed from London by the SED, or from Edinburgh by Anglicized university professors, but were to be found at the heart of Scottish educational culture.

When the 1873 Code was issued, the section on history was drawn up by the Board of Education, and expressed Scottish priorities. In Standard IV pupils were to study the outlines of Scottish history, from Bruce to 1603; in Standard V they looked at it from Bruce to 1707, with special attention to any events connected with their own district. Only in Standard VI was British history taught, from 1603 to 1820. There was a similar scheme for geography, which started with outlines of Scotland, focused on the locality in Standard V, and moved on to the British Isles and the rest of the world in Standard VI. After a few years,

---

[45] Hansard, 5th series 84, 18 July 1916, 922; cf. H. Craik, *A Century of Scottish History, from the Days before the '45 to those within Living Memory* (Edinburgh, 1901), ii. 443–50.

[46] *EN* 3 Jan. 1885, 9 (J. Macarthur).

[47] Hansard, 3rd series 300, 3 Aug. 1885, 923.   [48] *EN* 7 Nov. 1885, 740.

the history syllabus was modified: British history from 1603 to 1820 was now taught in Standard V, and studied in more detail, with local references, in Standard VI. But when history became a class subject in 1886, the Scottish and local emphases were abandoned. British history from 1603 to the present was to be studied chronologically in Standards IV to VI, and similar changes were made in geography. The earlier history of Scotland was pushed back into Standard III, where pupils would study 'leading facts in the lives of Bruce and Mary Queen of Scots'; one inspector suggested 'that the teacher . . . should give some slight sketch of the history that connects Robert the Bruce with Queen Mary, so that the pupils may not imagine they are father and daughter'.[49]

These changes no doubt reflect the take-over by Craik, but the inspectors' reports had already revealed a strong hostility to Scottish history. 'In Standard IV.', one remarked in 1878,

a wise and skilful instructor may possibly add some human interest to the ghastly line of battles, feuds, and violent deaths that form the salient points of Scottish history from the death of the Bruce to the Reformation, and may even give his pupils some conception of the social life of the time, but in the hands of the great majority of teachers the history of this period can be little else than a matter of burdensome and profitless rote. From a moral stand point, too, one must question the value of a school history that lands a child in the midst of loose laws and looser passions, and unquestionably helps . . . to maintain the sentimental Scotch antipathy to England.[50]

Scottish history was commonly dismissed as a squalid chronicle of violence, of 'barren events in which we trace little development or progress among the people'.[51] It had few civic lessons to teach, and was all too liable to sectarian bias: in the 1880s Episcopalians were protesting about the treatment of the seventeenth century in the textbooks used by Edinburgh school board.[52]

There was also the business point of view, expressed by the chairman of Govan school board in 1886: Scottish history and geography begat 'provincialism', but Britain was an imperial and commercial country, and children should be taught that they were citizens of a 'greater Britain' before they were English or Scots. Modern history should concentrate on the forces which have 'revolutionised the face

[49] PP 1888, XLI, *CCES Report, 1887–8*, 248 (W. Bathgate).
[50] PP 1878, XXXI, *CCES Report, 1877–8*, 141 (A. Barrie).
[51] PP 1878–9, XXV, *CCES Report, 1878–9*, 154 (A. Dey).
[52] *EN* 25 Nov. 1882, 760; 19 Jan. 1884, 61; 26 Jan. 1884, 70–1.

of Europe' since 1789; for older children, classical history was more useful than Scottish, for 'from Roman history we learn of national progress—of strength, order, and law. . . . From Greece we learn what should beautify our individual lives; from Rome we learn that which fits us to be better citizens, especially in relation to our duties to the State.'[53] When the Code was revised in 1890, the SED withdrew for a time from this controversial field: no curriculum was officially pre-scribed, and teachers were to devise their own. Most teachers probably continued to teach Scottish history as anecdotes about romantic indi-viduals for younger children, with only a token presence in the narra-tive of British history since 1603; that was certainly the approach used in the textbooks produced by the numerous educational publishers in Glasgow and Edinburgh who specialized in the Scottish school market. Elementary teachers were not specialists, and with both history and geography there was little incentive to go beyond the rote learning of facts and dates, in preparation for stereotyped examinations. In 1896, a revision of the Code which reduced the number of class subjects nor-mally taken from three to two led many schools to drop history alto-gether, but the subject was to revive after the recasting of the Code in 1899.

The attitudes of inspectors were even more vehement towards Gaelic. The 1873 Code, under pressure from the Board of Education, allowed Gaelic to be used in examining the Standards in order to test pupils' comprehension of English. This did not go very far, and certainly not far enough for those who were now trying to rescue the language and encourage bilingual teaching. The MP for Inverness, C. Fraser Mack-intosh, was an indefatigable campaigner, and was backed up by the Gaelic Society of Inverness, a scholarly body founded in 1871, and by the old Gaelic School Society in Edinburgh, which kept its own schools going because of dissatisfaction with the 1872 Act. Another prominent figure was the professor of Greek at Edinburgh University, John Stuart Blackie, who campaigned to raise funds for a chair of Celtic, efforts which bore fruit in 1882. This movement could be seen as part of a Celtic revival shared with Ireland and Wales, but the Scottish cam-paigners had the most difficult task, given a hostile educational tradi-tion and the dissociation of the language from Scottish national feeling; there was to be no Gaelic equivalent of the educational advantages gained for Welsh by the early twentieth century.

[53] *EN* 23 Jan. 1886, 67–9, and cf. 2 Jan. 1886, 13 (G. Crichton).

Most of the SED's inspectors, including the Gaelic speakers in the highland districts, regarded the revival campaign as the work of sentimentalists and outsiders—Scottish exiles in London, or non-highlanders like Blackie—who did not reflect the true feelings of highland people and school boards, and were more interested in preserving the highlands as a picturesque tourist reserve than in economic progress. 'I should regard the teaching of Gaelic in schools, in any shape or form, as a most serious misfortune' was the verdict of one inspector. According to another, highland patriotism would be more usefully employed in

gathering and conserving, ere it be too late, the antiquities, traditions, and disjointed fragments of the literature of the country, than in the effort to ignore the force of irresistible social laws through means which may retard the civilisation of the people. But though almost infinitely inferior to English, Gaelic may very usefully be employed by teachers in remote corners to explain their lessons to the children, just as Broad Scotch is employed in several parts of the country.[54]

The inspector most favourable to the Gaelic cause, William Jolly, was an Englishman who did not speak the language.

These expressions of 'cultural imperialism' (Durkacz) were thought tactless even at the time, and the SED could not ignore an issue which had reached Parliament.[55] In 1876 it sent a circular to highland school boards. Contrary to the claims that Gaelic agitation did not have local support, 65 out of 103 boards supported the Gaelic School Society's proposal that extra grants should be given for Gaelic teaching, and they identified 208 schools which would make use of them, in only one in six of which was Gaelic currently taught.[56] The SED responded by inserting footnotes in the 1878 Code allowing a teacher of Gaelic to be paid for out of grants. This was a significant concession. The Napier commission of 1883 included the new Edinburgh professor, Donald MacKinnon, and its report observed that Gaelic 'is entitled to something more than permissive recognition, and a place in a footnote along with drill and cookery'. The overriding aim was still defined as 'to

[54] PP 1878–9, XXV, *CCES Report, 1878–9*, 222 (D. Sime), 195 (D. Ross).
[55] V. E. Durkacz, *The Decline of the Celtic Languages: A Study of Linguistic and Cultural Conflict in Scotland, Wales and Ireland from the Reformation to the Twentieth Century* (Edinburgh, 1983), 204; cf. 117–18, 173–5, and C. W. J. Withers, *Gaelic in Scotland, 1698–1981: The Geographical History of a Language* (Edinburgh, 1984), 158–60, 242–4.
[56] *EN* 21 Apr. 1877, 194; 8 Mar. 1879, 142. See Parliamentary Return in PP 1877, LXVII.

enable every Highland child as soon as possible to speak, read, and write the English language correctly', but for this very reason they ought first to learn to read Gaelic. The report recommended that suitable teachers should be appointed in all schools in Gaelic-speaking areas, that inspectors should ensure that the language was used, and that it should become a specific subject. Craik's report in response agreed that 'the bilingual faculty is one which should not be thrown away as a means of cultivating the intelligence', and its tone was not unsympathetic, but it also stressed the hostility of many school boards and the practical difficulty of finding teachers.[57] Gaelic became a specific subject in 1886 (though in 1899 only 343 pupils were presented for examination[58]) and the issue of teacher supply was referred to the Parker committee, after which some measures were taken to encourage recruitment to the training colleges. But the SED set its face against any compulsion on school boards, and although campaigns for the language continued the only further concessions were its inclusion in the Leaving Certificate in 1904 and an extra grant for Gaelic-speaking teachers in 1906. There was more sympathy for Gaelic as an academic study than as a living language, and one chief inspector remarked in 1896 that Gaelic 'will be of much more value and interest when it is dead'.[59] Before 1918, the movement for cultural revival in the highlands took place largely without help from the public educational system.

The fundamental perception was that Gaelic, like Scottish history, reflected a parochial and backward-looking patriotism which stood in the way of wider loyalties. History, however, was to enjoy a revival because of its obvious relevance to citizenship. Another reason was the introduction of history in the university syllabus in the 1890s. The new departments took their professors from England, and the courses largely ignored Scotland, concentrating on the kind of constitutional and diplomatic history taught at Oxford. As Bruce Lenman puts it,

academic history was primarily the corporate worship of the origins and development of the contemporary parliamentary establishment at Westminster, which both the Scottish and English middle classes regarded as the supreme embodiment of their national, class and communal interests.[60]

---

[57] PP 1884, XXXII, *Report of Her Majesty's Commissioners of Inquiry into the Condition of the Crofters and Cottars in the Highlands and Islands of Scotland*, 77–81; PP 1884–5, XXVI, *Report on Highland Schools by Henry Craik, Esq., LL.D.*, 6.

[58] PP 1900, XXIV, *CCES Report, 1899–1900*, 13.

[59] PP 1896, XXIX, *CCES Report, 1895–6*, 400 (T. A. Stewart).

[60] B. P. Lenman, 'The Teaching of Scottish History in the Scottish Universities', *SHR* 52 (1973), 174.

University history did not have a direct influence on training elementary teachers, but did help to stimulate interest in the subject. EIS meetings often heard talks from history professors, notably Richard Lodge, who was at Glasgow and Edinburgh successively, and who had a strong interest in questions of citizenship and social reform. Moreover, there was a parallel movement for the serious study of Scottish history: Edinburgh acquired a chair of Scottish history in 1901, and the *Scottish Historical Review* was founded in 1903.

As early as the 1880s, school boards were complaining about the use of 'English' rather than 'British' in history textbooks, and in the 1900s this grievance was taken up by bodies like the Scottish Patriotic Association of Glasgow and the St Andrew Society of Edinburgh. Theirs was a limited form of nationalism, which demanded not so much the separate teaching of Scottish history, as a fair appreciation of the Scottish contribution to the union. As the Association's circular to school boards in 1906 put it, pupils should receive 'a just and honourable conception of the relation of Scotland and England, and would be enabled to understand the beginnings and making of the British Empire as it is to-day'.[61] The campaign was targeted at school boards and town councils, and had considerable success. It won over Edinburgh and Glasgow school boards and the Convention of Royal Burghs, and questions were soon being asked in Parliament.[62] The SED responded sympathetically to a deputation from the Convention, and publishers climbed on the bandwagon. John Cormack of Edinburgh pointed out that

my History Books are written precisely from the standpoint taken by the Convention, viz., the authentic Scottish standpoint. . . . My Histories were produced especially to promote the teaching of Scottish History in Schools. . . . They are written in stirring and vigorous language, and on every page they enforce the lessons of patriotism and endurance to which the narrative so eminently lends itself.[63]

In 1907 the SED reached history in its series of memoranda on teaching, and this document was notable both for stressing that history should not be taught as a collection of facts but for its moral and intellectual value, and for insisting that at all levels Scottish history

[61] *EN* 7 Dec. 1906, 955. Cf. D. Macrae, *Scottish History in our Schools: Urgent Need for Reform* (Glasgow, n.d. [*c*.1905]).

[62] Hansard, 4th series 123, 18 June 1903, 1369; *EN* 25 Mar. 1905, 232–3; 29 July 1905, 550–1; 12 Aug. 1905, 594–5; 16 Nov. 1906, 872.

[63] Advertisement in *EN* 2 Sept. 1905, 639.

should be fundamental to the curriculum. It recommended a 'concentric' method, moving out from Scottish to general history at each stage, and stressing Scotland's role in the Empire.[64] John Cormack was ready with 'Cormack's Caledonia Readers' embodying this approach, and other publishers followed suit, Oliver and Boyd commissioning textbooks from the leading academic specialists, H. W. Meikle and P. Hume Brown. Thus while complaints about the neglect of Scottish history continued—the Scottish Patriotic Association was active in the 1909 school board elections—the schools came to take it more seriously than is usually thought. An inspector spoke of 'that interest in our own history and literature which was at present advancing like the flowing tide', and there was talk of a 'Scottish Renaissance' in history.[65] In 1911 the Historical Association of Scotland was founded, and a chair of Scottish history and literature was established at Glasgow out of the proceeds of the 1911 International Exhibition, after a campaign headed by the aptly named editor of the *Glasgow Herald*, William Wallace. Scottish literature and the Scots language had also been the focus of patriotic campaigns, though less intensively than history, and the SED's memorandum on English, issued in 1907, had responded by stressing the value of teaching in the 'mother tongue', whether Scots or Gaelic.[66]

Yet the 1900s also saw the celebration of Empire Day in schools, and a growing cult of the Union Jack. Flags were exchanged with schools in other parts of the empire, and there were ceremonies like the 'Children's Day' at Edinburgh in 1908, a gathering of 1,500 schoolchildren where a flag was presented to each school by the Victoria League; Lord Rosebery was on hand with a speech on imperial unity and citizenship.[67] The *Educational News* was soon complaining that 'what between Boys' Brigades, Boy Scouts, Girl Guides, Navy Leagues, Union Jack Leagues, and other organisations, there is ground for fear that there is just a little too much "flag-wagging" business in our schools.'[68] But there was no suggestion that British and Scottish patriotism were incompatible. In 1914 the *News* published a special number to commemorate the 600th anniversary of Bannockburn. The lesson was the familiar one: Scots and English were once enemies, but are now

---

[64] PP 1908, XXVIII, *CCES Report, 1907–8*, 291–310.

[65] *EN* 31 Jan. 1908, 120; 24 July 1908, 831–2; 11 Dec. 1908, 1394. Cf. (especially on the Leaving Certificate) B. J. Elliott, 'Early Examination Reform in Scotland and the Crisis in History, 1888–1939', *JEAH* 24 (1992), 47–58.

[66] PP 1907, XXIII, *CCES Report, 1906–7*, 275–303, and cf. *EN* 12 Apr. 1907, 337–8.

[67] *EN* 28 Feb. 1908, 228–9.   [68] *EN* 26 Nov. 1909, 1248.

citizens of a great empire. The issue included a message to the boys and girls of Scotland from Rosebery:

Are we worthy of these men, of Bruce and his fellows? Do you children feel that you, too, might grow up to be heroes like them; to be ready, if necessary, to die for your country, your freedom, and your king; and if that chance do not come, as I hope it may not, to be heroes, as you may all be in your daily lives, winning little Bannockburns for yourselves over the forces of evil?[69]

The chance for heroism was to come all too soon, and the response to the outbreak of war suggested that the lessons of citizenship and loyalty had not been taught in vain.

[69] *EN* 19 June 1914, 574.

9

Schools and Schooling after 1872

In Chapters 4 and 5, variations in school provision, attendance, and literacy were used to illustrate the social dimensions of education. After 1872 this is a less fruitful exercise, as school boards extended their control and compulsory attendance was enforced. The process took some time, but as the memory of older customs of flexibility and intermittent attendance faded, and as the first generation of children subjected to compulsion themselves became parents, regular attendance passed into custom. The abolition of fees in 1890 was significant both for this and for finishing off most of the non-board schools which had managed to survive 1872. School boards now found themselves as the main providers of education in their areas, obliged to cater for a wide social range, and where formerly there had been independent schools charging different fees, there was now social differentiation within the public system, with consequences for the links between elementary and secondary education to be discussed in the next chapter.

1. SCHOOL BUILDING AND REORGANIZATION

The two main tasks of school boards were enforcing attendance and building schools, and the latter was the more urgent. The total number of schools declined as smaller ones were closed. As Chapter 4 showed, there were probably well over 5,000 schools in the 1860s, and the 1873 school board survey found 4,819. A first wave of closures took place as church schools were transferred or abandoned, and a second followed the reform of endowments and the abolition of fees. The number of board schools, which passed 2,000 in 1876 and 2,500 in 1884, did not reach 3,000 until 1910, and the total number of public schools (board plus denominational schools) stabilized before 1900 at just over 3,000 (not 80,000, as claimed by one patriotic historian),[1] then rose to

---

[1] N. Stone, *Europe Transformed, 1878–1919* (Glasgow, 1983), 32. For school numbers, see Table IV in Appendix 1.

3,370 in 1913. Vigorous school-building in the 1900s was due to sub-urban growth in the cities, the rapid development of the Fife and Stirlingshire coalfields, and the vitality of Catholic schools in the west.

While urban education was expanding, fewer schools were needed in the countryside. Rural depopulation was a long-established phenom-enon in the highlands and islands, and by the 1881 census it was be-ginning in the borders and south-west, and in some other rural counties like Perthshire and Banff. This reflected a shift from arable to pastoral agriculture as well as migration to the towns. Many remote or 'side' schools were no longer needed, and rural school boards were able to concentrate their efforts; 'there are few rural parishes', it was reported in 1879, 'in which two or more schools have not been swallowed up in one central school.'[2] Every rural board inherited a parish school, which could usually be adapted as the new 'public' school. In Langholm, for example, a typical small town, there had formerly been five schools: the parish school, a Free Church school, an infant school maintained by a wealthy individual, a private school for young ladies, and a dame school. The school board acquired the Free Church school by transfer and bought the infant school. The three schools were then amalgamated into a single public school which employed all the existing teachers: it had a head, six certificated assistants, and eleven pupil-teachers; the dame school closed down, and its teacher became the board's sewing mis-tress. The 'separate system' of independent teachers was thus replaced by class teaching based on the Standards.[3]

In rural parishes, when walking was the only way for children to reach school, extra schools were usually needed, but former Free Church, General Assembly, or girls' schools could be retained to serve outlying districts; boards often saved money by replacing male teachers with women, a process encouraged by the SED, but opposed by parents who wanted to have the full range of subjects, including Latin, at their doorstep. In the remotest areas, side schools of the traditional type might still be found, and the Code permitted unqualified teachers and lower attendance rates where numbers were small. By the 1900s, with the arrival of motor transport, the SED hoped that side schools could be eliminated by the 'conveyance' of children, but progress was slow, and they remained necessary in the highlands. In 1912 there were fifty-seven in the Inverness district, of which some were like orthodox schools, others

[2] *EN* 1 Nov. 1879, 567.   [3] *EN* 19 Oct. 1878, 511–12.

meet either in an erection of corrugated iron specially built for the purpose, or in an improvised room of a vacant dwelling or outhouse; and a third, and by far the least satisfactory class, is that where the pupils are taught at their own fireside. Here the teacher, who is usually a girl with qualifications not beyond the Merit Certificate, has, as a rule, to divide her time among several families living some distance apart.[4]

Urban school boards had no direct legacy of elementary schools, and were confronted with unexpectedly large building programmes. The Presbyterian churches were only too eager to give up their schools, and often simply closed them down at short notice, forcing the boards to use emergency accommodation to house the extra pupils. In other cases legal problems hampered the transfer, and even when existing buildings were taken over, most were cramped and old-fashioned and soon needed to be replaced. Thus according to the reports of the Board of Education, which supervised this process, only 147 of the 548 Free Church schools had been transferred by 1875; by the end of 1877, only 514 schools of all kinds had been transferred to school boards, whereas over 1,500 had closed.[5] In Glasgow, the school board's initial survey discovered several thousand children escaping school altogether, and there were plans to build thirty new schools to hold 22,000 children. Edinburgh and Dundee planned seven, Leith six, Govan and Paisley five, and so on. By the end of 1873, 1,685 applications for building grants, to provide 250,000 places, had been received by the SED.[6] But the initial estimates were soon overtaken: by 1891, for example, Govan had twenty schools providing over 21,000 places—seventeen newly built, two purchased, and only one transferred.[7]

The larger school boards had most of their children in newly-built schools within ten years of 1872, and the large schools built in the 1870s and 1880s became a feature of the urban landscape. Built on restricted sites amid the tenements, they usually rose to three or four

---

[4] *SED Reports, 1911–12*, Highland Division, 9. Cf. *SED Reports, 1914–15*, Northern and Highland Divisions, 26–7. (From 1908 the sections of the SED annual report were paginated separately. They were published together, though no longer as a Parliamentary Paper, under the title *Scotch Education Department* [later *Education (Scotland)*], *Reports, &c., Issued in* . . . They will be cited as in this footnote.)

[5] PP 1875, XXVI, *Second Annual Report of the Board of Education for Scotland*, pp. xi–xii; PP 1876, XXV, *3rd Report*, pp. v–vi; PP 1878, XXX, *5th Report*, 70.

[6] PP 1874, XX, *First Annual Report of the Board of Education for Scotland*, pp. xii, xx–xxi; PP 1875, XXVI, *2nd Report*, pp. ix–x; PP 1878, XXXI, *CCES Report, 1877–8*, p. viii. Cf. J. M. Roxburgh, *The School Board of Glasgow, 1873–1919* (London, 1971), 52–70.

[7] *EN* 28 Nov. 1891, 797.

storeys, and were designed to serve an extended neighbourhood. Schools with over 1,000 pupils were common, and those with over 2,000 by no means unknown. Camphill school in Paisley, with 2,500, had the dubious honour in the 1890s of being the largest in Scotland. Classes were correspondingly large. In the 1870s the Code allowed a staff–student ratio of sixty children per adult teacher with an additional forty for each pupil-teacher; later these limits were reduced to fifty and twenty-five, but since they were staffing averages for the whole school, actual classes were often bigger, being handled by a teacher and pupil-teacher together. At Edinburgh in 1895, there were 'girls struggling with classes of over a hundred with a single pupil teacher'.[8] The typical classroom was designed to hold at least eighty children, and some early board schools still consisted of a large schoolroom holding several groups, with one or more smaller classrooms attached. An inspector in 1887 condemned 'the huge room in which probably half-a-dozen teachers have to spend their energy in roaring each other down, and the pigmy class-room, where a standard has to be packed together like herrings in a barrel'.[9] This pattern was soon thought obsolete, as qualified assistants replaced pupil-teachers, and was followed first by the 'central hall' plan, with classrooms of equal size around a hall and glass partitions allowing the head to supervise the assistants, and later by more flexible corridor or pavilion plans. By the 1890s the most modern schools in the cities had rooms for art, needlework, cookery, science, and woodwork; there were halls which could be used for drill or exercise, and in some cases gymnasiums and swimming-pools. After the abolition of the pupil-teacher system in 1906, the SED sought to reduce the average class size to fifty, with a maximum of sixty. A regulation to this effect was issued in 1911, but the likely expense of rebuilding schools and recruiting new teachers caused an outcry from school boards and denominational schools, and this measure was suspended annually until it was overtaken by war.

2. SURVIVALS AND SOCIAL DIFFERENTIATION

Apart from Catholic and Episcopalian schools, school boards eventually established a virtual monopoly of elementary education, but other types of school lingered into the 1890s. Some church schools survived for a time because they were former sessional schools with a reputation

---

[8] *EN* 20 July 1895, 481. [9] PP 1887, XXXII, *CCES Report, 1886–7*, 225.

which justified higher fees, others were simply kept going until a respected teacher retired. Rural schools financed by landowners were
seldom maintained, but industrial employers were more reluctant to
hand over schools which were often part of the fabric of the works, and
gave them some control of community life. Works schools were particularly useful where half-time working was in force, and the Coats
firm of Paisley built an architecturally lavish one at Ferguslie as late as
1887. But the Truck Act of the same year, which gave parents a choice
of school where school fees were deducted from wages, the abolition
of fees, and the decline of half-time working made works and colliery
schools obsolete. Endowed schools also survived for a time, but with
few exceptions the commissions of 1878 and 1882 either closed them
or transferred them to school boards; this could be controversial, because at the time it meant a change from free to fee-paying education.
The Heriot's free schools, for example, passed to Edinburgh school
board in 1886 amid bitter opposition, and there was similar feeling in
Glasgow over the transfer of Alexander's School.[10] Controversy could
also arise where an endowment combined a secondary school with
elementary education for the whole parish, as at Madras College, St
Andrews or Dollar Academy: here the elementary pupils were ejected,
and the endowment became the monopoly of the middle classes.[11] In
most cases, however, schools were handed over amicably, retaining
their names as a token of the past. These handovers, and the diversion
of charitable funds to supporting the board schools, showed the strength
of the Scottish belief in public education and in the school boards as
community agencies.

This belief also worked against private schools. As we saw in Chapter 4, historians of English education have recently stressed their role
in working-class education. This continued after 1870, despite the hostile attitudes of school boards, until the abolition of fees made competition hopeless. In Scotland, the statistics suggested that private schools
had only a small share of the market before 1872, though direct evidence was limited. This evidence becomes more abundant with three
parliamentary returns of 1880, 1888, and 1897, which purported to list
every school in Scotland.[12] According to these surveys, which are not

[10] *EN* 7 Aug. 1886, 555.

[11] See R. D. Anderson, *Education and Opportunity in Victorian Scotland: Schools and
Universities* (Oxford, 1983), 187–8.

[12] See Appendix 1 for sources, and summary of totals in Table III. The 1880 return
showed the number of school places, but not actual attendance.

very reliable, there were 508 non-state elementary schools with 8 per cent of the school accommodation in 1880; they had declined to 351 with 4 per cent by 1888, when the share of actual attendance was 3.5 per cent; by 1897 there were only 188 schools and 9,000 pupils—1.5 per cent of the attendance. Study of the actual lists shows that many of these schools were endowed schools or reformatories and similar institutions, not private adventure schools. In Aberdeen in 1880, for example, there were twenty-five non-state schools, but eleven were public institutions; in Edinburgh, the thirty-one schools listed included the thirteen Heriot's schools. If half of the 508 schools in 1880 were private adventure or dame schools, they might have had 4 per cent of the working-class market, which seems compatible with their already declining share before 1872.

Under the 1872 Act parents had to send their children to a school 'recognized as efficient', and it was school boards which awarded recognition. By prosecuting parents who used unrecognized schools, they could drive them out of business, and the survival of private schools therefore depended partly on local policy. Glasgow seems to have been especially hostile. In 1880 William Mitchell, chairman of its attendance committee, proclaimed that the erection of the board's fine new schools

has had the effect . . . of stamping out of existence a large number of small, wretched, unhealthy so-called schools, of which, in Glasgow, we had many notable specimens. The genus is not quite extinct with us yet, but will soon be numbered among the barbarous relics of a bygone age.[13]

According to the school board, 144 schools in Glasgow closed down between 1873 and 1885, of which sixty-four were private; perhaps these included middle-class schools, for in another version of the figures there were forty-nine elementary private schools in 1873 with more than 6,000 children, reduced to fourteen with 1,000 pupils in 1883.

There were always schools cropping up here and there, one could not tell how—opened by discarded teachers in little schools and rooms; but the system had not taken very great root in the city, and wherever they had been able to point to a school where the education was actually inefficient, they had been able before very long to have that school shut.[14]

[13] *EN* 17 Jan. 1880, 45.
[14] PP 1884–5, XI, *Report from the Select Committee on School Board Elections (Voting)*, 271; *EN* 17 Mar. 1883, 180 (including quotation).

At Aberdeen, there was a similar decline of adventure school children, from 1,805 in 1873 to 550 in 1883.[15] Sometimes, however, a board might prefer to keep such schools going to relieve their building funds. At Fraserburgh, for example, the SED rejected the school board's argument in 1878 that private schools were adequate, and forced it to provide 600 new places; later in the year, the board took action against a dame school of the classic type, when it 'resolved not to recognise the school in Back Street, conducted by an old lady, as affording efficient education. It was stated there were 43 scholars in attendance, while the room was barely 14 feet square and 6½ feet high, and was crowded with pots, pans, and other utensils.' With unconscious (or perhaps deadpan) humour, the board went on to reject 'a proposal to connect cooking classes with the Board'.[16] In 1880 the school board at Coatbridge moved against a 'school' consisting of three children taught in an ironmonger's shop, but at Airdrie the sheriff refused to co-operate when the board tried to stamp out adventure schools through test prosecutions.[17]

In 1877, the inspector for south Lanarkshire thought that inefficient private schools had grown since 1872 as a way for parents to comply with the law,[18] and this was especially the case where schoolmasters' certificates were needed for the factory acts. The chief example was Dundee, the stronghold of the half-time system, where the school board was accused of complaisance towards employers and failing to act against private schools which handed out attendance certificates indiscriminately. The parliamentary returns seem to confirm this: in 1880 Dundee had more non-public schools than any other town in Scotland (forty-two, compared with thirty-nine in Glasgow). But by 1888 there were only fourteen non-public schools, and the private adventure ones had vanished. The law had been tightened up in 1883, and half-time pupils were concentrated either in works schools or in special schools built by the board itself; in 1886 there were seven half-time schools in Dundee, five connected with works and two run by the board.[19]

Before 1872 private schools had a niche because they provided either for the very poor, or for those willing to pay for social exclusivity. Towns had many small schools, clustered in no clear geographical pattern, and serving different layers of the working class defined by the fees paid. These were now replaced by large neighbourhood schools

---

[15] *EN* 24 Feb. 1883, 133.   [16] *EN* 20 July 1878, 350; 30 Nov. 1878, 588.
[17] *EN* 2 Oct. 1880, 581; 16 Oct. 1880, 622; 23 Oct. 1880, 628.
[18] PP 1877, XXXII, *CCES Report, 1876–7*, 162.
[19] PP 1886, XXVII, *CCES Report, 1885–6*, 232,

('territorial' schools in the phraseology of Chalmers), and this could create difficulties when the respectable working class were brought into contact with those who had formerly run wild in the streets, or been segregated in mission and adventure schools. 'If a score of filthy ragged waifs go in at one door of a school', said one inspector, 'probably twice as many children of respectable people will go out at the other.'[20] School boards were thus tempted to make special provision for the poorest, especially as parents might be unable to pay the standard fee; as before 1872, this was typically 3*d*. or 4*d*. a week. In 1876, the old Govan parish school was reopened as 'a lower grade school at a lower fee'; Ayr followed suit in 1878, and by 1884 both Edinburgh and Glasgow had schools for 'ragged' children which provided free meals.[21]

W. E. Marsden has shown how in England between 1870 and the 1890s urban school boards used differential fees to reflect social stratification, and the same was true of Scotland.[22] One of the arguments against the abolition of fees was that parents' freedom of choice would be lost if boards forced them to use the nearest school. The fact that schools had their own social character made school organization a sensitive matter, as Greenock found in 1887 when it reshuffled teachers following the take-over of the endowed Highlanders' Academy. The consequences included children's demonstrations, street violence, the opening of a private school by disgruntled parents, and a stormy board election. The outcome was that in 1888 Greenock had three grades of school, with fees beginning at 4*d*., 8*d*., and 1*s*.; the Highlanders' Academy was one of three schools in the top grade.[23] In Glasgow the social character of the district determined both the fees and the method of payment—weekly, monthly, or quarterly—and they ranged from a penny a week to 12*s*. 6*d*. a quarter. This system was defended as having 'arisen historically from the fact that in dealing with schools in different districts in the city they found traditional fees suited to the habits and resources of each district, and these were continued'.[24] When fees were abolished, this overt differentiation disappeared, but the marked

[20] PP 1874, XX, *CCES Report, 1873–4*, 35, and cf. 15.

[21] *EN* 16 Dec. 1876, 634; 5 Oct. 1878, 489; 19 Jan. 1884, 50, 57; 26 Jan. 1884, 77.

[22] W. E. Marsden, 'Social Stratification and Nineteenth-Century English Urban Education', in R. K. Goodenow and W. E. Marsden, *The City and Education in Four Nations* (Cambridge, 1992), 111–28.

[23] *EN* 12 Nov. 1887, 798–9; 10 Dec. 1887, 867–8; 19 May 1888, 356; 7 July 1888, 468.

[24] Roxburgh, *School Board of Glasgow*, 152; Hansard, 3rd series 338, 22 July 1889, 1015 (C. S. Parker).

social differences between residential areas in the bigger towns no doubt perpetuated it in another form. Moreover, the schools with higher fees formed the basis of 'higher grade' secondary education, which will be examined in the next chapter.

3. ENFORCING ATTENDANCE

Recent studies of the enforcement of attendance in England have tended to stress the imposition of alien patterns on working-class life, and the resistance of pupils and parents. These included waves of school strikes in 1889 and 1911, in which Scotland was involved.[25] But the only detailed Scottish study of compulsion is Roxburgh's of Glasgow, which takes the orthodox view of an enlightened school board struggling to enforce the law over the selfishness of parents and employers. Glasgow was undoubtedly committed to enforcing attendance, and used a range of methods to achieve it. It could not be divorced from the problem of destitute and neglected children, and in 1878 Glasgow secured a special act allowing 'day industrial schools' to which persistent truants could be committed, a measure not extended to the rest of Scotland until 1893.

Other school boards, dominated by employers or farmers, might be more sympathetic than Glasgow to the demand for child labour, and even when prosecutions were brought sheriffs and magistrates were not always willing to penalize parents. Full-time attendance until a fixed leaving age might suit the prosperous stratum of urban workers, but it was less convenient for rural families aware of the seasonal opportunities for children to make money, or for families living on the margin of poverty or dependent on casual work. As in other matters (notably the stress on the domestic role of women), educational policy was based on a model of the working-class family able to live on the father's wages and not requiring work from other members. To insist on a child giving up work might force a family onto the Poor Law, and school boards often accepted the parents' case, though they were probably more willing to allow girls to stay at home than to sanction evasion of the law by boys. Large families or those dependent on casual

---

[25] S. Humphries, *Hooligans or Rebels? An Oral History of Working-Class Childhood and Youth, 1889–1939* (Oxford, 1981), 90–120. Cf. C. M. Heward, 'Compulsion, Work and Family: A Case Study from Nineteenth-Century Birmingham', in Goodenow and Marsden, *City and Education*, 129–57.

work were also disadvantaged by the fee system. School boards were not allowed to give free education. Pauper children had their fees paid, and other parents could apply to the Poor Law authorities, but this carried a heavy stigma, and the numbers involved were always small: 26,938 pauper children and 9,317 others in 1880, about 6 per cent of the total on the roll.[26] The working poor, above the poverty level but unable to pay full fees, were caught in a poverty trap. Official statements always claimed that poverty was not a cause of non-attendance, but it could not be denied that attendance improved after fees were abolished.

The law prescribed attendance between 5 and 13—raised to 14 in 1883—but the reality was always different. For one thing, compulsory attendance at 5 was out of line with Scottish habits. According to the *Educational News* in 1878, it was 'not the custom in Scotland to send children to school until they are nearly six years of age; and School Boards need expect very little assistance from the Sheriffs in any attempt to send them sooner'.[27] School boards did not press the issue, nor did the SED; even in the 1900s, it was tacit policy in Glasgow not to enforce attendance until the age of 6, and it was said that less than half of 5-year-olds in the city were at school. There was a 'vague feeling among parents' that 6 was actually the legal age, and the more negligent waited until 7.[28] It made more sense to concentrate on enforcing regular attendance once children had started; besides, the earlier children started school, the earlier they were likely to leave, since until 1901 the law allowed them to take up full-time work once a specified standard had been reached. After the 1872 Act had been strengthened on this point in 1878, the SED fixed Standard V as the criterion for the 'labour certificate' (a colloquial rather than official term), and Standard III as the level at which children could leave for half-time work, corresponding roughly to ages 12 and 10; no child under 10 could be exempted. Practical difficulties arose in reconciling these exemptions with the factory acts, until the Education (Scotland) Act of 1883 embodied the SED's regulations in law, and raised the statutory leaving age to 14, as was already the case in England.[29] Under this act inspectors had no choice but to give certificates to qualified children, but in

---

[26] PP 1881, XXXIV, *CCES Report, 1880–1*, pp. xiii, 92.

[27] *EN* 9 Mar. 1878, 123.

[28] PP 1904, XXI, *CCES Report, 1903–4*, 247–8; *EN* 12 Feb. 1909, 151.

[29] For details of the difficulties, see PP 1883, XXVI, *CCES Report, 1882–3*, pp. xii ff., 38–69.

1901 the emphasis was reversed: exemptions had to be specially re-
quested if a child was to leave school before 14, and school boards had
the power to refuse them, or to impose conditions such as part-time
attendance at evening classes. The 1901 Act also raised the minimum
age of employment from 11 (as it had been since 1891 under the factory
acts) to 12.

In 1883 about 27,000 children were working as shop assistants or
errand-boys under half-time certificates, and another 8,394 in factories,
at least 4,500 of them in Dundee.[30] Half-time education under the factory acts was confined to the textile industry, but for some decades after
1872 it remained widespread in areas like the borders (wool), Kirkcaldy
(linoleum), and the Vale of Leven (dyeing and cotton-printing). It declined with the cotton industry itself in Glasgow, and disappeared in the
remaining cotton towns, including Paisley, as technical progress made
child labour obsolete.[31] But the jute employers of Dundee and neighbouring towns like Brechin and Arbroath maintained that they could
not do without child labour (mostly female), and strenuously opposed
the 1883 Act; their claim that two-thirds of their half-timers would have
to be dismissed if the rule on passing Standard III was enforced cast a
revealing light on the state of education in the city.[32] By 1900 nearly
all the half-timers in Scotland were in the Dundee district, and their
number was steadily declining, from 2,033 in 1902 to 269 in 1914, by
when there was only one half-time school left in the city.[33] This contrasted with England, where the system remained common in Lanca-
shire, but its lingering in Dundee contributed, along with notoriously
poor housing, to the city's reputation as an educational black spot.

As before 1872, while industrial work took children permanently
away from school, in the countryside the problem was more one of
irregular and seasonal attendance, and school boards dominated by
landlords and farmers were likely to be sympathetic to requests for
absence. The rigidity of the law conflicted with traditional habits of
reconciling school and work, and seemed unnecessary in communities
where literacy was long established. Though statistics to illustrate it are
hard to come by, the difference between winter and summer attendance
did not disappear at once. In Orkney, for example, where children were

[30] Hansard, 3rd series 276, 9 Mar. 1883, 1920–6, 1929–30.
[31] For Glasgow, see Roxburgh, *School Board of Glasgow*, 71–97.
[32] *EN* 10 Mar. 1883, 169.
[33] PP 1902, XXXIII, *CCES Report, 1901–2*, 749; *SED Reports, 1914–15*, Northern
and Highland Divisions, 22.

used for herding animals, an inspector in 1887 saw 'a survival of the old Scotch system of winter schooling'.[34] Other demands on child labour were the herring fishery, which was responsible for large seasonal migrations, and the tourist industry, which employed teenagers as beaters or golf caddies. On the other hand, the use of children at harvest time declined with the introduction of the mechanical reaper-binder. Formerly each village had taken its school holiday when the harvest was ripe, but now this was replaced by a standard holiday period starting in July. In the east of Scotland, children were still needed for the potato harvest in October or November, and it became normal either to allow special exemptions for this, or to split the vacation into two halves with a period of schooling between.[35] Agriculture remained labour-intensive, and the demand for child labour still existed. It was to increase during the First World War, but a study of rural childhood in the early twentieth century based on oral reminiscences suggests that children did normally stay at school until 14, and did not do much part-time paid labour before they left.[36] In the towns, far more casual work was available, and many schoolchildren ran errands or delivered milk and newspapers, work which was increasingly (though probably ineffectively) limited by law. But in 1914 only 8,828 children were given formal exemptions from school after the age of 12, and 5,607 of those were conditional on part-time or evening attendance; figures for previous years since 1901 were similar, and confirm that the leaving age of 14 was a reality.[37]

4. ATTENDANCE STATISTICS

Two sets of figures are available to illustrate the growth of schooling after 1872: the annual totals published by the SED for public schools, which exclude secondary and private pupils, and the periodic census reports, which cover all children, and perhaps err on the optimistic side. These are combined in Table 9.1, in a format comparable with that of Table 5.1, and showing the standard measure of pupils per thousand

---

[34] PP 1887, XXXII, *CCES Report, 1886–7*, 230.

[35] *EN* 22 July 1905, 535; 21 Oct. 1905, 781–2.

[36] L. Jamieson and C. Toynbee, *Country Bairns: Growing Up, 1900–1930* (Edinburgh, 1992).

[37] *SED Reports, 1914–15*, General Report, 54.

TABLE 9.1. *School Attendance, 1871–1911*

Year	Category	Total	Per 1,000 population
Pupils in public elementary schools			
1881	On roll	544,982	146
	Average attendance	409,966	
1891	On roll	677,948	168
	Average attendance	538,365	
1901	On roll	767,421	172
	Average attendance	636,374	
1911	On roll	845,055	178
	Average attendance	755,988	
Censuses: persons in receipt of education			
1871	Aged 0–15	552,020	164
	All ages	574,121	171
1881	Aged 0–15	689,466	185
	All ages	720,099	193
1891	Aged 0–15	760,417	189
	All ages	783,967	195
1901	Aged 0–15	849,703	190
	All ages	873,028	195

Sources: see Appendix 1.

population. In 1870 219,444 pupils were presented for examination in state-aided schools, and the average attendance was 203,522; by 1881 numbers had more than doubled, but this obviously reflected the school board take-over as well as the enforcement of attendance. However, the census figures suggest there was a large real increase in the 1870s. From the 1880s, growth was more gentle, but it continued to outpace the rising population; there are no census figures for education in 1911, but the abolition of exemptions in 1901 must have raised the participation rate still further. In 1913 attendance stopped growing for the first

TABLE 9.2. *School Attendance as Percentage of Age-Group, 1871–1901*

Age	1871		1881		1891		1901	
	B	G	B	G	B	G	B	G
3	2	2	3	3	2	2	1	1
4	9	9	12	11	13	12	10	10
5	52	48	51	48	58	56	64	62
6	76	73	82	80	88	87	95	95
7	87	84	93	91	95	94	100	99
8	91	89	95	94	96	96	100	100
9	92	89	96	95	97	97	100	100
10	90	88	96	95	96	96	100	100
11	84	83	95	94	95	95	100	99
12	70	72	90	90	86	87	97	98
13	41	40	65	67	59	63	82	85
14	23	22	32	34	30	32	33	37
Total 5–14	70		79		80		87	

Sources: see Appendix 1.

time since 1872, and fell off slightly in later years, suggesting that until the leaving age was raised again saturation point had been reached.[38]

The censuses also show school attendance by annual age-group, and Table 9.2 compares 1871 and later years. In discussing the figures for 1871, it was argued that in most areas nearly all children were attending school at some point, and that deficiencies in the national figures reflected problems in the industrial cities and in the highlands. A comparison of 1871 and 1881 shows the filling of these gaps, and again makes the point that the law on compulsion had real work to do. It made a comparatively small difference at the core ages of 8 and 9, but a significant one in bringing in older children; reluctance to start school at 5, on the other hand, was only slowly overcome. Compulsion also narrowed the gap between boys and girls: there was still a smaller proportion of girls attending in the middle of the age-range (concealed in the table by the rounding up of percentages), but this was evened out by their tendency to stay on longer. Thus in 1901, the overall percentage of 87 for the 5–14 age-group represented 86.8 per cent for boys and 87.4 per cent for girls. Regional differences were also evened out,

[38] For 1870, PP 1871, XXII, *CCE Report, 1870–1*, p. x; for the annual figures from 1872, see Table IV in Appendix 1.

TABLE 9.3. *School Attendance as Percentage of Higher Age-Groups, 1871–1911*

Age	1871		1901		1911	
	B	G	B	G	B	G
14	23	22	33	37	39	38
15	13	13	12	16	13	13
16	7	7	5	8	7	9
17	4	4	2	4	4	6

Sources: see Appendix 1.

and by 1901 were of no real significance; the north-east and the borders were still a percentage point or two ahead of other regions, but the highlands now matched the national average.

Scotland comes well out of international comparisons. One statistical compendium, which uses attendance in the 5–14 age-group as a standard measure, puts Scotland second only to France among advanced European countries: in 1910–11 the figures were France 85.8 per cent, Scotland 81.9, England and Wales 78.6, Ireland 78.3, Germany 71.9, Holland 70.3, and Switzerland 70.2, with Austria and the Scandinavian countries in the upper 60s.[39] But if Scottish school attendance until 14 was high, after that age it fell off very sharply, as shown in Table 9.3, based on the censuses. This table suggests that while elementary education expanded between 1871 and 1911, the length of élite schooling did not, despite radical changes in the quality and organization of secondary education. It is difficult to distinguish secondary from elementary attendance at a time when schools were defined by their social function rather than by stage, and when 14 was a common leaving age even for middle-class children: SED figures for state secondary schools in 1912 showed that they had 10,079 pupils aged 14, but only 2,012 aged 17.[40] Using Table 9.3, one can perhaps say that the 15 age-cohort, when some 13 per cent were at school, corresponded to the number getting some sort of secondary education, and to the middle class in a

[39] P. Flora (ed.), *State, Economy and Society in Western Europe, 1815–1975: A Data Handbook in Two Volumes*, i: *The Growth of Mass Democracies and Welfare States* (Frankfurt, 1983), 630. The age-group is the same as for Table 9.2, but the percentage is lower because Flora only counts children in public elementary schools, and because the censuses are always more generous than school-based figures.

[40] Anderson, *Education and Opportunity*, 248.

broad sense. But those getting an élite secondary education of the type familiar in other countries might be represented by the 17 age-cohort, of whom only about 4 per cent were at school—a figure in fact typical for European countries.[41] Another measure of complete secondary education is the Leaving Certificate, usually confined at this time to those aiming at higher education. On the eve of 1914, about 1,700 full certificates were awarded every year, equivalent to 1.8 per cent of the age-group. This fits in with university statistics: the total number of students was just under 8,000, which would correspond to some 2,000 entrants a year. About 23 per cent were women, probably as high as was practicable when few graduate occupations were open to them.[42] Even among men, the proportion of the age-group getting a university education can hardly have been more than 2 per cent, so that working-class children who achieved this ambition were not only a minority of a minority, but a tiny fraction of their own class. This needs to be borne in mind when discussing the issue, to which contemporaries attached such importance, of access from elementary schools to secondary and higher education.

[41] See also R. D. Anderson. 'Education and Society in Modern Scotland: A Comparative Perspective', *History of Education Quarterly*, 25 (1985), 459–81.
[42] Anderson, *Education and Opportunity*, 357.

10

The Secondary Connection

THE expansion of national systems of secondary and higher education was a general phenomenon between the middle of the nineteenth century and 1914, and has attracted rather more theoretical and comparative attention than elementary education.[1] One common theme is that as societies became industrialized their educational systems became more hierarchical and 'systematized', corresponding to the deepening of class divisions. Not only did élite and mass education develop in separate compartments, but within the secondary sector itself expansion was marked by 'segmentation', with new demand being diverted into cheaper and shorter forms of education. Institutionally, this might be expressed in the creation of a second layer of quasi-secondary schools alongside the traditional type; in terms of the curriculum, it meant concentrating on scientific or modern subjects, reserving the prestige of the classics for the social élite which had its eyes on the professions, the bureaucracy, and the universities. Social control was preserved through a stricter regulation of the channels of mobility, and some historians have argued that these were narrower by 1914 than under the less systematized arrangements of the early nineteenth century.

Another interpretative idea, inspired by the French sociologist Pierre Bourdieu, is that the function of the educational system was to reproduce the distribution of power within society, in terms of gender as well as class. This proved compatible with formal equality of opportunity because of the 'cultural capital' which middle-class children were able to bring to the educational process. The ideology of meritocracy, and the existence of a limited amount of social mobility for individuals, created a myth of equality which legitimized the reproduction of the existing social structure. Furet and Ozouf, for example, argue that in France the working class were won over to this ideology:

---

[1] See especially F. K. Ringer, *Education and Society in Modern Europe* (Bloomington, Ind., 1979) and D. K. Müller, F. Ringer, and B. Simon (eds.), *The Rise of the Modern Educational System: Structural Change and Social Reproduction, 1870–1920* (Cambridge, 1987).

we may readily grasp the connection between their thirst for education and the requisites of the liberal bourgeoisie: the religion of merit, the image of individual success within a framework of never-ending collective progress; . . . The poor child who succeeds, a central figure in the mythology of the 19th century school, could well, in the eyes of the bourgeoisie, have been the exception that justified the entire system, while for the working people it stood as a collective, quasi-religious, hope.[2]

Much of this makes sense in Scottish terms, and Houston uses these ideas in his critique of the democratic myth. But given the link between parish schools and universities, there could never be a hermetic seal between élite and mass sectors, and when the development of secondary education was discussed the preservation of opportunities for lads of parts was never far from Scottish minds. The argument here (already put forward elsewhere) is that the secondary system in place by 1900 was a relatively open and permeable one, growing in many cases from the top of elementary schools.[3] There was no real segmentation within secondary education, and the same liberal curriculum was taught in all schools; on the other hand, especially after 1903, a sharp distinction was drawn between this curriculum and that judged suitable for older children who stayed in elementary schools, where the onward connections were with evening classes and technical colleges. There was thus a form of segmentation determined by transfer from elementary to secondary schools. Opportunities for individual advancement were extended rather than restricted, but the accepted limits to this process remained narrow, and there was as yet little thought of organizing education in 'horizontal' stages related to age instead of vertical sectors related to class.

In England, the prestige of the public schools meant that their curriculum and values were imitated in the new state grammar schools, in a relationship analogous to that of the English civic universities with Oxford and Cambridge. The schools to which working-class children gained access through scholarships formed part of a second stratum of education at one remove from the real centres of power. In Scotland, this was much less the case. The burgh schools were modest institutions by the standards of élite education in other countries; they could

---

[2] F. Furet and J. Ozouf, *Reading and Writing: Literacy in France from Calvin to Jules Ferry* (Cambridge, 1982), 130.

[3] R. D. Anderson, *Education and Opportunity in Victorian Scotland: Schools and Universities* (Oxford, 1983), 162 ff. Cf. id., 'Education and Society in Modern Scotland: A Comparative Perspective', *History of Education Quarterly*, 25 (1985), 459–81.

not dictate the pattern, and being public institutions they were themselves remoulded as part of the new, more open system. The aims of Scottish education were defined by a university tradition which was popular rather than élitist, and by the parish school, now a myth from the past rather than a living reality. Reference to the parish schools and the democratic glories of Scottish education was constant, and although this was partly a mystification which discouraged Scots from taking a hard look at their own society, it was also a political force with its own creative power.

1. EDUCATION AND OPPORTUNITY

Between the 1860s and the 1890s both secondary schools and universities (the subject of major legislation in 1889) were remodelled in response to the growth of the middle classes and to the professionalization of middle-class occupations. The task of preparing for the universities, and for the many business occupations which took boys who left school at 14 or 15, had long been shared between burgh schools, parish schools, and the more select church or private schools in the towns. Boys could pass directly from parish schools to universities, but the idea of a systematic transfer of pupils to secondary schools hardly existed. After 1872, however, while school boards developed a homogeneous system of public elementary education, the trend of reform in middle-class education was to build up strong secondary schools with an academic curriculum oriented to the universities. The introduction of the Leaving Certificate in 1888 and the restriction of university entry to those who had reached this standard in 1892 marked the success of this policy, and by the end of the century it was difficult to reach the university except through a secondary school. The number of these was restricted as advanced education was squeezed out of elementary schools, and chances for working-class children came to depend on scholarships and on changing schools at the age of 12.

The form which these changes took was the result of a complex process of debate and political controversy, already outlined in Chapter 7. All agreed that opportunities for individuals needed to be maintained, but they disagreed on the method. The 'secondary' party thought that secondary education (or 'higher' education, as it was often called) should be concentrated in true secondary schools, staffed and equipped for the purpose, and soundly financed by charging adequate fees.

Promising children should be supported by scholarships, and transferred from elementary schools at an early age. In a favourite image of the time, selected individuals should climb the ladder of opportunity: the 'ladder from the gutter to the university' was the phrase invented by the scientist T. H. Huxley. The alternative view was that the elements of secondary education should be widely available to all, as in the parish schools; as late as the 1890s, it was being argued that a school teaching secondary subjects should be within walking distance of every child. There should be no rigid selection, and higher education should grow organically out of elementary subjects. It was admitted that distinct secondary schools were needed, but they should not be socially exclusive; they should charge low fees, or none at all, so that access did not depend only on scholarships, which were in any case likely to be exploited by middle-class families. The anti-secondary view was most clearly held by the EIS, which had the advantage of the *Educational News* to put its point of view. But politicians and practical educationists tended to come down on the secondary side. They accepted the value of the parish school tradition, but justified the 'grading' of schools and the selection of individuals as a modern interpretation of the principles of John Knox. This was the view of Playfair, a great exponent of Knoxian rhetoric, and of men like Craik, Laurie, C. S. Parker, or Balfour of Burleigh; it was to prevail in the reform of endowments, which stressed merit rather than poverty as the criterion for aid.

In the 1870s, as we have seen, the Board of Education criticized the SED's narrow definition of elementary education, and wanted to keep university preparation alive in ordinary schools through specific subjects, while the Colebrooke commission and the Association for the Promotion of Secondary Education sought the development of secondary schools. Promotion of secondary schools naturally encouraged the idea of a scholarship ladder. There had been some discussion of this by the Argyll commission, but it was then a minor theme. In the 1870s, it can be seen developing in the annual reports of the school inspector John Kerr. In 1872 he stressed that in Scotland even the sons of the poorest should have a stepping-stone to the university, and that it was in the state's own interest to help the clever few as well as the future 'hewers of wood and drawers of water'. He hoped that the 1872 Act would allow 'in each district or centre to be hereafter fixed, a type of school which is the link between the lower and higher education'. In 1875 he looked forward, though still seeing it as a distant prospect, to a time when it may be thought right in order to utilize the best brain of the country from all classes, to connect the primary with the higher class school by small bursaries offered for competition to the élite of the primary school, and so complete the chain, the last link of which is the university.

In 1878 he argued for supporting Latin through specific subject grants: classics

supplies the ladder by which the poor boy with more than average brains can rise to the social position corresponding to his natural ability. . . . If, therefore, it is desirable that the best brain of the country from whatever class should be utilised; that advancement in social position should be possible for all who are worthy of it; and if advancement in several important lines can be most easily attained through the university, it seems clear that as long as the university door remains what it is now [i.e. via Latin], a national system of education should furnish to those worthy, few though they be, the means of opening it.

By 1881, he saw the bursary ladder becoming a reality through endowments reform, so that 'the elementary school, the secondary school, and the university, will . . . so dovetail into each other' as to create a 'thoroughly national system of education, symmetrical and compact from foundation to apex, in which pupils of ability from whatever social class may, with creditable industry, rise to the level for which nature intended them'.[4]

The 'democratic' nature of these views should not be exaggerated. One of Kerr's arguments for encouraging social mobility was that it prevented talented men from becoming 'seditious demagogues' and 'political firebrands'. As another inspector put it, 'the communist of Paris or the republican of London becomes the clergyman, the doctor, the lawyer, or the schoolmaster of Scotland'. Laurie joined in, asking 'those who tremble before the secret and assured advance of communism, by what counter-theory can they hope to meet it and destroy it, save by the theory of individualism, which involves a free and open field for the intellect of those who have been born poor?'[5] Although the Paris Commune of 1871 and the stirrings of socialism gave a new edge to these arguments, their basic point would not have been out of place

[4] PP 1872, XXII, *CCE Report, 1871–2*, 93, 99–100; PP 1875, XXVI, *CCES Report, 1874–5*, 78–9; PP 1878, XXXI, *CCES Report, 1877–8*, 183; PP 1881, XXXIV, *CCES Report, 1880–1*, 134–5.
[5] PP 1872, XXII, *CCE Report, 1871–2*, 93; PP 1878–9, XXV, *CCES Report, 1878–9*, 166 (J. Macleod); S. S. Laurie, *The Training of Teachers, and Other Educational Papers* (London, 1882), 156 (written 1879). See also R. D. Anderson, 'In Search of the "Lad of Parts": the Mythical History of Scottish Education', *History Workshop*, 19 (1985), 82–104.

in the Old Statistical Account. But Kerr's talk of brainpower reflected a new idea of selective meritocracy inspired by efficiency thinking. 'Can a great empire like ours continue to subsist', asked Laurie in the passage just cited, 'if we do not lay under contribution all the best brains in this small, but imperial island? Assuredly not; for all the intellectual needs of the State, we require to draw forth the best intellects of the community.'

G. G. Ramsay, professor of Latin at Glasgow University, a leading figure in the secondary party and in the reform of endowments in Glasgow, put it this way in 1876:

Statesmen are beginning everywhere to recognise the fact that . . . one of the main factors, if not *the* main factor, in the continued prosperity of a nation, in these days of complex civilisation, is the disciplined intelligence of the great bulk of the community; and that if we permit ourselves to fall behind rival nations in this essential respect, we cannot hope to retain our place among them. . . . We cannot trust only to the intellect of our well-to-do classes; we cannot afford to allow humbly-born ability to take its chance of being able, by rare good fortune, to struggle out into usefulness and recognition; we must go to meet it, search it out wherever it is to be found, and, by a carefully organised system of graded education, placed within the reach of all such as are able to profit by it, do everything that is possible to swell the bulk and improve the quality of the national intelligence.

Twenty-six years later, in an address on 'Efficiency in Education' to the Classical Association of Scotland, Ramsay could proclaim that

the nation has at last been roused to the necessity, which many of us have been preaching all our lives as a matter of national concern, of training to the utmost the brain-power of the community, and of bringing within the reach of every capable mind, in every class, the benefits of a liberal education.[6]

In 1890 Haldane declared that he would 'take for his watchword and goal for the educational policy of this country, the maxim of equality of educational opportunity for rich and poor, for great and small alike'.[7] By the 1900s the phrase 'equality of opportunity' was in common use, expressing the idea of a scientific selection of merit. This was especially striking in Darroch, who saw education as a mechanism for directing talent to where it could best serve the state. It was the duty of the state to 'endeavour to equalize the opportunities to all capable of profiting by any form of secondary or higher education'—but also to

---

[6] *Fraser's Magazine*, NS 13 (1876), 596; *Classical Association of Scotland, Proceedings 1902–3*, 3.
[7] *EN* 30 Aug. 1890, 579 (speech at Auchterarder).

exclude those who were not, and to divert them to more suitable types of school. As part of this, Darroch believed strongly that girls' education should be directed towards their destiny as wives and mothers. He was critical of the concept of the ladder to the university because it distorted the system in an academic direction, and encouraged too many children to embark on an over-ambitious curriculum. This was also the view of Laurie, who caused something of a stir by saying that 'the gospel of "getting on" is after all a devil's gospel'.[8] For behind all these theories of social mobility and equality of opportunity was the assumption that only the 'very best brains of the poorest classes' (Laurie) or the 'picked boy' (Craik) might be expected to benefit.[9] Clever children needed to be identified and isolated from the mass, but even Playfair put the percentage which might benefit from secondary education at only 7 per cent. Looking back in 1926, Craik put it at 5 per cent, or 10 at the outside, and in Parliament in 1892 there were arguments for and against 4 per cent.[10]

Thus there is reason to say that the rhetoric of opportunity concealed and legitimized a very narrow concept of democracy, and there was certainly no shortage of such rhetoric. From the 1870s onwards, a romantic aura began to gather around the parish school, as memories of the reality receded and the 'old parochial' teachers died off. Knox was invoked on all sides, and there was much reference to 'lads of pregnant parts', though it was not until 1894 that the phrase 'lad of parts' (or 'lad o' pairts' in reinvented Scots), since often used as a shorthand description of the democratic ideal, was put into circulation by the 'kailyard' writer Ian Maclaren. Dominies and lads o' pairts were favourite figures in the popular tales of rural Scotland which catered for the nostalgia of town-dwellers and Scottish exiles, as the real Scotland turned into an urban and industrial country.

2. PROBLEMS OF URBAN EDUCATION

One virtue claimed for the parish school was its mixture of social classes. But this ideal was difficult to transfer to urban conditions, and

[8] A. Darroch, *Education and the New Utilitarianism, and other Educational Addresses* (London, 1914), 39, 129; S. S. Laurie, *The Training of Teachers and Methods of Instruction: Selected Papers* (Cambridge, 1901), 196 (written 1893).

[9] Laurie, ibid.; Craik in *EN* 9 Feb. 1912, 119.

[10] Playfair in Hansard, 3rd series 273, 2 Aug. 1882, 541; Craik in *National Review*, 86 (1925–6), 261; Hansard, 4th series 3, 31 Mar. 1892, 423–4.

the 1880s saw the elaboration of social divisions with the appearance of 'higher grade' schools, especially in Glasgow. These could be seen as offering new opportunities to children from elementary schools, but their origin lay just as much in the need for school boards to provide a range of schools serving all classes, and in the disappearance of private alternatives. Since former burgh schools were now mostly controlled by school boards, it might be thought that they could create integrated local systems and forge the organic connections lacking before 1872. But in practice this was far from straightforward. Schools designated as 'higher class' could not be subsidized from the school rate, and although this was modified in 1878 it was still necessary to charge high fees in order to balance the books. School boards were conscious of the traditional prestige of these old-established schools, and were usually anxious not to lower academic standards. The schools consequently remained middle-class institutions, and generally had their own primary departments charging high fees. Burgh schools had few scholarships attached to them (Scottish benefactors had preferred to create university bursaries), and there was no public money available for this purpose; in 1876 the Board of Education agreed to the designation of Hamilton Academy as a higher class school, but only on condition that funds were raised privately for scholarships for elementary pupils.[11] In the 1880s endowments reform did produce scholarship schemes, but it was still difficult for elementary scholars to transfer into schools where children of the same age had already started Latin.

They might also meet social prejudice from middle-class parents, pupils, and teachers. Much evidence of this was presented to the Elgin committee, which discussed the distribution of state grants to secondary schools in 1892, and it continued in later years. At Perth Academy in 1899, protests from parents forced the school board to cut back a scheme for free places, while at Arbroath in 1907 it was reported that the fee-paying pupils had a pronounced 'class feeling towards the free scholars'.[12] The level of fees in high schools was a persistent subject of local controversy: 'working men's' representatives objected to spending any money on schools from which working-class children were excluded, but if the fees were lowered the schools would become unviable; even within the middle class, there might be tensions between those prepared to pay high fees for a full liberal education and those seeking a more

[11] *EN* 15 July 1876, 365.
[12] E. Smart, *History of Perth Academy* (Perth, 1932), 190–1; *EN* 22 Mar. 1907, 273.

practical and accessible education. Nor were burgh ratepayers willing to subsidize schools which also served surrounding areas. Some of the problems were illustrated at Stirling, where the school board had spent heavily on extending the High School, with the help of the local Educational Trust formed by consolidating endowments. According to the Revd J. P. Lang, chairman of the board, about 40 per cent of the pupils came from outside the town, mostly the children of farmers and 'very well-to-do families'; the children from the town came more from 'the shop-keeping class' and 'the better-off members of the working class'. The school had its own fee-paying primary department. The board was anxious to encourage children from its elementary schools, and charged them half fees. But the full fee averaged £6 a year, and the school's survival would be threatened if pupils were drawn away by new secondary centres in towns like Alloa, or if (as Craik was proposing at that point) a maximum fee of £3 was imposed. Another of the town's clergymen pondered the question in 1894: 'It was a very great problem and a very difficult one, how to utilise such an institution as the High School for the benefit of the community, not merely the middle class, but the working class and the community generally.' Scholarships had proved to have limited appeal, and

it appeared as if it would revert to its original character, to be really an institution for the middle class, for those who could afford to pay high fees for their children, and who preferred to send their children to a school where they would only meet the children of their own class. Sons of working men had a natural hesitation to go to a place where they stood alongside others better dressed, possibly pluming themselves on their better manners, and belonging to a different class of society. They had a natural objection to that, and he did not wonder at it.[13]

In any case, the historic legacy of burgh and endowed schools left many areas unserved, both in smaller towns and in the expanding suburbs of the cities. The 1870s and 1880s saw a boom in middle-class education. In Edinburgh, the reorganization of the Merchant Company endowments in 1870 (the only significant result of the 1869 endowments act) produced four large schools, two for boys and two for girls, which satisfied demand in the city for some years to come, and led to the closure of many private schools; the scheme also included

---

[13] PP 1892, LXII, *Minutes of Evidence Taken by the Committee Appointed to Inquire as to the Best Means of Distributing the Grant in Aid of Secondary Education in Scotland*, 125–30; *EN* 31 Mar. 1894, 212 (J. M. Robertson).

James Gillespie's, a school for 'the upper ten of the working classes'.[14] In Glasgow, the 1870s saw the foundation of Kelvinside Academy in the fashionable West End, the creation of the Hutchesons' endowed grammar schools for boys and girls, and the opening of Bellahouston Academy, 'erected by a company of gentlemen residing in the neighbourhood of Paisley Road, Glasgow, to supply a superior educational institution for the south western district of Glasgow'.[15] Proprietary schools like Kelvinside and Bellahouston charged high fees and were entirely closed to elementary pupils.

The development of girls' secondary schools in the big cities also offered little to working-class pupils. In most towns the burgh schools were mixed, but this had never been the case in Aberdeen, Glasgow, or Edinburgh, where most private and endowed schools were also segregated by sex. The whole ethos of the lad of parts, and the definition of social opportunity in terms of university entry, excluded girls whether of the middle or working class. In England, the development of academic girls' education began in the 1850s, and led to university education for women in the 1870s. In Scotland legal obstacles kept the universities closed until 1892, and though parish and burgh schools might be mixed, the tradition of graduate teachers meant that there were few teaching posts for women at the higher level; the training college and the elementary school were almost the only outlet for women's professional ambitions. In the 1870s, some girls' secondary schools on the modern pattern were founded, especially in Edinburgh and Glasgow, but they were mostly on a proprietary basis and thus socially exclusive. It was not until the 1880s, after the 1882 endowments act required the Balfour commission to make proper provision for girls, that the equal presence of girls in elementary schools was reflected in bursary schemes and secondary schools. But this was also a field where higher grade schools could provide a real enlargement of opportunity.

Élite schools could survive even though they charged high fees. Below this level, however, the middle classes were beginning to expect the public system to meet their needs; since school boards were already in the business of middle-class education through the ex-burgh schools, they had no difficulty in seeing themselves as providers for the whole community. This was reinforced by three factors. First, it soon became clear that many working-class children passed through the six Standards,

---

[14] *EN* 2 Aug. 1884, 501.   [15] *EN* 2 Sept. 1876, 445.

yet could still profit from staying at school, either because of their talent, or because their parents were willing to pay. It seemed to make sense to concentrate these 'ex-VI' pupils in schools with specialized teaching. Second, the years after 1872 saw a great expansion of lower-middle-class or white-collar occupations in commerce and services: among them clerks, shopkeepers and shop assistants, commercial travellers, and the elementary teachers themselves. These inhabitants of the respectable inner suburbs used the board schools from the start, but expected more than basic literacy for their children. They might not be interested in university entrance and the classics, but their needs suggested a new concept of short and practical 'intermediate' education. The 'higher primary schools' in France or the *Realschulen* in Germany were models often cited. Thirdly, the small private schools which before 1872 had satisfied the demands of such families for commercial training and social differentiation began to collapse before board school competition.

Some of the schools taken over by boards, like former sessional schools, had themselves charged relatively high fees, and it seemed natural to maintain these. It could be argued that 'if a sufficient number of parents are prepared to pay liberally for a little social exclusion, it is only fair that they should have it if at all possible', and that a true national system was one which embraced all social classes.

The tendency is to classify schools according to a gradation of fees, and therefore of social status. The old Scotch idea of national education seems to be gathering additional strength and consistence from the maxim that those who pay the educational rate should profit from it; and therefore there is a growing desire to discountenance adventure establishments, and to bring a higher social grade within the sphere of the public schools, to multiply schools that meet the needs of the large commercial and middle classes that our modern conditions develop.[16]

Similar ideas were expressed in 1883 by Glasgow school board, replying to an SED circular, and by Craik in an article of 1885 which argued strongly for the duty of the state to 'organize, test, and stimulate the education of the middle classes'.[17] The *Educational News* celebrated

---

[16] Inspectors' reports in PP 1880, XXIV, *CCES Report, 1879–80*, 157; PP 1882, XXV, *CCES Report, 1881–2*, 151–2.

[17] Glasgow letter reprinted in PP 1888, XLI, *Third Report of the Committee Appointed to Inquire into Certain Questions Relating to Education in Scotland*, 165; *Fortnightly Review*, NS 37 (1885), 485–7.

'the union of social grades in our Board schools' as a return to Scottish tradition, and an inspector declared in an after-dinner speech that

the Boards have been steadily drawing within the influence of their schools a higher social class, and the idea that there is anything incompatible with gentility in having one's children at a Board School is rapidly disappearing. (Applause.)[18]

One symptom was that while in 1876 the gentlemen of Bellahouston founded their own school, by 1884 a meeting of 'influential gentlemen resident in Lenzie' (part of the Glasgow commuter belt) were demanding that in return for their rates they should get a 'high-class' school.[19] The two school boards in the area agreed, and bought the private Lenzie Academy. Indeed, Bellahouston Academy itself failed, and was bought by the Govan board for use as a higher grade school.

The term 'higher grade', borrowed from England, became normal from about 1885, but Glasgow school board had been experimenting with the policy since 1878, when it opened the City Schools (one each for boys and girls). Others were added later, and the number eventually settled at five. They charged relatively high fees, paid by the quarter, and were described by the board as 'secondary', although they were not intended to compete socially with the High School. They offered the model of an 'organic' curriculum, built on top of the Code yet covering the full range of secondary subjects. Most pupils left at 15 or so for commercial occupations, but the schools offered a clear road to the universities and professions for those who wished to take it, and soon began to score university successes. Glasgow's claim that the schools inherited the tradition of the parish schools had some justification. There was a similar policy in Govan, which placed a school in each of its main districts; the most successful was Hillhead, which soon adopted the name of High School and was considered of full secondary status. Other boards serving the Glasgow suburbs also opened higher grade schools. In all these cases, the higher grade department was part of a school covering all ages: pupils from other elementary schools could be transferred to them, including those benefiting from new scholarship schemes, but their basic function was to serve the districts where they were set, which were chosen because of their relatively middle-class character.

Similar schools developed in several towns. At Perth, it was an endowed school, Sharp's Institution, which had this role. At Ayr, the

---

[18] *EN* 8 Nov. 1884, 733; 11 Oct. 1884, 669.   [19] *EN* 22 Mar. 1884, 194.

school board had a Grammar School aimed at a lower clientele than its Academy. In some cases the school board had the incentive of not controlling the former burgh school—those under mixed management before 1872 were not automatically transferred. At Inverness, for example, the Academy was independent and socially exclusive, and the school board deliberately charged lower fees at the High School, which it had inherited from the Free Church. At Dundee, the school board failed in its attempt to get legal control of the High School, and set up Harris Academy with the aid of a private donation, Mr Harris's explicit aim being to save the exclusivity of the High School. When Harris Academy opened in 1885 it was intended to give 'secondary education at moderate fees to the children of the working classes', and it was noted that they came mostly from 'higher class adventure schools'. They were described in 1892, however, as 'the children of foremen, mill managers, shop-keepers, and a few of the clergy'.[20] Later the school board also acquired Morgan Academy, converted from a hospital by the Balfour commission. In Edinburgh, on the other hand, the school board encouraged the teaching of specific subjects in ordinary schools, but made no move to found higher grade schools. It was unable to challenge the Merchant Company, which did not want competition for its schools, and had a strong voice on the burgh secondary education committee after 1892. At Aberdeen, the board at first maintained several 'quarterly' schools (charging fees by the quarter) with advanced teaching,[21] but in the 1890s it adopted a model unusual in Scotland: the 'central' higher grade school, which did not have an elementary department of its own, but took ex-VI pupils from all over the city. In smaller towns, although higher grade schools were not set up under that name, it became usual to concentrate higher work in a single school, providing a framework for later secondary development. This was not always popular with the teachers at other schools, who did not want to lose their older pupils, and who argued that working-class children were more likely to leave early than to move to an unfamiliar school.

Higher grade schools proved controversial, being opposed from one direction by full secondary schools, public and private, which complained of unfair competition from subsidized fees, and from another by the free education lobby, notably James Caldwell, who condemned

---

[20] *EN* 12 Sept. 1885, 591; PP 1887, XXXII, *CCES Report, 1886–7*, 225; PP 1892, LXII, *Minutes of Evidence*, 199.
[21] PP 1888, XLI, *Third Report*, 121.

those in Glasgow (and the new Lenzie Academy) as middle-class schools maintained at the expense of the working-class ratepayer. A fierce battle was fought before the Balfour commissioners when they held Glasgow hearings, before the Parker committee, and in Parliament through to the Equivalent Grant debate in 1892. One victory was gained by the radicals. Under the Code, a school could not normally get a grant if its fees averaged more than 9*d.* a week. After pressure from the Glasgow and Govan boards, the SED agreed in 1884 to allow exceptions to the rule. But Caldwell and his allies forced the government auditor to declare this illegal, and the SED had to reinstate the 'ninepenny rule'. None the less, the higher grade schools continued to flourish, and the stratification of public provision was underlined when fees were abolished in 1890. School boards were allowed to retain fee-paying schools under the Code as long as free education was available elsewhere; all the forty or so schools on the fee-paying list were urban, either higher grade schools in the cities, or the main school (often a former burgh school) in towns without a higher class school.[22] This development was naturally opposed by the radicals, especially in Glasgow. Caldwell and Cameron formed a Glasgow and District Free Education Association, which won five seats in the Glasgow school board elections of 1891, but they failed to prevent the retention of fees in the higher grade schools.[23] When their colleague Trevelyan became Secretary for Scotland in 1892, he brought pressure on school boards to abolish fee-paying, and succeeded in forcing Leith to make its new higher grade school free. The issue was controversial in several other places, and one board, Eastwood in suburban Glasgow, conducted a plebiscite through postcards on whether its new higher grade school at Shawlands should be fee-paying; fees won the vote.[24] Aberdeen school board, unusually, retained fees in a purely elementary school, Ashley Road, and the secondary schools complained about this use of board schools by the middle classes. Of its 776 pupils, 358 were the children of 'shipmasters' or men in independent business, 101 of clergymen, accountants, and clerks, and 25 of commercial travellers. There were 220 children of foremen and master tradesmen, but only 18 whose fathers were labourers.[25] At Dundee, by contrast, though fees continued in the two academies, a

---

[22] A Parliamentary Return listing them (obtained by Caldwell) is in PP 1890, LVI.
[23] *EN* 1 Mar. 1890, 158; 22 Nov. 1890, 804–5; 13 Feb. 1892, 120.
[24] *EN* 9 Apr. 1892, 249.
[25] *Association of Teachers in the Secondary Schools of Scotland: Report of General Meeting, 19th October, 1889* (Edinburgh, 1889), 13.

proposal to retain them in selected elementary schools was defeated on the grounds that it 'would accentuate class distinctions, and . . . it was their duty as a Board rather to try to break those down'.[26] Edinburgh also abolished all its fees after 1890, but this was easier because, although some of its schools were more middle-class than others, it had no true higher grade schools.

The case against fees was that they reinforced class barriers. According to Trevelyan,

Up to this time there has been no class distinction in Scotland, but now that the Government have justified and sanctified this idea of class distinction I venture to say that within three years we shall not find a single person who sets up to be 'smart' or to belong to or be near the upper classes sending his children to a school where fees are not paid, if he is within a railway journey of a school where fees are paid.[27]

The argument on the other side was that fees attracted middle-class custom, brought in useful income, and reflected the realities of urban life. Equality might prevail in the country, but 'it is not so in large towns, and it is idle to suppose that in the towns you can have the same mixture of stations in life as you have in the schools in the country.' As for class distinctions,

in the existing state of things they cannot be avoided. There may be something very grand, and very Scotch, and very patriotic in the idea that the sons of the poor man and the nobleman should be educated together; but we know that that is not what actually goes on in the different communities with which we are acquainted, and I think we must be content to take the 19th century as it is, and endeavour to develop our views of education in accordance with existing circumstances.[28]

3. THE EVOLUTION OF SED POLICY

From 1885, Craik had a clear policy of extending state inspection and financial aid to the endowed and higher class schools, hitherto starved of public support. Where practicable, secondary education should be concentrated in these schools, but in compensation they should be made more accessible socially through moderate fees and free places. Craik used his membership of the Parker committee to push opinion in this

---

[26] *EN* 27 Feb. 1892, 146.   [27] Hansard, 3rd series 342, 13 Mar. 1890, 825.
[28] Ibid. 822 (J. A. Campbell); 3rd series 349, 3 Feb. 1891, 1702–3 (M. Stewart).

direction, and its report recommended that secondary schools should receive state grants in return for free places open to competition from elementary schools. When the Equivalent Grant became available in 1892, Craik favoured using capitation grants to impose lower fees, but was overruled for political reasons.[29] The grants were not administered directly by the SED, but paid to the county secondary education committees, which could draw up their own plans for subsidies and bursaries. Endowed and higher class schools benefited from these plans, but so did city higher grade schools as well as the Catholic sector, where serious secondary work was only now beginning. In county areas, the committees sometimes used their money for completely new secondary schools (Duns, Stranraer), but more often to build up a network of secondary departments in smaller towns. In Perthshire, for example, the committee supported higher class schools at Perth, Crieff, and Callander, and secondary departments at Aberfeldy, Blairgowrie, Alyth, Coupar Angus, and Pitlochry. Where the parish school tradition was still strong, as in Aberdeenshire or Banff, the money could be spread even more widely. Thus some sort of secondary education was put within geographical reach of most of the population, and since few new fee-paying schools were authorized after 1890 much of it was free. Although the term 'higher grade' was not yet applied outside the cities, many schools now offered the same continuum of elementary and secondary curricula, with the possibility of taking education through to university level. Schools might differ in legal status and social prestige, but there was no 'segmentation' of the curriculum. There was thus a compromise between elementary and secondary ideals, and the old controversies died down, one symptom being that the Leaving Certificate was now opened to all schools. By 1900, 348 state schools were presenting 11,464 candidates, compared with 5,307 candidates from 83 higher class schools, public and private.[30]

These developments had clear implications for elementary education. A circular of 1895 spoke of the need to make it the foundation for secondary and university work,[31] and in 1898 the SED embarked on a new policy initiative, signalled in speeches by Balfour of Burleigh as well as official circulars. The aim was to build an integrated national system in which

---

[29] See, for the whole of this section, Anderson, *Education and Opportunity*, ch. 6.

[30] PP 1900, XXIV, *CCES Report, 1899–1900*, 394.

[31] PP 1895, XXX, *CCES Report, 1894–5*, 164.

every school must bear a share in what is a connected work—viz., the construction of an educational highway from the infant class to the ultimate entry upon the business of life. Along which highway all must travel, so far as circumstances and mental capacity enable each one to go.[32]

The execution of this policy (and the terminology of Scottish education) was complicated by the separate financial status of 'endowed and higher class' schools and those under the Code, which persisted until 1918. Craik continued to think that the former were under-financed, and he ensured that new grants were controlled by the SED, not devolved to the county committees. Further changes in local finance in 1898 and the SED's take-over of the Science and Art grants for Scotland led to a Minute of 1899 on grants to secondary schools which was the precursor of the Secondary School Regulations of 1907. For schools financed under the Code, developments were more complicated, as work beyond the Standards still depended on the rather miscellaneous specific subject grants. But in 1898 and 1899 these were swept away, and with them the last vestige of payment by results. Instead, secondary-type teaching was to be given in Advanced Departments. These had no specified curriculum, and each school could submit its own for approval. The SED was generous in recognizing Advanced Departments, and by 1903 there were nearly 400, including many small rural schools. The 1899 Code was thus hailed by traditionalists as a vindication of the parish school tradition: it allowed 'liberal' education including Latin to be continued wherever there was a demand, and in areas like the northeast, Advanced Departments were seen as giving 'official sanction to the immemorial usage of Scottish schools'.[33] Laurie welcomed the 1899 Code because it 'was humanistic, and went right in the teeth of the attempts to turn our schools into ante-chambers of alkali works and engineering shops'.[34]

The same could not be said of a second aspect of the 1899 Code, which took up the term 'higher grade' officially for the first time, but applied it to a specially designated group of secondary schools. As legatee of the Department of Science and Art, the SED was conscious of its duty to promote science, and floated a policy of 'higher grade science schools' in 1898. In 1899 this was expanded to allow either scientific or commercial specialization. To a common base including a

[32] Lord Balfour of Burleigh, *Higher Education in Scotland: Address Delivered at Paisley, September 14, 1898* (Edinburgh, 1898), 7.
[33] PP 1900, XXIV, *CCES Report, 1899–1900*, 575.   [34] *EN* 21 Oct. 1899, 723.

modern language but excluding Latin, the science course added manual work as well as laboratory-based science, and the commercial course added bookkeeping and shorthand. But although the new policy finally induced Edinburgh school board to found two higher grade schools, no schools devoted themselves exclusively to this new curriculum. Higher grade departments coexisted with classical teaching, and the commercial course proved more popular than the scientific. By 1903 only 36 schools had taken up higher grade status, and few pupils reached the third year. The policy could not be considered a success, and in 1903 the cards were reshuffled again.

The Advanced Departments of 1899 were based on the assumption that most advanced work had secondary aspirations. But after the abolition of exemptions in 1901, schools retained a mass of pupils between 12 and 14 to whom this academic approach was ill suited. This was the main reason for the change in policy, which introduced a much sharper distinction between secondary education proper and prolonged or 'supplementary' elementary education. Secondary schools under the Code were now all to be called Higher Grade—a third meaning for the term—and secondary teaching was to be concentrated within them. Advanced Departments were abolished; most of the schools which had them became Higher Grades, but others were pushed back into the elementary ranks, a development seldom welcomed locally. The system soon stabilized, and on the eve of the First World War there were 249 secondary schools: 57 higher class and endowed, 179 higher grade, and 13 Roman Catholic. Of these, 78 charged fees and 171 were free.[35] Some of these schools only gave a three-year 'intermediate' education, but the curriculum was essentially the same in all types of school. The idea of scientific or commercial specialization was virtually abandoned, though the SED insisted on a balanced curriculum with full attention given to modern subjects. The Leaving Certificate remained the standard goal, and was reorganized with an 'intermediate' certificate taken at 15 and a 'higher' one two years later; it was also 'grouped' so that candidates taking isolated subjects did not get a full certificate, which discouraged the presentation of non-secondary pupils.

For those who stayed on after 12 without transferring to secondary schools or departments, advanced education was now to be given in Supplementary Courses, lasting two or three years, and entered after passing a Qualifying Examination. These courses were to be strictly

[35] Anderson, *Education and Opportunity*, 244–6.

practical and to follow one of four curricula: industrial, commercial, rural, and one for girls. The name Merit Certificate, used since 1892 for an examination taken at the end of the Standards, was transferred to one taken after the second supplementary year. Thus the vocational specialization which had failed when applied to middle-class education was now imposed on the working classes, and while curricular segmentation had been avoided in secondary education itself, it was enforced in the division between the two sectors. The reform was justified in 'Circular 374' on supplementary courses, which argued that 'the tendency . . . to make one and the same school with one and the same staff serve many different functions is the weak point of educational organisation in Scotland as compared with that of other countries', and that 'increasing division of function as between different types of schools is an essential condition of further educational progress'. Thus pupils interested in secondary education should be transferred to proper secondary schools by the age of 12, and the education of the remainder should bear directly on 'the probable practical requirements of the pupils' after-school life'. Certainly, supplementary courses should have a liberal element, and 'aim at producing the useful citizen, imbued with a sense of responsibility and of obligation towards the society in which he lives', prepared moreover for 'the rational enjoyment of his leisure time'. But the academic element in this general education was to consist essentially of English literature, and there was definitely to be no teaching of Latin or other languages.[36]

Speaking just after he left office in 1903, Balfour of Burleigh claimed that the policies pursued since 1898 amounted to 'the organisation of a comprehensive and coherent system of national education'.[37] The SED's official statements stressed the continuity of policy, and glossed over changes of direction; one MP complained with some justice of 'the multitude of Blue-books, Reports, Circulars and Minutes with which the department, like a cuttle-fish, darkened all around it, and endeavoured to baffle the public'.[38] But the shift in 1903 was a real one, and although Craik did not retire until 1904, it seems certain that Struthers was behind the changes. According to the *Educational News* this was an open secret, and it added that the new secretary 'teems with ideas'.[39] The keynote of these ideas, tenaciously defended by Struthers throughout

[36] PP 1905, XXIX, *CCES Report, 1904–5*, 281–90.
[37] *EN* 17 Oct. 1903, 789.
[38] Hansard, 4th series 197, 24 Nov. 1908, 152 (Norman Lamont).
[39] *EN* 31 Dec. 1904, 957–8.

his period of office, was functional specialization, and there was a close correspondence with the educational theories of Darroch. Craik, by contrast, though old-fashioned in his limited views of social mobility, also had an old-fashioned belief in liberal education and in the unique value of the classics.

Nor was he alone. Those like Laurie who had welcomed the 1899 Code reacted indignantly against Circular 374. For him the 1903 Code was 'little short of a national calamity', and he objected on principle to the utilitarian approach:

The object of the State in educating the people is not so much the equipping of future citizens for their work in this or that special industry as the disciplining of the young to the vigorous exercise of their intelligence; and above all, training them up to the moral and religious ideal of the nation to which they belong. . . . The primary school, above all, should, in my opinion, be sacred to a liberal education, and technical instruction should be postponed to a later stage.

For those who valued the parish school ideal, the diversion of country children into a 'rural' vocational course was especially repugnant: 'the bridge over which for generations many a poor country boy in Scotland has passed to professions which he has adorned will be broken down.'[40] Struthers's policy of 'centralizing' rural secondary education encountered much local opposition, and criticism reached its height in 1912 with the formation of an Association for Securing Higher Instruction in Rural Schools, which attracted significant political support.[41] One of its organizers, and a particular thorn in Struthers's flesh, was the Revd John Smith, chairman of Govan school board, of the Church of Scotland's Education Committee, and of the Scottish School Boards Association. In 1913 he published an attack on SED policy under the title *Broken Links in Scottish Education*. But the SSBA did not speak for all the school boards, and the critics were not typical of educational opinion. By 1914 the system established in 1903 had gained general acceptance.

A final element in the pattern was the reform of teacher training. Pupil-teachers originally studied for their examinations in the schools where they were apprenticed, but from 1880 they could be brought together centrally for part-time tuition. Glasgow was one of the first to try this. Its 'pupil-teacher institutes' were separate, but in most places

---

[40] S. S. Laurie, *Dick Bequest Trust: General Report to the Governors, 1890–1904* (Edinburgh, 1904), 31, 32, 44–5; cf. Laurie in *EN* 6 June 1903, 427–31.
[41] Anderson, *Education and Opportunity*, 237–43.

these classes were given in a higher grade or secondary school, and provided a useful nucleus of scholars financed by the state. The recognition of university-based training in 1895 reflected the new demand for teachers in higher grade schools, and in the 1900s the training system struggled to cope with changes such as the abolition of exemptions, the drive for smaller classes, and the creation of supplementary courses. The churches lacked the resources for expansion, and in 1907 the Presbyterian colleges were handed over to the state. Those in Edinburgh, Glasgow, and Aberdeen were amalgamated, and a new one created at Dundee. They were administered by 'provincial committees' which included university representatives, and new training structures were devised which integrated university courses and professional training, and reflected the classification of schools. Broadly speaking, under the 1906 regulations Honours graduates went to secondary schools, Ordinary graduates to Higher Grades, and non-graduates (who by now included few men) to primary schools.[42] The pupil-teacher system was abolished; instead the state supported 'junior students', who studied in secondary schools. They had a special curriculum reflecting the new vocational emphasis in primary education, but could aim at the Leaving Certificate and university entry. The policy was criticized at the time for underlining the cultural division between secondary and elementary sectors, but in practice the junior student system could promote both social mobility and intellectual emancipation. C. M. Grieve, the future poet Hugh MacDiarmid, the son of a postman at Langholm, was able to go as a junior student in 1908 to Edinburgh's higher grade school at Broughton, and it was not the system's fault that his career in education ended abruptly when he left under a cloud.[43]

4. SUPPLEMENTARY COURSES AND THE DEMOCRATIC IDEAL

Supplementary courses were the main development in elementary education after 1903. In principle they were available to all children, and were offered in about two-thirds of the schools. But since they required specialized staff and equipment it was natural to concentrate supplementary work in selected schools. Glasgow and Aberdeen held out

[42] M. Cruickshank, *A History of the Training of Teachers in Scotland* (London, 1970), 138–9.
[43] A. Bold, *MacDiarmid: Christopher Murray Grieve, a Critical Biography* (new edn., London, 1990), 56–72.

against this policy, but Edinburgh and Dundee built new and elaborately equipped central schools, at Tynecastle and Stobswell respectively. This recalled the concentration of 'ex-VI' pupils which had led on to higher grade schools, and central supplementary schools could be seen as the beginnings of a new quasi-secondary wave. Many of them, indeed, were to become the 'junior secondary schools' of the 1940s and 1950s. The SED encouraged school boards to provide a third year of supplementary education, thus taking children to 15, and from 1914 three-year schools which met certain conditions could earn the same grants as higher grade schools; but Struthers refused to take the next logical step, which was to create a three-year certificate as a vocational equivalent of the intermediate Leaving Certificate. The EIS supported this idea, and there were some who thought it time to acknowledge that 'all education after the Qualifying Stage is Secondary Education'.[44] But SED policy insisted rigidly on the separation of the two kinds of education. Even where a higher grade school was used as the central supplementary school, as was common in smaller towns, the SED forbade children to be taught together, and it resisted pressure from school boards to include secondary subjects in supplementary curricula.

At Stranraer, for example, the same building housed the Academy, an elementary school run by the school board, and the High School, a fee-paying secondary school under the county committee. The school board wanted to teach Latin, French, and mathematics in the Academy, since elementary pupils were 'placed in an unhappy social environment in the High School classes'. But the SED insisted that the Academy must confine itself to the supplementary syllabus.[45] The SED also stressed the vocational emphasis of the schools. The 'industrial' course was perhaps the least satisfactory, since the teaching of science was limited, and practical training usually consisted only of woodwork, in the Sloyd tradition. Domestic courses for girls, however, could be quite elaborate. In Glasgow one school was converted into a centre for girls from surrounding schools; in Stirling, two rooms were fitted up as a parlour and bedroom, where 'the senior girls of all the schools in the Burgh will be taught how to arrange a dining table and how to make up a bedroom and keep it tidy'; and in Elgin existing courses were reorganized as a Girls' Technical School with the same purpose.[46]

In theory, children took the Qualifying Examination—soon familiar

---

[44] *EN* 25 Oct. 1912, 994.   [45] *EN* 12 Sept. 1903, 676–7.
[46] *EN* 30 Dec. 1905, 966–7; 18 June 1904, 454; 4 Mar. 1905, 163–4.

in school lore as the 'Qualy'—at 12, spent two years taking supplementary courses, and left school with the Merit Certificate to show for their pains. The reality was often different, and fell well short of the rhetoric about preparation for the world of work and citizenship. For one thing, entry to the courses depended on passing the examination; those who failed were left to repeat elementary work until they left school. For another, not all reached the Qualifying standard, supposedly based on seven years' work, by the age of 12. Late starting, poor attendance, and large classes took their toll. Thus there might be time for only one supplementary year. In Aberdeen in 1912, only 36 per cent of school-leavers had the Merit Certificate; a further 28 per cent had undergone some supplementary instruction, but 36 per cent left without even reaching the supplementary course; this picture of two-thirds 'qualifying' and one-third reaching the Merit Certificate seems to have been typical for the cities. The low numbers achieving the Merit Certificate were 'the darkest blot on our educational record'.[47] In many places, only the first year was properly organized, and three-year courses were exceptional.

Supplementary courses were also weakened because the more able or ambitious pupils spurned vocationalism, and parents put them in a secondary course even if they had no intention of keeping them there to complete it. In the west of Scotland in 1908, 24 per cent of those qualifying went on to higher grade courses.[48] But only a minority stayed more than a year or two. Attempts to exclude these pupils by devices such as exacting pledges to attend for three years proved useless, and

the social aspect of the question is not without its weight. It is considered a more 'genteel' thing for a boy or girl to be in the Intermediate Section of the school than in the Supplementary Course. . . . the fact is again and again forced on one's notice that, if a Supplementary Course be found in a Higher Grade School, it not unfrequently has the savour about it of a 'duffers'' class.[49]

And of the supplementary curricula, the commercial was the most popular: as the *Educational News* pointed out, 'under past and present conditions the Office has superior attractions to the Workshop, the Foundry, or the Factory', and boys were not easily to be attracted from the 'seductive delights of clean collars and inky fingers'.[50] The SED

[47] *SED Reports, 1913–14*, CCs & CIs, 90; *SED Reports, 1914–15*, Northern and Highland Divisions, 11, and cf. Western Division, 27.
[48] PP 1908, XXVIII, *CCES Report, 1907–8*, 446.
[49] *SED Reports, 1908–9*, Western Division, 65–7.   [50] *EN* 2 May 1903, 343.

continued to maintain that for those leaving at 14 'the advantage to be got from a sound Supplementary Course training is beyond all comparison greater than any that could be derived from following a truncated Higher Grade curriculum', but it failed to convince parents.[51] As the *News* had predicted in 1903 when Balfour of Burleigh was claiming that the courses would have parity of esteem, 'the logic of events proves the fact to be quite the contrary. Social status, the income, even the ambitions of parents, are potent factors in his classification, in spite of his excellent intention.' It might work in an ideal society, but not in a socially stratified one, for we were still 'very far from free and equal opportunity for every boy and every girl'.[52]

Parents were free to choose secondary rather than supplementary courses because the Qualifying Examination led to both. Originally this examination was non-selective, and there was no numerical limit on entry to secondary courses. It was not an external examination, but administered within the school by head-teachers. But the idea soon arose that it might be used to pick out those best suited to secondary education. Govan, for example, 'on their own responsibility, have instituted an examination by means of which those who cannot profit by a predominantly literary and linguistic curriculum are riddled out from the multitude who have satisfied formally the qualifying test'. The inspector cautiously approved, and suggested a common 'control test' supervised by the inspectorate.[53] In 1912 the SED encouraged local experiments of this kind, despite hostility from teachers who saw it as a return to the days of payment by results: 'The re-introduction into the public schools of a fixed ceremonial day of juvenile execution by means of external examinations has met with opposition in all parts of the country.'[54] But use of 'control' papers, ostensibly to maintain common standards, became established in various districts, and the Qualifying Examination, already seen like the original Merit Certificate as the natural point of transition from primary to secondary schooling, became the embryo of a selective 'twelve plus'.

'The severe demands which modern conditions impose are every day strengthening the necessity for specialisation of functions', argued the SED. 'One may regret this tendency on general grounds, but it would be idle to try and withstand it. We ought to be well content if we can secure that no individual misses his opportunity because of a too

[51] *SED Reports, 1911–12*, Secondary Education, 5.
[52] *EN* 17 Oct. 1903, 787.
[53] *SED Reports, 1911–12*, Western Division, 27.   [54] *EN* 12 July 1912, 645.

mechanical system of organisation.'[55] By 1914 specialization of functions was a reality: outside a few rural areas where remote schools were
allowed to retain advanced teaching, secondary education was given
only in secondary or higher grade schools, and access to it was by
formal promotion or transfer at the age of 12. But had opportunities for
individuals been secured? The general view was optimistic, and self-
congratulation was a common theme in educational debate. According
to the president of the EIS in 1903,

The ideal of free opportunity in education for all . . . , whether properly called
a democratic or a national ideal, is one still vitally active in the Scottish people.
However checked, diverted, or modified that ideal may have been by the current of events during the last generation, and notably by Scotland's ever increasing industrial prosperity, with its consequent social cleavage . . . , it is still
to be calculated on by those who seek to fashion our educational system, as a
whole, in accordance with our traditional spirit.[56]

The ideal of the lad of parts was given classic expression by one MP—
who remembered to include girls, as many did not—in 1904:

education was not to be treated as the possession or privilege of the few, but
it was the right of every boy or girl, however humble his or her origin, and
however remote the place was in which he or she resided, to receive the education best calculated to fit him or her for the career of the greatest usefulness
which his or her capacities rendered possible.[57]

Andrew Carnegie, himself an exemplary case of individual achievement, promoted it both as an ideal—he published a life of James Watt
in 1905—and in a practical way through the Carnegie Trust scheme,
beginning in 1900, which paid the university fees of Scottish students
whatever their means.

According to Carnegie, John Knox 'made Scotland a democracy while
England remains a nation of caste', and this contrast was a common
theme. In England, there was a 'barbed-wire fence' between elementary
and secondary schools, and contemporary developments were deemed
to be inspired by a spirit of class distinction alien to Scotland.[58] After
the 1902 Act the secretary of the Board of Education, Robert Morant,
directed the new grammar schools along a strongly academic road,

[55] *SED Reports, 1909–10*, General Report, 18.
[56] *EN* 3 Jan. 1903, 9–10 (A. T. Watson).
[57] Hansard, 4th series 134, 2 May 1904, 129 (A. W. Black).
[58] Carnegie in *EN* 5 Sept. 1903, 654; editorial in *EN* 9 Mar. 1901, 175.

distinguishing them sharply from 'higher elementary' education. According to historians critical of Morant this was a surrender to the values of the English public schools, and abandoned the scientific and democratic traditions built up since the 1870s by the English higher grade schools, though others have argued that Morant's policy was designed to give grammar-school scholars a chance to compete on equal terms with the privileged.[59] Scottish supplementary courses bore more than a passing resemblance to higher elementary schools, but the general development of Scottish education since the 1880s meant that secondary education was already widely available in towns of all sizes and linked with the elementary curriculum. Moreover, although Scotland did have schools outside the state system which were entirely closed to those who could not pay the fees, there was no equivalent of the dominant position of the English public schools; to enter a Scottish secondary school was to gain access to the best education available, not to a second-rank system. There was, it is true, no Scottish equivalent of the 'free place' scheme introduced by the Liberal government in 1907, by which state-aided secondary schools had to give at least 25 per cent of their places to elementary scholars. But whereas Morant's policy insisted on secondary schools charging fees, many Scottish ones were free, and the Education Act of 1908 encouraged county committees to develop generous bursary schemes.

There are therefore a priori or structural reasons for thinking that the educational ladder was relatively accessible. Indirect evidence comes from the universities, where records of students' social origins show that working-class students, now including women, were more numerous in the 1900s than in the 1860s.[60] The means of ascent, once haphazard and individualistic, had been regularized through scholarship systems, but were no less extensive than before. This case was argued vigorously by Struthers, and he published statistics which showed that by 1914 over half of all pupils in the first secondary year were transferred from primary schools (the remainder coming from the primary department of the same school), and that 80 per cent of Scottish primary schools were sending children forward. One in six or seven children—say 15 per cent—embarked on a secondary course; in England

[59] For a brief summary, see M. Sanderson, *Educational Opportunity and Social Change in England* (London, 1987), 18–25.

[60] Anderson, *Education and Opportunity*, 308–18; id., *The Student Community at Aberdeen, 1860–1939* (Aberdeen, 1988), 138–41.

the figure was one in twenty-two.[61] But most of these pupils would not stay for very long (as the statistics on attendance cited in Chapter 9 confirm), and they chose secondary education in the face of the SED's efforts to encourage them into supplementary courses, so here Struthers was making a virtue of necessity. One of the signs of democratic vigour was indeed parents' persistence in seeing shorter or more practical forms of education as inferior alternatives designed to close off their children's opportunities, and their refusal to accept official categorizations, a mentality which derived ultimately from the traditional prestige of liberal education and the professions to which it led.

But the efficiency of the educational ladder should not be exaggerated. Official language, having at last adopted the term 'primary', might speak of primary education leading to different options at the age of 12, but the schools themselves were still organized as parallel streams, not successive stages. Everything depended on the transfer of talented children into secondary schools, but there was no fixed age for this, and no systematic attempt to pick out the most able. Without a scholarship, staying at school after 14 was usually impossible, and even when there were no fees, few parents could afford to support their older children or forfeit their wages. The scholarships themselves, because they were open and competitive, were often captured by lower-middle-class children or those higher up in the social scale. They favoured children from cultured and socially ambitious homes who were well prepared, highly motivated, and already familiar with the literary subjects favoured in secondary schools. In short, there were cultural as well as social barriers to mobility, and the dice were loaded against the working-class pupil; even the ability to study at home was a luxury when, as was still the case in 1911, half the Scottish population lived in houses of one or two rooms.[62] As in the past, the lad of parts ideal worked better in rural areas and small towns than in the class-segregated cities, and for skilled workers or the lower ranges of the middle class than for the really poor. For the great mass of school-leavers, it was the field, the pit, or the factory which beckoned, and universities and secondary schools were part of an alien world.

---

[61] *SED Reports, 1912–13*, Secondary Education, 5; *SED Reports, 1913–14*, Secondary Education, 3; *SED Reports, 1914–15*, Secondary Education, 3; G. Sherington, *English Education, Social Change and War, 1911–20* (Manchester, 1981), 7.

[62] T. C. Smout, 'Scotland, 1850–1950', in F. M. L. Thompson (ed.), *The Cambridge Social History of Britain, 1750–1950*, i: *Regions and Communities* (Cambridge, 1990), 254.

11

Technical and Continuing Education

THE early history of 'adult' education has been discussed in Chapter 6. Most of it took the form of evening classes directed at adolescents or young men and women, providing an alternative form of social mobility and self-improvement for those who could not afford secondary schools. Only part of it can be classified as technical education, which was slow to develop as a full-time affair. Indeed, the failure of the state to devote significant resources to it was a constant complaint of the science and technology lobby in the nineteenth century, and has been taken up since by historians in search of an explanation for Britain's economic decline. By some it has been seen as part of a wider cultural phenomenon, the 'decline of the industrial spirit', in which the 'aristocratic' values of the ancient universities and public schools in England undermined the entrepreneurial dynamism of the middle class.[1] On the face of it, this argument would seem less applicable to Scotland, which lacked this aristocratic bias in its élite education. But Scotland had anti-utilitarian prejudices of its own, and although the broad history of technical education is the same for the two countries, there were some significant variations. It would be desirable to ask how far technical education met the actual needs of industry and commerce, but the research needed to answer this question has not yet been done. It does seem, however, that policy was driven as much by political imperatives such as national strength or the desire to distinguish working-class from middle-class education as by strictly economic criteria, and in the 1900s there was a strong concentration on 'continuation classes' as a way of prolonging the general education of adolescents rather than as an investment in skills.

1. TECHNICAL EDUCATION AND INTERNATIONAL COMPETITION

The state's interest in technical education began in the 1850s, and was spurred by fears that Britain was falling behind industrially. When a

[1] M. J. Wiener, *English Culture and the Decline of the Industrial Spirit, 1850–1980* (Cambridge, 1981); this subject has now given rise to a large literature, none of which says much about Scotland.

second wave of concern began in the late 1860s, international competition was again a central theme, though Germany rather than France was now seen as the model to be imitated. For a time in the 1870s, the pace was set by scientists, and the Devonshire commission, which reported in 1875, concentrated on scientific research and teaching in the universities. This was followed by a royal commission on Scottish universities which included Lyon Playfair and T. H. Huxley, whose report in 1878 was strongly pro-scientific but had no immediate results. In the 1880s, attention switched back to technical education. It is striking how much attention was given to the question in the *Educational News*, although it might not be thought a natural interest of Scottish schoolteachers. Editorials in favour of technical education, stressing the theme of international rivalry, accompanied frequent articles on foreign countries, especially Germany, whose technical high schools and municipal trade schools were much admired; it was assumed without much argument that lavish expenditure on these was a direct cause of Germany's economic prosperity.

Promoting technical education was one of the duties given to the Balfour commission in 1882, and it took some important initiatives, to be described later. At the national level, the Samuelson commission, whose main report appeared in 1884, was also inspired by foreign examples, and recommended new powers for local authorities to support technical schools and colleges. One result was the Technical Schools (Scotland) Act of 1887, but this provided no extra funds, and champions of technical education remained dissatisfied: 'it is only the State', said the *News*, 'that can set up useful school systems. Technical education, in the right sense, can never be established in this country except by the Government. . . . Hard cash will alone suffice.'[2] The agitation developed into a general campaign for state intervention, in which technical and secondary education tended to be seen as two aspects of the same need. In 1887 a National Association for the Promotion of Technical Education was founded in London, which included Scots like Rosebery. Later 'Secondary' was added to the title. Local committees for promoting technical education appeared in Dundee in 1888 and Aberdeen in 1891, and further moves led in 1893 to the formation of a separate Scottish Association for the Promotion of Technical and Secondary Education, which attracted a wide array of politicians and educationists,

[2] *EN* 29 Oct. 1887, 768.

including Lord Elgin, Lord Reay, C. S. Parker, Laurie, Flora Stevenson, and the sociologist Patrick Geddes.[3]

One specifically Scottish element in the debate was the identification of a cultural prejudice against practical and utilitarian education. The prestige of the classics and the universities meant that socially mobile Scots aimed at the church and teaching rather than commerce or industry, while at a lower level the products of the elementary schools wanted to become clerks or white-collar workers rather than dirty their hands in industry. For Playfair, one of the arguments against dividing Scottish and English administration in 1885 was that it would reinforce this prejudice, and in 1892 he found his forebodings justified:

all the ideas of the Education Department of Scotland are simply for the old-fashioned education, and not for extending a useful technical education to different parts of Scotland in the same way as is being done in England. As long as you have a Central Department with an extremely able Secretary, you will have education going through one groove instead of consulting localities as to their wants.'[4]

Craik certainly had little personal enthusiasm for technical education, but it was Laurie (despite his membership of the SAPTSE) who most clearly voiced the traditional view. While he admitted that technical colleges could be 'centres of a vast civilising influence amongst the largest part of the population', and give 'to the artisan class that discipline and culture which secondary schools and Universities were supposed to give to the middle class', he warned that

we must not allow ourselves to be led astray by the technical instruction boom: with a nation as with an individual, it is moral energy and intellectual vigour which make it and bring all arts in their train. The Shorter Catechism has done more to make Scotland efficient in the world's work than mathematics and chemistry can ever do.[5]

Laurie's suspicion of vocationalism and preference for liberal, character-forming education were widely shared.

This bias was difficult to overcome, and discussion of technical education was often hampered by ambiguity about its aims and potential clientele. It was generally agreed that industry could no longer rest on empirical practice, and needed a systematic intellectual foundation.

---

[3] *EN* 10 Mar. 1888, 174; 25 Apr. 1891, 285–6; 7 Nov. 1891, 755; 19 Dec. 1891, 857; 27 May 1893, 354; 19 Aug. 1893, 545–6.

[4] Hansard, 4th series 3, 31 Mar. 1892, 405–6.

[5] *EN* 8 Nov. 1884, 730; *Scottish Review*, 19 (1892), 168.

For some, the aim was to create full-time technical institutions at the secondary and higher levels, which would train the officers and NCOs of industry, and compete for prestige with traditional schools and universities. Others pointed to the decline of apprenticeship, and saw skilled workers as the beneficiaries, though they also argued that there must be a theoretical element to distinguish it from mere craft training. Others again saw technical education as a specifically popular or working-class sphere of education, offering a route forward from elementary schools through evening classes to its culmination in colleges like the Watt Institution. W. B. Hodgson, professor of political economy at Edinburgh University, speaking at the Watt in 1879, asked

whether this great and now flourishing Institution shall be a mere ante-room or off-chamber of the workshop, or whether it shall be the true College, or rather University, the *alma mater*, the bountiful mother of the industrial classes, rich in all means and instruments of the most generous culture for the majority of our people who have no time for the discipline of the ordinary university.

The present system of 'individual selection' widened the gulf between the so-called lower and higher classes, but the new education should demonstrate 'the compatibility of a widely liberal culture with industrial and economic pursuits', and its aim should be 'the raising of the whole platform of industrial life, much more than the elevation of this or that individual out of the industrial into the professional sphere'.[6] Hodgson's Saint-Simonian vision of the 'industrial classes' was a broad one, but to set technical against professional education did not encourage the middle classes to accept it as a prestigious alternative, and perhaps only reinforced suspicion that it was intended to divert children away from more desirable careers.

2. EVENING CLASSES AND TECHNICAL COLLEGES

Some evening classes, mainly in elementary subjects, were supported by the SED, since the Code had always given grants to classes run by schoolteachers. But scientific or technical subjects were the preserve of the Department of Science and Art, whose classes continued with little change on the lines already established. Their stereotyped nature, dependence on examination results, and bias towards elementary science

[6] *EN* 22 Nov. 1879, 603.

rather than the technical needs of industry attracted criticism. Evening classes were organized in various centres by local committees, and often bore the title 'school of science and art', but they relied almost exclusively on part-time teachers and borrowed premises. Some, as at Leith, lasted for many years and established a reputation, but there was no guarantee of continuity. Only the art schools dating from the 1850s, notably at Edinburgh, Glasgow, and Aberdeen, had a clear identity as distinct institutions. Perhaps the most notable of the technical schools was the Gartsherrie School of Science at Coatbridge, established by David Ross in 1867. Ross had been appointed to teach classics at Gartsherrie Academy, a school supported by the Baird iron firm, but had soon realized the need for practical education. Ross left in 1878 to become rector of the Church of Scotland Training College in Glasgow, and a leading figure in the educational world, but the school continued to flourish; it taught mechanical, civil, and mining engineering, and sent students on to Glasgow University and the Royal College of Mines in London. Yet all its students came in the evening, and it had no premises of its own.[7]

Another successful school was the former Mechanics' Institution in Glasgow, renamed the College of Science and Arts in 1881. This now offered daytime classes in mathematics, drawing, and mechanics to young men between 14 and 21 who aimed to enter engineers' and architects' offices, or engineering and shipbuilding apprenticeships. It provided most of the Scottish winners of the Whitworth scholarships, the blue riband of the South Kensington system, and seems to have been considerably more lively at this time than its parent body, Anderson's College.[8] The latter had renounced the title of university in 1877, and though it had a large number of students it did not depart from the usual pattern of evening classes over a wide and unco-ordinated range of subjects. The same was true of the Watt Institution, which in 1880 had 2,004 students, including 232 women.[9] In addition, both Glasgow and Edinburgh universities had chairs of engineering, founded in 1840 and 1868 respectively. Their professors were active in the technical education movement, but their courses made little general contribution to it, being tied to the top levels of the engineering profession.

[7] *EN* 24 Nov. 1883, 780–1; 18 Oct. 1890, 711–12; 21 July 1894, 479.
[8] *EN* 4 Feb. 1882, 76–9; 22 Sept. 1883, 609 (advertisement); 27 Aug. 1887, 594. Cf. A. H. Sexton, *The First Technical College: A Sketch of the History of 'the Andersonian' and the Institutions Descended from it, 1796–1894* (London, 1894), 84–6.
[9] *EN* 24 Apr. 1880, 248.

That the 1880s saw important advances in the cities was due largely to the Balfour commission. Reformers in Edinburgh had always identified the endowed hospitals as a potential source of funds,[10] and the commission approached the question at both higher and secondary levels. In Edinburgh, part of the Heriot endowment was diverted to the Watt Institution, which became Heriot-Watt College (1885). In Glasgow, Anderson's College was amalgamated in 1887 with the College of Science and Arts and a Weaving School opened in 1877 to form the Glasgow and West of Scotland Technical College, which was also supported by diverted endowments. These institutions had the potential to develop into technical universities. Aberdeen was not given a separate higher college, but evening technical teaching was centred on Robert Gordon's College, which the Moncreiff commission had already converted from a hospital to a day-school, and Gordon's was linked in 1886 with the School of Art built by John Gray, a local engineer, at his own expense 'to provide a better means for technical artisan education than at present existed in the city', which had already absorbed the old Mechanics' Institution.[11] In Dundee there were few endowments to draw on, but 1883 saw the opening of University College, Scotland's only contribution to the civic university movement, mainly financed by Mary Ann Baxter, a member of one of the city's wealthiest industrial dynasties. At the opening ceremony, the Cambridge don James Stuart, a Scot who had been the main creator of the university 'extension' movement in England, described the mission of such colleges to 'the democracy of our great cities' and predicted that

applied science ... will form the basis of the new extended liberal education for which there is a demand, and the liberal education of the masses of our people, rich or poor, engaged in the arduous daily life of a great town will ... grow up and circle round their technical instruction as a nucleus.[12]

In fact the college taught medicine and arts subjects as well as science, and later became affiliated to St Andrews University. It did not satisfy the need for ordinary technical classes, for which the Technical Institute, also paid for with Baxter money, was opened in 1888.

The Colebrooke commission had seen in Heriot's Hospital

an opportunity for establishing a school somewhat after the model of the Realschulen—one in which the basis of education shall be mathematical and

---

[10] e.g. Playfair in Hansard, 3rd series 197, 17 June 1869, 155–6; Principal Grant in A. Grant (ed.), *Recess Studies* (Edinburgh, 1870), 142–7.
[11] *EN* 22 Sept. 1883, 619.   [12] *EN* 13 Oct. 1883, 680–1.

practical to the same degree that in our ordinary Secondary schools the basis is classical. Indeed, we should be disposed to recommend the exclusion of classics, believing that where a classical education is given, it is apt, as being the more fashionable, to oust or starve the modern instruction that may be given alongside of it.[13]

The Balfour commission acted on this, and three schools—George Heriot's, Robert Gordon's, and Allan Glen's in Glasgow—emerged as secondary schools of a special type, all for boys only. Allan Glen's, a former charitable day-school which had already been modernized in 1876, was described by the Samuelson commission in 1884 as 'one of the very best examples of a secondary technical school . . . that we have met with in the course of our investigations'. A science-based general course down to the age of 14 was followed by two years of technical education oriented to the chemical and engineering industries.[14] To reinforce the technical link, Allan Glen's and Heriot's were put under the same boards of governors as the Glasgow and West of Scotland and Heriot-Watt colleges. The three schools were thus given an 'artisan' mission thought appropriate to their charitable origins. They were equipped with workshops and laboratories, had low fees and numerous bursaries, and were intended to offer a practical, modern curriculum. The schemes for Heriot's and Allan Glen's forbade them to teach Greek, in the hope of discouraging university ambitions, though Latin was allowed as a general educational subject. But Colebrooke's forebodings were soon borne out; Allan Glen's remained closest to the original plan, but all three schools began to develop classical teaching and send boys to the universities, though their wide social recruitment lasted into the twentieth century. One of the problems of endowments reform was that once the initial scheme was put into operation there was no continuing control to ensure that governors remained faithful to the original policy.

The 1887 Act was followed by a circular from the SED which urged school boards to set up 'secondary technical schools' giving full-time education to pupils of 13 upwards, with a curriculum devised in consultation with local industrial and commercial interests.[15] But nothing

[13] PP 1875, XXIX, *Third Report of the Royal Commissioners Appointed to Inquire into Endowed Schools and Hospitals (Scotland)*, 52.

[14] PP 1884, XXIX, *Second Report of the Royal Commissioners on Technical Instruction*, i. 489; XXVII, *First Report of the Educational Endowments (Scotland) Commission*, 177–8.

[15] PP 1888, XLI, *CCES Report, 1887–8*, 90–5.

came of this. The only board which took immediate advantage of the act was Old Monkland (Coatbridge), whose Technical School of 1891 was really a new home for the Gartsherrie Science School. Elgin opened its Victoria School of Science and Art in the same year, though this was not run directly by the school board. By 1914, technical colleges had been built in towns like Paisley (on a site donated by Coats), Motherwell, Kilmarnock, and Inverness, but they usually depended on voluntary appeals, and progress was slow. Despite the 'whisky money' paid to town councils from 1890, it was school boards which were more active in the burghs: in 1891 Glasgow school board had some 10,000 pupils in evening classes, which were carefully organized and publicized.[16] Counties made better use of the grant, and county councils like Lanarkshire and Fife appointed full-time organizers and worked out schemes for distributing resources rationally. Many county councils, dominated by farming interests, were more interested in agriculture than industry, and agricultural education began to get special grants from the government in the 1890s in an attempt to palliate the agricultural depression. By the 1900s the state was supporting agricultural colleges in Glasgow (with an outlying dairying institute in Kilmarnock), Aberdeen, and Edinburgh. These colleges, whose roots lay in the 1880s, had the special function of organizing local classes throughout their region, and eventually passed under the separate control of the Scottish Board of Agriculture.

The case of Dunfermline shows how little local enthusiasm there might be for technical colleges. The idea was floated in the 1880s, and in 1891 the school board decided to adopt the 1887 Act. But in 1893 the 'working men's' representatives opposed it on grounds of cost. The *Educational News* claimed that the true interests of the workers were being manipulated by politicians in search of cheap popularity.

The technical school is now the working man's college. There he can qualify himself for rising in the world—for acquiring wealth and distinction. Dunfermline is essentially a technical school district. Its industries [mainly high-class linen manufacture] are highly technical; and their further development will tax all the resources of technical skill to keep the well-trained foreigner at a safe distance.[17]

Despite the offer of aid from Andrew Carnegie, the local manufacturers joined in the agitation against the supposed burden on the rates, and the

---

[16] *EN* 17 Jan. 1891, 44–7.
[17] *EN* 20 May 1893, 335. Cf. 25 Feb. 1888, 140, 143; 12 Dec. 1891, 835; 3 June 1893, 361.

chairman and four members of the school board resigned in protest against this obscurantism. Nothing was done, and in 1896 the *News* returned to the charge. The town was complaining of loss of trade, but it had

> freely enough spent on kirks and clergymen the profits which should have been devoted to weaving schools, and schools of design; . . . its prosperity depends a good deal more on teachers than on preachers. No continental manufacturing city of the importance of Dunfermline is without technical schools thoroughly adapted to its requirements, and manned by specialists ever on the watch for opportunities of improving on the past, and of reducing the cost of production.[18]

The Technical School eventually opened in 1899, the expense of £12,000 being borne by Carnegie; it was named after George Lauder, leader of the original campaign (and a relative of Carnegie).[19] This was not Carnegie's only intervention in this field, since he gave £5,000 to the Sutherland Technical School at Golspie, opened in 1904. This was financed by millionaires—Carnegie, who had his castle nearby at Skibo, the Canadian-Scottish Lord Strathcona, and the Duke and Duchess of Sutherland, based at Dunrobin Castle—but it was the brain-child of the duchess. It took boarders from all over the northern highlands to study agriculture as well as technical crafts, and was more a secondary school with progressive ideas about practical education than a technical school in the usual sense.[20] It was the model for the Kintyre Technical School, established in 1915 at Keil, near Campbeltown.

When businessmen financed technical colleges (or sat on school boards) it was from a sense of paternalistic social obligation rather than as part of an industrial strategy. For one significant weakness of the technical education movement was its lack of corporate industrial support. The SAPTSE brought together educationists and politicians, but only two businessmen played much part in it: Robert Pullar, of the Perth dyeing firm, and the Greenock shipbuilder Robert Caird. Others who showed an interest in technical education were the borders woollen manufacturers, who set up a college for their industry at Galashiels, and the Fife coal-owners, whose mining school operated first at Dunfermline, later at Cowdenbeath. The shipbuilding and engineering industries of the west, the core of Scottish industry, did not play any conspicuous role. Even Caird saw technical education mainly as something for boys

---

[18] *EN* 7 Nov. 1896, 753.   [19] *EN* 21 Oct. 1899, 727.
[20] *EN* 8 Oct. 1904, 725–6. Cf. E. Beaton, 'The Sutherland Technical School: Pioneer Education for Crofters' Sons', *Review of Scottish Culture*, 7 (1991), 35–51.

of 14 to 16, to fill the gap between school and apprenticeship, and the interest of heavy industry in higher technical education for its experts and managers was very limited.[21] Whether they were being fatally short-sighted in ignoring technical education, or taking an economically rational view in finding current notions of it irrelevant to their needs, is difficult to say in the absence of much research in this area. But it is understandable that Clydeside industrialists, at a time when they still seemed to dominate world markets, with a work-force of highly skilled craftsmen at their disposal, did not share the sense of crisis stirred up by the propagandists.

Commercial employers took more interest, to judge by the activity of chambers of commerce. Commercial subjects, and preparation for civil service examinations, were always an important part of evening class activity, and here there was rivalry from private colleges, of which the best-known was Skerry's in Edinburgh and Glasgow. Commercial education was increasingly significant, not just because of the growth of white-collar jobs and the entry of women into offices, but also because when concern about international rivalry revived at the end of the 1890s (after a lull earlier in the decade) attention switched from industry to commerce. In 1897 the *Educational News* proclaimed that 'the nation is at present face to face with commercial collapse', and in 1898 an MP complained that 'young men from Germany and other countries in the world have now quite cut out the Scotch boy and the Scotch young man from the positions they used to occupy', and hoped that with its take-over of the Science and Art Department the SED would be able to stop the rot, so that we 'shall be sending Scotchmen all over the world to take charge in the great manufacturing places where they have been so successful in the past'.[22] This new wave of agitation focused on the threat from Germany, and attributed her capture of international markets to superior salesmanship and attention to the customer's demands.

One demand which had little success was that the universities should introduce degrees in commerce and give modern languages equal status with the classics. But at a rather lower level, the need was identified for a type of commercial education based on economics, geography, and languages, to supplement or replace practical training in merchants' offices. The London Chamber of Commerce had already

---

[21] *EN* 11 Feb. 1893, 95–7. Cf. P. L. Robertson, 'Technical Education in the British Shipbuilding and Marine Engineering Industries, 1863–1914', *Economic History Review*, 2nd series, 27 (1974), 222–35.

[22] *EN* 4 Dec. 1897, 825; Hansard, 4th series 64, 5 Aug. 1898, 336–7 (G. B. Clark).

created certificates at lower and higher levels, and in Scotland action was taken locally either to organize training for the London examinations, or to set up local schemes; in 1892, in concert with the South of Scotland Chamber of Commerce in the borders, the EIS itself had produced a scheme.[23] The difficulty was—as a report published by the commercial organizations of Edinburgh and Leith in 1900 showed—that the enthusiasm of chamber of commerce activists was seldom shared by ordinary firms, which still preferred to take boys of 14 or 15 and train them on the job, and to use German clerks for their foreign correspondence.[24] When the SED introduced a commercial variant of the Leaving Certificate in 1902, it was a complete failure; 'matters will never be put on a really solid basis', concluded Struthers, 'until business men give the whole problem much more earnest attention than it receives at present from any but the very select few who are familiar with what our most formidable rivals in trade find it well worth their while to do for the training of the future merchant.'[25]

3. CENTRAL INSTITUTIONS

In 1898 the SED took over the work of the Department of Science and Art. Some of its grants for drawing and science had gone to ordinary day-schools, and these were now absorbed into the general funding system. The SED reorganized its own evening classes in 1893 (in line with England) under a separate Continuation School Code, designed 'as a means of enabling scholars who have left elementary schools to acquire something more than elementary knowledge, and especially of giving them opportunities of learning the scientific principles which underlie the employment upon which they have entered'.[26] In 1901 a new Continuation Code was issued, integrating the former science and art classes. 'Continuation classes' remained the official term to cover a huge variety of work at every level, including elementary remedial classes, art, commerce, trade and technical classes, and recreational subjects for adults. Grants were still generally tied to individual courses; most local technical colleges depended on this system, and the SED did

---

[23] *EN* 9 Jan. 1892, 35–6; 28 May 1892, 357.
[24] R. D. Anderson, *Education and Opportunity in Victorian Scotland: Schools and Universities* (Oxford, 1983), 225–6.
[25] *SED Reports, 1908–9*, Secondary Education, 32.
[26] PP 1893–4, XXVIII, *CCES Report, 1892–3*, 87.

TABLE 11.1. *Central Institutions, 1912–1913*

	No. of students	
	Day	Evening
Aberdeen: Robert Gordon's Technical College	380	456
Dundee: Technical College and School of Art	142	1,130
Dunfermline: College of Hygiene and Physical Training	33	0
Edinburgh: Heriot-Watt College	256	2,837
Edinburgh: College of Art	391	464
Edinburgh: School of Cookery and Domestic Economy	1,660	253
Glasgow: Royal Technical College	583	4,298
Glasgow: School of Art	362	348
Glasgow: Athenaeum Commercial College	90	1,037
Glasgow: Glasgow and West of Scotland College of Domestic Science	730	34
Leith: Nautical College	179	46
Total	4,806	10,903

Source: *SED Reports, 1913–14*, CCs & CIs, 162–3.

not give them any special encouragement. Instead it concentrated on two aspects of policy: classes for school-leavers designed to prolong their exposure to a coherent educational experience, and the development of higher technical education in 'central institutions', so called because they received a block grant from the SED.

In English cities, local authorities had taken a lead in developing technical colleges from the 1880s onwards, creating powerful municipal institutions which often worked in harmony with the new civic universities. Their position was further strengthened after the authorities absorbed the school boards in 1902, and a body like London County Council was a major force in technical education. In Scotland, the history of educational grants and local government reform had worked differently: neither town councils nor school boards had become dominant, and most technical colleges were run by independent boards of governors or committees. The SED was thus able to intervene creatively to form a uniform system, and it encouraged amalgamations to form larger specialized colleges. By 1913 the list of central institutions was as shown in Table 11.1. Edinburgh and Glasgow had schools of domestic science (now also branching out into social work training), Leith of navigation, Glasgow of commerce, but in the other cities these functions were performed within the general colleges. There were also three agricultural and two veterinary colleges, transferred from the SED to the Scottish Board of Agriculture in 1912.

Unlike local technical colleges, the central institutions had significant numbers of day students, though they were not necessarily studying full-time, nor were many of them at an advanced level. Since their reorganization in the 1880s, the Glasgow and West of Scotland and Heriot-Watt colleges had been developing higher work leading to three- or four-year diplomas, and setting up research laboratories related to local industries. Ambitious buildings were constructed (as also at Dundee and Aberdeen) with the help of local appeals; the Glasgow college raised £360,000 in the 1900s, and built what was claimed to be the largest single educational building in Europe, while Aberdeen launched an appeal for £100,000 in 1907. The growth of these ambitions can be traced at Heriot-Watt. In 1886 the governors commissioned a report from the English expert Philip Magnus, which envisaged

an institution in which (1) artisans, clerks, and other persons occupied in trade and commerce may supplement their previous education by evening instruction, and in which (2) youths leaving school at about the age of 15 may continue their education during the day time for two or three years before entering some industrial occupation.

The new principal, F. Grant Ogilvie, added to this the sons of manufacturers, engineers, architects, et cetera entering their father's profession, and saw the Glasgow and Edinburgh colleges as a national resource for this élite.[27] In 1888, the new building opened and day classes began. But the achievements were modest, and in 1901 Craik was pressing the governors to make the college 'a great technical school for the East of Scotland. Hitherto it has been little more than a huge overgrown night school.'[28] In 1900, Grant Ogilvie was succeeded by A. P. Laurie, the son of S. S. Laurie. Unlike his father, Laurie was an enthusiast for utilitarian education and for things German—an enthusiasm which was to lead him astray politically in the 1930s.[29] In 1908, following the opening of a new engineering department, he declared that 'the Heriot-Watt College is rapidly becoming a technical university', and compared

[27] *EN* 10 Apr. 1886, 273; 12 Feb. 1887, 120–2.   [28] *EN* 16 Nov. 1901, 814.
[29] R. Griffiths, *Fellow Travellers of the Right: British Enthusiasts for Nazi Germany, 1933–9* (Oxford, 1983), 308.

it directly with the German model. He was able to point to courses in mechanical, mining and electrical engineering, technical chemistry, and brewing; to collaboration with the university, including the joint use of laboratories; and to sandwich courses arranged with local engineering firms. The attitudes of employers, however, still held back progress:

It is . . . absolutely necessary, if this country is to hold its industrial position, that we should cease playing at technical education and living under the delusion that all that is wanted is the teaching of a smattering of science to our artizans. . . . the real weakness of the position lies in the ignorance of the employer, not the employed, and the consequent absence of the highly organised technical research by scientific experts in all branches of industry.[30]

The SED too liked to think that the central institutions 'may be described as industrial universities'.[31] It claimed that of the 1,740 students who gained the Leaving Certificate in 1913, 961 entered universities and 319 central institutions, which would suggest that the latter had established a serious reputation among the middle classes.[32] Unfortunately this was an isolated statistic, and it is difficult to say how many students were studying at the highest level. At Heriot-Watt, with well over 3,000 students, only eight or nine diplomas were awarded each year. The Glasgow college, renamed the Royal College of Technology in 1912 and formally affiliated to Glasgow University in 1913, awarded forty or fifty, and was perhaps the only central institution really comparable to a university.[33] Even at Edinburgh and Glasgow, as the figures show, the bulk of the work was in evening classes, and many of these were either 'trade' classes for the building trades, printing, tailoring, and so on, or courses in office skills, with the students themselves coming from skilled working or white-collar occupations.[34]

Among the specialized colleges, the SED made a particular effort to build up the Glasgow Athenaeum (which traced its origins to the 1840s) as a 'great commercial central institution' and 'a coping stone in one direction to that system of education which the Department wished to carry out for Scotland';[35] in 1914 it was renamed the Glasgow and West

---

[30] *EN* 23 Oct. 1908, 1199–1202.

[31] PP 1906, XXX, *CCES Report, 1905–6*, 31.

[32] *SED Reports, 1916–19*, Report for 1917–18, 14.

[33] Details in the annual *Calendars* of the colleges.

[34] For a time in the 1900s students' occupations were printed in the annual reports: see for example PP 1905, XXIX, *CCES Report 1904–5*, 908–9 (Edinburgh), 919–20 (Glasgow).

[35] *EN* 3 Dec. 1904, 886.

of Scotland Commercial College. But much of the teaching remained elementary (typing, shorthand, or bookkeeping), and there were few takers for the four-year diploma, the familiar reason being 'the profound distrust of the ordinary business man for all forms of education that have not been acquired in counting-house or warehouse'.[36] Another part of the SED's strategy was to create a single Art College in Edinburgh, combining the original school of art of 1858, a School of Applied Art founded in 1892 by the architect Robert Rowand Anderson, and the art classes of Heriot-Watt College; the town council was persuaded to finance this, and the new college opened in 1908.[37] In Glasgow, the School of Art established its reputation long before it became a central institution. Francis Newbery, director since 1885, emphasized design and applied art, giving special opportunities to women artists. The school became famous for the group of artists and craft workers around Margaret Macdonald, as well as for its building designed by her husband Charles Rennie Mackintosh.[38] Their products for the wealthy consumer may not have had much to do with the heavy industries of contemporary Glasgow, but they did wonders in the long run for the Glasgow branch of the heritage industry.

4. CONTINUATION CLASSES

Systematic part-time education for school-leavers was one of the many ideas taken from Germany, and there were suggestions even in the 1880s that it might be made compulsory. Under the 1901 Act, exemptions could be made conditional on attendance at continuation classes, and the idea became part of the general concern about adolescence and the dangerous period of transition to the adult labour market. It was especially associated with the English educationist Michael Sadler, but Craik was also an enthusiast, seeing it as analogous to military service. In his last speech as an official, opening a new gymnasium at Dingwall Academy, he declared his personal belief in compulsory continuation classes for men between 14 and 18 who did not join the Volunteers: every youth should learn,

[36] *EN* 12 Jan. 1917, 36.
[37] *EN* 15 Mar. 1902, 184; *EN* 13 Apr. 1906, 279; S. McKinstry, *Rowand Anderson: 'the Premier Architect of Scotland'* (Edinburgh, 1991), 139–44, 163–4, 168–9.
[38] J. Burkhauser (ed.), *Glasgow Girls: Women in Art and Design, 1880–1920* (Edinburgh, 1990), 63–6, 71–4.

whether or not he was to serve in the ranks, whether or not he was to be a military conscript, whether or not that was to be the particular form of service which the State demands of him—that it was absolutely inevitable that the debt must be paid, a debt that would bring home to him the sense of civic responsibility.[39]

Again in 1907,

He believed there was an immense wastage . . . in those three or four years that followed the life in the elementary school. . . . the State might fairly require, in connection with these continuation classes, that each young citizen should make himself fit to serve his country in her need. (Applause.) He knew people said this would promote militarism,

but they were wrong to object to 'compulsory physical training'. In the debate on the 1908 Act, Craik again spoke up for 'the duty of service to the State', and for compulsory military drill in continuation classes.[40]

Compulsory military training was never on the political cards, but in 1906 the Liberal Scottish Secretary Sinclair announced his support for compulsory continuation;[41] permissive powers were included in the 1907 bill, and became law in 1908. School boards could make by-laws imposing continuation classes until the age of 17, and could establish juvenile employment bureaux, another popular idea of the time for guiding adolescents. Although there were opponents of the compulsory principle, it went through with relatively little debate, except over the maximum age, and it seems that the opportunity was taken to experiment with an idea which might be introduced later in England. The act was followed in 1909 by a circular from the SED which pointed out that 'everywhere the progressive nations of the world are bestirring themselves to make the proper instruction, control, and discipline of adolescents a matter of State concern'. Scots should be pleased that 'the Legislature has seen fit to permit this momentous experiment to be made first of all in that portion of the United Kingdom'. In this 'stupendous' task, school boards must 'join hands with every agency having for its object the industrial efficiency and social well-being of the community', including employers, and one suggested task was the compilation of a 'census' of young persons between 14 and 18 in order to decide whether compulsion was necessary.[42]

[39] *EN* 31 Dec. 1904, 953.
[40] *EN* 12 Apr. 1907, 327–8; Hansard, 4th series 196, 10 Nov. 1908, 198.
[41] Hansard, 4th series 158, 14 June 1906, 1179.
[42] *SED Reports, 1908–9*, Minutes and Circulars, 55–9. This circular was reprinted annually as part of the Continuation Code.

However, there seems to have been little popular demand for the new powers. The SED refrained from putting pressure on school boards, and at first it was only a few rural boards which acted. In rural areas the SED allowed the Supplementary Courses to double up as continuation classes, and this could be seen as a revival of the old habit of returning to school in the winter. In towns, however, few children were able to attend during the day, except in a few cases where courses were organized at the workplace. Even in Edinburgh, which devoted great efforts to continuation classes and was regarded as the model authority, the board preferred to wait until the voluntary system had exhausted its possibilities. A census of 14- to 18-year-olds in the city in 1910 showed that only 27 per cent were in evening classes; 22 per cent were still at school, and 51 per cent escaping education altogether. At Greenock at the same period, 25 per cent were in continuation classes, and this seems to have been typical.[43] By 1912, it was claimed that Edinburgh had reduced the proportion of non-attenders to 30 per cent, and by 1914 the SED estimated, surely over-optimistically, that continuation classes nationally were reaching nearly half the adolescent age-group; they had 145,000 students compared with 78,000 in 1901.[44] Since only eighteen school boards had adopted compulsory by-laws, this could be considered a success for voluntary persuasion, but it would be difficult to raise the proportion further without making compulsion universal. One Edinburgh enthusiast who hoped that continuation classes would 'lead up to the Central Institutions of the country, so that "the lad o' pairts" may rise from the lowest rung of the ladder to the very highest' had also to admit that 'the picture palaces which are increasing so rapidly in number, provide excitement, beside which the most attractive evening school must seem dull to the adolescent of the average type'.[45]

By far the most important board to adopt the act was Glasgow: in 1911 compulsion was introduced for children without the Merit Certificate. By 1914, 8,513 of the 30,000 students in continuation classes were there under the by-law.[46] But this met the resistance of employers and teenagers alike. Engineering firms like Barr and Stroud and the Albion Motor Company were willing to encourage their apprentices to attend in the evenings, but not to release them during the day; since

[43] *SED Reports, 1910–11*, CCs & CIs, 28 (Greenock); *EN* 17 Mar. 1911, 273 (Edinburgh).

[44] *SED Reports, 1912–13*, CCs & CIs, 8; *SED Reports, 1913–14*, General Report, 33; *EN* 12 Sept. 1913, 795–6.

[45] *EN* 31 May 1912, 500–1.   [46] *EN* 20 Mar. 1914, 260–2.

they worked alongside adults, this 'would completely dislocate the "squad system" of working and would inevitably throw some men out of employment'. Another problem was that since only the Glasgow board had acted, some workers were affected and others were not. Moreover, continuation classes were counted as work for the purposes of the factory acts, so reducing the hours available to employers, and the fact that prosecuting employers rather than pupils was the means of enforcing the act did not help to win over the former.[47] As for the pupils, those now forced to come back to school after a day's work were precisely those who had profited from it least before, 'the derelicts of our educational system'. It was not surprising that they resented the experience, and sabotaged the classes by indiscipline or refusal to work; the lot of the teachers drafted to cope with these hard cases was unenviable.[48] The organized labour movement was also against compulsory continuation, preferring to raise the full-time leaving age. Glasgow was in any case a city where an exceptionally high proportion of young men went into skilled trades,[49] and starting work traditionally depended on apprenticeship, family contacts, and religious allegiance rather than formal educational qualifications.

The Continuation Code covered all types of technical and commercial education, and both Edinburgh and Glasgow had extensive systems of evening classes, with full-time organizers and elaborate publicity, co-ordinated with the technical colleges to avoid overlapping. But Edinburgh gave particular attention to the post-school classes favoured by the SED, and the chairman of its continuation committee, Councillor Leishman, was recognized as an expert. It was one of the first boards to set up an employment bureau, and in 1908 it brought the German authority Dr Kerschensteiner, director of education at Munich, over to lecture in the four Scottish cities.[50] When Edinburgh built its central supplementary school at Tynecastle in 1912, it was also used for continuation classes, in the hope of a painless transition from full-time to part-time education. The school had a range of twelve workshops for skilled trades like pattern-making, joinery, upholstering, and tailoring, as well as five rooms for cookery and laundrywork. It was described

---

[47] *SED Reports, 1910–11*, CCs & CIs, 30–5; *EN* 6 Sept. 1912, 770; *EN* 31 Oct. 1913, 1016.

[48] *EN* 15 Dec. 1911, 1253–4; 22 Oct. 1915, 767–8.

[49] J. Springhall, *Coming of Age: Adolescence in Britain, 1860–1960* (Dublin, 1986), 237.

[50] *EN* 24 Apr. 1908, 449–52.

as 'an important "Trade School," largely on the lines of Continental practice', and 'a connecting link between the day school and the workshop or factory'.[51] The SED, however, saw continuation classes as combining general and vocational education, and encouraged a balanced syllabus similar to that of supplementary courses, including English literature as well as training in citizenship and (for girls) domestic science. Part-time compulsory education was to be a surrogate for further raising of the leaving age, and a preparation for it.

The SED's concentration on school-leavers at one end of the spectrum and Central Institutions at the other meant that technical education for the ordinary worker was neglected—as was 'liberal' education for adults, left to bodies like the Workers' Educational Association, which was slow to catch on in Scotland. There were other weaknesses in the SED's approach to the question. Although it constantly urged local authorities to set up advisory committees of businessmen and experts, it did not take its own advice, and policies on supplementary courses and continuation classes do not seem to have been based on any systematic analysis of the needs of industry or commerce. Craik and Struthers were bureaucrats responding to political pressures and prejudices, and their solutions were often bureaucratic in a negative sense, based on theoretical schematizations which bore little relation to social realities or local conditions. After 1903, for example, the educational system was presented in terms of three pillars, primary, 'intermediate', and secondary, with leaving ages of 14, 15, and 17, leading respectively to continuation classes and working-class jobs, to commerce, industry and Central Institutions, and to the professions and universities. But in reality there was no 'intermediate' sector of schools, and to link technical education with early leaving and part-time attendance inevitably damaged its prestige. Michael Sanderson has argued in relation to England that the crucial weakness in the twentieth century has been the failure to develop high-status secondary technical schools, and the same may be true of Scotland.[52] And yet, if Scottish educational culture had a persistent 'academic' bias, it is difficult to blame the SED for this. With the higher grade schools of 1899, supplementary courses, continuation classes, and 'industrial universities', there was no shortage of attempts to stress the practical and the vocational. But like the Balfour commission's

[51] *SED Reports, 1912–13*, CCs & CIs, 8; *EN* 5 Jan. 1912, 4; 26 Jan. 1912, 67.

[52] M. Sanderson, 'Education and Economic Decline, 1890–1980s', *Oxford Review of Economic Policy*, 4/1 (1988), 38–50.

secondary technical schools of the 1880s, they foundered on the indifference of employers and the refusal of parents to accept what was seen as an inferior alternative. For in Scotland Latin, university culture, and liberal education were not 'aristocratic', but the symbols of a national democratic tradition.

12

The Twentieth Century

THE intensity of educational development after 1900, and the placing of the school within a broader framework of social welfare, made school boards look increasingly obsolete. Although they had perhaps rooted themselves more deeply in local life than their English equivalents, they were too small and numerous, and lacked a proper connection either with the secondary education committees or with other local agencies of social policy. The English Act of 1902 seemed to provide a model for reform, but political difficulties were to stand in the way, and although the Education Act of 1908 was the most comprehensive piece of legislation since 1872, school boards survived until 1918. The Act of 1918 reflected the new mood of social and democratic reform created by the First World War. But its most radical provisions did not survive the post-war financial crisis, and there was little in the act which had not been discussed at length before 1914. The war should therefore be seen as accelerating trends already in progress and dismantling former political barriers to change, rather than as the source of a wholly new mood of reform.[1]

1. ABORTIVE BILLS AND THE 1908 ACT

The 1902 Act for England and Wales, the work of a Conservative government, aroused bitter controversy because it put denominational schools 'on the rates', though not under the direct control of the local authorities. This aspect had no great resonance in Scotland, but Scottish opinion was attracted both by the idea of unitary authorities and by the Consultative Committee of experts, which had been set up in 1899 when the old Education Department and the Department of Science and Art were merged into a new Board of Education. The Scottish demand

---

[1] This chapter is more tentative than others. From the 1890s the records of the SED in the Scottish Record Office are substantial, especially those connected with legislation. To have given the detailed account allowed by this evidence would have unbalanced the book, and I have therefore excluded it.

for a local input to policy-making had been unsatisfied since the abolition of the Edinburgh Board of Education in 1878, and the 'autocracy' of the SED was a favourite theme of complaint, especially among Liberal MPs.

In 1900 Balfour of Burleigh introduced a bill which left school boards intact, but proposed county 'higher education' committees with independent rating powers. The various grants to secondary and technical education which had grown up since 1890 were to be consolidated into a single fund; this rationalization was a priority in all the subsequent bills. Reflecting the hostility of the SED to any weakening of its authority, Balfour refused the Liberal demand for a consultative committee. Otherwise the Liberals supported the bill. It was passed by the Lords, but soon ran into a problem which was to defeat all subsequent efforts, the political sensitivity of any change in the distribution of the rate burden. The bill's provisions for raising the effective leaving age to 14, which were supported by all parties, were detached and passed into law in 1901. A period of legislative frustration reminiscent of the 1850s then followed. Parliamentary priorities made it difficult to get a Scottish bill through unless it was generally agreed by the Scottish MPs; an obstructive minority was able to block comprehensive legislation, and minor but worthwhile and uncontroversial reforms suffered from the delay. The divisions were no longer over religion, but were again within the Liberal party, between the 'establishment' leadership, which was in broad agreement with the Conservatives, and a knot of radicals with a special interest in educational issues. There was a direct link with the disputes of the 1880s: James Caldwell, once the scourge of school boards over the grading of schools, now emerged as their champion, opposing their abolition and praising them as models of popular control. The future of the administrative authorities joined rating as a political issue.

The EIS was keen to see legislation, if only for professional reasons. It wanted statutory security for teachers, and improvements in the teachers' pension scheme which had been introduced in 1898. It had little love for school boards, which had often been oppressive employers, and favoured large unitary authorities controlling all levels of education. The 1900 bill was thus found inadequate. In 1902 Balfour of Burleigh made a speech promising to create large authorities, but not committing himself to a specific plan. There was no bill in 1903, but that year saw the publication of *Scottish Education Reform* by C. M. Douglas, a Liberal MP, and Henry Jones, the Glasgow philosophy professor, with a preface by Haldane. This was generally seen as the policy manifesto of the Rosebery group, and its two main demands were for 'district' education authorities, smaller than counties but larger than school boards, and for a Scottish Council of Education representing the spectrum of educational interests.[2] When Balfour introduced a new bill in 1904, therefore, it was after widespread public discussion, and since this bill was close to the Liberal proposals the way seemed clear for agreed action. There were to be 107 district school boards, replacing the existing 972 boards and the secondary education committees. A national advisory council was still rejected, but there were to be four provincial councils, based on Edinburgh, Aberdeen, Glasgow, and—unexpectedly—Inverness. The bill attempted to defuse opposition by retaining the existing system of parish rates instead of giving the new boards general rating powers, but this raised many practical difficulties, and the bill expired amid technical discussion of local government finance. The units of administration were also controversial—county councils were opposed to the loss of their powers as well as school boards—and there were those who preferred a 'municipal' solution, using the general local authorities as in England, to the *ad hoc* authorities proposed in the bill.

In 1905 the bill was reintroduced, with the rating proposals altered and St Andrews replacing Inverness as the seat of the fourth provincial council. But this came to grief on the opposition of the smaller school boards (the large urban boards would have survived in a new guise). Their spokesman was Caldwell, and he forced an amendment to retain school boards which divided the Liberals: the party leader Campbell-Bannerman supported him, but Douglas and Haldane were among those who sided with the government.[3] In the face of this dissension at a stage when time was running out, the government dropped the bill, and the Liberal divisions were underlined by the formation of a Scottish Education Reform Association which had a programme based on the book by Douglas and Jones, and included Unionists as well as the Rosebery wing of the Liberals and various educational and university leaders.[4] Later in 1905 the Liberals came to power, and in 1906 they won a famous election victory. According to one MP, they were elected 'with a mandate to make Scottish education democratic'.[5] But the party

[2] C. M. Douglas and H. Jones, *Scottish Education Reform: A Scheme of District School Boards and a National Council* (Glasgow, 1903).
[3] Hansard, 4th series 149, 14 July 1905. Cf. *EN* 22 July 1905, 533–4.
[4] *EN* 7 Oct. 1905, 744.
[5] Hansard, 4th series 158, 14 June 1906, 1195 (A. W. Black).

division over educational authorities meant that when the new government did turn to reform it carefully abstained from disturbing the school boards or the secondary education committees. There was no bill in 1906, when the government was preoccupied with a controversial and unsuccessful attempt to overturn the English act of 1902. But in 1907 a Scottish bill was introduced which became the 1908 Education Act. This finally carried out the amalgamation of most of the state grants into a single Education (Scotland) Fund. The SED retained the bulk of this for distribution centrally, but the local grants reappeared as 'district education funds' administered by the county secondary committees. These were given more flexibility in matters such as bursaries, and in the absence of other county-wide authorities they acquired some non-secondary functions such as the co-ordination of medical inspection. Within the limits of what was politically feasible, the 1908 Act did introduce more unity into educational administration, and school boards were also given more powers; the financial restrictions on higher class schools, for example, were abolished. But the Liberal government refused to set up advisory councils, national or provincial.

All these bills went beyond administrative reorganization, and incorporated changes of various kinds as they appeared on the political agenda. Those which reached the statute-book in 1908 included reform of the school board franchise, public provision of school meals and medical inspection, concessions to the teachers' professional demands, and a move towards compulsory continuation classes. The assimilation of school boards to the general local government franchise was uncontroversial. The abolition of the cumulative vote was also included in all the bills, and nearly went through in 1908. Catholics then mounted opposition to this threat to their special position, and mobilized the Irish MPs: an attempt to retain the system failed at the committee stage, but succeeded in the final stages of discussion.[6] The cumulative vote survived, but there were many suggestions that proportional representation (then being widely discussed as a general political principle) would be a better way of preserving minority rights. The religious issue had also arisen in 1904, when the bill included powers for school boards to aid denominational schools from the rates. This question was at the heart of the party dispute over the 1902 Act, and would certainly have proved controversial in Scotland if the bill had gone further; inevitably, it was dropped in the Liberal bills. The 1908 Act did allow school

---

[6] The debates in the Scottish Grand Committee, not in Hansard, can be found in *EN*.

boards to provide free books for children in denominational schools, but even this modest attempt at equity stirred up sectarian trouble in school board elections, notably in Edinburgh. Not until the war years was a serious attempt made to grapple with the denominational problem.

The movement to give schools a wider welfare role was discussed in Chapter 8. The most controversial aspect was the power to provide school meals. It was the chief educational priority of the Labour party, which was now flexing its muscles as a Liberal ally, and in 1906 the government introduced bills for England and Scotland. These were referred to a Select Committee, which included Craik, now an MP and a strong opponent. Although the committee was in favour of change, the Scottish witnesses showed little demand for it, Edinburgh and Glasgow school boards being decidedly hostile.[7] Scotland was cut out of the legislation by the House of Lords, but it went ahead for England. In 1907 Ramsay MacDonald introduced a Labour bill for Scotland,[8] and this was eventually subsumed in the general education bill. A Liberal government with Labour links was also more responsive than a Unionist one to the grievances of teachers, most of which were met in 1908 with the introduction of an improved pension scheme and a right of appeal to the SED against dismissal.

2. FROM 1908 TO THE FIRST WORLD WAR

The 1908 Act did not satisfy all parties. The Education (Scotland) Fund turned out to have less money in it than was expected, and there was much dispute about the allocation of district funds to the county committees. School boards complained that new responsibilities were being placed on them without the state providing extra finance, and denominational schools found it increasingly difficult to keep up with the complexities of modern education. As we have seen, the SED was forced to postpone indefinitely plans to reduce the size of classes. On the political front, various MPs continued to demand that school boards should give way to larger units, that proportional representation should replace the cumulative vote, that the SED should be renamed 'Scottish' and moved to Edinburgh, and that the autocracy of Struthers should be

---

[7] PP 1906, VIII, *Special Report and Report from the Select Committee on the Education (Provision of Meals) Bill, 1906; and the Education (Provision of Meals) (Scotland) Bill, 1906.* Cf. summary in *EN* 11 May 1906, 341–2; 18 May 1906, 366–8.

[8] See debate in Hansard, 4th series 170, 1 Mar. 1907.

tempered by an advisory committee or council: 'the veiled prophet of Dover House was pre-eminent among the oligarchy of eminent public servants which dominated Scottish affairs', complained R. Munro-Ferguson.[9] These grievances were at their height in 1912–13, and some MPs wanted a royal commission on Scottish education. But although the SED had opened an Edinburgh office in 1908, policy continued to be made in London.

The First World War led to a new Education Act in 1918, but many of its provisions were unfinished business from 1908 rather than the product of reconstructionist idealism. The absence of county education authorities, for example, was increasingly seen as an anomaly, and by 1914 school boards in several counties had anticipated change by forming county associations.[10] In 1912 the government planned a new education bill for England, and Struthers was included on a policy committee of officials and ministers headed by Haldane, now Lord Chancellor but still seen as the Liberals' chief educational philosopher.[11] In 1913 Haldane revealed some of the government's thinking, and though the details were not publicized, and the commitment of the Cabinet to the plan seemed lukewarm, the emphasis was clearly on equality of opportunity and on opening up the universities. In Scotland, where the educational ladder was already fairly complete, longer school attendance seemed to be the next step demanded by progress. Since the achievement of school meals, raising the school leaving age to 16 was the main Labour demand, but more orthodox opinion looked to the extension of compulsory part-time attendance, for which experience with continuation classes since 1908 paved the way.

A second issue of growing importance was the position of denominational schools.[12] The educational innovations of the 1900s put a heavy strain on their finances, and their teachers were notoriously poorly paid. During the 1900 general election, when putting denominational education on the rates was in prospect in England, the Catholic Archbishop of Glasgow had issued a pastoral letter welcoming this solution. But the church showed no willingness to relax its grip on school management,

---

[9] Hansard, 4th series 196, 10 Nov. 1908, 130.

[10] *EN* 15 Aug. 1913, 719–20; 30 Jan. 1914, 96.

[11] G. Sherington, *English Education, Social Change and War, 1911–20* (Manchester, 1981), 22.

[12] See M. Skinnider, 'Catholic Elementary Education in Glasgow, 1818–1918', in T. R. Bone (ed.), *Studies in the History of Scottish Education, 1872–1939* (London, 1967), 41–57; Brother Kenneth, 'The Education (Scotland) Act, 1918, in the Making', *Innes Review*, 19 (1968), 91–128.

which was a prerequisite for change. The Conservative education bills of 1904 and 1905 would have given permissive powers for rate aid, but by now Catholic opinion preferred to concentrate on securing higher grants from Whitehall. This was the policy of a Catholic education conference at Dumfries in 1903, and in 1906 a Catholic Education Council for Scotland was formed in anticipation of Liberal legislation.[13] But despite the intervention of Irish MPs during the debate on the 1908 Act, no firm promises were gained, and by 1911 grants or rate aid were on the political agenda once more. In 1911 and 1913 there were Catholic negotiations with Glasgow school board, and in 1915–16 Catholics and Episcopalians had joint discussions with Edinburgh school board and worked out a transfer scheme which foreshadowed that of 1918. But it needed national legislation to solve the problems of finance and management.[14] The Episcopalians, unlike the Catholics, had now come to see their ailing schools as more a burden than an advantage, and contemplated handing them over if some kind of religious guarantee could be secured: in 1900 they seemed willing to accept Episcopalian religious instruction within state schools; in 1904 they offered to give school boards a share in management in return for the grants proposed by the education bill; and in 1905 they offered to transfer their training college to the state given suitable safeguards. This did not happen, and by 1913 the college was in such straits that closure was only averted by staff and salary cuts.[15]

A third pre-war development was the growth of militancy in the EIS, and moves towards amalgamation with the secondary teachers. The 1908 superannuation scheme had serious teething troubles, and inflation began to put strain on teachers' salaries. For the first time, the EIS began seriously to consider national salary scales, and there were demands, though they were rejected by the union leadership, for a policy of equal salaries for men and women.[16] There were now younger teachers in the ranks inspired by socialism, and many wanted the EIS to follow the more political and trade-unionist stance of the National Union of Teachers in England. In 1911 Scotland saw its first teachers' strike, at Barrhead, over the appointment of a head rather than a class teacher

[13] *EN* 3 Oct. 1903, 751–2.

[14] *EN* 4 July 1913, 623–4; 17 Oct. 1913, 967–8, 980; 31 Oct. 1913, 1007, 1012; 12 Mar. 1915, 169.

[15] *EN* 28 Apr. 1900, 282; 7 May 1904, 330–1; 6 May 1905, 334; 16 May 1913, 444.

[16] H. Corr, 'Politics of the Sexes in English and Scottish Teachers' Unions, 1870–1914', in H. Corr and L. Jamieson (eds.), *Politics of Everyday Life: Continuity and Change in Work and the Family* (London, 1990), 186–205.

as a continuation class organizer.[17] It was surely no coincidence that Barrhead was the residence of the socialist Annie Maxton and her brother John. The strike was officially supported by the Scottish Class Teachers' Federation; both Maxtons were active in the EIS, and John Maxton was on its national council.[18]

In 1909 there was an amalgamation, hailed by the *Educational News* as 'an important step in the process of systematizing Scottish education',[19] of the two secondary teachers' unions. These were the Association of Teachers in the Secondary Schools of Scotland founded in the 1880s, and the Scottish Association of Secondary Teachers, which had started in the west of Scotland and represented the higher grade teachers and their ethos. The new union was the Secondary Education Association of Scotland, and it published the *Secondary School Journal*. By spring 1914 the EIS was considering a single teachers' union, to include this Association and the Class Teachers' Federation. The idea of unity was linked both with the trade-union approach and with the concept of a national system of education without divisive 'grades'.[20] Negotiations started in 1914, but proved laborious, and it was not until September 1917 that the new body, which retained the name of the EIS, was inaugurated. It could claim 20,000 members. The unions' journals were also amalgamated, and the venerable *Educational News* gave way in 1918 to the *Scottish Educational Journal*.

Teacher militancy had been increased by such wartime developments as the SED's pressure to allow unqualified teachers to fill the gaps left by those who joined the army, the pursuit of policies of 'economy' by school boards, and the steep rise in prices, which required the payment of 'war bonuses' and led in 1917 to a committee on teachers' salaries headed by Craik, which prepared the way for the national salary scales introduced by the 1918 Act. Other wartime problems caused administrative headaches for school boards and the SED, but did not raise issues of policy. Schools and technical colleges were commandeered by the military, and buildings often had to be used in shifts, while additional places were needed urgently in areas like Gretna where huge munitions factories were established. Women's work took more mothers out of the home, leading to the extension of school meals and the provision of 'play centres' by school boards. The most serious effects of the war were the result of the demand for labour, both in industrial

---

[17] *EN* 19 Sept. 1913, 878.
[18] Cf. G. Brown, *Maxton* (Edinburgh, 1986), 35.   [19] *EN* 19 Feb. 1909, 173.
[20] *EN* 15 May 1914, 439–40; 5 Feb. 1915, 88–9; 12 Feb. 1915, 103–4, 109.

areas, where continuation classes suffered from the ready availability of
work, and in the countryside, where it was difficult to resist the pleas
of farmers to allow exemptions. General levels of attendance suffered,
and moralists complained of the rise in juvenile delinquency and
indiscipline. On the other hand, in Scotland as in England, the war also
led to more children staying on and entering secondary education, which
perhaps reflected hopes for a more open society after the war, and made
the breaking down of social barriers one of the themes of the 1918 Act.
One inspector commented on

the increased interest taken in education by the general public, the enhanced
esteem in which it is held, and the larger expectations based on education as
a main instrument for the bringing in of a newer and better order.... It is
apparent also in the world of labour from the demand made by many of the
most intelligent of labour's representatives, not for the traditional ladder of
opportunity, up which a few may climb, but for the extension to the whole of
the proletariat of the benefits of a prolonged course of secondary education.[21]

One of the first-fruits of the teachers' unity movement was the setting up in 1916 of a Scottish Education Reform Committee, headed by
Alexander Morgan, principal of the Edinburgh training college, to draw
up post-war plans. Not surprisingly, it concluded that better pay and
status for teachers was the most urgent reform, but the report was
thorough and progressive, and included separate sections on women's,
technical, and moral education. It brought together the various strands
of pre-war thinking, and recommended raising the leaving age to 15,
with compulsory continuation classes until 18. The report broadly endorsed SED policy, particularly the specialization and functional differentiation in force since 1903, and did not put forward any radical
educational vision.[22] It was launched at a special New Year congress in
1917, where Morgan identified two priorities: equality of opportunity
(here Knox and the *First Book of Discipline* were invoked), and moral
education, which would 'utilise more fully for the good of humanity the
spiritual forces of the nation'. The example of Germany showed the
danger of merely material efficiency. Yet Germany's war effort also
commanded reluctant admiration for her industrial organization, and
the war years saw a revival of the rhetoric of international competition,

---

[21] *SED Reports, 1916–19*, Report for 1918–19, 5. For numbers in secondary schools,
see Table V in Appendix 1.

[22] *Reform in Scottish Education: being the Report of the Scottish Education Reform
Committee* (Edinburgh, 1917).

which was expected to be fiercer than ever once peace was restored: 'the future position of our country as a great power', said Morgan, 'depends upon our training and organising to a far higher degree than ever before the intellectual and moral capacity, and the productive power of the nation. . . . Never before have the brain-power and trained intelligence of the country been put to the test as they will be in the coming generation.'[23] As an MP put it in the debate on the 1918 Act, 'German brains are more to be feared than German bullets.'[24]

3. THE 1918 EDUCATION ACT

The government moved more slowly than the Scottish teachers. After Lloyd George became prime minister at the end of 1916 education had a higher salience, and there was a committee on educational reconstruction, including Struthers as a member, which took the government's pre-war plans as its starting-point, but no separate reconstruction committee was ever set up for Scotland. Nevertheless, Haldane received the Reform Committee's proposals favourably, and the Scottish Liberal MPs set up their own committee to advance Scottish educational affairs.[25] The Reform Committee remained in being, and was in touch with bodies like the Workers' Educational Association and the Scottish Trades Union Congress. A Scottish education bill was introduced at the end of 1917. The main point of controversy was the proposal to replace school boards not by *ad hoc* authorities, but by county and city councils. This was what the Reform Committee had recommended, but it was opposed by the Scottish School Boards Association, still led by the Revd John Smith of Govan, by Labour members who preferred smaller district authorities, and by the churches, which wanted *ad hoc* authorities where their influence would survive. A compromise was reached in which the county was retained as the unit of administration, but with directly elected education authorities, including separate ones for Glasgow (incorporating Govan), Edinburgh, Dundee, Aberdeen, and Leith. The cumulative vote was abolished, and the authorities were elected by proportional representation, using the single transferable vote; until abolished in 1929 as part of a reform of Scottish local government,

---

[23] *EN* 5 Jan. 1917, 12.
[24] Hansard, 5th series 107, 26 June 1918, 1143 (E. Parrott).
[25] *EN* 12 Jan. 1917, 22–3; 2 Mar. 1917, 119.

these authorities provided one of the few examples of working PR in Britain.

Prior negotiations had also achieved a religious compromise.[26] The provisions of the 1918 Act, which were very similar to proposals made by Struthers to the Catholics in 1911, allowed denominational schools to be transferred to the education authorities, which would henceforth maintain them and appoint and pay the teachers. Guarantees were provided for the continuation of religious instruction and for the teachers' religious faith, but transferred schools became public schools over which the religious authorities had no direct control. Many Catholics—notably the Archbishop of Glasgow, whose archdiocese contained three-quarters of the Catholic schoolchildren—were unhappy with this, and it was dissension among Catholics rather than any anti-Catholic feeling which threatened to delay the settlement. The Presbyterian churches did mount an agitation on the grounds that Catholics were being given what the majority had been refused in 1872, a statutory guarantee of religious instruction; but this was appeased by reproducing in the 1918 Act the 'use and wont' preamble from 1872. Although Episcopalians were also able to transfer their schools, the 1918 Act is remembered above all as the founding charter of Scottish Catholic education, when it at last gained financial security and equality of resources—though of course it did not mark the beginning, as is often popularly supposed, of state aid to Catholic schools. The drawbacks of the settlement—the entrenchment of sectarian divisions, and their import into the new education authorities—were matters for the future.

These compromises were agreed before the bill was reintroduced in 1918, and it passed through Parliament with relatively little controversy and much Scottish self-congratulation. When introducing it, the Scottish Secretary Robert Munro stressed the twin themes of equal opportunity and international competition. It was necessary to 'mobilise the intellectual resources of the nation as against those arduous times which are in front of us, when brains developed by education will be of more and more account'.[27] The leaving age was raised to 15, and there was to be compulsory continuation education, at first until 16 and later to 18. But these provisions, like similar ones in the English act, were overtaken by financial crisis and remained a dead letter; the leaving age was not raised from 14 until 1945. Munro also stressed secondary

---

[26] Skinnider, 'Catholic Elementary Education', 57–70; Br. Kenneth, 'Education (Scotland) Act, 1918'.
[27] Hansard, 5th series 107, 26 June 1918, 1082.

education, which needed to expand far beyond the current output of 2,000 a year if the needs of industry and commerce as well as the liberal professions were to be met. Education authorities now had to provide free secondary education for all requiring it, although they could, and did, retain a limited number of fee-paying schools in addition; this was a reform not achieved in England and Wales until 1944. The act was silent, however, about the organization of schools, and post-war hopes were disappointed by an SED circular of 1921 which followed the segregationist policies of 1903 rather than introducing 'secondary education for all' by giving equal status to all post-qualifying education. 'Circular 44', issued while Struthers was still in office, aroused much controversy, not least because it went against the recommendations of the Advisory Council which the 1918 Act had at last introduced. Back-bench pressure also produced one symbolic gesture: the SED was now Scottish rather than Scotch.

13

Conclusion

ACCORDING to one MP, the 1918 Act was 'in accord with the best traditions of the village schools of Scotland, which so often have been the common schools of all classes of the people'.[1] Writing a general history of Scottish education in 1927, Alexander Morgan claimed that the 1918 Act carried out 'almost in the letter the ideals of Knox and the other great educational reformers', and that 'most of the progress in Scottish education since Knox's day has consisted in advancing towards his ideals. The great Education Acts of 1872 and 1918 are but modern expressions of some of his ideals, others having still to be fulfilled.' The reformers 'cast the mould in which the Scottish character and intellect have been formed for nearly four centuries'.[2]

This stress on continuity and development has been characteristic of Scottish thinking about the educational system. Yet for the historian, the discontinuities seem more striking. The most obvious is the impact of urbanization and industrialization: few countries changed more radically in this respect between 1750 and 1914 than Scotland. The central story of this book has been the construction of a system of public elementary education for the working class, and although Scotland started from a different base, it ended up with the same kind of mass education as every advanced country, and the new urban schools had little direct connection with their parish predecessors. This change was accompanied by a cultural shift, from an educational world which was part of Scotland's religious culture to one which was tied to the state, secular, and pluralistic. The parish teacher, a kind of subordinate clergyman, gave way to the massed ranks, predominantly female, of a new profession. Before 1872 the parish school enjoyed great prestige, and probably gave a better education than the hard-pressed urban schools created to cope with expanding working-class demand. By 1914, though rural life remained vigorous enough for the tradition to seem intact in the schools which were still at the centre of life in every village, the

[1] Hansard, 5th series 110, 17 Oct. 1918, 387 (J. H. Whitehouse).
[2] A. Morgan, *Rise and Progress of Scottish Education* (Edinburgh, 1927), 53, 190.

advantages were mostly the other way. It was the urban child who enjoyed the widest choice of subjects, the most modern buildings and equipment, and the newest methods, and urban school boards could offer salaries and careers to attract the ablest teachers. Rural education, from being the spiritual heart of Scottish education, was pushed to the margins, and defined as a problem area. The apparatus of education created in the cities was to survive, with the inter-war stagnation of the Scottish economy, until well after the Second World War, becoming in its turn the object of a nostalgia for tenement life, skilled industrial work, and vibrant working-class communities, which replaced the Victorian nostalgia for village schools, dominies, and lads of parts. Yet the hold which the old ideal had over the Scottish mind showed that the cultural shift was not complete. It is easy for historians to show that the myth of Scottish democracy had become detached from reality, yet the myth was also a creative force, which helped both to form the concept of 'national' education which lay behind the 1872 Act, and to ensure that the links between elementary and secondary schools were wide and flexible. It also had a negative side, as the history of technical education shows, in reinforcing the prestige of the professions and keeping alive prejudices against utilitarian and vocational education.

Part of the history of educational change in the nineteenth century lies in systematization: an undifferentiated system, in which parish schools, burgh schools, and universities had overlapping functions and were loosely linked by the same religious and classical culture, gave way to a hierarchy of schools with different functions, linked by formal systems of transfer and examination. Education became, more than ever before, the mechanism which determined occupations and social privileges. Those who climbed the educational ladder were few in number, and the doctrine of individual opportunity concealed and legitimized the division between the superior education allowed to the chosen few and the basic education—a 'sham education' in Christopher Smout's words—reserved for the masses. But as Smout says, this sort of selective meritocracy had always been the real meaning of Scotland's 'democratic' tradition.[3] In any case, the class-based structure of the system in the early twentieth century did not differ from the European norm at that time, and Scotland compared favourably with other countries both in the relatively open structure of its educational hierarchy and in international league tables of attendance.

[3] T. C. Smout, *A Century of the Scottish People, 1830–1950* (London, 1986), 2, 212, 218–30.

Smout also questions the democratic credentials of Scottish education by pointing out that its prevailing ethos was conformist, disciplinarian, and deferential. Teachers were a timidly conservative body with little interest in new ideas: 'it is in the history of the school more than in any other aspect of recent social history that the key lies to some of the more depressing aspects of modern Scotland.'[4] But there was nothing new about that either, for instilling conformity and reinforcing the social order had always been one of the purposes of popular education, whether the language used was that of religious orthodoxy, moralization and social control, efficiency and citizenship, or functional differentiation in the style of Darroch and Struthers. The history of state intervention must be explained at least partly in these terms, as must the movement, common to all countries in the nineteenth century, to a more formal, institutionalized type of schooling which classified children by class, age, and gender.

The state, which had no active role until the 1830s, had a virtual monopoly of Scottish education by 1918. The Presbyterian churches, after playing a vital part in expansion in mid-century, lost virtually all their influence in 1872. Behind this lay class factors as well as the broader trend of secularization. The urban middle class challenged the grip of landowners and clerics over education, acting at first within the churches and through voluntary action, later through elected school boards. Local democracy enjoyed its heyday in the late nineteenth century, but after that power moved to the centre as the growing complexity of education and its use as a tool of social reform made school boards inadequate. In the 1880s, they had pioneered the higher grade schools; by the 1900s, changes like smaller classes and medical inspection were coming from the SED, and were often resisted by parsimonious school boards. As democracy became broader with the rise of the labour movement, it was to national rather than local politics that progressive reformers looked.

Until the 1840s Scottish education was able to develop without reference to England. But the Disruption, which ruled out simple control by the established church, coincided with the beginnings of state action. Since religion was the deepest source of cultural difference between Scotland and England, secularization itself removed some of the national features of Scottish education, and once it was financed from London assimilation of standards was inevitable. This was at its most

---

[4] T. C. Smout, *A Century of the Scottish People, 1830–1950* (London, 1986), 229.

irksome at the time of the Revised Code, and over the issue of state finance for secondary schools. After 1872, and even more after 1885, there was more administrative freedom, but even then it was difficult for the systems to diverge very widely. A great deal has been said about the Anglicization of the Scottish universities in this period, with the implication that the schools remained authentically Scottish. Yet as far as its curriculum and organization went, a Scottish elementary school in the 1900s was much more like its English counterpart than a Scottish university was like an English one. The difference was that in the schools, unlike the universities, nearly all the teachers and pupils were Scottish: schools drew their 'Scottish' character as much from the community which they served as from distinctive educational characteristics.

The 1872 Act forms a convenient marker in the narrative of educational change, but it should not be seen as a breach in continuity. Its significance was political and administrative, but it is clear that the main work of schooling the masses was complete by 1872. The achievement of the act was above all to iron out the remaining inequalities—between highlands and lowlands, between towns and country, between boys and girls, between prosperous and poor workers—and to extend the same basic standards to all. The statistics on literacy and school attendance before 1872 seem to confirm this. They underline the importance of regional and local variations, and do not permit any simple conclusion about whether Scottish education was on a career of constant progress, or had to struggle for a time to overcome the challenges posed by town life, factories, and migration. The interpretation offered here inclines to the second of these alternatives. But by 1872 interaction between the supply of schools from above and demand from an increasingly stable and prosperous working class had broken the back of the problems. Moreover, the creation through education of 'modern' mentalities—loyalty to the British state, participation in written culture, religious devotion based on rationality rather than superstition—was also largely complete before the state came on the scene, in the rural lowlands perhaps even before 1750. Scottish education had been precocious in its early development; by 1914 other countries had caught up. But that does not make its history less distinctive or less interesting.

Appendix 1: Statistical sources

Tables I–V are at the end of this Appendix.

Early Surveys

A number of surveys of education were carried out in the early nineteenth century under parliamentary auspices. Most of them purported to list all schools, with statistics or comments, and they are a valuable and under-used source for local history. But they also had many deficiencies, and depended on the local informants, usually the minister or schoolmaster. National totals derived from them can only be considered approximations.

PP 1819, IX (Part 3), *A Digest of Parochial Returns made to the Select Committee Appointed to Inquire into the Education of the Poor: Session 1818, Vol. III*

There are many gaps, e.g. there are few returns from Edinburgh. The figures in Tables 4.1 and 5.1, Map 5.1, and Table II are from the unpaginated summary table opposite p. 1450.

PP 1826, XVIII, *Parochial Education, Scotland, Returns to an Address of the Honourable House of Commons, dated March 30th, 1825*

This did not include standardized statistics.

PP 1837, XLVII, *Education Enquiry, Abstract of the Answers and Returns made Pursuant to an Address of the House of Commons, Dated 9th July 1834*

This is used for Table 5.1 (p. 743) and Map 5.3 (p. 745). It was the only inquiry to take account of seasonal variations. Ministers were asked to estimate the lowest and the highest numbers in attendance in summer 1833 and winter 1833–4. With the addition of an estimated percentage to cover defective returns, this produced figures of 189,266 to 260,853 (summer) and 208,384 to 286,798 (winter). These four totals were then averaged to produce the figure of 236,325 shown in Table 5.1. This shows how arbitrary these statistics are. Map 5.3 is based on the figures for maximum winter attendance.

PP 1841, XIX, *Answers Made by Schoolmasters in Scotland to Queries Circulated in 1838, by Order of the Select Committee on Education in Scotland*

This included statistics, but they do not seem reliable enough to use. There was a large number of non-returns, and the total number of pupils counted (for 1837) was only 190,239.

Literacy

The percentages on which Figure 5.1 is based are derived from C. Cipolla, *Literacy and Development in the West* (Harmondsworth, 1969), 121–5. Table I gives these at five-year intervals, with the same figures for England and Wales.

The literacy of brides and bridegrooms was recorded in the reports of the Registrar-General, but the percentages used in Maps 5.7 and 5.8 and Table 5.2 are from a summary for the years 1861–70 in the 1871 census: PP 1873, LXXIII, *Eighth Decennial Census of the Population of Scotland taken 3d April 1871, with Report*, vol. ii, p. clxix. The data are set out below in Table II.

The figures for denominations in Table 5.3 are in PP 1872, LXVIII, *Eighth Decennial Census of the Population of Scotland taken 3d April 1871, with Report*, vol. i, p. xliii.

Censuses 1851–71

The totals in Tables 5.1 and 9.1 from the general censuses are based on:

PP 1852–3, LXXXVIII, vol. 2, *Census of Great Britain, 1851, Population Tables, II. Ages, Civil Condition, Occupations, and Birth-Place of the People*, 908, 911.

PP 1864, LI, *Census of Scotland, 1861, Population Tables and Report*, vol. ii. 95, 106.

PP 1873, LXXIII, *Eighth Decennial Census of the Population of Scotland taken 3d April 1871, with Report*, vol. ii, p. xxiv.

In 1851 there was also the special census of education: PP 1854, LIX, *Census of Great Britain, 1851, Religious Worship, and Education, Scotland, Report and Tables*. The reference for Table 4.1 is p. 36, and for Table 5.1, Maps 5.2 and 5.4, and Table II it is pp. 53 ff.

The 1871 census has the age-group figures used for Figure 5.2, Maps 5.5–6, Tables 5.4, 5.6, and 5.7, and Tables 9.2–3. See above for the source reference: the figures for counties are on pp. 78–9 down to age 14, and p. cxlviii from 15 upwards (for corresponding age-group figures, see pp. 2 – 6). Below county level, see table XI. Since this census and subsequent ones to 1901 show attendance for each parish they are a rich but unused source susceptible to computerized analysis.

The Argyll Commission

The Argyll commission's statistical work had two weaknesses, which have sometimes led historians astray. The first was its calculation of school attendance by relation to the age-group, as discussed in Chapter 5. The second was reliance on the civil registrars for information. They refused to provide it for nearly all the towns, so that reliable statistics were only collected for about two-thirds of the country. The details of schools in Table 4.1, for example, refer only to the areas covered. There was a special report on Glasgow, but no inquiries in other towns. The total of 418,367 pupils shown in Table 5.1 was arrived at by extrapolation. The detailed survey found 312,795 pupils, the report on Glasgow 41,248. The commission assumed that Glasgow was typical, and applied the same pupil/population ratio to other towns to produce notional figures. Since Glasgow was probably not typical at all, the total is likely to be an underestimate.

The published reports are:

PP 1865, XVII, *First Report by Her Majesty's Commissioners Appointed to Inquire into the Schools in Scotland* [mainly oral evidence]

PP 1867, XXV, *Appendix to First Report by Her Majesty's Commissioners Appointed to Inquire into the Schools in Scotland* [mainly written evidence]

PP 1867, XXV, *Second Report by Her Majesty's Commissioners Appointed to Inquire into the Schools in Scotland* [main report on elementary education]

PP 1867, XXV, *Report on the State of Education in the Country Districts of Scotland* [by C. F. Maxwell and A. C. Sellar]

PP 1867, XXV, *Statistical Report on the State of Education in the Lowland Country Districts of Scotland*

PP 1867, XXV, *Report on the State of Education in Glasgow* [by J. Greig and T. Harvey]

PP 1867, XXV, *Report on the State of Education in the Hebrides* [by A. Nicolson]

PP 1867, XXVI, *Statistics Relative to Schools in Scotland Collected by the Registrars of Births, Deaths, and Marriages under Instructions from Her Majesty's Commissioners Appointed to Inquire into the Schools in Scotland* [includes details of individual schools in areas covered]

PP 1867–8, XXIX, *Third Report of Her Majesty's Commissioners Appointed to Inquire into the Schools in Scotland, with an Appendix, Burgh and Middle-Class Schools* [by T. Harvey and A. Sellar]

PP 1867–8, XXIX, *Report on the State of Education in the Burgh and Middle-Class Schools in Scotland. Vol. II: Special Reports*

References: for Table 4.1, *Second Report*, p. 24; for Table 5.1, *Second Report*, pp. clxxiii–clxxiv; for Table 5.7, *Second Report*, p. lxi and map opposite p. xlvi, and *Report on Glasgow*, pp. 126, 132–3, 137.

Statistics after 1872

The annual reports of the SED provide a continuous series of basic statistics for public schools, which are given in Table IV. These figures include denominational schools and secondary pupils in higher grade departments, but not higher class and endowed schools.

Statistics for secondary schools are given separately in Table V. The figures are for average attendance. Those for higher grade schools only include pupils in higher grade departments, and down to 1904 are limited to specially designated schools, as explained in Chapter 10. The statistics for endowed and higher class schools (not collected in earlier years) included younger children in primary departments; some, but not all, of these were excluded from 1914. The source for this table is *SED Reports, 1914–15*, General Report, 53, and subsequent annual reports.

School boards carried out a census of all schools in 1873, and this provides the total of 515,353 in Table 5.1. Source: PP 1878, XXX, *Fifth Annual Report of the Board of Education for Scotland*, Appendix II, pp. 13 ff.

The only sources which purport to list every school in Scotland are the Parliamentary Returns of 1880, 1888, and 1897 published in PP 1880, LV, PP 1888, LXXVIII, and PP 1897, LXXI. These returns are summarized in Table III. Detailed scrutiny suggests many gaps and anomalies (e.g. in whether private schools were classified as 'elementary' or 'higher class'). The 1880 return gave figures for accommodation, but not for attendance. The 'technical' category in 1897 is an arbitrary definition without significance.

The censuses of 1881, 1891, and 1901 included details of attendance by age-group on the same lines as in 1871, including a breakdown to parish level. As in 1871, they give a maximal view of attendance. Only the 1901 census had information for children over 14, as did the 1911 census, which otherwise omitted detailed coverage of education. These censuses form the basis of Tables 9.1–3; in some cases the information for one census is only printed in the next one. The source references are:

PP 1883, LXXXI, *Ninth Decennial Census of the Population of Scotland taken 4th April 1881, with Report*, vol. ii, pp. xvii–xix, 78.

PP 1893–4, CVII, *Tenth Decennial Census of the Population of Scotland taken 5th April 1891, with Report*, vol. ii, Part I, pp. xvii–xviii, xxviii, 62–3.

PP 1903, LXXXVI, *Eleventh Decennial Census of the Population of Scotland taken 31st March 1901, with Report*, vol. ii, pp. xxvi–xxvii, xxxvii, 280 ff.

PP 1913, LXXX, *Census of Scotland, 1911, Report on the Twelfth Decennial Census of Scotland*, vol. ii. 296–7.

TABLE I. *Literacy of Brides and Bridegrooms, 1855–1900*

| | Percentage able to sign names | | | |
| | Scotland | | England and Wales | |
	Men	Women	Men	Women
1855	89	77	70	59
1860	90	78	74	64
1865	89	78	77	69
1870	90	80	80	73
1875	91	83	83	77
1880	92	85	86	81
1885	94	89	89	87
1890	96	93	93	92
1895	97	95	96	95
1900	98	97	97	97

TABLE II. *Regional Variations in Education and Literacy*

	Pupils per 1,000 population		Literacy 1861–70 Percentage	
	1818	1851	Men	Women
Far North				
Caithness	72	132	95	89
Orkney	60[a]	77[a]	99	95
Shetland			90	68
Highlands				
Argyll	108	102	88	78
Bute	102	103	91	87
Inverness	76	87	64	53
Ross and Cromarty	82	91	65	49
Sutherland	76	112	88	73
North-east				
Aberdeen	66	121	98	93
Banff	71	130	96	86
Kincardine	70	127	98	92
Moray	81	129	96	89
Nairn	60	94	89	75
Eastern lowlands				
Angus	78	101	90	75
Clackmannan	107	136	96	87
East Lothian	103	112	90	83
Fife	97	131	97	92
Kinross	127	141	98	97
Midlothian	n.a.	118	95	90
Perth	99	129	97	93
Stirling	108	113	88	79
West Lothian	73	109	84	74
Western lowlands				
Ayr	90	107	87	75
Dumbarton	99	94	83	72
Lanark	94	87	85	69
Renfrew	97	86	83	69

TABLE II. *Continued*

	Pupils per 1,000 population		Literacy 1861–70 Percentage	
	1818	1851	Men	Women
Borders				
Berwick	101	140	98	97
Dumfries	99	121	97	94
Kirkcudbright	100	131	96	94
Peebles	115	124	99	98
Roxburgh	116	127	97	94
Selkirk	86	119	99	97
Wigtown	85	108	90	85
SCOTLAND	84	108	89	79[a]

[a] Figures combined.

TABLE III. *Returns on School Supply, 1880–1897*

Type of school	1880	1888		1897	
	Schools	Schools	Attendance	Schools	Attendance
Public elementary (school board)	2,503	2,652	414,503	2,741	523,172
State-aided elementary	605	522	89,123	393	81,426
Non-public elementary	508	351	18,307	188	9,007
Public higher class	17	20	5,441	35	7,241
Non-public higher class	260	217	17,512	166	17,075
Technical				10	1,379
Total	3,893	3,762	544,886	3,533	639,300

TABLE IV. *Annual Statistics of Public Education*

Year	Number of Schools							Number of pupils	
	School Board	Church of Scotland	Free Church	Episcopalian	Roman Catholic	Other	Total	On roll	Average attendance
1872		1,306	550	58	65		1,979	267,048	213,549
1873		1,341	560	84	65		2,050	280,581	220,508
1874	1,352	607	275	75	79		2,388	344,628	263,748
1875	1,945	476	151	66	92		2,730	402,633	303,536
1876	2,099	420	136	70	104		2,829	433,749	329,083
1877	2,271	372	116	72	112		2,943	472,668	360,413
1878	2,342	352	125	74	118		3,011	494,488	377,257
1879	2,383	126[a]	45[a]	73	127	265[a]	3,019	508,452	385,109
1880	2,442	146	39	74	127	236	3,064	534,428	404,618
1881	2,468	126	35	77	133	238	3,077	544,982	409,966
1882	2,477	124	32	78	138	227	3,076	555,660	421,265
1883	2,494	120	30	76	139	233	3,092	569,241	433,137
1884	2,536	112	27	77	150	230	3,132	587,945	448,242
1885	2,511	100	27	74	148	222	3,082	592,266	455,655
1886	2,528	94	26	75	150	220	3,093	615,498	476,890
1887	2,570	86	25	72	152	208	3,113	631,865	491,735
1888	2,580	80	25	72	156	195	3,108	641,540	496,239
1889	2,616	72	22	72	160	176	3,118	648,089	503,100
1890	2,590	69	19	74	163	163	3,078	664,466	524,326
1891	2,653	55	18	71	166	143	3,106	677,948	538,365
1892	2,595	50	19	70	173	127	3,034	666,992	554,685
1893	2,580	51	18	73	174	112	3,008	664,838	562,426
1894	2,643	44	15	71	172	109	3,054	686,335	567,442

Year									
1895	2,621	42	16	70	179	106	3,034	692,202	575,305
1896	2,687	37	11	71	181	96	3,083	709,478	592,934
1897	2,705	34	9	69	182	87	3,086	716,893	605,389
1898	2,687	35	8	71	183	83	3,067	717,747	605,776
1899	2,694	31	8	69	184	76	3,062	731,272	612,457
1900	2,774[b]	27	6	68	189	71	3,135	756,558	629,038
1901	2,788	24	4	67	189	69	3,141	767,421	636,374
1902	2,786	21	4	66	190	78	3,145	768,528	649,501
1903	2,793	20	4	66	192	74	3,149	785,473	669,289
1904	2,834	18	6	66	196	69	3,189	793,492	682,269
1905	2,882	20	6	66	201	69	3,244	804,162	696,381
1906	2,903	18	6	62	208	65	3,262	806,737	706,062
1907	2,922	18	6	61	213	65	3,285	811,000	711,228
1908	2,951	11	1	59	218	72	3,312	812,346	712,076
1909	2,979	9	1	57	220	65	3,331	826,223	727,244
1910	3,000	8	1	57	220	61	3,347	843,242	743,217
1911	3,020	8	1	57	223	60	3,369	845,055	755,988
1912	3,015	7	1	56	222	57	3,358	844,715	757,993
1913	3,030	7	1	54	224	54	3,370	845,879[b]	753,906
1914	3,028[c]	6	1	54	225	52	3,366	843,309	754,183
1915	3,026	6	1	53	227	51	3,364	844,843	752,566
1916	3,034	5	1	53	224	47	3,364	841,207	744,469
1917	3,030	5	1	53	226	48	3,363	839,002	743,725
1918								840,475	743,199

Figures refer to the school year ending in the year shown. Some of them represent a choice between variants, as the SED was in the habit of revising them retrospectively. The attendance totals are more reliable than those 'on the roll'.

[a] Classification changed.

[b] Basis of counting changed.

[c] This and subsequent figures on types of school from Hansard, 5th series 101, 17 Jan. 1918, 522.

TABLE V. *Annual Statistics of Public Secondary Education*

Year	Higher Grade		Endowed/higher Class	
	Schools	Pupils	Schools	Pupils
1900	27	2,561		
1901	34	3,270		
1902	35	3,821	55	16,264
1903	36	4,548	55	16,507
1904	74	10,107	55	16,619
1905	121	14,508	55	16,688
1906	137	17,150	55	16,840
1907	147	18,467	55	16,928
1908	169	19,932	55	17,549
1909	182	22,118	57	19,480
1910	191	24,095	57	19,965
1911	196	24,083	56	19,353
1912	194	24,201	56	19,458
1913	193	24,817	56	18,315
1914	195	25,913	56	18,742[a]
1915	196	27,102	56	18,448
1916	196	28,234	56	19,338
1917	196	29,198	56	18,989
1918	196	30,509	56	20,765

[a] Some primary pupils excluded from this year.

Appendix 2: Summary of Legislation

This Appendix gives brief chronological details of legislation and administration. It does not cover legislation which affected education indirectly, such as the Factory Acts (which were very complex) or the laws on industrial and reformatory schools and child welfare.

The *Act for Settling of Schools 1696* remained the basis of the law until 1872. Main provisions: a school and schoolmaster to be provided in every parish, 'by advice of the heritors and minister'; heritors to provide 'a commodious house for a school' and a salary between 100 and 200 merks per annum; money raised by a tax on property split equally between owners and tenants. (The merk was a unit of Scottish currency worth $1s$. $1\frac{1}{3}d$. sterling; to the nearest penny, 100 and 200 merks corresponded to £5. $11s$. $1d$. and £11. $2s$. $3d$.).

The Act 43 Geo. III chap. 54, sometimes called the *Schoolmasters Act*, was passed in 1803, and specified many points which were already customary. Main provisions: salary limits raised to 300 and 400 merks (£16. $13s$. $4d$. and £22. $4s$. $5d$.); schoolhouse to include dwelling-house and garden; dwelling-house need have no more than two apartments including kitchen; in large parishes, additional masters may be appointed (side schools), with salary limit raised to 600 merks for all teachers, but in this case no obligation to provide schoolhouse; confirmed that legislation does not apply to royal burghs; schoolmasters to be examined by presbyteries as to morality, religion, and literary qualifications, and to take oath of loyalty to king and sign Confession of Faith; heritors and minister to fix school fees, and may require schoolmaster to teach poor children free; presbyteries have power to make regulations on hours of teaching, and powers of discipline over schoolmaster; only heritors with land valued at £100 Scots annual rent may attend and vote at meetings concerned with school.

Under the 1803 Act salaries were to be revised after 25 years in line with the price of oatmeal. This was done in 1828, when the limits were raised to £25. $13s$. $3d$. and £34. $4s$. $4d$. But when this was next due in the 1850s, the price of meal had fallen, and the existing salaries were maintained by temporary enactments until the 1861 Act.

The Act 1 & 2 Vict. chap. 87, usually known as the *Highland Schools Act*, was passed in 1838. It provided a government grant for salaries of additional teachers in specified highland parishes; heritors must provide a schoolhouse (unlike side schools under 1803 Act). These were 'parliamentary' schools, a term applied only to the small number (about 30) which came under this act.

The system of state grants to schools starting in 1833 was not based on statute, but on annual parliamentary vote. An Order in Council of 1839 created the Committee of Council on Education, a committee of the Privy Council; its political head was the Lord President of the Council. Its regulations were expressed in Minutes, e.g. those of 1846 which instituted the pupil-teacher system, later brought together in the annual Code. Its powers extended to Scotland, with minor variations (e.g. in the appointment of school inspectors) to take account of the religious situation.

The Department of Practical Art was founded in 1852 under the Board of Trade. In 1853 it became the Department of Science and Art. In 1856 the DSA was transferred to the Committee of Council on Education, which was also given a Vice-President, who was in effect minister of education, though the Lord President remained the formal head. The DSA and the Education Department remained distinct, each having its own officials. The DSA operated throughout the United Kingdom (including Ireland), and this continued after 1872.

Main provisions of the *Parochial and Burgh Schoolmasters (Scotland) Act 1861*: salary limits raised to £35–70 sterling, or total salary £50–80 where divided between two or more teachers; heritors and minister may appoint a female teacher, with salary not above £30, to give instruction in 'industrial and household training' as well as elementary education (heritors' girls' schools); examination of newly appointed teachers transferred from presbyteries to examiners appointed by the four universities; parochial schoolmasters no longer to sign Confession of Faith, but must declare that they will not 'teach or inculcate any opinions opposed to the divine authority of the Holy Scriptures, or to the doctrines contained in the Shorter Catechism'; disciplinary powers of presbytery transferred to sheriff court; dwelling-houses to have minimum of three rooms plus kitchen; schoolmasters may be required to resign for reasons of age, infirmity, negligence, etc.; heritors to pay 'retiring allowance' (annual pension) to masters who retire or resign;

burgh schoolmasters exempt from Confession of Faith and authority of presbyteries, and not required to make any religious declaration.

Main provisions of the *Education (Scotland) Act 1872* (sometimes known as Lord Young's Act):

1. Every parish and burgh to have a school board, elected triennially; electors are owners or occupiers of property above £4 annual rental, and each has as many votes as boards have members (cumulative vote); vacancies filled by co-option.
2. Separate Committee of Council on Education in Scotland, known as Scotch Education Department. Temporary Board of Education in Edinburgh to supervise initial application of act (wound up 1878).
3. All parochial and burgh schools vested in school boards. They may also accept transfer (without compensation) of any denominational or subscription school. Power to raise rates.
4. SED makes grants to public schools, and continues direct grants to existing denominational etc. schools. New non-public schools may be aided when SED is 'satisfied that no sufficient provision exists for the children for whom the school is intended, regard being had to the religious belief of their parents'. Building grants may be claimed by school boards before end of 1873, but then to cease; no further building grants to non-public schools.
5. Higher grants in districts with low rate income, and further special grants in specified highland counties.
6. Preamble: 'whereas it has been the custom in the public schools of Scotland to give instruction in religion to children whose parents did not object to the instruction so given . . . it is expedient that the managers of public schools shall be at liberty to continue the said custom' (use and wont). Religion excluded from grants and inspection. Every school open to children of all denominations; parents may withdraw children from religious instruction (conscience clause). This applies to all grant-aided schools, including denominational.
7. Duty of parents 'to provide elementary education in reading, writing, and arithmetic' for children between 5 and 13. May apply to parochial board (Poor Law authority) for payment of fees. Exemption from attendance allowed if inspector gives certificate of knowledge of three Rs (no minimum age specified).
8. Every principal teacher must hold certificate of competency granted by SED.

9. Care to be taken in Code that 'the standard of education which now exists in the public schools shall not be lowered' (part of s. 67).
10. Former burgh schools in which education is not chiefly elementary given status of higher class schools (eleven scheduled initially). May not receive grants, or (with minor exceptions) expenditure from rate fund.

The act referred to 'elementary education', but not to elementary (or secondary) schools. The term in common usage was 'public schools'; in a strict sense this meant schools run by school boards, others being 'state-aided', but it was often used to refer to both types. The term 'denominational' was in general use; 'board school' and 'voluntary school', though sometimes used, were really English terms.

Under the 1872 Act the SED did not have a separate Secretary or ministers; the Lord President and Vice-President were the responsible ministers. In 1885 the SED gained autonomy, and came under the authority of the Secretary for Scotland, who was Vice-President of the Committee of Council on Education in Scotland. The Lord President remained the formal head, but took no active part.

The *Elementary Education Act 1876* was an English act, but sections relating to conditions on which grants could be made applied to Scotland. Some minor legislation (e.g. the *Highland Schools (Scotland) Act 1873*) dealt with anomalies in the 1872 Act, and this continued in the *Education (Scotland) Act 1878*. Its significant provisions were: procedures for enforcing compulsion improved; SED to lay down conditions for exemption, with minimum age 10; school boards to maintain buildings of higher class schools from rates, along with other expenses approved by SED; SED given powers of inspection of higher class schools. The *Public Schools (Scotland) Teachers Act 1882* (Mundella Act) laid down a special procedure before teachers could be dismissed. The *Education (Scotland) Act 1883* raised the age of compulsory education to 14, and gave statutory force to the SED's regulations for exemption.

Legislation on endowments began with the *Endowed Institutions (Scotland) Act 1869*. This provided for voluntary reform, but did not set up commissioners. The *Endowed Institutions (Scotland) Act 1878* set up the Moncreiff commission, but without compulsory powers. The *Educational Endowments (Scotland) Act 1882* gave the Balfour of Burleigh commission compulsory powers. All these acts expired after a fixed term, and residual powers remained with the SED.

The *Technical Schools (Scotland) Act 1887* authorized school boards to maintain technical schools. The *Technical Instruction Amendment (Scotland) Act 1892* extended the powers of county and burgh councils in this field. The *Education of Blind and Deaf-Mute Children (Scotland) Act 1890* gave school boards a duty to educate these categories, and the *Day Industrial Schools (Scotland) Act 1893* recognized this type of school, maintained by school boards or others. They already existed in Glasgow under the optimistically-named *Glasgow Juvenile Delinquency Prevention and Repression Act 1878*.

The allocation of revenue grants to educational purposes began with the *Local Government (Scotland) Act 1889* (Probate Grant, used to abolish fees). The *Local Taxation (Customs and Excise) Act 1890* created the Residue Grant (whisky money, allocated to town and county councils for technical education). The *Education and Local Taxation Account (Scotland) Act 1892* created the Equivalent Grant, used for secondary education and allocated to county secondary education committees, with joint representation of local authorities and school boards. The *Local Taxation Account (Scotland) Act 1898* provided further funds for secondary and technical education, as did the transfer of Science and Art grants in 1898. After the Education Act of 1902 for England and Wales, a further 'equivalent' known as the General Aid Grant was given to Scotland. The *Education (Scotland) Act 1897* increased the grants to 'voluntary' schools, in line with similar changes in England and Wales.

The *Elementary School Teachers (Superannuation) Act 1898* created a contributory scheme common to England, Wales, and Scotland. The *Education (Scotland) Act 1901* restricted exemption to children over 12. Cases to be approved individually by school boards, and conditions may be imposed. The *Education of Defective Children (Scotland) Act 1906* gave school boards powers to provide for epileptic, crippled, and 'defective' children.

Main provisions of the *Education (Scotland) Act 1908*:

1. School board franchise assimilated to local government franchise (= parliamentary franchise plus women). Amalgamation of school boards made easier.
2. Enlarged powers for school boards include: restrictions on higher class schools removed; supply of meals; paying travel and lodging expenses; supporting employment bureaux; provision of books and stationery, for all state-aided schools. May, and where required by

SED must, organize medical inspection, appoint medical officers and nurses, provide 'appliances' (but not treatment).

3. School boards must provide continuation classes; may make by-laws enforcing attendance to age 17.
4. Grants under Acts of 1890, 1892, 1898, and General Aid Grant combined to form Education (Scotland) Fund. Part used centrally, part allocated as district education funds to secondary education committees. (Town and county councils lose direct role in technical education.)
5. Duties of secondary education committees include: supporting secondary and technical education (less local discretion allowed than before), and providing specialist teachers; preparing comprehensive bursary scheme; paying part of cost of medical inspection.
6. Central institutions given statutory recognition.
7. Teachers may appeal to SED against dismissal. Improved superannuation scheme.

The *Education (Scotland) Act 1913* allowed school boards to provide medical and dental treatment. The *Education (Scotland) (Provision of Meals) Act 1914* clarified their powers under the 1908 Act.

Points in the *Education (Scotland) Act 1918* which are only relevant to the period after 1918 are omitted. Main provisions:

1. School boards and secondary education committees replaced by education authorities for counties and cities, elected by proportional representation. Cumulative vote abolished.
2. Secondary education must be available free, though limited number of fee-paying schools may be retained.
3. Nursery schools may be provided.
4. Leaving age raised to 15, minimum exemption age to 13. Compulsory continuation classes up to 16 at first, 18 later.
5. Voluntary schools may be transferred to education authorities by sale or lease, to become public schools. Teachers appointed by education authority, but must satisfy denominational representatives 'as regards their religious belief and character'. Religious instruction to continue, with conscience clause. SED may authorize new denominational schools. No further grants for voluntary schools not transferred.
6. Preamble of 1872 Act on religious instruction incorporated in Act.
7. Advisory Council set up; national salary scales for teachers; SED renamed Scottish Education Department.

Bibliography

This bibliography is intended as a guide to scholarly work, and does not include all the books cited in the footnotes. It omits most older books, and general works on Scottish history unless they make a substantial contribution to the history of education. It does not cover secondary and university education, for which an updated bibliography is available in the 2nd edn. (Edinburgh, 1989) of R. D. Anderson, *Education and Opportunity in Victorian Scotland: Schools and Universities*. Annual lists of new publications appear in the *SHR*, *SESH*, and *Economic History Review*.

1. GENERAL

Knox is a brief factual introduction. Scotland commands respect as the only modern attempt at a comprehensive account, but lacks wider historical awareness. Craigie's books are indispensable guides to sources. Smout's work is full of insights on education, and Brown, Campbell, Fry, and Hutchison also relate it to the general Scottish context. Green and Maynes are pioneering attempts at a comparative account of popular education.

ANDERSON, R. D., *Education and Opportunity in Victorian Scotland: Schools and Universities* (Oxford, 1983).

—— 'Education and Society in Modern Scotland: A Comparative Perspective', *History of Education Quarterly*, 25 (1985), 459–81.

—— 'In Search of the "Lad of Parts": the Mythical History of Scottish Education', *History Workshop*, 19 (1985), 82–104.

BROWN, C. G., *The Social History of Religion in Scotland since 1730* (London, 1987).

CAMPBELL, R. H., *The Rise and Fall of Scottish Industry, 1707–1939* (Edinburgh, 1980).

CHECKLAND, O., *Philanthropy in Victorian Scotland: Social Welfare and the Voluntary Principle* (Edinburgh, 1980).

CORR, H., 'An Exploration into Scottish Education', in W. H. Fraser and R. J. Morris (eds.), *People and Society in Scotland, II: 1830–1914* (Edinburgh, 1990), 290–309.

CRAIGIE, J., *A Bibliography of Scottish Education before 1872* (London, 1970).

—— *A Bibliography of Scottish Education 1872–1972* (London, 1974).

FRY, M., *Patronage and Principle: A Political History of Modern Scotland* (Aberdeen, 1987).

GREEN, A., *Education and State Formation: The Rise of Education Systems in England, France and the USA* (London, 1990).

HARVIE, C., 'The Folk and the *Gwerin*: The Myth and the Reality of Popular Culture in 19th-Century Scotland and Wales', *Proceedings of the British Academy*, 80 (1991), 19–48.

HUMES, W. M., and PATERSON, H. M. (eds.), *Scottish Culture and Scottish Education* (Edinburgh, 1983) [cited as Humes and Paterson].

HUTCHISON, I. G. C., *A Political History of Scotland, 1832–1924: Parties, Elections and Issues* (Edinburgh, 1986).

KNOX, H. M., *Two Hundred and Fifty Years of Scottish Education, 1696–1946* (Edinburgh, 1953).

MAYNES, M. J., *Schooling in Western Europe: A Social History* (Albany, NY, 1985).

MCPHERSON, A., 'An Angle on the Geist: Persistence and Change in the Scottish Educational Tradition', in Humes and Paterson, 216–43.

ROBBINS, K., *Nineteenth-Century Britain: Integration and Diversity* (Oxford, 1988).

SCOTLAND, J., *The History of Scottish Education* (2 vols., London, 1969).

SMOUT, T. C., *A History of the Scottish People, 1560–1830,* paperback edn. (n.p., 1972).

——*A Century of the Scottish People, 1830–1950* (London, 1986).

—— 'Scotland, 1850–1950', in F. M. L. Thompson (ed.), *The Cambridge Social History of Britain, 1750–1950,* i: *Regions and Communities* (Cambridge, 1990), 209–80.

SUTHERLAND, G., 'Education', in F. M. L. Thompson (ed.), *The Cambridge Social History of Britain, 1750–1950,* iii: *Social Agencies and Institutions* (Cambridge, 1990), 119–69.

2. LOCAL STUDIES

These vary in quality, and tend to stop in 1872. Bain, Beale, and Boyd are the best of the county studies. See also Section 5(*c*) below on the highlands.

BAIN, A., *Education in Stirlingshire from the Reformation to the Act of 1872* (London, 1965).

BEALE, J. M., *A History of the Burgh and Parochial Schools of Fife* (n.p., 1983).

BOYD, W., *Education in Ayrshire through Seven Centuries* (London, 1961).

BUCHAN, J., *From Parish School to Academy: The Story of Education in the Parish of Peterculter* (Aberdeen, 1967).

CORMACK, A. A., *Education in the Eighteenth Century: Parish of Peterculter, Aberdeenshire* (Peterculter, 1965).

CRUICKSHANK, M., 'The Dick Bequest: The Effect of a Famous Nineteenth-

Century Endowment on Parish Schools of North East Scotland', *History of Education Quarterly*, 5 (1965), 153–65.

DONNACHIE, I., and HEWITT, G., *Historic New Lanark: The Dale and Owen Industrial Community since 1785* (Edinburgh, 1993).

GILCHRIST, A., 'The Parish School Buildings of Upper Clydesdale, 1872–1975', *Scottish Local History*, 17 (1989), 10–13.

HUTCHISON, H., 'Church, State and School in Clackmannanshire, 1803–1872', *SES* 3 (1971), 25–38.

JESSOP, J. C., *Education in Angus: An Historical Survey of Education up to the Act of 1872, from Original and Contemporary Sources* (London, 1931).

LAW, A., *Education in Edinburgh in the Eighteenth Century* (London, 1965).

ROXBURGH, J. M., *The School Board of Glasgow, 1873–1919* (London, 1971).

RUSSELL, J. A., *History of Education in the Stewartry of Kirkcudbright, from Original and Contemporary Sources* (Newton Stewart, 1951).

—— *Education in Wigtownshire, 1560–1970* (Newton Stewart, 1971).

SIMPSON, I. J., *Education in Aberdeenshire before 1872* (London, 1947).

WOOD, S., 'Education in Nineteenth-Century Rural Scotland—an Aberdeenshire Case Study', *Review of Scottish Culture*, 7 (1991), 25–33.

3. LITERACY

Houston's *Past and Present* article should be read along with his *Scottish Literacy*. Several comparative works are included here, as it is a topic which benefits especially from this approach. For the nineteenth century, Webb has not been superseded. See also Section 5(*e*) below.

CIPOLLA, C. M., *Literacy and Development in the West* (Harmondsworth, 1969).

FURET, F., and OZOUF, J., *Reading and Writing: Literacy in France from Calvin to Jules Ferry* (Cambridge, 1982).

GRAFF, H. J., *Literacy and Social Development in the West: A Reader* (Cambridge, Ind., 1981).

—— *The Legacies of Literacy: Continuities and Contradictions in Western Culture and Society* (Bloomington, Ind., 1987).

HOUSTON, R. A., 'The Literacy Myth?: Illiteracy in Scotland, 1630–1760', *Past and Present*, 96 (1982), 98–9.

—— 'Literacy and Society in the West, 1500–1850', *Social History*, 8 (1983), 269–93.

—— *Scottish Literacy and the Scottish Identity: Illiteracy and Society in Scotland and Northern England, 1600–1800* (Cambridge, 1985).

—— *Literacy in Early Modern Europe: Culture and Education, 1500–1800* (London, 1988).

—— 'Scottish Education and Literacy, 1600–1800: An International

HOUSTON, R. A., (*cont.*):

Perspective', in T. M. Devine (ed.), *Improvement and Enlightenment* (Edinburgh, 1989), 43–61.

—— 'Literacy, Education and the Culture of Print in Enlightenment Edinburgh', *History*, 78 (1993), 373–92.

SMOUT, T. C., 'Born Again at Cambuslang: New Evidence on Popular Religion and Literacy in Eighteenth-Century Scotland', *Past and Present*, 97 (1982), 114–27.

STEPHENS, W. B., 'Literacy in England, Scotland, and Wales, 1500–1900', *History of Education Quarterly*, 30 (1990), 545–71.

STONE, L., 'Literacy and Education in England, 1640–1900', *Past and Present*, 42 (1969), 69–139.

WEBB, R. K., 'Literacy among the Working Classes in Nineteenth Century Scotland', *SHR* 33 (1954), 100–14.

4. PERIODS

(a) Eighteenth and early nineteenth centuries

This period is dominated by the work of Withrington. Saunders is still a stimulating read. There is a large literature on the Scottish Enlightenment, but Scottish educational thinking remains unexplored.

ANDERSON, R. D., 'Education and the State in Nineteenth-Century Scotland', *Economic History Review*, 2nd series, 36 (1983), 518–34.

—— 'School Attendance in Nineteenth-Century Scotland: A Reply', *Economic History Review*, 2nd series, 38 (1985), 282–6.

BROWN, S. J., 'The Disruption and Urban Poverty: Thomas Chalmers and the West Port Operation in Edinburgh, 1844–47', *SCHSR* 20 (1978–80), 65–89.

GLAISTER, R. T. D., 'Rural Private Teachers in 18th-Century Scotland', *JEAH* 23/2 (1991), 49–61.

MASON, D. M., 'School Attendance in Nineteenth-Century Scotland', *Economic History Review*, 2nd series, 38 (1985), 276–81.

MITCHISON, R., 'Scotland, 1750–1850', in F. M. L. Thompson (ed.), *The Cambridge Social History of Britain, 1750–1950,* i: *Regions and Communities* (Cambridge, 1990), 155–207.

O'DAY, R., *Education and Society, 1500–1800: The Social Foundations of Education in Early Modern Britain* (London, 1982).

PAZ, D. G., *The Politics of Working-Class Education in Britain, 1830–50* (Manchester, 1980).

SAUNDERS, L. J., *Scottish Democracy, 1815–1840: The Social and Intellectual Background* (Edinburgh, 1950).

WEST, E. G., *Education and the Industrial Revolution* (London, 1975).

WITHRINGTON, D. J., 'The Free Church Educational Scheme, 1843–50', *SCHSR* 15 (1963–5), 103–15.

—— 'Lists of Schoolmasters Teaching Latin, 1690', in *Miscellany of the Scottish History Society*, x (Edinburgh, 1965).

—— 'Education and Society in the Eighteenth Century', in N. T. Phillipson and R. Mitchison (eds.), *Scotland in the Age of Improvement: Essays in Scottish History in the Eighteenth Century* (Edinburgh, 1970), 169–99.

—— '"Scotland a Half Educated Nation" in 1834? Reliable Critique or Persuasive Polemic?', in Humes and Paterson, 55–74.

—— 'What was Distinctive about the Scottish Enlightenment?', in J. J. Carter and J. H. Pittock (eds.), *Aberdeen and the Enlightenment: Proceedings of a Conference Held at the University of Aberdeen* (Aberdeen, 1987), 9–19.

—— '"A Ferment of Change": Aspirations, Ideas and Ideals in Nineteenth-Century Scotland', in D. Gifford (ed.), *The History of Scottish Literature*, iii: *Nineteenth Century* (Aberdeen, 1988), 43–63.

—— 'Schooling, Literacy and Society', in T. M. Devine and R. Mitchison (eds.), *People and Society in Scotland I: 1760–1830* (Edinburgh, 1988), 163–87.

—— 'Adrift among the Reefs of Conflicting Ideals? Education and the Free Church, 1843–55', in S. J. Brown and M. Fry (eds.), *Scotland in the Age of the Disruption* (Edinburgh, 1993), 79–97.

(b) 1850–72

BAIN, W. H., '"Attacking the Citadel": James Moncreiff's Proposals to Reform Scottish Education, 1851–69', *SER* 10/2 (1978) 5–14.

CRUICKSHANK, M., 'The Argyll Commission Report, 1865–8: A Landmark in Scottish Education', *BJES* 15 (1967), 133–47.

MYERS, J. D., 'Scottish Nationalism and the Antecedents of the 1872 Education Act', *SES* 4 (1972), 71–92.

SCOTLAND, J., 'The Centenary of the Education (Scotland) Act of 1872', *BJES* 20 (1972), 121–36.

WILSON, T., 'A Reinterpretation of "Payment by Results" in Scotland, 1861–1872', in Humes and Paterson, 93–114.

WITHRINGTON, D. J., 'The 1872 Education Act—a Centenary Retrospect', *Education in the North*, 9 (1972), 5–9.

—— 'Towards a National System, 1867–72: The Last Years in the Struggle for a Scottish Education Act', *SES* 4 (1972), 107–24.

(c) 1872–1918

See also Roxburgh in Section 2 above. This is the period least well covered. Hendrick and Humphries are important books, but only refer to Scotland incidentally. The work by Jamieson and Toynbee is based on oral history research.

FINN, M. E., 'Social Efficiency Progressivism and Secondary Education in Scotland, 1885–1905', in Humes and Paterson, 175–96.

HENDRICK, H., *Images of Youth: Age, Class, and the Male Youth Problem, 1880–1920* (Oxford, 1990).

HUMPHRIES, S., *Hooligans or Rebels? An Oral History of Working-Class Childhood and Youth, 1889–1939* (Oxford, 1981).

JAMIESON, L., 'Growing Up in Scotland in the 1900s', in Glasgow Women's Studies Group, *Uncharted Lives: Extracts from Scottish Women's Experiences, 1850–1982* (Glasgow, 1983), 17–34.

—— 'We All Left at 14: Boys' and Girls' Schooling circa 1900–1930', in J. Fewell and F. Paterson (eds.), *Girls in their Prime: Scottish Education Revisited* (Edinburgh, 1990), 16–37.

—— and TOYNBEE, C., *Country Bairns: Growing Up, 1900–1930* (Edinburgh, 1992).

LENMAN, B., and STOCKS, J., 'The Beginnings of State Education in Scotland, 1872–1885', *SES* 4 (1972), 93–106.

OSBORNE, G. S., *Scottish and English Schools: A Comparative Survey of the Past Fifty Years* (London, 1966).

WADE, N. A., *Post-Primary Education in the Primary Schools of Scotland, 1872–1936* (London, 1939).

5. THEMES

(a) Curriculum

The history of girls' education is the most lively area. Markus and Hamilton are interesting on teaching methods and their architectural implications.

CORR, H., 'The Schoolgirls' Curriculum and the Ideology of the Home, 1870–1914', in Glasgow Women's Studies Group, *Uncharted Lives: Extracts from Scottish Women's Experiences, 1850–1982* (Glasgow, 1983), 74–97.

—— '"Home-Rule" in Scotland: The Teaching of Housework in Schools, 1872–1914', in J. Fewell and F. Paterson (eds.), *Girls in their Prime: Scottish Education Revisited* (Edinburgh, 1990), 38–53.

ELLIOTT, B. J., 'Early Examination Reform in Scotland and the Crisis in History, 1888–1939', *JEAH* 24 (1992), 47–58.

HAMILTON, D., *Towards a Theory of Schooling* (London, 1989).

MARKUS, T. A., 'The School as Machine: Working Class Scottish Education and the Glasgow Normal Seminary', in T. A. Markus (ed.), *Order in Space and Society: Architectural Form and its Context in the Scottish Enlightenment* (Edinburgh, 1982).

—— *Buildings and Power: Freedom and Control in the Origin of Modern Building Types* (London, 1993).

MOORE, L., 'Invisible Scholars: Girls Learning Latin and Mathematics in the Elementary Public Schools of Scotland before 1872', *History of Education*, 13 (1984), 121–37.

—— 'Educating for the "Woman's Sphere": Domestic Training versus Intellectual Discipline', in E. Breitenbach and E. Gordon (eds.), *Out of Bounds: Women in Scottish Society, 1800–1945* (Edinburgh, 1992), 10–41.

WITHRINGTON, D. J., 'Scots in Education: A Historical Retrospect', in J. D. McClure (ed.), *The Scots Language in Education* (Aberdeen, n.d.).

(b) Teachers

BAIN, A., *Patterns of Error: The Teacher and External Authority in Central Scotland, 1581–1861* (Edinburgh, 1989).

—— *From Church to State: The Significance of the Education Act of 1861 in East Central Scotland* (Dundee, 1993).

BELFORD, A. J., *Centenary Handbook of the Educational Institute of Scotland* (Edinburgh, 1946).

BONE, T. R., 'Teachers and Security of Tenure, 1872–1908', in T. R. Bone (ed.), *Studies in the History of Scottish Education, 1872–1939* (London, 1967), 71–135.

CORR, H., 'The Sexual Division of Labour in the Scottish Teaching Profession, 1872–1914', in Humes and Paterson, 137–50.

—— 'Politics of the Sexes in English and Scottish Teachers' Unions, 1870–1914', in H. Corr and L. Jamieson (eds.), *Politics of Everyday Life: Continuity and Change in Work and the Family* (London, 1990), 186–205.

CRUICKSHANK, M., *A History of the Training of Teachers in Scotland* (London, 1970).

MYERS, D., 'Scottish Schoolmasters in the Nineteenth Century: Professionalism and Politics', in Humes and Paterson, 75–92.

(c) Gaelic and the Highlands

Durkacz and Withers are definitive on the history of the language. Highland schools are quite well covered.

BEATON, E., 'The Sutherland Technical School: Pioneer Education for Crofters' Sons', *Review of Scottish Culture*, 7 (1991), 35–51.

CHAMBERS, D., 'The Church of Scotland's Highlands and Islands Education Scheme, 1824–1843', *JEAH* 7/1 (1975), 8–17.

DURKACZ, V. E., *The Decline of the Celtic Languages: A Study of Linguistic*

Durkacz, V. E., (*cont.*):
and *Cultural Conflict in Scotland, Wales and Ireland from the Reformation to the Twentieth Century* (Edinburgh, 1983).

Harding, A. W., 'Gaelic Schools in Northern Perthshire, 1823–1849', *TGSI* 52 (1980–2), 1–19.

MacKinnon, K. M., 'Education and Social Control: The Case of Gaelic Scotland', *SES*, 4 (1972), 125–37.

Macleod, M., 'Gaelic in Highland Education', *TGSI* 43 (1960–3), 305–34.

Murchison, T. M., 'Raining's School, Inverness: A Seed-Bed of Talent', *TGSI* 52 (1980–2), 405–59.

Smith, J. A., 'The 1872 Education (Scotland) Act and Gaelic Education', *TGSI* 51 (1978–80), 1–67.

—— 'An Educational Miscellany', *TGSI* 53 (1982–4), 248–309.

Thompson, F. G., 'Technical Education in the Highlands and Islands', *TGSI* 48 (1972–4), 244–338.

Withers, C. W. J., 'Education and Anglicisation: The Policy of the SSPCK toward the Education of the Highlander, 1709–1825', *Scottish Studies*, 26 (1982), 37–56.

—— *Gaelic in Scotland, 1698–1981: The Geographical History of a Language* (Edinburgh, 1984).

—— *Gaelic Scotland: The Transformation of a Culture Region* (London, 1988).

Withrington, D. J., 'The S.P.C.K. and Highland Schools in Mid-Eighteenth Century', *SHR* 41 (1962), 89–99.

(d) Catholic Schools

Sound work has been done on these, whereas there is nothing on Episcopalian schools.

Dealy, M. B., *Catholic Schools in Scotland* (Washington, DC, 1945).

Fitzpatrick, T. A., 'Catholic Education in Glasgow, Lanarkshire and South-West Scotland before 1872', *Innes Review*, 36 (1985), 86–96.

—— *Catholic Secondary Education in South-West Scotland before 1972: Its Contribution to the Change in Status of the Catholic Community of the Area* (Aberdeen, 1986).

Kenneth, Brother, 'The Education (Scotland) Act, 1918, in the Making', *Innes Review*, 19 (1968), 91–128.

McGloin, J., 'Catholic Education in Ayr, 1823–1918', *Innes Review*, 13 (1962), 77–103 and 190–216.

Skinnider, M., 'Catholic Elementary Education in Glasgow, 1818–1918', in T. R. Bone (ed.), *Studies in the History of Scottish Education, 1872–1939* (London, 1967), 13–70.

Treble, J. H., 'The Development of Roman Catholic Education in Scotland, 1878–1978', *Innes Review*, 29 (1978), 111–39.

(e) Working-Class Reading and Adult Education

Aitken and Kelly are standard works. The early history of libraries has attracted considerable attention, but Smith on Dundee is the only modern study of a Scottish mechanics' institute.

AITKEN, W. R., *A History of the Public Library Movement in Scotland to 1955* (Glasgow, 1971).

CARTER, I. R., 'The Mutual Improvement Movement in North-East Scotland in the Nineteenth Century', *Aberdeen University Review*, 46 (1975–6), 383–92.

CRAWFORD, J. C., 'Denominational Libraries in 19th-Century Scotland', *Library History*, 7 (1985–7), 33–44.

DONALDSON, W., *Popular Literature in Victorian Scotland* (Aberdeen, 1986).

JACKAMAN, P., 'The Company, the Common Man, and the Library: Leadhills and Wanlockhead', *Library Review*, 29 (1980), 27–32.

KELLY, T., *A History of Adult Education in Great Britain* (Liverpool, 1962).

McDONALD, W. R., 'Circulating Libraries in the North-East of Scotland in the Eighteenth Century', *The Bibliotheck*, 5 (1967–70), 119–37.

MOWAT, I. R. M., 'Literacy, Libraries and Literature in 18th and 19th Century Easter Ross', *Library History*, 5 (1979–81), 1–10.

SIMPSON, J. M., 'Three East Lothian Pioneers of Adult Education', *Transactions of the East Lothian Antiquarian and Field Naturalists' Society*, 13 (1972), 43–60.

SMITH, J. V., *The Watt Institution, Dundee, 1824–49* (Dundee, 1978).

—— 'Manners, Morals and Mentalities: Reflections on the Popular Enlightenment of Early Nineteenth-Century Scotland', in Humes and Paterson, 25–54.

—— 'Reason, Revelation and Reform: Thomas Dick of Methven and the "Improvement of Society by the Diffusion of Knowledge"', *History of Education*, 12 (1983), 255–70.

THOMPSON, A. R., 'The Use of Libraries by the Working Class in Scotland in the Early Nineteenth Century', *SHR* 42 (1963), 21–9.

TYRRELL, A., 'Political Economy, Whiggism and the Education of Working-Class Adults in Scotland, 1817–40', *SHR* 48 (1969), 151–65.

(f) Miscellaneous

Robertson deals incidentally with Scotland, but otherwise Scottish technical education is a historical blank.

BONE, T. R., *School Inspection in Scotland 1840–1966* (London, 1968).

BROWN, C. G., 'The Sunday-School Movement in Scotland, 1780–1914', *SCHSR* 21 (1981–3), 3–26.

KNOX, H. M., 'Simon Somerville Laurie: 1829–1909', *BJES* 10 (1961–2), 138–52.

MACKIE, P., 'The Foundation of the United Industrial School of Edinburgh: "A Bold Experiment"', *Innes Review*, 39 (1988), 133–50.

—— 'Inter-Denominational Education and the United Industrial School of Edinburgh, 1847–1900', *Innes Review*, 43 (1992), 3–17.

RALSTON, A. G., 'The Development of Reformatory and Industrial Schools in Scotland, 1832–1872', *SESH* 8 (1988), 40–55.

ROBERTS, A. F. B., 'Scotland and Infant Education in the Nineteenth Century', *SES* 4 (1972), 39–45.

ROBERTSON, P. L., 'Technical Education in the British Shipbuilding and Marine Engineering Industries, 1863–1914', *Economic History Review*, 2nd series, 27 (1974), 222–35.

THOMSON, I., 'The Origins of Physical Education in State Schools', *SER* 10/2 (1978), 15–24.

Index